the

practice ᵒᶠ **E**veryday **L**ife

Volume 2

Also from the University of Minnesota Press

The Capture of Speech and Other Political Writings
Michel de Certeau
Edited and with an Introduction by Luce Giard
Translated and with an Afterword by Tom Conley

Culture in the Plural
Michel de Certeau
Edited and with an Introduction by Luce Giard
Translated and with an Afterword by Tom Conley

Heterologies: Discourse on the Other
Michel de Certeau
Foreword by Wlad Godzich
Translated by Brian Massumi

The

Practice *of* Everyday Life

Volume 2: Living and Cooking

Michel de Certeau • Luce Giard • Pierre Mayol

New Revised and Augmented Edition

Edited by Luce Giard • Translated by Timothy J. Tomasik

University of Minnesota Press
Minneapolis • London

Originally published as *L'invention du quotidien, II, habiter, cuisiner,* copyright 1994 Éditions Gallimard. "Introduction to Volume 1: History of a Research Project," by Luce Giard, was originally published as the Introduction to *L'invention du quotidien, I, arts de faire,* copyright 1990 by Éditions Gallimard.

Published by the University of Minnesota Press
111 Third Avenue South, Suite 290
Minneapolis, MN 55401-2520
http://www.upress.umn.edu

Library of Congress Cataloging-in-Publication Data

Giard, Luce.
   [Habiter, cuisiner. English]
   The practice of everyday life. Volume 2, Living and cooking /
Michel de Certeau, Luce Giard, Pierre Mayol ; translated by Timothy
J. Tomasik. — New rev. and augm. ed. / edited by Luce Giard.
     p.   cm.
   Rev. translation of v. 2 of L'invention du quotidien, with
additional articles by P. Mayol and articles by M. de Certeau who
did not contribute to the original ed.
   Includes bibliographical references and index.
   ISBN 0-8166-2876-9 (alk. paper). — ISBN 0-8166-2877-7 (pbk. :
alk. paper)
   1. France — Social life and customs — 20th century.   2. Life skills —
France.   3. Cookery, French.   4. Conduct of life in literature.
I. Mayol, Pierre.   II. Certeau, Michel de.   III. Title.
DC33.7.G4413   1998
306'.0944—dc21   98-10876
                                             CIP

Printed in the United States of America on acid-free paper

The University of Minnesota is an equal-opportunity educator and employer.

20 19 18 17 16 15 14 13   10 9 8 7 6 5

Contents

Translator's Note
Timothy J. Tomasik

At the risk of adding to an already highly charged introductory section, a few comments about the English translation of *The Practice of Everyday Life*, volume 2, *Living and Cooking* seem in order.[1] Luce Giard's "History of a Research Project," which introduces the 1990 revised French edition of volume 1, explains the genesis of the two-volume joint project with Michel de Certeau and Pierre Mayol. An introduction written for the 1994 revised French edition of volume 2, her "Times and Places" details the preparation of *Living and Cooking*. My comments here involve the difficulties encountered in translating this volume into English.

In "Times and Places," Giard refers to the enthusiastic reception of Michel de Certeau's work in volume 1, which appeared in English via Steven Rendall's translation in 1984.[2] She adds that: "Not having been translated at this time, volume 2, which the American publisher had judged too closely linked to something specifically French to interest the American public, was less read." What the American publisher found to be "too closely linked to something specifically French" can in part be explained in light of the French concept of *terroir*, the difficult translation of which itself illustrates one difficulty in translating *Living and Cooking*.

According to its etymology, *terroir* is rooted in the popular Latin *terratorium*, referring to earth, land, or soil, which is an alternation of *territorium*, referring more specifically to territory.[3] *Terroir* is often employed in the context of food products that come from or have a flavor unique to a particular region. Cheese, for example, that comes from the Languedoc-Roussillon in France does not have the same savor as that from Normandy. This difference can be explained in part by differing production methods, but the concept of *terroir* suggests that such difference stems from local geographic, geologic, climatic, and other distinctions, which in turn affect the soil that produces the plants that nourish the animals whose milk is then made into Roquefort or Camembert.

Giard evokes the concept of *terroir*, particularly in chapter 11, by referring to the borrowing of regional cuisines. She maintains that when regional specialties are borrowed by other countries, their duplication seems "to uproot a regional cuisine from the tang of its soil [*terroir*]." The danger in this uprooting is that the results become "pale copies" of the original. In terms of translating *Living and Cooking* one difficulty involves how to carefully "uproot" that which is specifically French without the result becoming a pale copy in translation. This task is not made any simpler in that cultural allusions, idiosyncratic expressions, and plays on words — examples of what I might call discursive *terroir* — abound in this text on cultural practices. Adding translator notes is one way to minimize the shock of uprooting the original French, but such tactics cannot eliminate all potential damage.

Moreover, this text teems with voices. We encounter the voices of three main authors who, though united in pursuit of a common task, maintain their own unique tonalities. In addition to the numerous citations of other authors brought to bear on this task, the authors of *Living and Cooking* have incorporated interviews in which "ordinary" people speak about their lifestyles. The translator is thus faced with the diverse prose styles of Certeau, Giard, and Mayol as well as the everyday spoken discourse of the transcribed interviews. Capturing the timbre of these multiple voices in translation presents obvious difficulties.

This chorus of voices creates a unique harmony out of what Mayol refers to in chapter 1 as "the *murmuring* of the everyday." But this harmony is further modulated by voices I have marshaled behind the scenes of the translation. For the references to Certeau's vocabulary in volume 1, I am indebted to Steven Rendall for his preparation of this fertile ground. My thanks, too, go out to those whose voices contributed to this translation in other myriad ways: to all those at the University of Minnesota Press who contributed to this project; to Tom Conley, who first proposed my name to the Press as a potential translator and whose translation experience served as a source of support; to Luce Giard for her generous explanations of problematic passages and her meticulous editing of the manuscript; to Françoise Charras and Frantz Coursière for their detailed clarifications from a native-speaker perspective; to Hélène Guastalla for her perspicacious insights into the art of translating; to Jim Fraser at Harvard's Widener Library for his help in locating English translations for works cited in this volume; most important, to Paula Shreve, to whom I owe more than gratitude for her timely typing and unstinting support throughout the duration of this project.

Unless otherwise indicated, all translations are my own. Where possible, I have located English translations for the secondary sources here.

The contributions of the individuals above have undoubtedly gone a long way in making this translation possible. Any shortcomings that remain are my own.

I dedicate this translation to the memory of my brother, Eric Tomasik.

Introduction to Volume 1:
History of a Research Project
Luce Giard

> Only the end of an age makes it possible to say what made it live,
> as if it had to die in order to become a book.
> Michel de Certeau, *The Practice of Everyday Life*, vol. 1, 198

In February 1980, the first French edition of *L'Invention du quotidien* appeared in paperback.[1] The fact that a previously unpublished work, presenting the results of a long-term research project (from the end of 1974 to 1978) of which only a few fragmentary insights had previously been in circulation, was published directly in paperback form was not customary.[2] Research reports generally await the highly regarded appearance in hardback, or more often disappear into purgatory, into the flotilla of "gray literature" bogged down in the secrecy of government ministries or research centers. The particular treatment received by this work, from the moment its writing was finished (September 1979), can be explained by the nature of the publishing series, the personality of the main author, and the internal logic of the intellectual project.

At that time, the 10–18 series was not just any paperback series. It had its specificity, its renown, its program, its ambitions. The director, Christian Bourgois, a publisher if ever there was one, publishes, on a large scale and at the lowest cost in a modest format, the recent production of the social sciences, which he places side by side with works of literature, among them a good number of translations, because he believes in the importance of a text's form as much as in a policy of quality and of a diversity of authors, genres, and styles. Within a joyous brouhaha of new ideas, of concepts knocked together, of anathema on the opposing school, and of sector-based jargon, the 10–18 series circulated the winds of words and ideas and published, amid mixed allegiances, anthropology, political economics, linguistics, philosophy, sociology, and so on. In those books, people debated with the *furia francese* about Marxism, structuralism, or Western ethnocentrism. The eclectic flair of the director, his curiosities, and a favorable economic context made this intellectual wager win out for a time. Prosperous and vaguely worried, post–1968 France believed in the effectiveness of the social sciences in digesting the modernization of its economy, its urbanization, and the mounting flow of graduates produced by universities. Thousands of students and their professors passionately debated the ideas of Marx, Freud, or Lévi-Strauss. People chose sides for Althusser, Chomsky, Foucault, Lacan, and a few others, or against them; they bought their work; they read their epigones or their adversaries. People still went into theory as if into religion or revolution in the past. Neither the lassitude of the "postmoderns" nor the ruin of the great ideological families had yet reached the crowd of authors and readers. Only a few visionaries traced out the barely visible rift where the tranquillity of the "glorious years" would soon founder, and sought to interpret society differently by shying away from the too-simple antagonisms that were still a big success.

Michel de Certeau is one of these anticonformist and perspicacious spirits. On the intellectual scene, he is a character apart, not true to the canons of a well-fixed discipline, and whose intellectual radiance follows paths that are strangers to the logic of institutions, whether these stem from the university, the church, or the state. A well-known historian, respected for his learned production on mysticism and religious currents in the sixteenth and seventeenth centuries, he is also feared for his demanding and lucid criticism of the epistemology that silently governs the historical profession. Some reproach him for relativizing the notion of truth, for being suspicious of the objectivity of scholarly institutions, for underscoring the weight of hierarchical dependency and complicity, and finally, for doubting the received models for which the French school of history is renowned. Some would soon reproach him for foregrounding the role of writing at the expense of the grasp of the "real" of which the historian wants to give a "true" description. Is he not too interested in the semiotic or psychoanalytic reading of situations and texts, all of them things foreign to the good historical method and that go against the (sacred) ideal of fixation on the archive, of accumulation of an (impossible) exhaustive documentation? These were repeated reproaches, unjust ones, irritated at being so, because on not one of these contentious points did people succeed in catching him in his practice of historical work. Thus, Emmanuel Le Roy Ladurie allowed his embarrassment to show through, as well as the irritation of the profession faced with the (too?) brilliant rereading of the Loudun affair under Richelieu: "for Michel de Certeau, theologian and historian, the devil is everywhere except in the precise place where the witch-hunters thought they had detected him." Certeau "knows how to make use of all locutors and take over successively all languages. He is in turn historian of medicine and society, theologian, psychoanalyst, quantifier, disciple of Freud or Foucault"; "he never lowers his guard. He remains indecipherable. By presenting his astute *Possession de Loudun*, Michel de Certeau thus wrote the most diabolical book of the year."[3]

Through the range of his scholarship interests, the multiplicity of methods that he practices without pledging allegiance to just one of them, and the diversity of abilities that he has acquired, Certeau intrigues and disconcerts. On the chessboard of a profession with rather sedentary tastes, he does not cease to move around and does not allow himself to be identified with one determined place. A Jesuit, he refused the social position that this belonging ensured for him, but he did not break ties to the Society. A historian who became a master in the most classic erudition, proved by his monumental edition of the *Correspondance* of Surin, a seventeenth-century mystic Jesuit whose "madness" rendered him suspect, Certeau does not content himself with the reputation for excellence on a certain topic of the past. He is interested in psychoanalysis, belonged to the École Freudienne of Jacques Lacan, as of its founding in 1964 and until its dissolution in 1980, and maintained an intellectual friendship with several great barons of Lacania.[4] But he deals just as much with linguistics, and assiduously frequented the semiotic seminars chaired by Algirdas Julien Greimas in Paris and the annual encounters in Urbino (Italy), discreetly orchestrated by Pino Paioni.

If a government agency asked him in 1974 to direct a research program on problems of culture and society (I will come back to the circumstances of this commission), it is because of another facet of his activity. In 1968, his reputation expanded beyond the milieu of historians where his works gained him his professional identity, outside of Christian networks where his Jesuit affiliation inserted him, but in which he refused to limit his intellectual and social circulation. From then on, he was invited to join numerous leftist intellectual circles, some political decision makers consulted him or had him consulted, and certain think tanks in high-level administration turned to him. He was thus associated, in an informal way, with the brain trust that collaborated with Edgar Faure in trying to reform the university during the summer of 1968 and create new foundations to organize the new academic year. Soon he was asked to teach history and anthropology in these places: he would be at Paris VIII-Vincennes from 1968 to 1971, then at Paris VII-Jussieu from 1971 to 1978.

This new role was born of his surprising ability to analyze, on the spot, between May and September 1968, the maelstrom of the "events," as people said at the time. In a series of dazzling articles, which remained so, appearing in the monthly journal of the Jesuits, *Études*, he gave an intelligent and generous reading about this uncertain time, a reading hospitable to change and free from the fear that paralyzed so many of his contemporaries.[5] He sought not to propose solutions, nor to posit a definitive diagnosis that would close off the future, but first of all to render what happened intelligible. His objective was not the froth of the day, the disarray of the political discourse, the lamentations of some, the reproaches of others, but the hidden meaning of that which, deeper and more mysterious, reveals itself as something essential in a large confusion of words. This turmoil, this disorder of words and barricades, this revolt and these strikes — what did they say about a society, about its latencies, about its hopes? In the rift between words and actions that he thought he had detected,[6] Certeau did not see a threat but a possibility for the future. He deciphered there the beginnings of a great social adventure and recognized, in front of the generation of fathers (his own) that did not know how to or could not assume its paternity, the legitimate impatience of a generation of sons that neither the mediocrity of small pleasures nor the management of social order would be able to fulfill.

May 1968 left Michel de Certeau intrigued, "affected," "altered" in his own words. This mark would be a definitive one on him. According to another of his phrases, coined to describe the contemporary situation of Christianity, it was for him at the time "a foundational rupture,"[7] not that he wanted to abandon, forget, or deny his former existence, but that henceforth his scholarship and intelligence, his social energy would be mobilized otherwise, in the service of an elucidating effort that had become a priority. From then on, he said that he had to "come back to this 'thing' that happened and understand what the unpredictable taught us about ourselves, that is, what, since then, we have become."[8] It was impossible to shirk this task: "I needed to clarify it. Not in the first instance for others. Rather, because of a need for veracity."[9] He did not know how to give reality to this radical quest; he hesitated, groped, sought a ground for action, instruments for analysis, and a way for adequate intervention. He reflected on educational matters, on universities, linguistic minorities, on what constitutes culture in any society. His thinking tried to find its direction and its object, but it had already identified the true question, the "indiscreet question... 'How to create *oneself?* '" This substituted for what had been "the imperious urgency that asked, 'Create *what* and how?'"[10] Within this very question, I recognize the first shapes of the perspective reversal that founds *L'Invention du quotidien* by displacing the attention from the supposed passive consumption of received products to anonymous creation, born of the unconventional practice of these products' use (32–33).

Because of the original stands he made in several studies that appeared after 1968, Certeau was asked to be the spokesperson for the Arc-et-Senans international colloquium (April 1972) where the Helsinki meeting of European Community ministers to define a European policy of culture was to be prepared (September of the same year). This work would be a decisive step in the crystallization of his reflection on cultural practices. In 1974, he brought together under the revealing title *La Culture au pluriel* the reports written for Arc-et-Senans and certain works concerning similar matters.[11] All by itself, the chosen title manifests the refusal of the uniformity that an administrative power would like to see reign in the name of a superior knowledge and of common interest. Throughout this collection of texts, one can follow just beneath the surface the research program of which *L'Invention du quotidien* would be the deployment. His "theoretical task," as he would say, was already clearly pointed out: one must be interested not in cultural products offered on the market of goods, but in the operations that make use of them; one must be concerned with the "different ways or styles of socially *marking* the gap opened up by a practice in a given form."[12] What matters is no longer — can no longer be — "learned culture," a treasure left to the vanity of its proprietors. It is no longer "popular culture," an appellation bestowed from the outside by some scholars who make an inventory of and embalm what one power has already eliminated because, for them and for this power, "the beauty of the dead" is all the more moving and celebrated the better that it is enclosed in a tomb.[13] From then on, one must turn toward the "disseminated proliferation" of anonymous and "perishable" creations that allow people to stay alive and cannot be capitalized.[14] A domain of research was circumscribed even if the theoretical means to work in it were still poorly defined. This domain would involve "the cultural operations [that] are movements" and whose "trajectories that are not indeterminate but that are unsuspected" constitute that whose formality and modalities are to be studied in order to give them intelligible status.[15] *La Culture au pluriel* can say no more about it; it would come down to the subsequent works to clarify the winding paths that the tactical ruses of ordinary practices follow.

This chance would be provided by the friendship and admiration of Augustin Girard. As head of the Service des Études et Recherches au Secrétariat d'État à la Culture [Department of Research at the State Office for Cultural Affairs], Girard had read and understood Certeau. He began by assuring Certeau's collaboration for a year thanks to an ad hoc study directorship in the department. This experience increased Girard's conviction that Certeau was the man for the situation, capable of defining this problematic of research and action on the culture that political decision makers and their administrations needed to orient their choices and decide on budgetary priorities. With skillfulness and a sure sense of opportunity, Girard advanced a timely proposal to the DGRST, where he sat on the leading committee (chaired by Paul Delouvrier) in charge of the "Cultural Development" program.[16] This was June 1974, the preparation of the Seventh National Plan was on the horizon, and the committee was in trouble because it did not have any clear ideas to propose to the delegate general (Hubert Curien, former director general of the CNRS [Centre National de la Recherche Scientifique] and future minister of research under the leftist government). Certain research credits still remained that had to be committed quickly, before, according to custom, the budgetary services froze the unspent surplus. Girard suggested a major project of reflection, sketched it out, proposed that Michel de Certeau be contacted, argued, persuaded, and finally prevailed. Soon Certeau was asked to produce a "synthesis taken at once from futurology, from concrete cases, and from the research milieu" (such were the committee's terms).

The commission took the official form of a research contract titled "Conjuncture, Synthesis, and Futurology," initially projected for two years and then prolonged for one year. The contract lasted financially from the end of 1974 until the end of 1977, and the final write-up of the work would be submitted in 1979 because in the meantime Certeau was teaching as a visiting professor at the University of Geneva in 1977–78, then as a full professor at the University of California, San Diego, as of September 1978. Certeau was left free to define the contents and methods of the contract; he alone ensured the scientific leadership of it and chose his own collaborators. He was assigned the report on futurology (technocrats at that time believed in this type of discourse) and a researcher in charge of working on it, but the latter would soon abandon the ongoing work, so that Certeau, in order to respect the letter of the signed contract, would have to resolve to form a small group for cultural futurology, considered "under its (own) scientific formality and as utopian literature" (according to a work document sent to the DGRST).[17] The critical reading of "scenarios for the future" and of grandiose projects for a "systemic(s)" supposed to establish order in the description of the present and to provide the possibility of forecasting the future would reveal itself to be deceiving, poor in conceptualization, rich in redundancies and numerical rhetoric, so that the announced study would not be written up. In the meantime, the wind had happily changed and the DGRST ceased believing in the importance of this nonsense.

The signed contract anticipated that Certeau would be able to benefit from the documentation and the experience accumulated by Girard's department. It had just published a vast study on cultural practices, providing a precise quantitative picture of modes of cultural consumption and of leisure occupations, divided according to age, gender, social category, residential zone, and so on.[18] Certeau himself intended to distance his project from this type of statistical study whose limits, because of the very nature of the procedures used, he perceived. It was not that he scorned figures, but such a step would allow everything that interested him to escape: the individual operations and customs, their sequences, and the changing trajectories of the practitioners. His introduction to volume 1 of *L'Invention du quotidien* would clearly summarize his criticism. Statistics "grasps the material of these practices, but not their *form*; it determines the elements used, but not the 'phrasing' produced by the *bricolage* (the artisan-like inventiveness) and the discursiveness that combine these elements, which are all in general circulation and rather drab. Statistical inquiry... 'finds' only the homogenous. It reproduces the system to which it belongs" (xviii).[19]

His criticism took its source from his reflection on the epistemology of history. He was, for his generation, one of the rare historians eager for new methods, ready to venture into them, and lucid about their determinations and their limits. Thus, he did not succumb to the siren's songs about quantitative data or to the modernist seductions of computerization; it was perhaps his love for the text (and his awareness of diverse reading methods) that protected him from some contemporary illusions. Likewise, he knew not to cede to the opposite bias that systematically denigrated recourse to figures, computers, or formal models. Finally, I believe his lucidity came from a philosophical education and an interest in epistemology; hence his insistence on the fact that statistical data have no other validity and pertinence than those of the conditions of collection. Treated manually or submitted to a sophisticated treatment by machine, data remain what they are at the moment of their production as such; their quality and informative meaning are proportionate to those of procedures used to define and construct the categories that organized this very production; the latter are worth as much as the former.[20] As a historian, Certeau was armed against the illusions of any scientific status [*scientificité*] gained through numbers, tables, and percentages. An analyst of culture, he had no reason to accept here what he had refused elsewhere.

Having defined his research framework in relation to the contract concluded with the DGRST, Certeau took charge of specifying its objective and major directions. A working document, sent to the DGRST in February 1975, emphasized "common and everyday culture inasmuch as that it involves appropriation (or reappropriation)," consumption or reception considered as "a way of practicing," and finally the necessity of "elaborating certain models of analysis that correspond to these trajectories (or series of operations articulated in time sequences)." Thus, an objective field, a line of inquiry, and a theoretical task were defined. It was a matter, said the text, of "sketching a *theory of everyday practices* in order to bring out of their murmuring the 'ways of operating' that, as a majority in social life, often only figure as 'resistances' or as apathies in relation to the development of sociocultural production." The essential of what would be done in *L'Invention du quotidien* was clearly stated and the general introduction to volume 1 would add nothing except that the "ruses of consumers compose the network of an antidiscipline which is the subject of this book" (xv).

Only one new term, "antidiscipline," intervenes in 1980, as an obvious echo of the work of Michel Foucault, whose masterpiece (in the eyes of Certeau), *Surveiller et punir* [*Discipline and Punish*], appeared in 1975 and caused a considerable stir.[21] It is not entirely right, however, to say that "there is an obvious and even claimed filiation" between the two works,[22] a filiation in which Certeau would have constructed volume 1 of *L'Invention du quotidien* in response and opposition to the analysis of Foucault, because Certeau's major themes are clearly articulated in his texts prior to the reading of *Surveiller et punir*. Thus, he was already using the vocabulary of "strategies" and "tactics" in an article that appeared in April 1974 and this vocabulary structured the internal work documents written for the DGRST in the definition phase of the contract in

June 1974 or addressed at the same time to those that Certeau intended to gather together in the "first circle" of interlocutors (I will come back to this point later on).[23] But it is true that the reference to Foucault is quite noticeable in the 1980 work. Quantitatively, Pierre Bourdieu is just as present in it, if not a bit more.[24] In fact, the two authors receive a comparable treatment and they share the same role as purveyors of strong theoretical propositions, read closely, with admiration and respect, carefully discussed, and finally ruled out.

If Foucault and Bourdieu serve together as opposed theoretical figures, it is because of some related reasons that are not entirely accounted for in the discussion of their theses. A difference comes into play here that precedes theory, a distance that one might qualify as an *elective anti-affinity* and that does not impede interest or fascination in proposing theses. With these words, I am pointing something out that would characterize the entire inspiration of a kind of thinking, its "style," its own tonality, in short its presuppositions, which do not stem from the critical awareness of the author and are never made explicit, but in which is rooted that which specifies a way of being in the world and rendering it intelligible. This involves the organization of the internal forces that govern the economy of a way of thinking, and determine its preferences and suspicions.[25] With Michel de Certeau one can always perceive an optimistic élan, a generosity of intelligence, and a trust given to others in such a way that no situation appears to him a priori fixed or hopeless. It seems that, beneath the massive reality of powers and institutions and without deluding oneself about their function, Certeau always discerns a Brownian motion of microresistances, which in turn found microfreedoms, mobilize unsuspected resources hidden among ordinary people, and in that way displace the veritable borders of the hold that social and political powers have over the anonymous crowd. Certeau often speaks about this inversion and subversion acted out by oppressed people, for example, the South American Indians subjected to forced Christianization by Spanish colonizers. Seeming on the surface to totally submit and conform to the expectations of the conqueror, they in fact "metaphorized the dominant order" by making its laws and representations function "in another register," within the framework of their own tradition (32).

This difference prior to theory stems from an ethical and political conviction; it is fed from an aesthetic sensibility that Certeau expressed through the maintained capacity for being filled with wonder. "Daily life is scattered with marvels, a froth...as dazzling as that of writers and artists. Lacking proper names, all kinds of language give birth to these ephemeral celebrations that surge up, disappear, and return."[26] If Michel de Certeau sees these wonders everywhere, it is because he is prepared to see them, as Surin in the seventeenth century was ready to encounter "the young uneducated man in the stagecoach" who would speak to him of God with more force and wisdom than all the authorities of Scripture or of the church.[27] His incredulity vis-à-vis the dogmatic order that authorities and institutions always want to organize, his attention to the internal freedom of nonconformists, even those reduced to silence, who turn imposed truth around and over, his respect for all resistance, however minimal, and for the form of mobility that this resistance opens up — all of this gives Certeau the possibility of firmly believing in the *truant freedom of practices.* From then on, it is natural for him to perceive microdifferences where so many others see obedience and standardization; it is natural that his attention focuses on the minuscule loose space that certain silent and subtle tactics "insinuate," as he liked to say, playing on the two meanings of this verb, within the imposed order. And it matters little that this order today involves consumer products offered by a mass distribution that wants to conform the crowd to imposed models of consumption, whereas in the past it was a matter of the order of dogmatic truths to believe and of their celebration rites to follow. The mechanisms for resistance are the same from one period to another, from one order to another, because the same unequal division of forces subsists and the same parrying procedures serve as the final recourse for the powerless, like so many ripostes and ruses that have come from "immemorial intelligence," rooted in the past of the species, in the "farthest reaches of the domain of the living," in the history of plants or of animals (xix–xx, 40) — an unexpected Aristotelian theme for someone who preferred the poetic style of Platonic philosophy to the naturalist logician of ancient Greece.

Certeau summarizes his position with a jest to be taken seriously: "it is always good to remind ourselves that we mustn't take people for fools" (176). In this trust of the intelligence and inventiveness of powerless people, in the extreme attention to their tactical mobility, in the respect accorded to the powerless who have neither belongings nor place, nimble at thus being deprived in face of the strategies of the powerful, owner of the theater of operations, stands out a political conception of action and of unequal relations between a government and its subjects. Here one may recognize the trace of an Ignatian conception of action. I am thus not pointing out the contents of a political plan defined by its relation to a time, place, and situation, but the very motivating forces behind the action such that Ignatius of Loyola puts them into play when stating his principles (for example, the directives of the *Spiritual Exercises* or the rules of the *Constitutions*). This conception of action is, for Michel de Certeau, inseparable from the reference to an "art," a "style," two notions equally familiar to Renaissance Jesuit culture. Both serve Certeau in volume 1 of *L'Invention du quotidien* for understanding cultural practices, as they served him elsewhere for interpreting mystical texts. In ordinary culture, he says, "order is *tricked* by an art," in other words, outsmarted and fooled; within the determinations of the institution "are thus insinuated styles of social exchange, technical invention, and moral resistance"; that is to say, "an economy of the *'gift,'*" "an aesthetics of *'tricks,'*" and "an ethics of *tenacity*" (26), three qualifications that put the finishing touches on the upgrading of ordinary culture and by rights give practices the status of a theoretical object. There then remained finding the way to "distinguish 'ways of operating,'" to think about "styles of action" (30), in other words, to theorize practices.

In order to realize this difficult task, a multiplicity of knowledges and methods was convened, applied according to varied procedures, and chosen according to the difference of the practices considered. But Certeau took care to dissipate all ambiguity about his intentions; he wanted to procure neither "a history of theories concerning practices" (62) nor "the constitution of . . . a semiotics" (39) that would seek to satisfy the eighteenth-century dream of finally having a complete and systematic description of the arts (66–67). He limited himself to proposing "some ways of thinking about everyday practices of consumers, supposing from the start that they are of a tactical nature" (39–40). In this intention, the analysis is organized on three levels: the modalities of action, the formalities of practices, and the types of operations specified by the ways of operating (29–30). Each theoretical proposition is immediately put to the test of a concrete practice, here walking in the city, there the description of a living space, elsewhere silent reading. It is not a question of elaborating a general model in order to pour into such a mold the totality of practices, but on the contrary of specifying "operational schemas" (30) and of seeing if there exists among them common categories and if, with these categories, it would be possible to take the totality of practices into account. Voluntarily, in its appropriateness to its concrete object, the analysis here is doomed to an incessant coming and going from the theoretical to the concrete and then from the particular and the circumstantial to the general. Certeau says this clearly about reading, of which he makes a central paradigm (xx–xxii): this analysis of practices "comes and goes, alternately captivated...playful, protesting, fugitive" (175), made in the image of the mobile reality that it aims at grasping.

In order to lead this ambitious and complex research program, Michel de Certeau tried to organize three collaborative circles, distinct circles with separate functions, but with points in common, certain members circulating from one to another. The "first circle" in chronological order appeared in June 1974. Certeau gathered together in this circle young researchers in the middle or at the end of their graduate studies with just a few exceptions; they did not yet have an institutional status or were starting research work alongside other wage-earning work. Their average age was right around thirty for the most experienced ones and did not go beyond twenty-five for most of the others. The initial proposal was addressed to Marie-Pierre Dupuy, Marie Ferrier, Dominique Julia (who declined the responsibility, absorbed as he was with his research in history), Patrick Mignon, Olivier Mongin, Isabelle Orgogozo, and myself; in July, Thomas Gunther (an American student), Pierre Mayol, and Pierre Michelin entered the "first circle"; this circle would spread no further, perhaps because of its ephemeral duration. In a circulated letter, Michel de Certeau proposed to the chosen collaborators "an engaged observational practice" in a Paris neighborhood to be determined by the group; but he specified that it involved neither joining together in a "commune" (born of the sixties, the communal dream was still attractive) nor constituting a closed group. On the contrary, he wrote, "our group is open to others who you think might be interested"; "we are forming a transitory space that one crosses through or leaves as amicably as one enters."[28] What he hoped for was a collaboration of work, a confrontation of experiences, and engagements with the young generation, but he did not want the adventure to end up being a "refuge" or with the formation of a sect, even if it were a thinking sect. He protected himself from these dangers, as he did the group (known by the vague and rarely mentioned title of "experimental group"), by refusing to set himself up as the charismatic leader or as the intellectual guide surrounded by disciples.[29] Even if the life span of the "first circle" had been ephemeral, the echo of this proposal can be found, almost stated in the same terms, in the opening to *L'Invention du quotidien*, whose two volumes written in collaboration allowed "the research to be pluralized and several passersby to cross paths," without erecting a unique space, nor amassing a treasure of which they would remain the proprietor. On the contrary, "this interlacing of journeys, far from constituting an enclosure, prepares for, so I hope, our progress toward becoming lost in the crowd."[30]

The "first circle" functioned from June 1974 until the spring of 1975, its activities declined in silence, and it silently disappeared. The participants, each one caught up individually in their own network, labor, and militancy, did not know how or could not invent for the group a common place of investment and investigation; their practices and interests were probably too divergent to agree on a project. Perhaps all they had in common was the impatience of their generation and their personal tie to Michel de Certeau, which was too little for a close-knit group to emerge inasmuch as its sponsor refused to be the group's motivation and glue. Perhaps Certeau's request was ambivalent and he allowed the circle to dissolve as he became aware of this ambivalence (I mean the ambivalence of his role in the group that he created, but in which he did not accept being the magnet and raison d'être). In any case, after a few months, it became obvious that the common insertion in a neighborhood had been a dream and would remain so. Another factor in this silent dissolution was the importance soon gained by the "second circle" and the vitality that came out of it. From the "first circle" would subsist among members links of variable intensity, a durable complicity, and the insistence placed on the need to refer to concrete cases in order to write their "description or historiography," a phrase used several times by Certeau in the internal documents of the "first circle." The "first circle" was not useless because it assembled people who, with very few exceptions, such as the inseparable duo of Patrick Mignon and Olivier Mongin (whose patronymic proximity seemed to cement the duration of their friendship), did not know each other previously; moreover, the actual collaborators in the research were eventually chosen by Certeau from the members of the "first circle," which certain of the other members felt as a form of repudiation in respect to them, as they explained to me years later.

The "second circle" of collaborators involved the doctoral seminar given by Certeau in anthropology at the University of Paris VII-Jussieu between 1974 and 1978 until his definitive departure for California. In truth, this was the anchoring post for the undertaking, an extraordinary place where people learned, confronted experience and questioning, drew theoretical schemata, and became educated in the range of social sciences, according to the French tradition, but also in the recent foreign production of Europe and America. There, every proposition was subject to common critique and likewise taken seriously because every theoretical position was defensible a priori on condition of being argued and referred to a concrete test. Certeau often cited the refutability of theories provided by Karl Popper as a criteria for scientific status and was inspired by it, without being Popperian with respect to the rest (he had frequented Hegel too much in the past and was too interested in Ludwig Wittgenstein during those years to be lured by Popper's claims). The seminar discussed with equanimity all the research stages, from the first badly roughed-out theoretical hypotheses with which one started on the quest for a "terrain," up to the final interpretations that shaped the obtained results. This was done in a climate of intellectual freedom and of equality for all participants, whether uncertain apprentices or experienced researchers, who were listened to and discussed with in the same way. No orthodoxy reigned and no dogma was imposed: the only rule (implicit but strong) was a desire for clarification and a cognitive interest about concrete living. It was a miraculous period; an air of intelligence floated there, a form of exhilaration in work that I have never encountered in the institution of knowledge. It was a ford on which the boatman encouraged, guided, and then stepped aside; each person was received with the same listening intensity, the same warmth, the same incisive attention; each person was treated as a unique and irreplaceable speaker, with an extreme delicacy, full of respect.[31]

In this fluidly, heterogeneously populated space, which attracted strangers, reigned a curious mixture of proximity and distance in relation to the person in charge, of availability for each person, and of reserve that simultaneously avoided familiarity, imitation, or the establishment of dependence. One passed through this place, then went on one's own way, and sometimes returned after a long absence as a psychoanalyst goes to another for a "check" at a difficult time. This "way of operating," which provided talent to so many students (testified to by the number of master's theses and Ph.D. dissertations that came out of the seminar) — Michel de Certeau took its secret with him all the way to California, but there remains a perceptible reflection of it in *L'Invention du quotidien* and it gives the work its particular savor.[32] The "second circle" basically constituted the place of experimentation and the echo chamber where the theoretical propositions of volume 1 were fashioned and tested in diverse contexts, at the crossroads of multiple field studies in and out of Paris. The seminar did not produce these theoretical propositions, the essential of which, as I have indicated, was already found in works by Certeau between 1968 and 1974, but it provided a place favorable to their refinement and final clarification.

The "third circle" was a small, restrained, and stable group composed of the direct collaborators on the contract with the DGRST. At
first there were Pierre Mayol and myself, then, in the final work phase,
Marie Ferrier. Pierre Mayol immediately gave himself the theme of the
practice of the city, in the relation between neighborhood and private
housing space. His collaboration was precious because he brought to the
Paris group the difference of an insertion in the provinces, in a working-
class neighborhood, and the material of a study taking time into account
through the consideration of three generations of a family that remained
attached to the same neighborhood. The object of my collaboration was
at first a request from Michel de Certeau, who hoped to find within the
logic of action (about which he had vaguely heard in some circles of semi-
oticians and of Chomskyan linguists) a theoretical model applicable to
practices. Soon I ended up with a negative diagnosis, which was difficult
to have him accept in the name of logical "neatness." I then broadened
my study to include the logic of time, modalities, and norms, in the hope
of finding a rigorous and precise kernel in order to analyze if not practices, at least the utterances that they involve. Later, I went on to study
the articulation between formal and natural language, basing it in particular on the contrasting theses of Wittgenstein (both the "first" and
the "second" Wittgenstein) and the logician Jaakko Hintikka. Certain elements of this work were incorporated into Part I of volume 1 of *L'Invention du quotidien.*

I intended to write separately a technical study on the problem of
those different types of logic and their way of "layering" the utterances
of language, but when the two volumes were finished in 1979, Michel
de Certeau and I decided to publish them without waiting for the completion of the third that we wanted to dedicate to the problem of those
logics and the question of language practices; this latter part would have
been written jointly by him and me. This project was first titled *Logiques
et ruses* [Logics and ruses] (in the intermediary documents written for
the DGRST), then *Dire l'autre* [Saying the other] (at the time our book
appeared in 1980), and finally the title that remained for us, *Arts de dire*
[The practice of speaking]. After 1980, we discussed the project over again
several times, redid the outline, tried to fix a writing schedule, and Certeau
dedicated some of his courses and seminars to it in California. But he
was absorbed in his history of mysticism and I by the history of logic
and languages during the Renaissance; time went on, and the third volume
never came into being.[33] He regretted this, just as he had the "missing
chapters," as he used to call them, from volume 1, which would have con-

cerned memory and museology, belief (of which chapter 13 is a sketch), torture, and finally scientific status (a dossier on which we had both worked a great deal together and of which I published my part in various articles, notably in *Esprit* between 1974 and 1981).

But my work in the "third circle" soon took an unexpected turn. Our trio was meeting for a weekly morning of discussion, that is, a trial of the theoretical analysis of concrete practices. I made a remark that women were strangely absent from this concrete music. I protested, I argued (it was the time of feminist awareness), and I did so well that we decided to remedy this serious gap—as soon as possible. I was charged with rapidly defining an object, a field, and a method because it was already spring 1976, time was of the essence, and the DGRST was asking for results. After some reflection and diverse discussions, I chose cooking for its primary necessity, its ability to cross over all divisions, and its intrinsic relation to *opportunity* and *circumstance*, two notions that had become central to our understanding of those who practice. To become familiar with the gestures of every day in all their hidden details, we thought of collecting from women of all ages and backgrounds, long interviews built on a rather flexible schema in order to allow comparisons without obtaining stereotyped responses. We hoped to see confidence appear in the dialogue so that certain things would be on the tips of their tongues, memories, fears, reticences, everything that usually remains unsaid about knacks for doing things, decisions, and feelings that silently preside at the accomplishment of everyday practices. This way of "giving the floor" to ordinary people corresponded to one of the main intentions of the research, but in collecting the interviews, the interviewer needed to give consideration without directing and to have an uncommon capacity for empathy.

This task was proposed to Marie Ferrier, then at the point of coming back from Greece where she had spent a long time working, and who had been a member of the "first circle" during its ephemeral existence. She accepted, became caught up in the game, fulfilled it quite well in 1977, and discovered how to strike up with her female interlocutors conversations of a marvelous freedom, rich in unexpected information. The "second circle," like our little trio before the arrival of Marie Ferrier, had thought for a long time about observation-participation techniques and of those for the collection of in-depth interviews, in relation to the classical methods of anthropology and in relation to the rediscovery, through linguistics, of the meaning in the distinction between oral and written. Marie Ferrier's work thus benefited from these prior theoretical explorations, as did Pierre Mayol's study of the Croix-Rousse neighborhood in Lyons. Thus, it was decided to publish in extenso in volume 2, one interview from each series (the neighborhood, the kitchen) to bear witness to the richness of speech among ordinary people if one takes the trouble to listen to them and encourage them to express themselves.[34] In so doing, the trio, which became a quartet, did not lose sight of the enterprise's primary intention—the refutation of the commonplace theses on the passivity of consumers and mass behavior.

The evocation of these three collaborative circles does not suffice to explain how the research was based on concrete experiences from diverse milieus. The contribution of numerous social action groups or research groups located abroad must be added. From 1974 to 1978, Michel de Certeau did not stop traveling. He was invited to teach, take part in, and supervise numerous programs of research or social action and he seized on these opportunities to amass an impressive documentation on problematics, methods, and cultural or social experimentation.[35] Some of these trips were long (a quarter) and so allowed him to directly participate in certain concrete experiences; others that were more brief only allowed him the time to listen to and discuss the reports of others. Thus was constituted an informal and active research network, from Europe to America, of which he was the pivot, thanks to an immense correspondence maintained with great regularity and always in a personal form in spite of the piling up of tasks and his numerous travels. The contributions of this informal network are visible everywhere in volume 1 of *L'Invention du quotidien*, whether it is about the narratives involving the great deeds of popular heroes in Brazil (15–16), the collection of oral culture in Denmark (131–33), the constructed space of the American city (91–93), or the way New Yorkers describe their place of residence (118–20). However, these elements, memories and testimonies about an elsewhere, do not function as decorative inlays or as exotic touch-ups; they are incorporated each time into the analysis itself and put into the service of the theoretical intention that unites the research program.

This diversified and multiple circulation across the social fabric was not limited to space located outside of France but had its equivalent in France within the most diverse groups: neighborhood militants mobilizing themselves against major urban planning operations decided on by a technocratic power, educators teaching in prisons or in deprived suburbs, associations assisting immigrants, architects responsible for the building of new cities in the Paris region, young women seeking to take back the management of their health, minorities defending a regional tradition and language against the centralizing and unifying state, and so on. All of these experiences, these encounters, these narratives and debates, and also an entire compost of tracts, ephemeral publications, and reports of studies produced by minuscule channels—all of these drops of water came along to irrigate the reflection, to enrich it at the same level as the perusal of the scientific literature and gray literature, piled up in research centers and ministries. Michel de Certeau in *L'Invention du quotidien* owes much to all these sources, as well as to all those interlocutors who remain anonymous, even if the trace of their contribution has melded into the mass of accumulated materials. Certeau knew of his debts to them and it is to them that are addressed the pages that make reference to the collective dimension of all scientific status (43–44), and it is also to them that the dedication that opens Part I of volume 1 must be rendered: "To the ordinary man. To a common hero, an ubiquitous character, walking in countless thousands on the streets" (v).

Chance (was that really it?) had it that I should see to the appearance of the first edition in 1980 while Michel de Certeau was teaching full-time in California. And now ten years later and almost five years after the death of its author, I am again bent over the text of volume 1 of *L'Invention du quotidien* to establish a second edition of it. I have brought a few minor modifications to the first published version, either to correct typographical errors from the preceding edition (of which the material production conditions did not allow a perfectly finished presentation of the printed text), or to take into consideration certain subsequent corrections indicated by Michel de Certeau on his own copy of the book. Thus were eliminated a few unfortunate repetitions between the development of the analysis and the "general introduction" written a posteriori in order to explain to the DGRST the nature of the obtained results. Also corrected were minute errors or inaccuracies noticed during the rereading carried out with translators of the work (English in 1984, Japanese and Spanish in 1987, German in 1988). As the author had decided in 1984 for the English version, the text of the overall presentation received the new title General Introduction, in accordance with its function.

In the notes for this introduction, I eliminated the three references that announced certain complementary studies to come, studies that we now know will never come into being; they involved, as I have already indicated, different types of logic, language practices, and futurology. I added a few footnotes, each signed with my initials, to provide minute explanations and to translate foreign-language quotations. While doing this, I noticed that these quotations, six in number, were in six different languages (English, German, Italian, Latin, Portuguese, Spanish). This range was not a conscious one, but I like the revealing role of chance, here once again, that "betrayed" (Michel de Certeau liked to play on the double meaning of this verb) a circulation from Europe to America, from the Old World to the New World, in the image of what François Hartog nicely described as "travel writing."[36] In the references given by the notes, I have standardized and completed the bibliographical information. For the texts by Certeau, I have each time mentioned the most recent edition or the collected edition of some of his articles.

I also added an index of authors cited in order to allow for intersecting itineraries. Reading an index is always instructive and indiscreet because it clarifies the secrets of a text's making. This allows us to see (it is no surprise for attentive readers) that the author most often made use of is undoubtedly Freud, present from one end to the other, a natural homage to the too-lucid author of a *Psychopathology of Everyday Life* (1901). Aside from Freud, the most profound influence is exerted not by Foucault nor by Bourdieu, whose theses are weighed and scrutinized in the same chapter; nor by Marcel Detienne and Jean-Pierre Vernant, whose Greek "ruse" played an essential role in the underscoring of the ruses of practitioners; nor by Claude Lévi-Strauss, whose "bricolages" were a triggering factor, but by Wittgenstein, to whom the maximum credit is accorded: this "fragmented and rigorous body of work seems to provide a philosophical blueprint for a contemporary science of the ordinary" (14). The rest of the index shows how much Certeau's thought, nourished from the complementary contributions of anthropology, history, linguistics, or sociology, is from the start structured by its philosophical entrenchment. All the periods of the philosophical tradition are made use of: antiquity with Heracleitus, Plato, and especially Aristotle; the early modern period with Hobbes, Descartes, Pascal, Diderot, Rousseau, Kant, and Condillac; the nineteenth century with Hegel, Marx, Nietzsche, or Peirce; our century with Wittgenstein, Heidegger, Quine, English analytic philosophy and French philosophy with Merleau-Ponty, Deleuze, Lyotard, or Derrida.

I regretted not being able to include in this index the gallery of legendary or fictional characters, heroes of Greek myths or from the "case studies" of Freud, that modern creator of myths. They are not authors. This close-knit troop traverses volume 1 of *L'Invention du quotidien*, just like the departed philosophers and poets in the cantos of Dante, sometimes as potential actors, sometimes as metaphoric carriers of meaning.

xxxii   History of a Research Project

Antigone, Sleeping Beauty, Cinderella, Daedalus and Icarus, Dora and
Little Hans, Émile, Figaro, Don Juan, Lady Macbeth, Oedipus, Robinson flanked by Friday, Scapin, Ulrich, and so many others people these
pages. Archetypal figures of an intermediate status, they act as go-be-
tweens, between known authors, named and renowned individuals, and
the anonymous crowd of inventive and cunning practitioners, "unrecognized producers, poets of their own affairs" (34). Their presence gives
this unclassifiable work a profound humanity, a poetic density in which
one recognizes "the artist, undoubtedly one of the greatest of our time,
through the grace of a permanent counterpoint between the rigor of his
writing and the richness of the metaphors that bring it to life."[37] An unclassifiable work of a "Jesuit who became a poacher,"[38] which one can assign neither to a genre nor to a discipline, it achieves this tour de force
of making the act of reading, an image of passivity for so many observers
and masters, into the example of an appropriation activity, an independent production of meaning, one might as well say "the paradigm of tactical activity."[39]

A praise of night and shadow (ordinary intelligence, ephemeral creation, opportunity, and circumstance), this philosophical journey through
"common life" is blind neither to political realities (treated by all of chapter 13) nor to the weight of temporality everywhere reaffirmed. Rereading the text as such ten years later, I am struck by an insistent, hidden,
maintained, and tenacious note that speaks of the presence of death
among the living. The death of God whose Word no longer inhabits the
world (136–37, 157), the death of societies (25, 197–98), the death of beliefs (180), the death to come for each of us (chap. 14). For Michel de
Certeau, death always refers back to the process of writing in which he
saw the matrix of Western societies, the means for this conquering rationality that spreads to the New World in the sixteenth century. This
hypothesis plays a central role in his thinking; put into place in *L'écriture de l'histoire* (1975) [*The Writing of History*, 1988] and already in the
articles collected in *L'Absent de l'histoire* (1973), it is reworked in *La Fable mystique* (1982) [*The Mystic Fable*, 1992]. Here, it structures the second half of volume 1 of *L'Invention du quotidien*, and on this thesis depends the place accorded to the theory of "narration," indissociable from
a theory of practices (78) and central for Certeau; for narration is the
language of operations, it "opens a legitimate *theater* for practical *actions*"
(125) and allows one to follow the stages of operativity; hence the attention given, for example, to spatial stories (chap. 9).

Since the Renaissance, God has withdrawn from the world and writing is no longer the interpreter of the hidden meaning of the Word. Thus, it has become the great fabricator (137), source of all power. For this new historical figure, Michel de Certeau found the perfect mythical expression in *Robinson Crusoe*, a text he never tired of reading and commenting on: henceforth, "the subject of writing is the master, and his man Friday is the worker, who has a tool other than language" (139). In this new form, writing has an intrinsic relationship to death; when writing, every writer is moving toward his or her own death. "In this respect, the writer is also a dying man who is trying to speak. But in the death that his footsteps inscribe on a black (and not blank) page, he knows and he can express the desire that expects from the other the marvellous and ephemeral excess of surviving through an attention that it alters" (198).

"A wonderful wreck," Surin would have said of this inscription of life in death, death in life, the image of the ordinary days of the innumerable crowd whose unflagging ruse carries these pages away.[40]

Times and Places
Luce Giard

It is a strange, bittersweet experience rereading and revising one's own text fourteen years later. Having appeared in their first edition in February 1980, the two volumes of *L'Invention du quotidien* had been finished the preceding summer. It was the outcome of a research contract, financed by the DGRST from 1974 to 1977, whose instigator was Augustin Girard, the person then in charge of the Service des Études et Recherches au Secrétariat d'État à la Culture [Department of Research at the State Office for Cultural Affairs].[1] My rereading is tinted with sadness. Michel de Certeau, the soul of this enterprise, passed away in January 1986 as had two other faces from the "first circle" of associates.[2] However, across these pages, a great movement of life comes back to me, a seething of ideas and plans, of laughter and voices, of naïveté and enthusiasm, and the all-too-rare feeling of participating in creation. As such, there were fierce discussions among us in which no one wanted to yield the advantage, points of view that intersected and more often that clashed unceremoniously, an entire unlikely and unusual élan that Michel de Certeau mysteriously aroused around him and enlivened with a strange generosity.[3] Later, during his stay in California (1978–84), I saw him produce the same alchemy with just as much success and just as light a touch, in spite of the difference of place, language, culture, and social context.

Where consumerism saw only the passive consumption of finished products, purchase volumes to be increased, or market shares moved from one brand to another, where Marxist vocabulary spoke in terms of exploitation, of imposed behaviors and products, of mass culture and uniformity, Michel de Certeau proposed as a primary postulate the creative activity of those in the practice of the ordinary and it was the responsibility of the ongoing study to bring "ways of operating" to the fore and to elaborate for them an initial theoretical mapping and shaping, which he called the "formality" of practices. From this work site, the master plan and the guiding lines were sketched out in informal meetings of the "first circle" and then clarified and pursued in more depth at the doctoral seminar in anthropology that Certeau gave at the University of

Paris VII, a seminar whose work was often prolonged in the small, smoky and noisy cafés of place Jussieu.

If Certeau inspired and led the enterprise from beginning to end, giving it his own style, his overall objective, his horizon of thought, this was never done by imposing his postulates and methods, nor by making our trio into an instrument of verification for his theory. During the research, he practiced—with an intelligent flexibility and the delicacy that he put into encounters with others—what he theorized. Thus, every research operation was conceived as the test for clearly stated hypotheses, with which one was supposed to faithfully treat the materials in an attempt at "bringing forth differences."[4] If he placed so highly the implementation of the analysis to be produced, it was because he was not satisfied with the divide established between disciplines of knowledge. He refused to believe that a "scientific status" was forever the privilege of certain fields of knowledge. On the link between the "sciences" and their exterior, he had more subtle ideas than the official vulgate at the time and his deep knowledge of the avatars of knowledge classifications allowed him to back history, like the other social sciences, with richer and more diversified conceptual references.[5]

Attentive to the explicit rigor of a method or of theoretical models, refusing to let himself be enclosed within the practice of one particular model or to accept the preeminence of a certain model, Certeau had an inveterate taste for controlled experimentation within the order of what is thinkable. Thus, there is nothing astonishing about his mistrust in regard to two tendencies, or temptations, common to the social sciences, and that he attributed to a gap in conceptual elaboration. The first of these tendencies is accustomed to thinking big, takes pleasure in pompous statements, and gives generalist and generalizing lectures about society. By nature having an answer for everything, such a discourse does not allow itself to be embarrassed by any contradiction; it always skirts around reality tests and never encounters a possible refutation. Certeau had in part read Karl Popper before 1970, before the first translations in France, perhaps under the influence of the information processing and criticism led by the *Archives de philosophie* under the direction of Marcel Régnier,[6] or from having circulated in Germany and across the Atlantic where the influence of Popper was massively exerted in the philosophy of science as in the social sciences. Popper's central thesis on the falsifiability of "scientific" statements, whose scientific status was precisely measured by the yardstick of their possible refutation, was made to please him. My first detailed discussion with him, much before the beginning of the joint work on practices, concerned the method of the history of science (in comparison to other specialized histories) and Anglophone epistemology. One of the recurrent themes was the problem of induction according to Popper, closely linked to the definition of the "demarcation criterion" between scientific theories and other theories.[7] Popper's thesis on the key role of falsifiability seduced Certeau through the modesty of its assertion, its economic character, in a sense, and through the provisional value that it gave to truth statements within a given theory. This satisfied his philosophical requirement and his experience as a historian. The problem of induction and of the demarcation criterion often led us to the question of skepticism and of the status of historical truth,[8] and thus brought back the reference, tinted with respect, to the work of Richard Popkin, uncontested master of the history of skepticism in its modern version.[9] Around 1970, for the series "Bibliothèque des sciences religieuses" of which he was in charge, Certeau had dreamed of having a collection of Popkin's articles translated.[10] This volume was never published because it proved to be difficult to put together and translate, but an impressive pile of Popkin's offprints figured in Certeau's personal library until the end.

His second aversion, or rather reticence, involved the erudition practiced as an end in itself, in order to avoid ideas and to shy away from the choice (and the responsibility) of an interpretation. Like all historians, he had learned about archival work, collating sources, and the minutiae of criticism, and he highly valued the "invention of the document," this moment when the historian, among the innumerable traces of the past, produces his or her material by defining relevant criteria, selection methods, and procedures for setting up series and parallels.[11] But this attentive and imaginative collection of sources did not suffice for him; he also believed in the benefits and the necessity of elucidation and explicit explanation in the "construction" of a research operation. This is why, at the very beginning of our trio's formation, it was clearly posited that our task would be neither to recapitulate the grand theories of the social by illustrating them, pro and con, or with ad hoc examples, nor, at the other extreme, to procure, through direct observation or by compiling earlier studies, an "encyclopedic description" of everyday life. Everything that up close or from a distance resembled an encyclopedic pretension made him recoil and I often wondered if a part of his Hegelian deception entered into this retreat—a plausible hypothesis, but no more than that.[12] He wished research work always to be clear-cut (a circumscription of a domain of objects, a statement of the study's methods, a proposition of theoretical hypotheses, a testing of the domain of objects retained in well-defined places, etc.).

Our own difficulties in conducting this study were born from this requirement. How could we grasp the activity of those who practice the ordinary, and how could we go *a contrario* from sociological and anthropological analyses? With our weak strength and without any illusion save our enthusiasm, we had to open up an immense construction site: we had to define a method, find models to apply to it, describe, compare, and differentiate activities that are by nature subterranean, ephemeral, fragile, and circumstantial—in short, seek by trial and error to elaborate "a practical science of the singular." We had to grasp the multiplicity of practices in action, not dream about them, succeed in rendering them intelligible so that others in turn might be able to study their operations. There was a desire at stake for a *reversal* of the analytic glance, and this desire was of course no stranger to the great disappointed commotion of May 1968; in order to succeed, this reversal had to be based on making practices factually visible and theoretically intelligible.[13] In retrospect, one may be amused by our audacity and optimism, and thinking about it now, it seems to me that both were justified. But that is up to the reader to decide.

In the setup phase, each of the three of us thus had to produce, in relation and in confrontation with the two others, his or her game of hypotheses and invent his or her material, in other words, determine a testing ground for these hypotheses. But first, one had to argue in defense of one's hypotheses, and then the first test came. At that point one often had to confess to the fragility of one's presupposition scaffolding. What seemed so attractive two weeks earlier collapsed like a house of cards or revealed itself to be perfectly useless for taking a real situation into consideration. Each of these stages was perilous. Although it was with great amiability, Michel de Certeau did not spare you or himself anything. Nuanced and subtle, his criticism was scathing because it went straight to the essential, with neither condescension nor pettiness. Because it did not grant itself more as the "authorized one," it deprived you of false theatrical exits and obliged you to really argue about the issue. Disarming, this criticism disarmed you, and in an instant you would lose your conceptual equipment and would realize that you had to start all over again from top to bottom. When, after several singeing experiences, a hypothesis finally survived this baptism by fire, you were still not at the end of your efforts. From then on, the difficulty concentrated on the fieldwork: good God how those who practice the ordinary became irksome, evasive, and uncertain in their "ways of operating"! One might even say that they had underhandedly decided to conspire against you and ruin the entire enterprise. It is useless to dwell on these phases of deception and discouragement; the standard literature contains quite a few nice stories about the trouble of the ethnologist or the sociologist confronted with his or her "terrain." Sometimes, after several deceptive and dismal weeks, the situation would suddenly be reversed, exaltation would overtake you and be communicated to your associates, and then a thousand contradictory details would make sense, all fitting together, just as the patient juxtaposition of small monochrome squares ends up composing the design of a mosaic.

This respite did not last long because soon a new difficulty had to be resolved. As voyagers in the ordinary, we had remained in a familiar world, inside a society to which everything attached us, our past, our education, our experiences, and our expectations. How were we rigorously to thematize this situation of "participating observation"? We knew *too much* about everyday life in France in the 1970s—our own lifestyle depended on it—and *not enough* because we were unable to benefit from any critical precedence, given the ambition of a "reversal" of the glance that we were pursuing. What meaning could we attribute to the microdifferences that we would find here and there? Would we have to ascribe them to the difference of generations, of family traditions, of local customs, of social groups, of ideologies, of circumstances? Did they stem from this circumstance or were they to be attributed to more profound regularities, buried within the secret of practices? Knowing my admiration for Aristotle, Certeau at that time would ask me, a bit mischievously, if the great one had a suggestion to offer in order to open up for us the path toward "a practical science of the singular." Based on my embarrassed and, in the end, humbly negative answer, Certeau would suggest that we might look for help from Freud or Wittgenstein. We thus learned together to travel from the same to otherness, each one with his or her favorite companions, Bourdieu, Foucault, Spinoza, Wittgenstein, and many others who were helpful to us, but strangely without any of us turning explicitly to Norbert Elias.[14] Then, little by little, a controlled and controllable distancing of our places and practices was constructed in order to enable us to marvel at them, interrogate them, and then give them back meaning and form in a sort of conceptual "re-creation"—a strange adventure that troubled us for a long time, absorbed us even more, and of which I retain a memory as being intellectually blissful.

Rereading today the parallel narratives of the journey across practices, two or three constituent traits appear clearly to me. We surveyed *urban spaces*, from small to large cities, each in our own way, spaces where there existed modes of *active sociability*, in the family, at school, in the neighborhood, among neighbors or work colleagues. What we paid close attention to stemmed from the common experience of a large segment of French society, considered at a particular moment in its history. Quite naturally, as all social description or experimentation, our work is dated and datable, limited and not exhaustive. Our interlocutors stemmed from the working class, from the lower middle class of employees and shopkeepers, and from the well-educated middle class; they shared the comfort and security of an "average condition" in the still prosperous France of the 1970s.

Undertaken today, an analogous study would have to explore an atomized reality where mounting unemployment has interrupted the functioning of procedures for social insertion through the work milieu and the corollary construction of social identities.[15] To the destructuration, for economic reasons, of the social fabric has been added the silent collapse of networks of belonging as well as other strongholds (political affiliations, trade unions, etc.). The transmission from generation to generation is becoming deficient.[16] Ordinary life has thus been profoundly reshaped whether in terms of the appropriation of private space or in the use of public spaces. The relation maintained between the neighborhood and the city has been transformed,[17] the generalization of the personal car has modified the alternating rhythm of work/leisure and accompanied the increase in the number of country homes toward which weekend travel has been multiplied. Likewise, much has changed in the preparation of meals, with the proliferation of semiprepared products (pie crusts) or ready-made meals to be reheated (frozen meals, which are nowadays very practical thanks to the microwave oven). Saving and spending behaviors and individual consumption practices are no longer the same because they are no longer exerted in the same economic and social context. In the same way, in the city, places and rites of merchant exchange have changed greatly.[18]

Today, to the reading of that which is written is added the intensive relation to the world of images through films, television, the use of the VCR, and the purchase of videotapes. New transforming practices of cultural products offered for consumption have appeared. Some people color in, paint over, and make double exposures of photographs. Others snatch up scraps of photocopies for artistic ends,[19] still others "mix" sound tracks and orchestrate a prerecorded melody using a "beat box," and so on. Everything is happening as if the generalization of reproduction devices (for images, sounds, and texts) had opened up users' imaginations to a new field of combinations and diversions. It would be along a range of these new practices that one would have to put the analytic schemata of *L'Invention du quotidien* to the test. From the initial trio, only Pierre Mayol remains to continue the investigation, which he is doing on youth culture and the whole of musical practices. Michel de Certeau is no longer and, as for me, a certain chain of circumstances associated me with this work for only a short time.[20] With this episode completed, I returned quite naturally to my province of origin, to the history and philosophy of science, and, as for the rest, rejoined the anonymous crowd of those who practice the ordinary.

Because of his ambition for a "reversal" of the glance, the two volumes of *L'Invention du quotidien* have been much read, discussed, and applied, imitated or copied, and sometimes unabashedly plagiarized. Each of us was able to recognize himself or herself, with or without quotation marks, under other pens and other signatures, but that just proved that we had had some attentive readers. Why had Certeau's theoretical propositions so often been silently reappropriated or pillaged without further ado? Why had people traced Pierre Mayol's methods of study, or my own, without saying a word? I would hypothesize that we did not belong to any school constituted within the market of ideas and methods, so we had no institutional identity; moreover, we exerted no power in the official administration of a discipline and this authorized the borrowings and minute conceptual pilferings. We had taken a certain pleasure in "crossing the borders" of fields of knowledge, methods, and literary genres; would it not be normal that we had to pay for it? In fact, in 1980, it was "transgressive," as it had been, in another form, back in May 1968, to believe in imagination, in the internal freedom of the "man without qualities." Our descriptive and interpretative hypotheses "disturbed" the established order, the hierarchy of abilities and knowledge. People sometimes treated us as "optimists" (as if that were an intellectual insult), and sometimes as "gullible fools" or as "dreamers," and people reproached us for not having revered God Marx the way his faithful understood that it should be done. Rereading our two volumes at present, I cannot stop thinking that on certain points, we had been correct in advance—may we be forgiven for it.

Next to the borrowers who did not recognize their debt, there were
those who, saying so, took up our hypotheses, our methods, our results
for their own and put them to the test, applying them by adapting them
to other situations. I have not drawn up a list of these successors and so I
will mention only a few recent works by Marc Augé, Anne-Marie Chartier
with Jean Hébrard, Marc Guillaume, or Louis Quéré.[21] Our work has
continued to serve social workers, counselors and trainers, and people
in the field, in the most diverse places;[22] I think Michel de Certeau would
have enjoyed this posterity the most because he would have felt that our
hypotheses were put forward to serve those who practice the ordinary.

In the Anglophone world, the circulation of our research has taken
place a bit differently. The translation of volume 1 and the strong presence of Michel de Certeau in California aroused a wide diffusion of his
ideas, which was continued and amplified after his death.[23] Not having
been translated at this time, volume 2, which the American publisher
had judged too closely linked to something specifically French to interest
the American public, was less read, but it did find perspicacious readers,
particularly in England — perhaps the European vicinity had something
to do with it. In any case, we, Michel de Certeau especially, Pierre Mayol
and myself to a lesser degree, have discovered a certain echo in English-
speaking countries right down to Australia, an echo in the disciplines of
urban sociology, cultural anthropology, "communication," or in a new
field, not yet recognized in France, cultural studies, a new way of writing the history and sociology of contemporary culture.[24]

This new edition, which I have established with the help of Pierre
Mayol for his own text, includes, in relation to the first edition, three
series of modifications, each one concerning one of the coauthors. First
comes the addition of two articles by Michel de Certeau, published after the appearance of volume 1 of *L'Invention du quotidien*, but that pursued its inspiration. This is why his name appears as a coauthor for this
second edition, contrary to what was done for the first. Along with Pierre
Mayol, we deemed it right and fair, legitimate as well, to salute his memory, to make visible his presence in this volume. Michel de Certeau had
aroused, enriched, and accompanied our research in so many ways that
it seemed quite natural to thus point out our debt to him. Each of us retains full responsibility for his or her part; I have already reminded the
reader that Certeau allowed us complete freedom to organize, each in
his or her own way, the monograph for which we were each responsible
and which was supposed to resonate with the analyses of volume 1. Right

from the composition of our trio, our two studies, on the practice of a
neighborhood through a family living in the Croix-Rousse neighborhood of Lyons, and the tactics of the Kitchen Women Nation [*le peuple
féminin des cuisines*], had been assigned the function of illustrating, through
the details of concrete cases, a common way of reading ordinary practices,
of putting theoretical propositions to the test, of correcting or nuancing
their assumptions, and of measuring their operativity and relevance.

In this new edition, Michel de Certeau is thus established at the
three main checkpoints whose titles are my own. As an "entrée" figures
the brief introductory text that had also opened the first edition of volume 2. For the "intermezzo," in order to conclude Pierre Mayol's study
of urban space, I selected Certeau's article on Paris, "Les revenants de la
ville" ["Ghosts in the City"], written at the request of Michel Vernes for
an issue titled "Paris, le retour de la ville" (*Architecture intérieure/Créé*
192–93 [January–March 1983]: 98–101). As an "envoi," I inserted an article that we had coauthored under the title "La culture comme on la
pratique" (*Le français dans le monde* 181 [November–December 1983]:
19–24). For "Les revenants de la ville," I followed the version, slightly
corrected according to indications written by Certeau on his own copy,
that I had edited for a republication as a tribute to him (*Traverses* 40, titled "Théâtres de la mémoire" [April 1987]: 74–85; this issue was dedicated to Certeau's memory as mentioned on pp. 4–5). For the coauthored text, I allowed myself to modify it, deleting some passages that
summarized the arguments of *L'Invention du quotidien*, clarifying other
points, but all in all without straying from his main line of argument. I
gave it a title based on a phrase that figured in his conclusion and that
perfectly summarized the intention of our work on ordinary culture.[25]

Pierre Mayol and I decided of a common accord to not yield to the
temptation of profoundly reworking our two studies. Because Michel de
Certeau did not have the chance to take up volume 1 again, rewriting
volume 2 would have introduced a gap between the two with this new
edition. We thus limited ourselves overall to touching up a few details
in order to eliminate repetition or stylistic heaviness, and to tighten, clarify, or nuance an expression here and there. Pierre Mayol has added about
twenty notes, each indicated by an asterisk, to update information and
point out a few recent studies. Moreover, he wrote up two "supplemental notes" on the present state of the Croix-Rousse neighborhood. They
are placed near the end of chapter 3; one involves the unemployment of
young people and the other analyzes recent demographic evolution in

light of the 1990 census. The work carried out by Pierre Mayol on his own part constitutes the second series of modifications mentioned earlier.

The third series concerns my part. I did not enrich the note system nor the bibliographic information in it for the simple reason that I have not pursued further research in this domain. On the other hand, I have added two articles that appeared shortly after the first edition of volume 2 and that complemented its analyses. The first of these texts, placed within the "intermezzo," treats the relation to private space and seemed to me to furnish a natural transition from the urban space studied by Mayol, and then evoked by Certeau, to the private space of kitchens, with which my part is concerned. A governmental agency for urban planning [*Plan-Construction*] had requested this article from me for the catalog of an exposition that it was organizing at the Trocadéro ("Lieu de corps, lieu de vie" [A place for the body, a place for life], in *Construire pour habiter* [Paris: L'Équerre and Plan-Construction, 1982], 16–17). I have amended it and added a few points. My other addition comes from another article, "Travaux de cuisine, gestes d'autrefois" (*Culture technique* 3, titled *Machines au foyer* [September 1980]: 63–71). I improved it and inserted it in what was the last chapter, "Gesture Sequences," of my part of the first edition. This led me to divide up the material from this chapter in a different way: its beginning, plus the article from *Culture technique*, have become chapter 12 in this edition while retaining the earlier title of the chapter. The rest of the first version of this chapter constitutes a new chapter 13 titled "The Rules of the Art," also modified and sometimes added to.

As for the interviews that made up the two last chapters of the first edition, neither Mayol nor myself has changed a single word of them. I have simply shifted their placement so that each one may conclude the study that it illustrates. The stories of Madame Marie and Madame Marguerite collected in Lyons now constitute chapter 7 at the end of Part I. The long interview with Irène on cooking makes up chapter 14 at the end of Part II. As for volume 1, I have edited the totality of this volume's text and established the index of names, which will allow the reader to judge the intellectual company that we kept and to follow the journeys of our interlocutors in the streets and shops of the Croix-Rousse or in the secrecy of kitchens, through this back-and-forth from the past to the present of the past, through practices of which certain ones have already receded from us. We were very fond of these intersectings of experiences and voices, these stories of times and places, these gestures that came from afar, fragments of life whose secrets and poetic ruses wove the fabric of a soon-to-be lost time, ephemeral inventions of the "ob-scure heros" of the ordinary, *arts de faire* that make up without saying so an *art de vivre*. The modifications and additions brought to this new edition had the sole intention of rendering more perceptible the music of these anonymous voices that speak the gestures of every day and the treasures of ingenuity that those who practice the everyday deploy there.

Entrée[1]

Michel de Certeau

The Annals of Everyday Life

Everyday life is what we are given every day (or what is willed to us), what presses us, even oppresses us, because there does exist an oppression of the present. Every morning, what we take up again, *on awakening*, is the weight of life, the difficulty of living, or of living in a certain condition, with a particular weakness or desire. Everyday life *is what holds us intimately*, from the inside. It is a history at the halfway point of ourselves, almost in a recess, sometimes veiled; we should not forget this *"memory world,"* to use Péguy's expression. We have our hearts set on such a world, a world of olfactory memory, memory of childhood places, of the body, of childhood gestures, of pleasures. We should perhaps underline the importance of the domain of this "irrational" history, or this "nonhistory," according to Alphonse Dupront. What interests the historian of everyday life is the *invisible*.[1]

It's not all that invisible. The intention of this second volume, an undoubtedly more important facet than the explanation of ways of operating and modes of action in the first one,[2] is precisely to trace the interlacings of a concrete sense of everyday life, to allow them to appear within the space of a memory. Only partial and necessarily limited, these annals of everyday life can only be, in a language of expectation, effects marked by those "obscure heroes" of whom we are the debtors and fellow creatures. This study, a haunted narrativity, thus does not seek to chase the living and the dead out of the house of the authors in which they live in order to make them into "objects" for analysis. It articulates itself by way of the relationship that their strangeness has with familiarity.

It is organized according to two motifs. On the one hand, living in a neighborhood according to family practices recalls the "swarming structure of the street,"[3] which is also the anthill-like structure of activities punctuated by spaces and relationships. On the other hand, culinary virtuosities establish the plural language of stratified histories, of multiple relationships between enjoyment and manipulation, of fundamental languages spelled out in everyday details.

These two studies, born of a common task, placed under the general rubric of everyday practices, have gained their freedom.[4] They escape. They follow their own paths. There should be many others, which in fact are not lacking. I am thinking of *Pedigree* by Georges Simenon, who said the following about his Old Désiré, living in Liège:

> He had arranged his days so that they were a harmonious succession of little joys, and the absence of the least of these joys threatened the whole edifice. A cup of coffee and a slice of bread and butter, a dish of bright-green peas, reading the paper beside the fire, a maidservant standing on a pair of steps and washing a window, a thousand quiet pleasures which were waiting for him at every turning of life, which he had foreseen and looked forward to, were as necessary to him as the air he breathed, and it was thanks to them that he was incapable of feeling any real suffering.[5]

"The annals of anonymity," as Valéry said.

But finally, their "meaning," linking a way of operating to a way of living, was written anonymously as a bit of graffiti in the rue des Rosiers in Paris: "When will you let yourself be happy?"

part I

Living

Pierre Mayol

Chapter 1
The Neighborhood

This study on the manners of city living aims at elucidating the cultural practices of city dwellers in the very space of their neighborhood. For a starting point, logical if not chronological, at least two problematics offer themselves as a way to implement the research:

1. *The urban sociology of the neighborhood.* It essentially privileges data relative to space and architecture; it takes measurements (surface area, topography, the flux of movements, etc.) and analyzes objective material and administrative constraints that enter into the definition of the neighborhood.

2. *The socioethnographic analysis of everyday life,* which proliferates from the erudite research of folklore specialists and historians of "popular culture," to the vast poetic, even mythic, frescoes that the work of a James Agee represents in an exemplary way.[1] From there, an unexpectedly lively offshoot detaches itself and becomes what one might call the hagiography of the poor, a literary genre of considerable success, whose "lives" more or less well transcribed by researchers, give the bittersweet illusion of rediscovering a people lost forever.[2]

These two opposed perspectives risked blurring the maps of our research by dragging us behind two *indeterminate discourses*: that of *regret* at not being able to propose a "fabrication" method for ideal spaces where dwellers could finally fully fit into their urban environment; and that of the *murmuring* of the everyday in which one can multiply the soundings indefinitely without ever locating the structures that organize it.

The chosen method consisted of joining these two sides of a similar approach in the hopes of establishing a system of control that would allow us to avoid indeterminate discursivity: to work at the objective matter of the neighborhood (external constraints, dispositions, etc.) only to the point where it becomes the terrain of choice for a "setting and staging of everyday life"; to work both setting and staging insofar as they concern the *public* space in which they are deployed. Some specific problems have come up: we were no longer working on objects carved out of the social field in only a speculative way (*the* neighborhood, *the* everyday life), but on *relationships* among objects, more precisely on the link that attaches private to public space. The mastery of this separation by the dweller, what it implies in terms of specific actions, "tactics," remains the essential foundation of this study: this is one of the conditions of possibility for everyday life in urban space, which decisively molds the notion of neighborhood.

Problematics

The organization of everyday life is articulated on at least two registers:

1. One is *behaviors*, whose system is visible in the social space of the street and which is translated by dress, the more or less strict application of politeness codes (greetings, "friendly" words, requests such as "how's the family?"), the rhythm of walking, the avoidance of, or, on the contrary, the frequent trips to a particular space.

2. The other is that of *expected symbolic benefits* gained through ways of "behaving" in neighborhood space: behaving well "yields a profit," but of what? The analysis here is extremely complex; it stems less from description than from *interpretation*. These benefits are rooted in the cultural tradition of the dweller, who is never totally aware of them. They appear in a partial, fragmented way within his or her walk or, more generally, in the mode in which he or she "consumes" public space. But they can also be elucidated through the *discourse of meaning* through which the dweller carries out the near totality of his or her steps. The neighborhood thus appears as the place where one manifests a social "commitment"; in other words, an art of coexisting with the partners (neighbors, shopkeepers) who are linked to you by the concrete, but essential, fact of proximity and repetition.

One regulation articulates both of these systems, which I have described and analyzed using the concept of *propriety*. Propriety is largely comparable to the system of the communal "kitty": it is, at the level of behaviors, a compromise in which each person, by renouncing the anarchy of individual impulses, makes a down payment to the collectivity with the goal of withdrawing from it symbolic benefits necessarily deferred in time. Through this "price to pay" (knowing how to "behave," to be "proper"), the dweller becomes a partner in a social contract that he or she consents to respect so that everyday life is possible. "Possible" is to be understood in the most banal sense of the term: not to make life "hell" with an abusive rupture of the implicit contract on which the neighborhood's coexistence is based. The compensation of this coercion for the dweller is the certitude of being recognized, "well thought of" by those around one, and of thus founding an advantageous relationship of forces in the diverse trajectories that he or she covers.

One can now better grasp the concept of a "cultural practice":[3] it is the more or less coherent and fluid assemblage of elements that are concrete and everyday (a gourmet menu) or ideological (religious, political), at once coming from a tradition (that of a family or social group) and reactualized from day to day across behaviors translating fragments of this cultural device into social visibility, in the same way that the utterance translates fragments of discourse in speech. A "practice" is what is decisive for the *identity* of a dweller or a group insofar as this identity allows him or her to take up a position in the network of social relations inscribed in the environment.

The neighborhood is, almost by definition, a mastery of the social environment because, for the dweller, it is a known area of social space in which, to a greater or lesser degree, he or she knows himself or herself to be recognized. The neighborhood can thus be grasped as this area of public space in general (anonymous, for everyone) in which little by little a *private, particularized space* insinuates itself as a result of the practical, everyday use of this space. The fact that dwellers have their homes here, the reciprocal habituation resulting from being neighbors, the processes of recognition — of identification — that are created thanks to proximity, to concrete coexistence in the same urban territory: all these "practical" elements offer themselves for use as vast fields of exploration with a view to understanding a little better the great unknown that is everyday life.

Having specified these analytic elements, I became attached to the monographic study of a family living in a neighborhood of Lyons, the Croix-Rousse. I myself come from this neighborhood. The division between the objective data of the study and my personal roots here is not obvious. Study of family members' personalities and of the relationships between them has been deliberately excluded to the extent that these did not concern the task's objective: the description and interpretation of the ways through which one takes possession of urban space in the neighborhood, in relation to which biographical or psychological considerations have only limited pertinence; I described less a family than the trajectories that it implemented in its neighborhood, and the way in which these trajectories are entrusted to one or another family member according to necessity. Moreover, I have retained only a few characters: Madame Marie, then age eighty-three, a former corset maker in a large downtown firm who was widowed in 1950;[4] Maurice, her elder son, sixty years old, a worker in a lumberyard of the west suburb, father of two sons, divorced; Joseph, the younger son, fifty-eight, single, a worker at the Rhône-Poulenc factory in the south suburb of Lyons (Saint-Fons); Jean twenty-five, a grandson, former gild worker in a jewelry store, currently a temporary worker, like many in his generation who are crushed by the economic crisis. I should also mention Michèle, Catherine, Benoît, Gérard, and so many others...[5]

Rightly or wrongly, I preferred to entrust the essential elements of the study to only a few people, while accumulating behind them the fruits of my prospecting within a much wider sphere of relationships. In this reconstruction, I endeavored to respect as much as possible the discourse of diverse generations, clearly privileging older people and adults because the time invested by them in the neighborhood facilitated one of the main lines of research polarized by the problem—a temporal one if nothing else—of *appropriation*.

What Is a Neighborhood?

To this embarrassing question, the work of sociology proposes several answers from which we will pull out some invaluable indications about the dimensions that define a neighborhood, about its historical, aesthetic, topographical, and socioprofessional characteristics.[6] I especially retain the proposition of Henri Lefebvre, for whom the neighborhood is "an entrance and exit between qualified spaces and a quantified space"—a key proposition for the inauguration of our first step. The neighborhood appears as the domain in which the space-time relationship is the most favorable for a dweller who moves from place to place *on foot, starting from his or her home*. Therefore, it is that piece of the city that a limit crosses distinguishing private from public space: it is the result of a *walk*, of a succession of steps on a road, conveyed little by little through the organic link to one's lodgings.

Faced with the totality of the city, obstructed by codes that the dweller has not mastered but that he or she must assimilate in order to live there, faced with a configuration of places imposed by urban planning, faced with the social unevenness inside urban space, the dweller always succeeds in creating places of withdrawal, itineraries for his or her use and pleasure that are individual marks that the dweller alone inscribes on urban space. The neighborhood is a dynamic notion requiring a progressive apprenticeship that grows with the repetition of the dweller's body's engagement in public space until it exercises a sort of appropriation of this space. The everyday banality of this process, shared among all urbanites, renders invisible its complexity as a cultural practice and its urgency in satisfying the *urban* desire of dwellers in the city.

As a result of its everyday use, the neighborhood can be considered as the progressive privatization of public space. It is a practical device whose function is to ensure a continuity between what is the most intimate (the private space of one's lodging) and what is the most unknown (the totality of the city or even, by extension, the rest of the world); "a relationship exists between the apprehension of lodging (an 'inside') and the apprehension of the urban space to which it is connected (an 'outside')."[7] The neighborhood is the middle term in an existential dialectic (on a personal level) and a social one (on the level of a group of users), between inside and outside. And it is in the tension between these two terms, an *inside* and an *outside*, which little by little becomes the continuation of an inside, that the appropriation of space takes place. As a result, the neighborhood can be called an outgrowth of the abode; for the dweller, it amounts to the sum of all trajectories inaugurated from the dwelling place. It is less an urban surface, transparent for everyone or statistically measurable, than the possibility offered everyone to inscribe in the city a multitude of trajectories whose hard core permanently remains the private sphere.

This appropriation implies actions that reconstruct the space proposed by the environment, to the extent of the subjects' investment, and that are the main pieces of a spontaneous cultural practice: without them, life in the city is impossible. First of all, there is the elucidation of a formal analogy between the neighborhood and one's home: each of them has, within its own limits, the highest rate of personal development possible because both are the only empty "places" where, in different ways, one can *do* what one wants. Because of the empty space inside constrained concrete layouts—the walls of an apartment, the facades of a street—the act of arranging one's interior space rejoins that of arranging one's own trajectories in the urban space of the neighborhood, and these two acts are the cofounders of everyday life in an urban milieu: to take away one or the other would be to destroy the conditions of possibility for this life. Thus, the limit between public and private, which appears to be the founding structure of the neighborhood for the practice of a dweller, is not only a separation, but constitutes a separation that unites: the public and private are not both disregarded as two exogenous, though coexisting, elements; they are much more, constantly interdependent because, in the neighborhood, one has no meaning without the other.

The neighborhood is also the space of a relationship to the other as a social being, requiring a special treatment. To leave one's home, to walk in the street, is right away to commit a cultural, nonarbitrary act: it inscribes the inhabitant in a network of social signs that preexist him or her (proximity, configuration of places, etc.). The relationship between entrance and exit, inside and outside, intersects with others such as between home and work, known and unknown, hot and cold, humid and dry weather, activity and passivity, masculine and feminine; this is always a relationship between oneself and the physical and social world; it is the organizer of an inaugural and even archaic structure of the urban "public subject" through the unflagging, because everyday, stomping around, which buries in a determinate soil the elementary seeds (decomposable into discrete units) of a dialectic constitutive of the self-awareness that, in this come-and-go movement, in this move between social mixing and intimate withdrawal, finds the certainty of itself as immediately social.

The neighborhood too is the place of passage by the other, untouchable because it is distant, and yet recognizable through its relative stability; neither intimate nor anonymous—a *neighbor*.[8] The practice of the neighborhood is, from childhood on, a technique of recognizing space as something social; everyone must have a turn at taking up a position in it: one is from the Croix-Rousse or from the rue Vercingétorix, just as one is known as Pierre or Paul. A signature attesting to an origin, the neighborhood is inscribed in the history of the subject like the mark of an indelible belonging inasmuch as it is the primary configuration, the archetype of every process of appropriation of space as a place for everyday public life.

By contrast, the relationship that links home to the workplace is, most generally in the urban space, marked by the *necessity* of a spatiotemporal coercion that requires traveling a maximum of distance in a minimum of time. Everyday language here provides an extremely precise description: "jumping out of bed," "eating on the run," "catching one's train," "diving into the subway," "arriving right on time"... Through these stereotypes, we see what "going to work" really means: entering into an undifferentiated, indistinct city, sinking into the magma of inert signs as in a swamp, guided only by the imperative of being on time (or late). Only the succession of the most univocal actions possible counts with a view toward improving the pertinence of the space-time relationship. In communication terms, one can say that the process (the syntagmatic axis) prevails over the system (the paradigmatic axis).

The practice of the neighborhood introduces gratuitousness instead of necessity; it favors a use of urban space whose end is not only functional. Ultimately, it aims at according *the maximum of time to a minimum of space* in order to liberate the possibilities for wandering about. The system carries over into the process; a stroller's walk in the neighborhood always carries several meanings: a dream of traveling in front of a particular display window, a brief sensual agitation, the arousal of the sense of smell under the trees in the park, memories of itineraries buried since childhood, joyous, serene, or bitter reflections on one's own destiny, as many "segments of meaning" as can be substituted for each other as the walk goes on, without order or constraint, aroused by chance meetings, incited by the floating attention to "events" that constantly take place in the street.

The city, in the strongest sense, is "poeticized" by the subject: the subject has refabricated it for his or her own use by undoing the constraints of the urban apparatus and, as a consumer of space, imposes his or her own law on the external order of the city. The neighborhood is thus, in the strongest sense of the term, an object of consumption that the dweller appropriates by way of the privatization of public space. All the conditions are assembled there to favor this exercise: knowledge of the surroundings, daily trips, relationships with neighbors (politics), relationships with shopkeepers (economics), diffuse feelings of being on one's territory (ethology), so many indices whose accumulation and combination produce and then organize the social and cultural apparatus according to which urban space becomes not only the object of a knowledge, but *the place of a recognition.*

Therefore, and to take up again a key distinction from Michel de Certeau, the practice of the neighborhood stems from a *tactic* whose place is "only that of the other." What the dweller gains in truly "possessing" his or her neighborhood neither counts nor is at stake in an exchange requiring a power relationship: the experience gained through habituation is only the improvement of the "way of operating," of strolling, of going to the market, through which the dweller can constantly verify the intensity of his or her insertion in the social environment.

Chapter 2
Propriety

Obligation and Recognition

The neighborhood is thus defined as a collective organization of individual trajectories; it involves places "close at hand" put at the dwellers' disposal in which they necessarily meet each other in order to provide for their everyday needs. But the interpersonal contact that takes place in these meetings is itself random, not calculated in advance; it is defined by chance comings and goings involving the necessities of everyday life: in the elevator, at the grocery store, at the market. By going out into the neighborhood, it is impossible not to come across someone you "already know" (a neighbor, a shopkeeper), but nothing can say in advance who or where (on the stairs, on the sidewalk). This relationship between the formal necessity of the encounter and the random aspect of its content pushes the dweller to behave as if "on guard" within precise social codes, all centered around the fact of *recognition* in the sort of indecisive collectivity—thus undecided and undecidable—that is the neighborhood.

By "neighborhood collectivity," I mean the raw, materially unpredictable fact of the encounter of subjects who, without being absolutely anonymous on account of proximity, are not absolutely integrated into the network of preferential human relationships (friendship, family) either. The neighborhood imposes a *savoir faire of simultaneously undecidable and inevitable coexistence*: the neighbors are there, on my floor, on my street, and it is impossible to avoid them forever; "one has to make do," to find an equilibrium between the proximity imposed by the public configuration of places and the distance necessary to safeguard one's private life. Neither too far, nor too close, so as not to be bothered and also not to lose the expected benefits of a good relationship with the neighbors: thus, one must win on all counts by mastering, without losing anything, the system of relationships imposed by space. Defined as such, the collectivity is a social place that induces a practical behavior by which each dweller adjusts to the general process of recognition by conceding a part of himself or herself to the jurisdiction of the other.

An individual who is born or moves into a neighborhood is obliged to take his or her social environment into consideration, to insert himself or herself into it in order to be able to live there. "Obliged" should not only be understood in a repressive sense, but also as something that "obliges," which creates obligations, *links* [*liens*], etymologically.[1] The practice of the neighborhood is a tacit collective convention, unwritten, but legible to all dwellers through the codes of language and of behavior; any submission to these codes, just as any transgression, is immediately the object of commentary: a norm exists and it is even weighty enough to play the game of social exclusion when faced with "eccentrics," those who "are not or do not act like us." Conversely, this norm is the manifestation of a contract that has a positive compensation: it allows for the coexistence on the same territory of partners who are, a priori, "not linked"; a contract, thus a "constraint" that obliges each person, so that the life of the "collective public" that is the neighborhood becomes possible for everyone.

To go out into the street is to constantly run the risk of being *recognized, thus pointed out*. The practice of the neighborhood implies adhesion to a system of values and behaviors forcing each dweller to remain behind a mask playing his or her role. To emphasize the word *behavior* indicates that the *body* is the primary, fundamental support for the social message proffered, without knowing it, by the dweller: smiling or not smiling, for example, is an opposition that empirically divides dwellers, on the social terrain of the neighborhood, into partners who are "friendly" or not; in the same way, clothing indicates an adhesion or not to the implicit contract of the neighborhood because, in its own way, it "speaks" the conformity of the dweller to (or his or her deviation from) what is supposed to be the "correct way" of the neighborhood. The body is the support for all the gestural messages that articulate this conformity: it is a blackboard on which is written—and thus rendered legible—the respect for codes, or the deviation from them, in relation to the system of behaviors.[2]

Transgressive deviation, moreover, possesses a wide range of possibilities: it can involve the minitransgression, in relation to the everyday continuum, that is the clothing of a woman who is "dressed to go out" one night ("She's dressed to the nines"; "You look wonderful tonight"), or, on the other hand, the complete dislocation of the recognition codes by an alcoholic under the influence who make noise at night. In short, the body, in the street, is always accompanied by a knowledge of the representation of the body whose code is more or less, yet sufficiently, understood by all dwellers and that I will designate with the word that is most appropriate to it: *propriety*.

This will appear to us as the conjunction of two lexicons associated with the same grammar: on the one hand, there is the lexicon of the body proper, the way of presenting itself on diverse occasions in the neighborhood (waiting in line at the grocer's, speaking loudly or softly, giving precedence or not to other partners according to the supposed hierarchical rank that dwellers believe they must maintain in certain circumstances); on the other hand, there is the lexicon of "benefits" expected from the progressive mastery of these occasions, based on habituation to the social space of the neighborhood. As for the grammar, it corresponds, one might say, to the space organized in trajectories around the living space, there where the dweller's body allows itself to be seen, and through which it brings home benefits acquired during its diverse prospecting.

Propriety

1. *Minuscule repressions.* Propriety first imposes itself on this analysis through its negative role: it is related to law, that which renders the social field heterogeneous by forbidding the distribution of any kind of behavior in any order at any time. It represses what is "not proper," "what one does not do"; it maintains at a distance, by filtering and exposing them, the signs of behaviors that are illegible in the neighborhood, intolerable for it, destructive, for example, of the dweller's personal reputation. This indicates that it maintains close relationships with educational processes implicit in every social group: it takes care of decreeing the "rules" of social custom, inasmuch as the social is the space of the other, and the medium for the position of self as a public being. Propriety is the symbolic management of the public facet of each of us as soon as we enter the street. Propriety is simultaneously the manner in which one is perceived and the means constraining one to remain submitted to it; fundamentally, it requires the avoidance of all dissonance in the game of behaviors and all qualitative disruption in the perception of the social environment. That is why it produces stereotyped behaviors, ready-to-wear social clothes, whose function is to make it possible to recognize anyone, anywhere.

Propriety imposes an ethical justification of behaviors that is intuitively measurable because it distributes them along an organizing axis of value judgments: the "quality" of the human relationship such that it is deployed within the instrument of social verification that is the neighborhood is not the quality of a social "know-how," but of a "knowing-how-to-live-with"; to the observation of contact or no contact with this other who is the neighbor (or any other "role" established by the internal necessities of neighborhood life) should be added an appreciation, I would dare say a fruition, of this contact.

We are now entering the field of the symbolic, not reducible, in anthropological analysis, to the statistical quantification of behaviors, nor to their taxonomic distribution. The field of the symbolic is "equivalently" that of the "cultural rule," of the *internal regulation* of behaviors as the effect of a heritage (emotional, political, economic, etc.) that overruns from all sides the subject implanted *hic et nunc* in the behavior that allows him or her to be located on the social surface of the neighborhood. Thus, some motivation is always added to the necessity of the encounter: like or dislike, "hot" or "cold," begins to superimpose itself on ("to color," as one might say) the system of "public" relations. The ethical axis of this motivation, what animates it from within, is the aim of *mediocritas* [moderation]. Not mediocrity, but the point of *social neutrality* in which the differences of individual behaviors are maximally abolished: one must respect the old proverb *in medio stat virtus* [excellence lies midway]. The bearing of the passerby must carry the least amount of information possible, to manifest the least amount of deviance in relation to the stereotypes allowed by the neighborhood; however, it must affirm the greatest participation in the standardization of behaviors.[3] The level of propriety is proportional to the lack of differentiation in the corporal manifestation of attitudes. To "remain a dweller in the neighborhood," and to benefit from the stock of relationships it contains, it is *not proper* to "be noticed." Every too-obvious deviation, especially in clothing behaviors, impacts this symbolic integrity; this is immediately echoed on the level of language in an ethical appreciation of the moral "quality" of the dweller, and the terms used can be extremely severe: "she's a slut," "he's just showing off," "he's snubbing us..." From the subject's point of view, propriety rests on an internal legislation that can be summed up in one phrase: "What are they going to think of me?" or "What are the neighbors going to say if...?"

2. *The social transparency of the neighborhood.* The neighborhood is a social universe that does not take transgression very well; this is incompatible with the supposed transparency of everyday life, with its immediate legibility; it must take place elsewhere, hide itself in the darkness of the "bad side of town," or flee into the private folds of the household. The neighborhood is a "diurnal" scene whose characters are, at every moment, identifiable in the role that propriety assigns to them — the child, the grocer, the family mother, the teenager, the retired man, the priest, the doctor — so many masks behind which the dweller of a neighbor-

hood is "obliged" to take refuge in order to continue collecting expected symbolic benefits. Propriety tends constantly to elucidate the nocturnal pockets of the neighborhood, an unflagging task of curiosity that, like an insect with enormous antennae, patiently explores all the nooks and crannies of public space, scans behaviors, interprets events, and constantly produces an irrepressible interrogative buzz: Who is who and who is doing what? Where is this new customer from? Who is the new tenant? Chatting and curiosity are internal impulses absolutely fundamental to the everyday practice of the neighborhood: on the one hand, they nourish the motivation for neighbor relations, but on the other, they constantly try to abolish the strangeness contained by the neighborhood; chatting is a repeated exorcism against the alteration of the social space of the neighborhood by unpredictable events that might cross it, it seeks "a reason for everything," and it measures everything against the backdrop of propriety. This being the point at which the character becomes legible to others, it is situated on the border that separates strangeness from what is recognizable. If one can say that every rite is the ordered assumption of an initial impulsive disorder, its symbolic "locking mechanism" in the social field, then *propriety is the rite of the neighborhood*: every dweller is subjected by it to a collective life whose lexicon is assimilated in order to prepare oneself for a structure of exchanges that will in turn allow him or her to propose, to articulate the signs of his or her own recognition. Propriety withdraws from social exchanges all "noises" that could alter the picture to be recognized; it filters everything that does not aim at obtaining *clarity*. But, and here is its positive side, if propriety imposes its own coercion, it is in the hopes of a "symbolic" benefit to acquire or maintain.

3. *The consumption and appearance of the body.* The concept of propriety becomes particularly pertinent at the level of consumption, as an everyday relationship with the quest for food and services. It is in this relationship that the accumulation of symbolic capital plays out best, and a capital from which the dweller will obtain expected benefits. The role of the body and its accessories (words, gestures) within the concrete event of the "presentation of self" possesses a key symbolic function on which propriety tends to base an order of equivalence where what is received is proportionate to what is given. Thus, buying is not just paying money for food, but in addition, being well served if one is a good customer. The act of buying is surrounded by the halo of a "motivation" that, one might say, precedes it before its completion: *faithfulness*. This uncountable surplus in the strict logic of the exchange of goods and services

is directly symbolic: it is the effect of a consensus, a tacit understanding between customer and shopkeeper that undoubtedly shows through at the level of gestures and words but is never mentioned explicitly in itself. It is the fruit of a long, reciprocal *habituation* in which each person knows what he or she can ask of or give to the other in hopes of an improvement of the relationship to the objects of exchange.

The economy of words, gestures, "explanations," as well as the economy of time, opens a path straight toward a growth in quality: the quality of objects for certain, but also the quality of the relationship itself. The latter functions in a special way: it does not proceed by way of a deepening as in friend or love relationships; it aims, on the contrary, at a sort of exaltation of the single process of recognition. It is necessary and it suffices to be recognized ("regarded," one might say) so that, for this one reason, the consensus will function, like a wink that would never go further than a blink except by improving itself through the simple act of repetition. Recognition becomes a process whose functioning is taken over by propriety. Between what is said (the shopkeeper's polite phrases, for example, whose content and intonation vary from customer to customer, adapted as they are to the habituation of each) and what is not (the calculation of the benefit in the relationship to objects), propriety gives rise to a complicity in which each person knows (not by a conscious knowledge, but by one acquired through the "circumstance" of the purchase)[4] that what one says is not immediately what is at stake and that, nevertheless, *this disparity between what is said and what is unsaid is the structure of the exchange* currently engaged, and that it is to this law that it is proper to consent in order to benefit from it. The relationship that links a customer to a shopkeeper (and vice versa) is made from the progressive insertion of an implicit discourse within the explicit words of conversation, which weaves between both partners in the purchase a network of signs, tenuous but efficient, favoring the process of recognition.

The deeds and gestures of propriety are the indirect style—the mask—of the benefit pursued through the relationships of the neighborhood. Thus, far from exhausting the possibilities of social space little by little, it favors, on the contrary, an undefined personal insertion into the collective fabric of the environment. That is why the time factor has such importance for dwellers, because it authorizes them to make demands that only habituation allows them to make. The level of consumption is, for the observer, one of the privileged places where the "socialness" of dwellers is verified, where the typical hierarchies of the street are elaborated, where the social roles of the neighborhood are polished up (the child, the man, the woman, etc.), and where the conventions agreed upon by characters momentarily assembled on the same stage are massed.

4. *The social task of signs.* This concept explains the complexity of relationships engaged in the small public space of the neighborhood. The signs of propriety are remarkable in that they are, with time, only rough sketches, incomplete linguistic strokes, barely articulated, fragments: a language of half-words, frozen in the smile of politeness, the silent compliment of the man who steps back to allow a woman to cut in front of him, or, conversely, the silently aggressive vigor with which one holds one's place "in line" ("I'm next..."), the furtive glances of the shopkeeper who, out of the corner of his or her eye, evaluates the behavior of a stranger or a newcomer, the automatic dialogues of the gossips who meet on the "doorstep," the unconscious recording of the neighbor's steps down the hall "who must be bringing back her shopping, it's about her time now..." These are worn-out, even hackneyed, stereotypes, but whose function is to ensure "contact" (the phatic function of language):[5] has communication been achieved or not? If so, going further does not matter! The symbolic equilibrium has not been ruptured and, for this reason alone, a benefit has been gained.

Fundamentally, the stereotypes of propriety are, through the presentation of the body, a manipulation of social distance and they are expressed under the negative form of a "how far is not going too far?" attitude, in order to retain the contact established by habituation and, at the same time, not become dependent on a too-close familiarity. The search for this equilibrium creates a tension that must continually be resolved by corporal bearing. For this reason, the quest for benefits is transformed into signs of recognition. The expected benefit cannot be brutally formulated: this would make the implicit spring forth directly into speech, without the mediation of the symbols of propriety. Supposing that the quest for the benefit is nakedly expressed ("serve me well and quick now because I'm a longtime customer"), this would break off, in one shot, the benefit of a contact accumulated over a long period of time: the dweller, like the shopkeeper, for that matter, must "behave well." The body thus bears a request that censorship covers up in the name of propriety by imposing controls that protect it against itself and therefore render it presentable within social space. One might say that propriety, with all its constraints, plays the role of a *reality principle* that socializes the demand by deferring its fulfillment. How can one behave at the butcher shop to calculate, "without seeming to," the price and quality of the meat, without it being perceived as mistrust? What can one say to the grocer, and at which moments (off-peak times, rush hour?), to continue being recognized without going overboard into a familiarity that is not proper because it exceeds the roles authorized by propriety? Over and over again, what are the appropriate signs that will clinch and stabilize the signs of recognition?

These signs, buried deep within the body, emerge on the surface, and slip toward the few points that are always before one's eyes: the face and hands. This fragmented body is the dweller's public face; a sort of "contemplation" is verified on it, that of a secret attention calculating the equilibrium between a demand and a response, providing a supplement of signs when, with equilibrium lacking, it is proper to reestablish it (a smile, an extra word, a slightly more insistent submission). The complementarity between demand and response is not static—it always aims at a sustained increase in the possibility for demanding and responding; there must be "something deferred," a remainder that will start the game of demand and response all over again because of the slight disequilibrium that it gives rise to.

To be "proper," one must know how to play "whoever loses wins," not to require everything immediately in order to always subsequently defer complete control of the expected benefit in the consumption relationship: the benefit also grows because it knows how to give up. The body knows it: it reads on the body of the other the discreet signs of exasperation when the demand far exceeds the foreseeable inscribed in habituation, but progressive indifference, on the other hand, when the demand falls short of it for too long. The body is truly a *learned memory* that records the signs of recognition: through the game of bearings at its disposal, it manifests the effectiveness of its insertion in the neighborhood, the detailed technique of a savoir faire that signs the appropriation of space. One could undoubtedly talk about an obsequiousness, but not in terms of dependence or submission; rather, in the manner of Spinoza, who speaks of "obedience" (*obsequium*) to a tacit law, "the constant will to execute that, which by law is good, and by the general decree ought to be done," in other words: obedience to the logic of the symbolic benefit of which all the agents of the neighborhood are, in different ways, the beneficiaries.[6]

Propriety is the royal road to this symbolic benefit, to the acquisition of this *surplus* whose mastery manifests the full insertion into the everyday social environment; it furnishes the lexicon of obedience and organizes from the inside the political life on the outside. The system of communication in the neighborhood is strongly controlled by conventions. The dweller, as an immediately social being caught in a relational public network that he or she has not completely mastered, is taken care of by the signs that secretly order him or her to behave according to the requirements of propriety. The latter occupies the place of law, a law stated directly by the social collective that is the neighborhood, of which no one dweller is the absolute keeper, but to which all are urged to submit in order, quite simply, to make everyday life possible. The symbolic level is none other than that where the most powerful *legitimization* of the social contract is born, that is, at its core, everyday life; and the diverse ways of speaking, of presenting oneself, in short, of manifesting oneself in the social field are nothing other than the ongoing assault of a "public" subject to join the likes of him or her. If one forgets this long process of habituation too much, one risks missing the true, though veiled, mastery with which the inhabitants of a neighborhood manage their own ascendancy over their environment and the discreet, though tenacious, way in which they insinuate themselves into public space in order to appropriate it for themselves.

Propriety and Sexuality

1. *The sexualized organization of public space.* As a practice of public space, crossed over by everyone, men and women, young and old, propriety cannot not take into consideration, in one way or another, the gender issue. It must confront this problem and try to manage it through its own capacities. The neighborhood is the traditional space of the difference in ages. It is also the space where boys and girls, teenagers, and men and women circulate and consequently meet and recognize each other. How will propriety legislate this gender difference? It first has at its disposal the code of politeness, which goes from familiarity (the "most common") to deference (the "most exquisite"); there are the winks (the pickup) that young men impose on young women in the street, and the indifference, irritation, or friendliness of the latter; there are public benches where young lovers clasp each other, where old couples rest; the parks where boys and girls run in most often distinct groups, where mothers walk with their infants during the week, where couples, this time on Sundays, stroll surrounded by their children. All these social manifestations respond to a gendered organization of society, each partner playing the role presented by his or her sexual definition within the limits imposed by propriety.

Certain places in the neighborhood are more specifically marked out by one or the other sex. The opposition between the café and the store is exemplary in this regard. The "neighborhood café"—in contrast to the "passing-through café," whose function is completely different—can in some ways be considered as the equivalent of the "men's club" of traditional societies. A "poor man's sitting room,"[7] it is also the vestibule of the apartment where men meet for a moment on their way from work before returning home for dinner; the café is a "transit zone," an air lock for readjustment to the social atmosphere, between the world of work and private life; that is why it is so regularly populated in the early evening on workdays and almost uniquely by men; that is also why it is an ambiguous space, at once highly tolerated because it is a "reward" for a day's work and terribly feared because of the propensity for alcoholism that it authorizes. Conversely, the grocery store plays the role of a "women's club," where what is usually called "the feminine" finds a place for its use: exchanges of words, family news, minor gastronomic remarks, the children's education, and so on.

This pinpointing of the occupation of a certain place by a certain sex at a certain moment is not sufficient to account for the extreme *practical subtlety* with which the gender difference is experienced in the space of the neighborhood. It becomes inadequate even when, basing itself on a naive psychosociology, it resorts to affirming, in the name of formal characteristics, the "essence" (masculine or feminine) of a certain portion of urban or private space: thus, straight, rectilinear, and hard would be the indisputable features for masculine spaces (the sacrosanct phallus), whereas soft and curved would be those for feminine space (the no less sacrosanct maternal womb). The mystification comes when one transfers supposed coherent criteria for the complementarity of the sexes to architectural data: hard and soft, dry and moist, logical and poetical, penetrating and penetrated, as if the division between the masculine and the feminine passed precisely along the genital or biological border that separates sexual partners. One thus overestimates the capacities of the space to account for sexual symbols, and one underestimates the extreme complexity of the symbolics of desire as it is elaborated by always approximate practices, shortcomings, dreams, slips of the tongue, and, as well, by itineraries within urban space.

2. *The problematic of sexual ambivalence.* A problematic of sexual ambivalence must be substituted for this dualism in the separation of the sexes: by that I mean the essentially polemical mode, never entirely elucidated and hence heavy going, difficult to manage, through which each sex constantly continues to maintain a relationship with the other, even

if this relationship is materially absent or, at least, strongly dominated from a numerical point of view; it is no longer a question of male or female space but, in the café as well as the store, in the kitchen as well as the park, of the very archaic work of the androgynous fantasy, the melodramatic muddle [*méli-mélo(drame)*] always tangled up in an unending dialogue, even if it takes a path other than that of self-evident speech. The same goes for the kitchen: rather than saying that it is a place for women because it is said that men are "often absent" from it (a statistical point of view), I prefer to begin with an analysis that would show that, through a procedure within the dialectic of the sexual separation of familial roles, men are *excluded* from it; there is another relationship here that inscribes negativity (and not absence) as an integral part of its function, and that allows men and women to be linked one to the other as sexual partners, up to their effacement.

I would like to try to locate this particular problematic within the *text* of propriety such that an attentive observer might understand it as soon as he or she is confronted with the microevents of everyday street life, a text that authorizes each of its "members" to articulate, even if unconsciously, their sexual attitude [*quant-au-sexe*] (as we say, personal attitude [*quant-à-soi*]). This supposes that one first analyzes the function of language between the contractual parties that are the dwellers in the same territory, in order to see how the discourse on sexuality succeeds in joining the game of neighborhood interrelationships (in the general sense of the term). How does one play with language in order to talk about sex? What type of behavior results? How does one express this specific statement? This investigation poses a serious methodological question: how can one clear a straight watershed path, the clear theoretical "vista," which not only avoids the gulf of psychosociology, but also the complicated, thorny, obscure paths through the fields of a "psychoanalysis of the social"?

I would like to situate myself on the side of an "anthropological" interpretation of stereotypes, clichés, and gestural and verbal conventions that allow propriety to tackle and manage, at its level, the problem of gender difference. I rely here on what Pierre Bourdieu calls "*the semi-learned grammar* of practices that we inherit from common sense, sayings, proverbs, riddles, secrets of specialists, gnomic poems.... This 'wisdom' hides the exact intellection of the system's logic in the very movement made to point it out," because it is "the sort of thing that turns away from a systematic explanation rather than introducing one.... Spontaneous 'theories' owe their open structure, their uncertainties, their inaccuracies, even their incoherence, to the fact that they remain subordinate to practical functions."[8]

3. *The status of the discourse on sexuality: double meaning and other figures.* The linguistic or behavioral material of propriety (this "semilearned grammar" of the "appearance" of language and the body in the public space of recognition) thus does not put forward a discourse on sexuality; the sexual life of the neighborhood (the language as well as the practices) is not locatable in a systematic that would reveal full social transparency to us. On the contrary, it only manifests itself there in brief sparks, in a twisted way, obliquely, "as if through the looking glass," by seizing the place of its utterance in "direct speech." In the street, at the café, in a shop, it is possible, and frequent, to speak clearly, in explicit terms, about political current events, employment, school, the kids, sicknesses. As soon as it becomes a matter of sexual allusion, the linguistic register changes immediately: one only speaks "around" sex, in a remote way, through a very fine, subtle manipulation of language, whose function is no longer to elucidate, but to "allow to be understood."

Sexuality is entrusted to allusion, innuendo; the words that talk about sex hover above the mystery of complicity, wake up latent echoes with something other than themselves, a "half-smile," an "equivocal" gesture; the statement about sex intervenes through a fracture of commonplaces, by metaphorizing "hack phrases," by playing on intonation (cooing, a toneless, muffled voice, interspersed with silent laughter), in order to ex-press (to push out in an embryonic yet effective way) an unexpected meaning; it is fundamentally the working over of language that functions by leafing through the possible meanings of the same expression that slip into the interdiction, opening on unplanned semantic spaces to a verbal exchange, but to the benefit of a relational mode that reinforces the permissiveness of propriety by enlarging the symbolic space of recognition. This everyday, frequent practice of semantic diversion finds its perhaps most accomplished form in the linguistic technique of the pun, of the play on words, of any speech act that, by the dislocation of conventional meaning, allows a *double meaning* to arise. Talking about sex is, in the register of propriety, talking about *the same thing in other words*: it implements a dehiscence that separates a signifier from its primary signified in order to place it beside other signifieds whose linguistic practice indicates that it carried them without knowing it; in its enunciation, talk about sex de-normalizes, de-stabilizes the conventional agreement between saying and what is said in order to carry out a substitution of meaning in the same utterance.

"To have a dirty mind" (as we say) is nothing more than the savoir faire of this "ironic" practice of language that understands or allows to be understood an "obscene" meaning (offstage, in the wings of propriety), through a play on intonation, the breaking out of laughter, punctuation, or a half-gesture. Talk about sex in a certain way is thus the intrusion of *emotion* into the clarity of everyday language; it only has a right to the status of an utterance by being pronounced at the same time on the level of transgression, in other words, that of the tolerance in action that the circumstance in which it takes place, *hic et nunc*, authorizes.

One can thus attend some truly oratorical jousts between partners taken up in the game of sexual complicity, which consists only of a revival of double meaning, of propriety's "pleasure of the text" that dislocates the game and overruns it on all sides so that the ambiguous meaning of sex stands out. The linguistic mode by which sexuality is semanticized in the neighborhood by the controls of propriety is especially *the ambiguity of meaning*. This particular status of sexual language has multiple causes. One might easily evoke the weight of moral, religious, or traditional constraints. But that does not sufficiently clean up in depth the problem of "public" sexuality, which, on all its borders, cannot not touch on the problem of prohibition. Indeed, the social transcription of this prohibition is expressed by behaviors that are more or less linked to the concept of *modesty*, which must not be perceived only as an exclusion of sex, but as the possibility of using cunning with prohibition: it then becomes possible to have "veiled" sexual speech, indirect, that is, not "shocking," in such a way that whatever the case, communication is not broken.

4. *Modesty and speech.* Double meaning, ambiguity, and wordplay are only a necessary duel that allows a neighborhood dweller to confront the limits of the forbidden in the relational game. Propriety authorizes one to say more than is proper, to produce a benefit that reinforces the process of recognition through a symbolic participation in the management of gender difference in a given area. Modesty is never just a reserve of fixed behaviors: little by little, habituation opens an itinerary of utterances to which the dweller, emerging from his or her "reserve," gives free rein, all the while knowing that it is a question of a game that, very precisely, is of "no consequence." Modesty is at the origin and at the end of the discourse on sexuality. It is first of all the practical limit in language that the game of double meaning or the pun transgresses,

because these make possible the utterance of a proposition marked as "erotic" in public space. But it also reemerges at the end of the operation insofar as it is what is to be protected from all "acting out."

This transgressive practice is a statement that never fails in the actual doing; it is a "poem," not a "praxis"—in the very materialistic sense of the transformation of concrete social facts. The "doing" (the real sexual practice) is inscribed in private life; if the acting out occurs (adultery, for example), the effects will make themselves felt only on the level of language, "comments" about the rumor, exclamations of amazement. But the neighborhood, as a public space, has no power of regulation or coercion at its disposal to subordinate the actual sexual practice of its dwellers to a collective will; it can, in no case, be the place of its proof or of its presentation openly and publicly. *It only has power over discourse*, over "what is said about sex"; words are the only social matter on which it can legitimately pass judgment within the very narrow margins, on its borders, that the behavioral system of propriety tolerates.

The ambiguity of talk about sex comes from the very ambivalence that authorizes for it on one level (what is said) what it forbids on the other (what is done). Right up to the permissive window of so-called risqué language, this ambiguity is also a law that is opposed to the illusion that everything is possible sexually in the public space of the neighborhood from a practical point of view. People are allowed to have a good laugh together, to "make a few allusions" by being clever with propriety in order to make a few erotic sparks fly out, but people are not allowed to "believe that they are allowed everything."

The innuendo is, structurally and quasi-legally, the expectation of propriety in regard to sexuality: no other means exists to utter it correctly (structure) and it is on this condition (jurisdiction) that propriety accepts it. The constraining character of this *ars loquendi* [art of speaking] comes from criteria that stem directly from the everyday face of "public morality"—not from a dogmatic morality, explicitly uttered, but from a practical morality more or less integrated into the heritage of social behaviors that we all practice. The randomness of encounters in the neighborhood limits all oral propensity for eroticism or smut; the risk of words explicitly termed "improper" is always insinuated in the very act of utterance. Propriety requires erotic discourse to adapt itself to the immediate social environment: crude jokes are toned down in the presence of children or young women or even elderly people judged to be respectable. Erotic speech is always subject to the system of the aside, of the lowered voice, of laughter. The erotic, smutty voice is always a vocal ornamentation for the displacement of signifiers, used in order to leave a space for double meaning.

5. *Three examples.* Be that as it may, tolerance in many places in the neighborhood is large. The markets are certainly the social spaces where erotic wordplay flourishes the most spontaneously. There are three reasons for this:

1. Markets are places in which the social environment is barely controllable because of the extreme complexity of the random relationships that overlap there. Consequently, it is very difficult for a market vendor to precisely take into consideration the "profile" (age, sex) of his or her clientele the way a shopkeeper who runs a store must.

2. Compared to shopkeepers or retailers, market vendors have a marginal position; they are more anonymous, more interchangeable, and their presence is more transitory. The relationships that they fashion with their customers are thus less organized by everyday propriety.

3. Finally, vendors are obligated by the profession to *hail* their customers; they have a vocal relationship with them that one might call hyperallocutive, often close to a yell. That is why they often deploy a vocal energy that forces them to go straight to the cut-and-dried essentials, either in order to extol their products or to attract customers. Hence the impressive number of mimed love declarations, of litanies of terms of endearment spread to the four winds ("my pet," "my beauty," "my dearie," "my little one," "my precious"), so many expressions "rendered permissible" by the market context.

In particular, I remember a vendor who, at a Parisian market, put forward the worst obscenities and only to his women customers (he practically scorned the men who "were doing the shopping," a slight macho remark); when women bought vegetables from him, it went from "mounds" of lettuce to "well-hung" onions, and moving on to carrots "that, when squeezed enough, the juice comes out"; all this to the point where one day, a deeply shocked woman customer publicly slapped him, to the amazement of everyone around—a supreme insult that the vendor succeeded in parrying by coming out with a superb curse, worthy of Georges Brassens: "Death to virtue, for Christ's sake!"

Examples of the eroticization of language also abound elsewhere, but in a less systematic way: the pressure of the social environment becomes more precise. It is then opportunity that makes the thief. For example, I enter a shop where everyone bursts out laughing; the origin of this euphoria is simple: the pleasure of a slip of the tongue. A small poster of a handwritten job notice is stuck to the display window: instead of stating "housemaid," it is written, in clumsy handwriting, "housemate."[9] No one had noticed or pointed out the mistake until the arrival of an old customer, a native of the neighborhood. He then abandoned himself to an improvisational sketch in which he allowed himself to make "propositions" to the women customers present and, naturally, the latter to take on airs of being offended as he would lay it on thick, to everyone's amusement.

Here is another example, in a café this time. Leaning with elbows on the counter next to the cash register, a middle-aged gentleman speaks to the woman at the register about another customer who is not there, a young, terribly sad alcoholic. The man says: "When I was his age, people used to go dancing" — he interrupts himself, outlines with one hand an evocative gesture (a woman's figure, a caress?), and begins again in a confidant tone: "How shall I say it?" with an "understanding" smile, while the woman at the register, blushing a bit, begins quickly to count her change, smiling herself as well.

One could add a multitude of other examples taken from everyday life in the neighborhood. One would quickly tire before the pointillist accumulation of facts. Each of these cited examples actively foregrounds the linguistic procedures that I have been trying to identify. Thus, the market vendor systematically uses the technique of *double meaning* through the metaphorization of the formal similarity of the objects he sells: mounds of lettuce become a pubic mound, onions become testicles, and as for the carrots, it is all too clear. The metaphoric movement and the swing into eroticism are only "suggested"; there is no true linguistic invention on the part of the merchant. He contents himself with superimposing within the same statement a realistic description of objects and an erotic description that their form evokes. People actually talk about mounds of lettuce; it so happens that onions are sometimes sold hung from a wooden stem like garlic or shallots in Provençal fashion; and finally it is well known that carrot juice is good for one's health and recommended for young children. These real details are doubled on a linguistic register that finds its root in spoken language: "Almond Joy's got nuts — Mounds don't,"[10] "to be well hung," "to come." It is thus by formal contamination that the erotic level is introduced. That these jokes are addressed only to women is the sociological sign that the vendor has, through his specific status (marginality, transitory presence), the right—he and he alone—to defy them on the level of language, that is, the right to be "improper" according to the consensus that forms the basis for the distribution of social roles in the neighborhood.

In the second case, it is a question of a *pun*, a play on words based on a similarity of sounds covering up a difference of meaning. The erotic transgression is made possible by the strange slip of the tongue on the job notice (the result of a certain misunderstanding of the French language if, as is most likely the case, it had been written by a foreign woman). Everything then plays out at the level of the "pleasure of the text" that allows an unexpected sexual meaning to come out before the decoding of the play on words: it is a fleeting permissiveness that metamorphoses an elderly customer into an imaginary and universal reveler thanks to a linguistic error.

The third example, the shortest to recount, is also the longest to decode. It is built on an *elliptical allusion*; one can unravel three simultaneous levels of reading. First of all, there is the hand gesture, at once furtive and specific, that takes the place of discourse; he says it "clearly," but in the place of speech: "When I was young, I didn't get bored dancing, please believe me. Back then, we knew how to have a good time..." Second, this call to the gallantry of yesteryear is for this man, he too a seasoned drinker, a way of distinguishing himself from the young alcoholic, who, moreover, is sad ("they don't know how to drink anymore"): on the one hand, to score a point against this antithetical adversary (young and sad versus middle-aged and happy) and to point out that middle age has nothing to envy of youth (in the connoted context of the "generation gap"); on the other hand, so that the woman at the register does not include both of them in the same judgment from the point of view of alcoholism: "I drink, perhaps, but I am not like the other guy, I am a bon vivant." Finally, the third level: the gesture was in essence rather audacious so that one might be allowed to think that the customer had felt himself authorized, very briefly, to "make advances" to the woman at the register. Even with a gesture to prove his good faith, he slipped in an attempt at seduction, hence a second-level double entendre! And the woman at the register was not wrong: by rushing to her change, she "made as if she had not understood," but her smile showed that she had understood quite well. In the end, it had all been a question of a very short comedy of manners in three small simultaneous acts: the past ("in the past, we knew how to have a good time"), the present ("it's no longer the case now; just look at all these young people"), and the future ("if you wanted to . . .").

6. *Semiotic volunteerism and the signifying practice.* In spite of the extreme diversity of their formulation and their dispersion in social space, these few examples all possess one common denominator: they are immediately locatable at the level of linguistic performance among speaking subjects, of what they say about sex; these subjects in essence override the codes of proper language in order to express its latent innuendo; they apply to linguistic conventions an activity of transformation that changes the semantic destiny of an utterance in the act of enunciation; in short, they "twist" respectability about in order to unveil the latent obscenity that it camouflages. This is to say that we find ourselves at the level of an activity of *conscious speech* that has for an indicator of its effectiveness only the time of its realization. As Louis-Jean Calvet says more precisely, in a synthetic expression, here we face a "semiotic volunteerism,"[11] a deliberately *active* mode of relationship to language, functioning through express manipulation of language signs.

The analysis has shown that we were dealing with linguistic and/or behavioral acts, aiming at introducing into the wonderful organization of propriety the disruptive ("troubling") code of eroticism (smut, pornography) through specific rhetorical work (parody, irony, double meaning) with a precise goal: to make people laugh, to seduce, to make fun of others, and so on. This mechanism can be observed in diverse strata of the population, from groups of teenagers to groups of adults; but for me, the effects in the wider social sphere seem to stem specifically from a prerogative of adult age, or, at least, to mark the entrance into professional life. The fact of being a man (a laborer, a wage earner, etc.) authorizes a more manifest deployment of eroticism in the social environment. If a high-school student or teenager publicly takes to this style of witty words, he would be considered a "misfit" or an "ill-mannered boy." This is why the erotic language of teenage groups almost never leaves the group; it is for internal use only.

Taken in this context, the term *semiotic* is charged with a specific meaning; it refers explicitly to the concept of a "signifying practice" as elaborated by Julia Kristeva.[12] She defines it as: "the constitution and crossing over of a sign system. . . . Crossing over the sign system is achieved by putting the speaking subject on trial, a subject who broadsides the social institutions in which he or she had previously been recognized, and coincides with a subject's moments of rupture, renovation, and revolution."[13] The signifying practice is the itinerary of rupture, the implementation of the unpredictable, the "poetics" of play, the disorganization of conventional arrangements, the social inscription of laughter and farce; it is the work of impulse, of an excessive *force*, never reduced, irreducible, injecting into the conventional organization of propriety's stereotypes an *internal semantic shock*, an explosion that disrupts the dominant social order (the most widespread, and not necessarily the most "repressive") of signifiers in order to introduce a carnivalesque process,[14] that is, very precisely, one of reversal. "The carnivalesque structure . . . *exists only in and through the process of relation.* . . . Carnival is essentially dialogic (made up of distances, relations, analogies, and nonexclusive oppositions). This spectacle has no footlights; this game is an activity; this signifier is a signified. Whoever participates in carnival is actor and spectator at the same time."[15]

The examples cited earlier are equally manifestations of this active reversal of supposedly coherent values in the relationships of everyday life. In propriety, in the social consensus that establishes the identity of a human group (like the neighborhood), there is an admittedly tenuous but structural *possibility* that authorizes eroticism to take up a position in public space, not as goods for consumption but as a social practice in the depth of language giving way to the collective repressed: "Having externalized the structure of well-thought-out literary production, the inevitable carnival reveals the unconscious that underlies this structure: sex, death. A dialogue is organized between them from which the structural dyads of carnival result: high and low, birth and death, food and excrement, praise and cursing, laughter and tears."[16]

A systematic analysis of linguistic practices in an urban neighborhood will certainly show the activity of these pairs whose internal tension creates unpredictable meaning in the text of propriety. The signifying practice is thus, if the analogy may be allowed, the performance of impulse in language, the manner in which it acts through and on language by way of a task of dismantling and reusing — transforming — codes, an itinerary drilled into the interior of words in order to undermine their peaceful social use. Words then live it up and become dangerous, susceptible to unleashing scandal (like the slap at the market); they then disrupt the rigid monument of seemliness, they point out its false windows, and they insolently reveal the cracks in the superb facade through which slip the fine wind of desire and the storm of lust; they detach with a finger the armor that protects the king in order to discover, through laughter, his nakedness.

The signifying practice here is none other than the implementation of the spontaneous theories of the *"semilearned grammar" of practices* (Pierre Bourdieu). It is this syntax's dynamism and sometimes even its frenetic implementation; pushed to the limit of its logic, the signifying practice implements the carnivalesque reversal of the codes of propriety. But it also means that, working along the borderlines of propriety ("at the limit of what is proper") that legislate public behaviors, the signifying practice too is unable to detach itself from it. It would risk disappearing into the worrisome world of anomie, into perversion, or into the codes of various social pathologies. This signifying practice is thus held in the snare of propriety by the very fact of the tolerance that the latter offers it. Finally, this practice is radically antitheoretical; it cannot be condensed into a systematic code; it signifies the diversion of proper meaning by a direct action on language, constantly pointing out the erotic flicker that, day after day, crosses everyday life right up into its deepest banality.

Chapter 3

The Croix-Rousse Neighborhood

Historical Elements

The neighborhood of Lyons that we will explore with the R. family is that of the Croix-Rousse; for a long time it was considered one of the more "working-class" neighborhoods of Lyons.[1] The territory designated by this name is vast: the Croix-Rousse is subdivided, from the point of view of the dwellers, into several subsets that are relatively autonomous in respect to one another, but globally comparable in the sociological composition of the population and in the external appearance of the most widespread housing, the *canut* buildings, inhabited in the past by Lyons silk workers [*canuts*].

Up until 1852, the Croix-Rousse was a district bordering on Lyons and separated from the latter by ramparts protecting the city in the north, most notably fortified after the *canut* insurrections in 1831.[2] We are located at the extreme southern point of the Dombes plateau that, at this point, descends in steep slopes into the confluence of the Rhône and the Saône, into the heart of the city, the Presqu'île (which was, until the Part-Dieu was brought into service, the active center of the town). On March 24, 1852, an imperial decree eliminated the municipal autonomy of the Vaise, Guillotière, and Croix-Rousse districts by including them within the city of Lyons.[3] Then, for ten years, through the impetus of the prefect Vaïsse, enormous public works transformed the center of the city, notably through the clearing done for the rue de l'Empereur and the rue de l'Impératrice (currently the rue de la République and the rue Édouard-Herriot); "and the Palais du Commerce was built, a temple to Industry and Business, which harbored a new and fascinating power: the Stock Exchange (place des Cordeliers)."[4] The slopes and plateau of the Croix-Rousse were to benefit from these urban transformations: on June 3, 1862, the first funicular railway in the world was inaugurated, linking the rue Terme (above the place des Terreaux) and the place de la Croix-Rousse higher up. On March 3, 1865, Louis-Napoléon Bonaparte declared in *Le Moniteur*: "I wish to replace the city toll wall, a work of suspicion from another age [an allusion to the 1831 and 1834 uprisings], with a vast landscaped boulevard, a long-lasting testimony of my trust in the common sense and patriotism of the Lyons population."[5] The clearing for the boulevard de la Croix-Rousse was to lead to the construction of a few villas and opulent-looking buildings where the rich silk producers, too constrained in the old buildings of the place Tolozan "down below," near the Rhône, would come to settle.

The *canut* buildings themselves result from a vast real-estate operation at the very beginning of the nineteenth century (1804–5). It undoubtedly involved the largest "working-class housing development" constructed in France at the time. The buildings encircle the Croix-Rousse along its slopes, from east to west, like a veritable shield. Many were built on the plateau after the district was included in Lyons.[6] The spectacular incline of the terrain and an initially very parceled-up cadastre (the multitude of religious properties turned into *biens nationaux* [during the Revolution], and of private properties bought up one by one by the promoters of the period) poorly reveal the coherence in the overall layout: one does not find the grid pattern of streets characteristic of "working-class housing developments" conceived by the urban functionalism of the 1960s (bar buildings and towers). On the other hand, the apartments were all conceived according to a standard model, submitted to a precise technological constraint: each was supposed to house a Jacquard weaving loom, a machine that measured more than thirteen feet high and weighed about half a ton:

> As of 1804, with the advent of the Jacquard weaving loom, the *canuts* moved to the new neighborhood [the Croix-Rousse]. With the vigorous return of Workmanship, after the Revolution, a veritable migration of *canuts* began from the Saint-Paul and Saint-Georges neighborhoods, "down below," on the other side of the Saône, right bank, toward the slopes of the Croix-Rousse where moderate rents could be found. The Jacquard loom allowed the silk trade to blossom and provoked the construction of these immense working-class hives that still cover the slopes of the plateau.[7]

These buildings all still have "lyonnaise" ceilings (short spans of support beams with very tight joists) that allow a great flexibility of surfaces so that they can bear the weight of the weaving loom.[8] Each apartment has two or three rooms; one is destined to house the loom and the others serve the family needs of the master worker or the journeyman. Because the rooms have very high ceilings, in the interior a cubbyhole [*soupente*] was built halfway up, a sort of balcony or mezzanine, converted into a bedroom. With only one water source near the entry door, the toilets were located in the stairway. There is not one elderly Croix-Rousse dweller who does not remember the "click-clack-wham-bam" of the weaving loom resonating in the street from five o'clock in the morning until eight or nine o'clock at night. Everyone knows these roomed apartments to be either cubical (more than thirteen feet by thirteen feet by thirteen feet, the necessary dimensions for the room that housed the loom), or narrow and with such high ceilings that one might think it was a box of matches resting on its smallest side and that it was almost impossible to heat these rooms in the winter.

The Croix-Rousse Today

Joined to the main arteries that precede it (the rue Terme, rue du Jardin des Plantes, rue de l'Annonciade, cours du Général-Giraud), the boulevard de la Croix-Rousse forms a veritable enclosure embracing the slopes that descend on the city: it climbs from the place des Terreaux in the south and, after a wide bend toward the west, it comes back to the Gros Caillou (a former glacial moraine, on view in a public park that closes off the boulevard), dominating the city in the east looking toward the Alps, with an itinerary slightly resembling the drawing of a crank start or a paper clip. In its last section (the east-west axis), the boulevard borders two distinct territories: there is the *plateau* itself where the highways that go toward the northeast begin (toward Bourg-en-Bresse, and further toward the Jura) on the immense zone caught between the north-south riverbed of the Saône and the east-west riverbed of the Rhône (the plateau of the Croix-Rousse corresponds to the fourth district of the city of Lyons); there are also the *hills* or the *slopes of the Croix-Rousse* (the first district of the city) advancing straight toward the heart of the city and whose sloping streets charge down onto either the banks of the Rhône to the east, those of the Saône to the west, or the place des Terreaux in the south, toward the center of the city.

One of the oldest and most famous main roads in Lyons, the montée de la Grande-Côte, links the place de la Croix-Rousse, on the plateau, to the place des Terreaux below by an exceptionally steep incline. The other, the montée Saint-Sébastien, links the place de la Croix-Rousse (more or less) to the place Tolozan on the Rhône. Between these two paths, which almost directly follow the line of slope, many streets and alleys open up, sometimes linked to each other by the famous "*traboules*,"[9] pedestrian passageways that pass from one street to another by crossing the interior of bordering buildings and that designate an alley network of rare complexity.

More precisely, the neighborhood that I studied is situated on the slopes of the Croix-Rousse descending toward the Saône, near the place

Rouville. It is located on the western flank of the first district. In its widest dimensions, it extends: (1) east to west, from the place Colbert up to and including the garden of the cours des Chartreux; the montée de la Grande-Côte, almost halfway between these two poles, is the veritable spinal column of this "enlarged" neighborhood; (2) north to south, from the last section of the boulevard de la Croix-Rousse above (around the square of the same name and the place des Tapis close to the fourth district city hall) up to the neighborhood of the Terreaux below, narrowly compressed by the double pressure of the Rhône and the Saône. In its restrained, everyday definition, the heart of the neighborhood is made up of the rue Rivet and the adjacent streets (rue Prunelle, rue Ornano, rue de Flesselles, rue Pierre-Blanc, rue de l'Annonciade). One will better grasp the apportionment of the neighborhood on the two maps and the diagram near the end of this chapter.

The R. Family in Its Neighborhood

Up until 1933, the R. family lived in the Saint-Jean neighborhood. Madame Marie was born there, at her parents' home; it was in this same apartment that she was married in 1917 while her fiancé was on leave from the army; it was also there that her first son Maurice was born. It was still common at this time for a young couple to live with the parents of one or the other, at least until the birth of the first child. This allowed them to "save up some money," but one would guess that this came at the price of certain family conflicts because the apartments were so tiny; people lived there one on top of the other without always being able to protect their privacy. The crisis engendered following World War I, the lack of savings that had been a result of the war (men were drafted and so they were not working and one could put nothing "aside") forced the young couple to remain for some years longer with Marie's parents. They did finally find a sort of miserable lodging in a neighboring street, a single room with an alcove and one tiny window opening on the north that afforded a view of the wall of the building across, only a few meters away in the narrow alley. Their second son, Joseph, was born there (1923). Humidity, darkness, lack of space: life became too difficult with two growing children. Finding nothing available on the premises, the R. family rented an apartment on the slopes of the Croix-Rousse whose lease was signed over to them by a lady friend. Marie was finally able to get decently set up in "her own home," *sixteen years after her marriage.*[10]

This apartment is on the fourth floor of a *canut* building, in the rue Rivet. From the time the R. family moved in in 1933, the managers have done nothing at all other than install a dim timed-light system in the stairway around 1960. The coats of paint are long gone, and wide patches of dampness eat away at the walls. The trash cans overflow in the alley, near the mailboxes; their odor mixed with that of the restrooms (which are in the stairway) is not easily dealt with in the summertime and sometimes attracts a fat rat. The stairs are wide open onto the street and so freezing in winter. This report of dilapidation and neglect completely corroborates the analysis of Michel Bonnet:

> When these *canut* buildings no longer served the textile industry and were emptied of their looms, the owners rented them out to make a profit but without doing any work on them. It was a fact that these apartments were designed for craft purposes and their entire equipment consisted of just one water source, with the bathrooms in the stairway...and no improvement was brought to their change in function.[11]

In their apartment, the R. family had a second faucet installed in the living room, with a "white porcelain sink" that was more functional than their small original sink hewn from stone and installed at the end of the long entry hallway. These household transformations date the internal history of the R. family by providing "befores" and "afters" from which a successiveness takes meaning, oriented toward "progress" or, at least, toward well-being.[12]

After an entryway hall that also serves another apartment (a tiny two-room apartment, one of which is still equipped with a cubbyhole), one follows a long corridor opening onto a large living room, which in turn opens onto two bedrooms, that of Madame Marie and that of Joseph. At the end of this chapter, one will find a detailed description of the two apartments along with a floor plan. In the main apartment, where the heartbeat of the family is, the living room is called, as is customary in Lyons, the "kitchen"; it is used for everything, the preparation of meals, watching television, listening to the radio, as a dining room, and for light domestic tasks; it is here, in fact, that all the heat is concentrated in the winter, a season during which the two bedrooms are not easy to heat, especially Joseph's, where sometimes, during "cold snaps," the temperature drops below freezing.

Maurice also lives in a *canut* building, in the rue Diderot. His apartment is on the sixth floor (which corresponds, in terms of the number of steps, to the ninth floor of a modern building). Jacquard looms were not put in this high up. In the past, these floors involved small apartments taken in the loft or in the attics that the young apprentices packed into for the night. The apartment is not very cheerful, but it is curiously refined by two series of objects that invade it in an almost fanciful way. Maurice is a collector who has a double passion in his life: music and scale models. His apartment resembles a Prévert poem: there is a bassoon, a flute, a recorder, a mandolin, a violin, a metronome, an old piano, musical scores of all sorts strung together in the corners (from Mozart to Tino Rossi [the crooner]), photos of famous artists, a few busts (Beethoven, Mozart),[13] and a harmonica, a Jew's harp, a choir conductor's baton, and so on, and there are hundreds of small automobiles, dozens of planes, locomotives, battleships, a few ancient sailing vessels, and I forget what else. The piano bridges the two systems of objects: it is a musical instrument, but it serves as an elegant shelf (with a long, faded, pink velour runner) for the most successful of the scale models. A strange universe secretly organized from the inside through an exceptional mastery of heterogeneity, for this entire inventory is held in less than 250 square feet. Like all true collectors, Maurice has an incomparable skill for order and secret hierarchies that are incomprehensible for the uninitiated. An astonishing erudition (on the history of transportation, of vehicles; on the history of music also) renders the apparent disorder of objects coherent when he starts to explain it.

The Population of the First District

Between 1962 and 1968, the population of the first district experienced a clear aging trend, a movement confirmed by the 1975 census, even if since then one perceives a slight rejuvenation of the local population, thanks to the arrival of students or young craftsmen attracted by very low rents. In 1968, the population of the district had diminished by 12.6 percent since 1962 and births by 5.6 percent, while the number of elderly persons sixty-five and over increased by 16.6 percent. Still in that same year, while households in Lyons as a whole had on average 0.79 children under sixteen years of age, the figure drops to 0.47 in the first district. Michel Bonnet's study shows that the number of children enrolled in elementary school diminished by 30 percent between 1968 and 1974. A decrease in birthrate and a considerable, almost abnormal, aging trend of the population in relation to national averages are the primary characteristics that one notices.

The R.'s live in Block 13 of neighborhood 2 in the first district (IN-SEE apportionment 1968), with the rue Rivet bordered in addition by

Blocks 8 and 12. In the strictest sense, a block is a "filled space" isolated by the "empty space" of the public roads; this filled space can attain a considerable surface area, as with the immense Block 8, surrounded by the rue Rivet, the cours du Général-Giraud, the rue Philippe-Gonnard and the rue Pierre-Dupont, the montée des Chartreux, and the rue Ornano; this block includes a school, a parish, a public housing complex, some old apartment buildings, a few nice estates, and all that on a surface area whose perimeter is about one and a quarter miles; thus, the dwellers grouped under the same block number do not necessarily know each other. An inventory should be done, insofar as possible, as a function of exits onto the same street rather than by considering the number of inhabitants of a block of houses, whatever the streets surrounding it may be! In the present case, it is impossible for me to use the numerical data of Block 8 because, in order to make a pertinent analysis, it would be necessary to extract from the data the inhabitants that live on the rue Rivet, thus to have infrablock data, which the statistics do not provide.

Block 13 (the half of the rue Rivet directly overhanging the place Rouville—the border marked off by the tiny rue Prunelle is not taken into consideration) provides some interesting information about the population of the street that one can extend to the part of the "rue Rivet" in Block 8. It shows a percentage of elderly persons clearly higher than the average, while Block 12 suffers from a lesser demographic tension, as table 1 illustrates.

The numbers for Block 13 are particularly abnormal at the two extremes of the age range: this block has the lowest percentage of young people (after Block 2: 15.4 percent; maximum: Block 6, 47.6 percent), and the highest percentage of elderly people, with the exception of

Table 1. Population of ordinary households
expressed in percentages by age

	0–19 years	20–64 years	65 years or more
Block 12	24.0	55.2	20.8
Block 13	16.8	57.3	25.9
Neighborhood 2	23.8	56.7	19.4
First district	23.4	59.9	16.6
Lyons	26.7	59.7	13.8
Metropolitan France	34.0	53.7	12.3

Source: INSEE 1968.

Block 2 (not shown in the table), which attains the extraordinary figure of 53.1 percent because it includes a "retirement home."

This relative aging trend should be read carefully because it manifests an ambivalence in social behavior. Certainly, many young people leave either for professional reasons or to find more modern buildings. But there is more: Madame Marie often told me that it was very difficult to find housing available in the neighborhood for the simple reason that *the inhabitants like it there* and have no desire to go elsewhere, in spite of the dilapidation of the premises. On the one hand, the rents there are still reasonably priced; on the other, the neighborhood is a ten-minute walk from the place des Terreaux, where numerous services are found and where downtown begins; finally, it has the advantage of being well ventilated (the people of Croix-Rousse are very proud of their "air") because it is in the hills, and it has at its disposal the ravishing Chartreux Park almost directly overlooking the sweep of the Saône. Madame Marie would not want to leave her street for anything in the world—undoubtedly an expected reflex in an elderly person, but one that I have found several times among younger adults, especially men, the women being more sensitive to the lack of comfort in the bathrooms and the mediocre cooking facilities. The aging trend stems less from a demographic abandonment than from the increase in the longevity of elderly persons who, to the extent that they feel well enough, prefer to remain at home rather than to enter an old folks' home or a hospital. An interesting study, in March 1975, showed the high percentage of inhabitants living for twenty years or more in the first district;[14] it included the following question: "How long have you lived in the Croix-Rousse?" (question 18). The results are given in table 2, with the neighborhood apportionment following the INSEE's nomenclature; the ZAD designates the Tolozan-Martinière sector then threatened with demolition, which took place after the enlargement of the place Tolozan.

These figures call for a few comments. One perceives first of all that in the total, the highest percentages (28.5 percent and 21.7 percent) are located in the extreme opposite columns. It is striking that, still in this total, the two right-hand columns (a duration of residence equal to or above twenty years) involve 42.1 percent of the people asked: it is the indicator of a strongly rooted settlement in the first district as a whole. A still more remarkable fact: the addition of these same two right-hand columns for the two neighborhoods on which I was working (2 and 3) equals 51.8 percent and 52.8 percent, respectively, the highest results for the group of neighborhoods considered. We are thus faced with a

Table 2

Neighbor-hood	Number of people asked	Refusals (%)	Years of residence				
			0–5 (%)	5–10 (%)	10–19 (%)	20 or more (%)	Still (%)
1	12	8.3	33.3	8.3	16.6	25.0	8.3
2	83	7.2	21.7	8.4	16.9	27.7	24.1
3	142	0.7	23.2	13.4	9.9	21.8	31.0
4	14	0.0	28.6	7.1	14.3	35.7	14.3
5	79	1.1	45.6	16.5	16.5	8.9	11.4
6	38	36.9	26.3	7.9	2.6	15.8	10.5
ZAD	117	12.8	39.3	13.7	12.0	11.1	11.1
Total	368	4.9	28.5	12.0	12.5	20.4	21.7

globally stable neighborhood at the time of the study, justifying the high percentages of elderly persons. The long practice of the neighborhood, the social osmosis that it induces, even ending up in a certain standardization of behaviors, all of this strongly enriches the feeling of "belonging." Perhaps it is this rather typical "ambiance" that explains the spectacular rise in percentages of new arrivals who have moved in since 1970: this phenomenon corresponds well to the renewal of interest manifested by young people after 1968 in popular neighborhoods that have maintained their own style and traditions.

The depopulation pointed out earlier (16 percent between 1962 and 1968) is above all the result of two factors: on the one hand, the disappearance of many small shops as of the years 1960–65 and, on the other hand, the nonrental of apartment or commercial space in the quite numerous places that were unhealthy, dark, and damp. But since then, one notices a certain renewal: empty shops have been bought up to be transformed into housing, and young craftspeople or shopkeepers (printers, booksellers, etc.) try to maintain themselves on the slopes of the Croix-Rousse; finally, the combination of the increase in immigrant workers in the last ten years, the unemployment crisis,[15] and, more locally, the demolition of one part of the Grande-Côte has required numerous families or inhabitants to make a virtue of necessity and to occupy again the abandoned housing of previous years. The renovation work undertaken in an authoritarian way had the effect of politically sensitizing these strata of newly established inhabitants (students, young craftspeople, and militants) by creating places of meeting and discussion that were completely novel in the social history of the neighborhood, where people are rather reserved. Unfortunately, this strong mobilization could not entirely oppose one demolition project (the upper montée de la Grande-Côte) that involved the blocks where the proportion of immigrants was the highest.[16]

The Working-Class Tradition of the Family[17]

From an objective and subjective point of view, the R. family (which, I remind the reader, is a synthesis of numerous testimonies) knows itself to be firmly ensconced in a working-class cultural tradition with which it strongly identifies. This means many things: first, there is the feeling of being urban from "generation to generation"; "we are workers as far back as you can go," says Madame Marie, which is a way of indicating that she no longer has any relationship with the possible peasant branches of the family. Next, the very notion of a worker does not exclusively refer to work in a factory but rather to the idea of a wage-earning class, whatever the trade carried out might be. By leafing through albums of yellowed photos, one sees "workers" surge forth from the past, pictured with their big caps and their heavy cloth vests leaving the factory; some city employees (a road repairman, a streetcar conductor); a simple postal worker, a city hall employee. One great-uncle worked in a weaving factory, another in an umbrella manufacturing workshop. Madame Marie's father was a jewelry-shop worker (a jeweler) in "a high-quality firm"; it seems that he worked admirably. The photograph depicts him as very dignified, with straight hair, and slightly bulging eyes from the hours of work on precious stones or metals. His wife, Marie's mother, was a stone polisher in another firm. As Madame Marie says laughingly: "At our house we did work with gold and silver, oh yes! But in terms of having it in the house, that was another matter!"

Being a worker is thus less being yoked to a specific task than participating—and this is fundamental—in a popular urban culture in which dominate essential values of identification revolving primarily around *solidarity practices.* In the absence of rites and peasant tales collected by folklorists, urban culture is founded on practices concerning specific relationships (friends and family). Taking up the categories proposed by Jacques Caroux, one can say that the R.'s and many of their neighbors fit into the class of *traditional workers* (whose companionesque ideology is the primary cement, proposing solidarity as a moral imperative) and of *transitional workers* (already trapped in a large firm far from home, but still benefiting from solidarity through the cultural environment's sociological inertia, when they are still living in traditional working-class neighborhoods).[18]

This entrenchment shows through vividly in the topography of the relational system. There is a continuity between social belonging and urban space, as shown by the breakdown of the R.'s anchorage points, in terms of friends and family, spread as follows throughout Lyons:

1. *The Croix-Rousse*: where Maurice, Joseph, Madame Marie, Madame Marguerite, and many of their friends live.
2. *Saint-Jean*: Madame Marie's and Amélie's neighborhood of birth and youth. Current place of residence for Amélie, Madame Marie's cousin.
3. *The Guillotière*: for some very close friends of the R. family.

In the suburbs, the family frequents:

1. *Oullins*: for one of Amélie's sons.
2. *La Duchère*: for another of Amélie's sons.
3. *Vénissieux*: for Amélie's third son.
4. *Villeurbanne*: where Jean rents a tiny studio in an apartment building targeted for demolition.
5. *Saint-Fons*: for other friends, and as a place of work.

For those familiar with Lyons, each of these localities connotes belonging to the working-class world (notably the suburbs, with the exception in part of Oullins, which includes a more "residential" area). This is still true for the Saint-Jean neighborhood, even though it has since undergone a major rehabilitation: there still remain a significant number of "good folk" (among them Amélie and Jacques) led little by little to leave their neighborhood to make way for more well-to-do classes fond of a "typical" neighborhood (a sociological phenomenon known under the English term *gentrification*).[19]

To these neighborhoods whose frequenting is, for the R.'s, hyper-motivated thanks to the family or friend relationships they have there, should be added what one might call intermediary neighborhoods or "passing through" neighborhoods (as Madame Marie calls them), often frequented by the R.'s for reasons having to do with their external characteristics, but in which their network of relationships is nonexistent. These involve downtown, in the part between the place des Terreaux and the place Bellecour, a very polyvalent urban space because the majority of cinemas (rue de la République), large department stores (place des Cordeliers, rue Grenette, rue Édouard-Herriot), and main public buildings are concentrated there.[20]

All that remains finally are the excluded neighborhoods. Some are excluded for reasons of indifference: they are too far away, we do not know any one there; there is never a reason to go there. People also speak about the "deep country of the eighth or third districts," "out back by Montchat," "after Grange-Blanche, near Vinatiers," all expressions emphasizing the inaccessible territorial limits, the extremes, the borders. Other neighborhoods are excluded for motivated reasons: the so-called "bourgeois," "well-off" neighborhoods, the "nice" neighborhoods to which the R.'s rarely go unless they have to follow main roads that pass through them, the "Presqu'île" for example, where the famous Ainay neighborhood is located (only the rue Victor-Hugo, a very busy street recently converted into a pedestrian street, is spared in the eyes of the R.'s), or the "chic" side in the Brotteaux neighborhood, the one that runs alongside the Tête d'Or Park (but the park itself, one of the most beautiful in Europe, is particularly appreciated by the people of Lyons, who like to take strolls there).

The system of human relationships induces a discriminating practice of urban space; it carves up portions of territory whose selection is significant because it has a value of opposition as much from the cultural as from the political point of view (in the most diffuse sense of the word *political*).[21] Belonging to a neighborhood, when it is corroborated by belonging to a specific social milieu, becomes a marker that reinforces the identification process of a specific group. At the level of representation, "being from the Croix-Rousse" excludes being simultaneously from Brotteaux or from the Presqu'île, in the same way that being a worker, a son of a worker, and so on, excludes belonging to other social classes populating the nice neighborhoods. But, on the other hand, this formula integrates whoever pronounces it within a process of recognition that shows that the territorial system correlates to the relational system. This process authorizes the appropriation of urban space to the extent that it is the place where social belonging and the network of urban itineraries charged with making it known are constantly joined. One knows oneself to be a "worker from father to son," a cousin of workers, living in a working-class neighborhood, having workers for friends, deeply inserted in this social fabric to which a specific urban fabric corresponds and of which the Croix-Rousse neighborhood is one of the most important stitches.

Family Relations in the Field

The preceding discussion, painted in broad strokes, marks the backdrop from which the everyday life of the R. family stands out. It remains now to touch on the types of relationships that each member of the family has with the others in order to see whether or not the relational combinations are pertinent to the analysis of the practice of the neighborhood.

First, the *proximity* factor: it is fundamental because it favors the frequency of visits, meetings, and especially, family meals. Indeed, in the case of the R. family at the time of the study, Madame Marie and Joseph are living in the same apartment and Maurice lives not very far away; only Jean is living on the other side of Lyons, but, on the other hand, he works nearby in the place Sathonay. Proximity in urban space is a decisive factor for the functioning of family relationships. The rue Rivet, rue Diderot, and the place Sathonay form an almost equilateral triangle; in any case, the distance between any two of these points does not exceed a ten-minute walk. With a temporary internal adjustment (Maurice makes a short detour on his way home from work, as does Jean, even though he lives much farther away), it becomes easy to meet at Madame Marie's home for the evening meal, starting from the principle that, whatever the case may be, it is much nicer to eat with others as a family than at home alone.

The second factor is already more subtle. One could call it the *inertial force of habit*: a slow inscription in the family annals that, with no peremptory reason and by the sole force of time, silently institutionalizes (without becoming aware at any moment of swinging from one system to the next: this movement is even forgotten) what, in the past, was only experienced as an exception. Thursday, for example, which was "Maurice's day," produced its own generalization: little by little, it became every workday of the week, by extension of the systematic habit that founded it. The inertial force of habit is thus the process by which a particular event, through its specificity, becomes a "model" that is generalized to practices of the same kind.

This introduces a subsidiary problem: in the old system, a qualifying interval separated workdays among themselves; Thursday was a bit more "festive" than the other days. Since the generalization of the process, the habit has smoothed over all qualitative difference. The family group thus now seeks to reintegrate some break in the weekly continuum. This intention was pushed back to Friday night, which became an open evening when each person could enjoy himself or herself as he or she wished and find "festive" possibilities elsewhere: the men each go out on their own and Madame Marie stays home alone, "for a little breathing space." The weight of habit, finally felt as an excessive introversion, was transformed into an extroversion: the group itself dissolves for one night in order to again practice a qualitative break in the way the week is organized. This small revolution is currently becoming prolonged on the weekend: from now on, each person feels more freedom to participate in the family meals or not, with the exception of a constantly maintained priority in favor of the family for Sunday dinner.[22]

One could draw up a table of the weekly participation of each person in the meals served at Madame Marie's, the center of attraction for the R. family. This especially has the value of a "methodological model" because the results are simplified considerably and only present the synthesis of many experiences and observations. What matters is the analysis of the principle according to which there is generally one relationship between a family mechanism (couples, generations, brotherhood/sisterhood) and its projection onto the social terrain of the neighborhood. (In table 3, I designate Maurice, Joseph, and Jean, respectively, by the abbreviations Mau, Jo, and Jn.)

This schema maps the logic of interfamily relationships (which take place only between the four subjects of the reference group) and internal ones (inside the apartment). They present a rather firm, regular, "well-oiled" coherence, anticipating the necessities of workdays and the "freedom" (the independence, the diversification of festive possibilities) of days off. But this system does not fold back on itself; it integrates other extrafamilial relationships (with cousins or friends) that attach themselves to it. "Visits" thus preferably take place at noon on Saturdays and Sundays rather than at night; during the week, they are almost nonexistent.

This division of visiting days is traditional: Saturday or Sunday afternoon is generally, in Croix-Rousse, a very favorable time for houseguests. Observation and experience show that the afternoon is more or less clearly divided into two periods that have opposite values. First of all, there is "coffee," which begins around four o'clock (in the afternoon) and ends around five-thirty; everyone gets together "at home" to

Table 3

Day	Noon	Evening
Monday	Mme Marie + Jn	Mme Marie + Jo + Mau
Tuesday	Mme Marie + Jn	Mme Marie + Jo + Mau + Jn
Wednesday	Mme Marie + Jn	Mme Marie + Jo + Mau
Thursday	Mme Marie + Jn	Mme Marie + Jo + Mau + Jn
Friday	Mme Marie + Jn	Mme Marie
Saturday	Mme Marie + Jo ± Mau ± Jn	Mme Marie + Jo ± Mau ± Jn
Sunday	Mme Marie + Jo + Mau ± Jn	Mme Marie + Jo + Mau ± Jn

drink coffee and eat pastries. This first period of the afternoon is still within the continuity of lunch.

When guests are invited for after five o'clock, the content and style change completely; I think a gastronomic rule is at the origin of this distinction: one works from the principle that at this time of day, with digestion finished, coffee becomes harmful because it will then prevent people from sleeping. The "coffee" ceremony is thus succeeded by what I have often heard described as a "light snack aperitif" or, more colloquially, using a Lyons term, as a *munch* [*mâchon*]. People drink wine, beer, and soft drinks as an accompaniment to deli meats, cheese, and/or pastries. This second period is clearly oriented toward dinner,[23] often light on nights when guests are invited, which assures a wait without impatience. The end of the afternoon is entirely appetite-inducing, whereas the first part is conclusive. This provides the diagram in table 4.

Now what happens when at least two members of the R. family go out on the town together? Can we locate a meaning in this scheme of going out either from the point of view of interfamily relations or from the point of view of the practice of urban space? Does a relationship exist between the organization of these relations and their projection into the field? After long observation, one arrives at the following results: as with the visits at the house, the interfamily going out takes place exclusively on Saturdays and Sundays. The sum, then, of the occasions that give rise to it can be reduced to the following cases: a meal in a restaurant, shopping, leisure time, market. We end up with the diagram in table 5.

Thus, Maurice neither goes out alone with his mother nor with his brother Joseph. It is extremely rare for him to go out with these two family partners. On the other hand, each time he comes by, his son Jean comes along. Consequently, the trio Mme Marie + Joseph + Jean can imply the presence of Maurice; in other words, "Maurice may go out

Table 4

Noon	Afternoon		Evening
1:00	4:00–5:30	5:00–6:30	7:30
lunch (full meal)	"coffee" with: coffee pastries	"snack-aperitif" or "munch" [*mâchon*] with: wine, beer, soda deli meats cheese pastries	dinner (full meal)

Table 5

	Restaurant	Shopping	Leisure
Saturday			
morning			
noon			
afternoon		Mme Marie + Jo ± Jn	Mme Marie + Jo + Jn
		Mme Marie + Jn	Mau + Jn
dinner			
evening			
Sunday			
morning		Jo (market)	
noon	Mme Marie + Jo + Mau + Jn		
	Mme Marie + Jo		
afternoon			Mme Marie + Jo + Mau + Jn
			Mme Marie + Jo + Jn
			Mau + Jn
dinner	Mme Marie + Jo + Mau + Jn		
	Mme Marie + Jo		
evening			

with Joseph and his mother as long as Jean is there." Conversely, the duo Mme Marie + Joseph necessarily implies Maurice's absence: "Maurice never goes out — or almost never — with Joseph and/or his mother in Jean's absence." Jean is thus in a mediating position between Maurice and the rest of the family; he makes for a going-out relation that, without him, would not exist. In their interfamily going out, the members of the R. family are divided up according to four scenarios:

1. Madame Marie + Joseph
2. Madame Marie + Joseph + Jean
3. Madame Marie + Joseph + Maurice + Jean
4. Maurice + Jean

The psychological or emotional reasons for this configuration of relations remain outside our subject. It suffices to show that the division of interfamilial relations is not exactly the same according to whether the family gathers inside or outside of Mme Marie's apartment. The phenomenon of *going out* redistributes the familial mechanism while maintaining certain distinctive traits: thus, Maurice never eats a meal alone with his mother at her place, and he never goes out alone with her.

From the point of view that interests us, these remarks direct us toward very significant observations. A topographical projection corresponds to each relational formula and the trajectories are not the same; thus, the incompatibility of certain combinations is less an outcome of psychological conflicts than the impossibility, for them, to meet on the same terrain simultaneously. Pushing this reasoning further, one could say that coexistence is impossible precisely because the terms for these combinations have not found a common ground where they can recognize one another in the neighborhood (though it is possible at home). We see from table 5, for example, that Joseph goes to the market regularly on Sunday mornings and that he goes there alone (a movement that I integrated into the "interfamily going out" because it involves an activity that explicitly serves the family). While at the market, he systematically stops in a café where he meets up with friends. (I will come back to this sequence later.) Does this mean that he alone has the right to go to this café? Yes and no. *No*, because Jean or Maurice can very easily go there at any time of the week; it is thus not a "secret" territory, reserved for Joseph's use alone. *Yes*, however, because no one in his family would think (outside of *foreseen* exceptions) of stopping by there on Sunday mornings. The sequence "Joseph goes to the market" excludes, at that time and place, any other interfamily combination because it would be felt as a disturbance in the system of relations: one does not mix up family relations and friendly ones in a café in just any way.[24]

Other examples: Table 3 shows that Jean has dinner at his grandmother's on Tuesdays and Thursdays. Before Jean returns home on the other side of the city, his father takes him to a café in the nearby rue Terme for a while where both have a beer before going their separate ways. Madame Marie and Joseph also are in the habit of stopping in this café, either the two of them, or even with Jean or Maurice. But they never go there on Tuesday or Thursday night; the café then is the intimate privileged meeting place between father and son with which, in one way or another, it would not be proper to interfere.

There is no explicit calculation, elaborate awareness of situations, or complex strategies of precedence. The territorialization of public space is infinitely more clever, woven into historical necessities and hardened in the process of recognition. It involves a practical diversification (I would almost say "praxical," because it is so attached to concrete modes of socialization) that aims at excavating (in the sense of "bringing out of the ground") specific places, and specific for a certain type of relation. Under these bundles of banal habits, it is not the humdrum appearance that one must aim for, not the peaceful pace of day after day as the weeks, months, and years go by; it is the rhythm produced in time by this family and through which it practices its singularity. The external (here, the neighborhood) has been internalized, and as a result the internal is externalized in this space that has been reappropriated, because it has become an exclusivity — in other words, something that draws its meaning through opposition. Laws of meaningful oppositions cross through the R. family to the extent that they authorize each member to articulate himself or herself in the socially structured environment that is the neighborhood.

Supplemental Note: Unemployment among Young People between Fifteen and Twenty-Four[25]

In 1975, I had taken a few notes on unemployment, of young people in particular, without using them, because it seemed that they did not directly concern my research. Events have decided otherwise. Rereading these notes while completing them with what one knows today, I notice that as of 1975–78, the duration of the fieldwork study and the writing based on it, unemployment among young people, especially those who are poorly qualified or unqualified, becomes worrisome and imposes itself as a new fact of social reality. It would thus be useful to take stock of the situation with the data from the INSEE, especially the remarkable *Annuaire rétrospectif de la France, 1948–1988* (Paris: INSEE, 1990), 658 pp.; on employment and unemployment, see pp. 50ff. and tables 8, 9, 27–30, and 35. For subsequent years, see the *Annuaire statistique de la France, 1991–1992* (Paris: INSEE, 1992), 824 pp. and index; pp. 102–4.

1. In 1955, when the young people I questioned in 1975 were being born or were in nursery school, France counted in total "only" 317,000 unemployed, that is, 1.7 percent of the working population of 19 million (the lowest proportion of unemployed was recorded in 1957: 1.0 percent, that is, less than 200,000 unemployed). In 1968, a year still fresh in everyone's memory, 584,000 were unemployed: 2.8 percent of the working population (20 million), of which already 251,000 unemployed were ages 15–24, meaning 5.2 percent of the working population of the same age (thus there were 4.5 million "young working people" that year); but proportionally, they represented 42.9 percent of the total number of unemployed, almost one out of two.

2. As of 1975, the *percentage of unemployed young people* among the working population from 15 to 24 increases a bit faster than that of the total percentage of unemployed: it brushes near and then surpasses the 10 percent mark. Table 6 shows the evolution of the situation from 1974 to 1988.

Comments on table 6:

- 1975: the total number of unemployed surpasses 1 million;
- 1974–81: during Valéry Giscard d'Estaing's seven-year presidential term, the total number of unemployed was multiplied by 2.4;
- 1982: the total number of unemployed surpasses 2 million;
- in 1984 and that year only, the number of unemployed young people surpasses one million. One worker out of four from 15 to 24 years of age is unemployed.

Between 1974 (8.5 percent) and 1984 (25.3 percent), the proportion of unemployed young people more than tripled and their absolute value was multiplied by 2.7. Rounding off, one counts one unemployed young person out of twenty working ones until 1970, one out of ten in 1975,

Table 6. Evolution of unemployed youth ages 15–24 in relation to the total number of unemployed in units and percentages

	Number of unemployed youth (units)	% of unemployed youth/active youth	Total unemployed (units)	Total % of unemployed/ active youth	% of unemployed youth/ total of unemployed
1974	414,000	8.5	848,000	3.8	48.8
1975	505,000	10.6	1,081,000	4.8	46.7
1976	517,000	10.9	1,100,000	4.9	47.0
1977	542,000	11.4	1,210,000	5.2	44.8
1978	617,000	13.2	1,360,000	5.9	45.4
1979	684,000	14.8	1,500,000	6.4	45.6
1980	744,000	16.5	1,650,000	7.0	45.1
1981	887,000	19.3	1,970,000	8.3	45.0
1982	898,000	19.6	2,010,000	8.5	44.7
1983	984,000	22.2	2,200,000	9.3	44.7
1984	1,120,000	25.3	2,540,000	10.6	44.1
1985	999,000	22.9	2,530,000	10.6	39.5
1986	955,000	22.5	2,620,000	10.9	36.4
1987	869,000	21.6	2,560,000	10.6	33.9
1988	793,000	20.9	2,530,000	10.4	31.3

one out of five from 1980 to 1982, one out of four in 1984, and then one out of five again in 1987.

The relative decline of unemployed people from 15 to 24 years of age, recorded after the black year of 1984, is explained, on the one hand, by the numerous social and professional integration measures put in place by the authorities (community work—the famous "TUC"s [*travaux d'utilité collective*]—local projects, work-solidarity contracts, revival of apprenticeships, tax reductions for employers of young people or when hiring young people who are getting their first job, establishment of the "RMI" [*revenu minimum d'insertion*, minimum income benefit] at the end of 1988, but this measure applies only to those over age 25), and, on the other hand, by the increase in the average duration of schooling and college studies. As table 7 shows, however, the proportion of unemployed young people from 15 to 24 remains, in 1991, twice as high as the national average (19.1 percent as opposed to 9.3 percent).

3. During 1954 and 1955, as table 8 demonstrates, for the total for men and women between 15 and 24, which is the synthesis of percentages of active workers for these ages, males (M) and females (F) together, *the activity rate for 15–24-year-olds* is very high, 62.9 percent: two out of three young people "work," as one called it at the time. The details show that this is the case for three out of four males (75 percent: 60 percent of 15–19-year-olds and 91 percent of 20–24-year-olds) and for one out of every two females (50 percent, of which 43 percent are 15–19 and 57 percent are 20–24). Then this synthesized rate does not cease to decline with 58.6 percent in 1962 before passing below the 50 percent mark precisely in 1975: 49.7 percent; then 49.5 percent in 1977, 48.0 percent in 1980 (these three years are contemporary to my research), 44.1 percent in 1985, 39.5 percent in 1988, 36.3 percent in 1990; finally, 33.8 percent in 1991, meaning one "actively working" young person between 15 and

Table 7. Synthesis of unemployment rates according to the BIT
(Bureau International du Travail, National Employment Bureau)
organized by gender and age (age as of December 31) (in percentages)

Unemployed	1954	1962	1975	1977	1980	1984	1985	1988	1990	1991
Total 15 years old and older	1.6	2.0	4.8	5.2	7.0	10.6	10.6	10.4	8.9	9.3
15–24	—	—	10.6	11.4	16.5	25.3	22.9	20.9	18.0	19.1

Source: Annuaire rétrospectif, table 28, p. 71, for 1954–88, and *Annuaire statistique 1991–1992.*

24, male or female, out of three. Between 1954 and 1991, the activity rate for young people, males and females between 15 and 24, had been divided almost in half. The most dramatic decline involves the activity rate of the youngest, between 15 and 19, divided by five for males (60 percent in 1954, 12 percent in 1991), by six for females (from 43 percent to 7 percent).

Moreover, in the period between 1950 and 1970, the activity rate for young people is clearly higher than the national average (62.9 percent in 1954 as opposed to 60.4 percent; 58.6 percent in 1962 as opposed to 57.5 percent), but passes below this average at the beginning of the 1970s (49.7 percent in 1975 as opposed to 55.4 percent) and declines all the way down to around 33 percent in 1991 (national average: 54.9 percent).

4. The Rhône-Alpes region followed the same evolution during the same period with, in general, one or two points better than the national average: a few more active workers, a few less unemployed (for example, 3.5 percent unemployed as opposed to the national average of 4.8 percent in 1975, 8 percent as opposed to 9 percent in 1982).

Thanks to the documents made for regions, departments, and communes by the INSEE (March 1990 census), I was able to draw up a table of percentages for the active working population and the unemployed (table 9), moving from the most general to the most particular: metropolitan France (F), the Rhône-Alpes region (RA), the Rhône department (Rh), the Lyons Urban Unit (UUL, which gathers together sixty-three communes within the COURLY [Communauté Urbaine de Lyon]),

Table 8. Falling activity rate based on census information by gender and five-year age groups, observed in March (age obtained in that year) (in percentages)

	1954	1962	1975	1977	1980	1985	1988	1990	1991
Men	82.5	78.8	71.0	70.3	69.7	66.7	64.8	64.0	63.8
15–19	60.2	49.2	29.1	27.6	26.2	19.5	15.0	14.5	12.3
20–24	91.0	88.1	81.5	81.2	80.4	78.2	71.2	65.1	62.0
Women	38.3	36.3	39.2	40.6	41.8	43.5	44.3	45.8	46.0
15–19	43.2	35.5	21.7	21.1	18.3	13.4	10.7	8.1	6.8
20–24	57.1	61.5	66.3	68.2	67.2	65.5	61.2	57.4	54.0
Total M + W, 15–24	62.9	58.6	49.7	49.5	48.0	44.1	39.5	36.3	33.8
Total M + W	60.4	57.5	55.1	55.4	55.7	55.1	55.1	54.9	54.9

Source: Annuaire rétrospectif, table 9, p. 56, for 1954–88, and *Annuaire statistique 1991–1992.*

Table 9. Active population rates including unemployment rates
according to the 1990 national census for metropolitan France, the
Rhône-Alpes region, the Rhône department, the Lyons Urban Unit,
the city of Lyons, and its first and fourth districts
(the Croix-Rousse) (in percentages)

	F	RA	Rh	UUL	Ly	1st	4th
% of active workers	55.1	56.6	57.8	57.6	55.5	56.7	54.9
15–19-year-olds	11.8	10.2	10.5	9.6	9.2	8.5	8.5
20–24-year-olds	63.7	64.0	58.6	55.9	47.8	44.8	55.0
25–29-year-olds	86.7	87.6	87.1	86.7	86.4	85.7	89.7
% of unemployed	11.1	9.1	8.7	9.5	9.2	11.4	7.9
15–19-year-olds	21.8	17.1	17.3	20.2	19.4	16.3*	14.4*
20–24-year-olds	20.3	16.3	15.1	16.6	14.5	17.2	15.2
25–29-year-olds	13.5	11.4	10.6	11.2	10.0	12.4	9.7

*22 subjects in these two cases.

Lyons (Ly), first (1st) and fourth (4th) districts, which represent the Croix-Rousse territory (Lyons consists of nine districts in all). I have retained the sorting into groups involving 15–19-, 20–24-, and 25–29-year-olds in order to complete the data for the preceding tables and commentary.

By summing up the results of the five right-hand columns (Rh to 4th), one will note that the activity rate is on average two points higher than the national average (about 57 percent as opposed to 55 percent), except in the fourth district. One will also notice that the unemployment rate is lower by one and a half points than the national average (about 9.5 percent as opposed to 11 percent), except in the first district, where it is slightly higher. The portion of actively working young people is clearly smaller in the city of Lyons and in the two districts than in metropolitan France, and the same difference is rated for the portion of unemployed young people (even though, in these two districts, it is not meaningful for the 15–19-year-olds because of the small size of the sample—twenty-two subjects). In the first case (activity), one obtains about 9 percent of actively working people from 15 to 19 as opposed to 11.8 percent in the national average, and about 50 percent of 20–24-year-olds as opposed to 63.7 percent. In the second case (unemployment), one notices that the proportion of young unemployed people from 20 to 24, around 15 percent for Lyons and its two districts, is as well clearly lower than the national average of 20.3 percent. An analogous assessment can be made for the older group of 25–29-year-olds (around 11 percent as opposed to 13.5 percent).

5. These results, which are rather positive in relation to the national averages, do not at all lighten the load of the "sociological destiny" (Pierre Bourdieu's phrase) that unemployment represents in the long term. A young person (a young man, but more so a young woman) with employment difficulties in Lyons at the time of my study in 1975 has many chances today of joining the ranks of the long-term unemployed or of benefiting, if one may say so, from the "minimum payment benefit" established by the law of October 1988 (the RMI), around 450 dollars a month. See Pierre Vanlerenberghe, ed., *RMI, le pari de l'insertion* (report of the National Commission on the evaluation of the minimum payment benefit), 2 vols. (Paris: La Documentation Française, 1992). For a summary presentation, see the interview with Vanlerenberghe in *Actualités sociales hebdomadaires*, no. 1777 (March 20, 1992); and *Économie et statistique*, no. 252 (March 1992).

This young person has even less chance of having found work, especially a stable job, if he or she has little or no education or is not professionally qualified. A "victim" of social exclusion—a phrase used today to describe the marginalization from all work structures and, more widely, from all recognized forms of work—this person will also have been a victim of the antischool ideology, which is opposed to the qualifications and diplomas representing "integration into the [discredited] system," an ideology born of the May 1968 events, theorized by highly educated intellectuals, which was still very much in force around 1975, when it was good form to have "dropped out of school or college." This utopia unfortunately backfired in relation to the socioprofessional realities of the time, much more severe than what was suspected by the "long procession of immobile discourses" (Roland Barthes).

Supplemental Note: The Croix-Rousse under Question[26]

What I wrote about the urban neighborhood "in general" has resisted time better than the chapters on the Croix-Rousse, which are dated from a demographic point of view. I used census data from 1962 to 1975. We did, however, already have a premonition about the increase of young people in the population, as well as about the beginnings of the establishment, noticed since then, of activities and services oriented toward the arts and culture (on "gentrification," see note 19 to this chapter), a tendency verified by the recent history of the Croix-Rousse, which has become a recognized place of attraction, with restaurants and living spectacle.

1. *In an initial period, the Croix-Rousse (first district) empties out and grows older.* The censuses of 1962, 1968, 1975, and 1982 record a con-

stant decline in the number of inhabitants: 47,000 in 1962, 41,200 in 1968 (12.3 percent less since 1962), 31,200 in 1975 (24.3 percent less), 25,600 in 1982 (17.9 percent less). In total, from 1962 to 1982, the first district lost 21,400 inhabitants—45.5 percent of its population. A decrease in birthrate, aging, and demographic hemorrhage, such were the "Croix-Roussian" criteria. Not until the March 1990 census did we see a slight comeback: 26,592 inhabitants, or 3.9 percent more than in 1982.

These demographic anomalies had not only negative aspects. The Croix-Roussian remained, and remains, very attached to his or her neighborhood and thus tends to grow old there, I might say, in spite of the long-standing legendary lack of comfort in the housing (see "The Population of the First District," earlier in this chapter, based on the study done in March 1975). Three values explained this entrenchment:

- "This neighborhood is not expensive." In 1975, one could still rent three- to four-room apartments for less than 100 dollars *every three months* (around 320 dollars today).
- "It's a nice neighborhood." People used to sing the praises of its tranquillity, its "good air," its market, its parks, and the trees along the boulevard. These qualities have not escaped the vigilance of developers, who will not rest until they turn the plateau, on the borders of the first and fourth districts, into a new residential neighborhood.
- It is close to *downtown*, which it in part contains (the first district extends to Saint Nizier's Church; city hall, on the place des Terreaux, is part of its territory) and to which it is properly linked by public transportation. Indeed, the "downtown" of cities is *always* more attractive than the outskirts. Why "get bogged down" in the suburbs when one can benefit at the same time from the advantages of tranquillity and proximity to downtown?[27]

2. *Beginning in 1975, the arrival of "young people" (or rather, those between 20 and 25) compensates for the neighborhood's aging.* Students, craftspeople, and artists are lured by the attractive rents for apartments, boutiques, and workshops. This influx of youth attacks the eastern hill on the "Rhône side," touching the streets and squares between the montée Saint-Sébastien and the montée de la Grande-Côte (or Grand'Côte). The other side, to the west, above the place Rouville looking straight down on the Saône, resisted these intrusions with a higher average age. With time, the advance of youth from east to west crosses the Grand'Côte, settles firmly for five or six years on the montée des Carmélites, which

Table 10. Division by large age groups of the population of metropolitan France, the Rhône-Alpes region, the Rhône department, the Lyons Urban Unit, the city of Lyons, and its first and fourth districts (the Croix-Rousse)

	F	RA	Rh	UUL	Ly	1st	4th
population*	56.4 M	5.35 M	1.5 M	1.215 M	422,444	26,592	30,552
0–19**	26.5	27.0	26.6	26.1	21.4	21.0	20.2
20–39	30.3	30.4	31.8	32.5	34.8	39.1	31.9
40–59	23.3	23.9	23.9	24.0	22.3	20.1	22.9
60–74	12.8	12.1	11.5	11.4	13.0	10.8	14.4
75 and above	7.1	6.9	6.2	6.0	6.5	8.9	10.2

*Population in millions (M), and then in thousands.
**Large age groups in percentages.

is parallel to it, as it were, then extends beyond it to finally touch the rue Rivet and the neighboring streets.

3. *The 1990 census sheds light on the demographic structure of this influx of youth.* Thanks to the data from the INSEE, I was able to set up a table of percentages for the population by "large age groups," from the most general to the most particular (table 10): metropolitan France (F), the Rhône-Alpes region (RA), the Rhône department (Rh), the Lyons Urban Unit (UUL), Lyons (Ly), first (1st) and fourth (4th) districts for the Croix-Rousse. I added sortings into age groups of 15–19, 20–24, and 25–29 to complete the demography of young people while refining it.

Table 10 shows that in Lyons and the Croix-Rousse (Ly, 1st, 4th) the proportion of 0–19-year-olds is clearly lower than the national average, 21 percent as opposed to 26.5 percent; thus, one finds a deficit of children and teenagers. On the other hand, one notices a high proportion of 20–39-year-olds, especially in the first district, where their rate is the highest, 39.1 percent as opposed to 30.3 percent for the general average. The 20–39-year-olds are thus the main source of the influx of youth under way on "the slopes."

This tendency is confirmed by table 11: in Lyons and in our two districts, the proportion of teenagers from 15 to 19 years of age is one and a half points lower than the national average—6 percent as opposed to 7.5 percent. But the combined rate of 20–24- and 25–29-year-olds in the three right-hand columns (Ly, 1st, 4th) is clearly higher than the general average, which it surpasses by two and a half points, 10 percent as opposed to 7.5 percent.

A more refined analysis (not in the table) on the population of the first district shows that in the "large age group" of 20–39-year-olds, it is

Table 11. Excerpts from the division by five-year age groups of
the French population according to the same categories as in table 10 for
15–19-, 20–24-, and 25–29-year-olds (in percentages)

	F	RA	Rh	UUL	Ly	1st	4th
15–19	7.5	7.5	7.4	7.3	6.1	6.0	5.9
20–24	7.5	7.7	8.7	9.1	10.1	11.2	7.6
25–29	7.6	7.6	8.4	8.8	9.9	11.3	9.3

the 23–27-year-olds who are the most numerous by age. In essence, whereas the average number of 20–39-year-olds is 520 per year, the number clears the 600 per year mark for those who are between 23 and 27: 629 are 23; 630, 24; 607, 25; 633, 26; and 624, 27. The 23–27-year-olds also constitute, in the 1990 census, the most significant age class for the first district: 11.7 percent of the inhabitants, or four more points than in metropolitan France, where the rate for 23–27-year-olds is, in relation to the population as a whole, 7.8 percent. In other words, and taking into consideration the time elapsed since the last census, 25–30-year-olds are currently, much more so than children and teenagers, the focal point for the demographic influx of youth in the first district.

4. *These statistical results confirm empirical observation.* Walking up and down the streets, one perceives this influx of youth as time goes on. The old grocery stores, artisan shops, and former bistros have been transformed into bookstores, galleries, or studios, or even into theaters or other places of living spectacle, right down to the spaces that could have been reasonably considered "beyond all hope" ten or fifteen years ago. The deadlock was broken, slow modifications transformed the walls, shops, courtyards, and apartments — these famous *canut* apartments with their "cubbyholes" that real-estate agents call mezzanines. The face-lift of the facade has built up this neighborhood whose general appearance was, not so long ago, heartrending in its dilapidation. To that can be added the growth in the number of associations — at least two hundred in the first and fourth districts (culture, leisure, sports, nonprofit restaurants, neighborhood committees, etc.).

5. *The young people who moved into the Croix-Rousse have especially developed artistic and cultural activities.* The study "Artistes croix-roussiens: les chiffres," published in *Le territoire du créateur* (a collection edited by Daniel Dhéret [see note 19 in this chapter]) took a census of the four hundred artists in the first and fourth districts, who represent 1 percent of the population between 19 and 74, but also 2 percent of the "actively working population." This proportion, which is significant for such a

specialized category of inhabitants, indicates that, since 1975–80, the Croix-Rousse has become a place with a strong concentration of artistic and cultural activities. The low rents explain (explained!) this attraction, but so does the special configuration of these apartments, which, designed for the Jacquard weaving looms, offer impressively high ceilings. This living space is particularly adapted to those who work with the plastic arts — the most numerous group, according to the study.

Besides artists, other professionals, booksellers, publishers, gallery owners, and restaurateurs enrich the palette with cultural activities and also give the neighborhood a strong symbolic surplus value.[28] Add to this a real-estate surplus value that, not long ago, backfired on them and chased them from an urban space whose value they themselves had enhanced. The renewal of leases takes place under devastating conditions and, if no solution is found, the fate of the artists and the entire cultural life there will be directly threatened.

6. The arrival of young people around 1975, including artists, did not slow down the demographic hemorrhage that continued, as we have seen, until 1982. But these young people integrated activities that, although they were new around ten years ago, are now easily recognized. This is so to the point that the Croix-Rousse is truly an *artists' neighborhood*, considered as such in Lyons, in France, and abroad. The Croix-Rousse would not be the *present-day* Croix-Rousse without its population of artists and professionals of cultural life. Furthermore, this relatively closed neighborhood has opened itself up to the rest of the Lyons agglomeration. Further still, *people go there: cultural exchange has henceforth become part of its everyday life, to the point that it has become one of its values.* A Saturday night in the Croix-Rousse around 1990 no longer has anything in common with a Saturday night in 1980: for every cultural event ten years ago, there are two or three today. Sometimes, festivals invade all of the slopes, festivals such as *La nuit des voraces*[29] on September 21, 1991, which allowed several hundred artists to show people their work and express themselves. The artists, cultural actors, spectators, and other night visitors really feel *at home* here, and this is what is new compared to 1975.

7. A last point must be emphasized: *the historic memory of the Croix-Rousse goes back to before the Roman occupation.* It rests on a number of factors, of which I would like to stress three points.

The martyrdom of Blandine and her companions in August 177 has become a pious imagery that masks the essential. In essence, the first Christians who disembarked here under the authority of Pothinus and

Irenaeus were the disciples of the apostle John, the most enigmatic of the authors of the New Testament. This perhaps explains the mystic, gnostic, and even esoteric Christianity of Lyons (the capital of gastronomy, Lyons is also the capital of spiritualism).[30]

The city has constantly turned toward the east. Silk—and thus quite directly the *canuts* of the Croix-Rousse—is the emblematic figure of this relation: Lyons was one of the banking, commercial, and intellectual poles of the Mediterranean basin. In its old cultural background, Lyons was eastern and Arab (which is testified to by its university tradition of oriental studies). North African immigration does not date back to the political and economic crises of the 1960s in this century but back to the middle of the nineteenth century. Its constitutive, *essential* relations with the east (Islamic or Christian) are a tradition in this city, a part of its history. If there is one city where racism and xenophobia should be banished, it is truly Lyons.

As another constitutive element of its history, the activity of the *canuts* was always accompanied by social cooperation, at the origin of numerous nonprofit mutual insurance companies and cooperatives born of the crises in 1831 and 1834. A plaque (at 95, montée de la Grand'Côte) recalls this: "Here in 1835 was founded, by Michel Derrion and Joseph Reynier, the first French consumption cooperative, 'Le commerce véridique et social.'" The current associative activity and the solidarity that goes along with it, solidarity between creators and solidarity with a place, are directly related to this well-known social tradition. It is an additional possibility for the Croix-Rousse to remain a "territory for creators."

The R. Family's Double Apartment

There are two adjoining apartments that share the same entryway—vestibule A. The first apartment, the larger one, which serves as the center of the family life, is made up of a corridor (B), a kitchen and living room (C), and two bedrooms (D and E). On the floor plan (see diagram), the hatch marks designate the rest of the building. In the main room (C), I have subdivided the space into three parts in order to organize the enumeration of furniture and various objects found there. The two apartments do not have bathrooms; the shared central toilets are situated outside them in the building's stairway.

First Apartment

Vestibule A leads to the right for the first apartment (about 650 square feet) made up of spaces B, C, D, and E; and to the left for the second

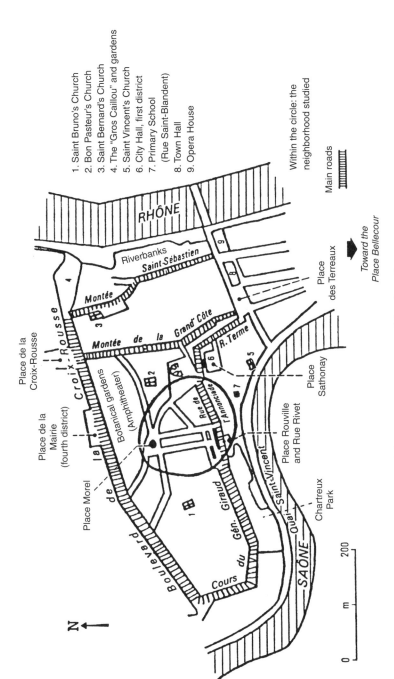

1. Saint Bruno's Church
2. Bon Pasteur's Church
3. Saint Bernard's Church
4. The "Gros Caillou" and gardens
5. Saint Vincent's Church
6. City Hall, first district
7. Primary School
   (Rue Saint-Blandent)
8. Town Hall
9. Opera House

Within the circle: the
neighborhood studied

Main roads

Simplified map of the Croix-Rousse neighborhood

64

1. RUE RIVET
2. RUE PRUNELLE
3. RUE DE FLESSELLES
4. RUE PIERRE BLANC
5. RUE ORNANO
6. Montée des Carmélites
7. PLACE MOREL
8. Rue des Chartreux
9. Rue de la Tourette
10. Rue du Bon Pasteur
11. RUE JEAN-BAPTISTE SAY
12. MONTÉE DE LA GRAND 'CÔTE
13. RUE NEYRET
    Bon Pasteur's Church

Note: the main roads of places most often used or cited have been capitalized.

14. Rue Imbert Colomès
15. RUE DIDEROT
16. Montée Saint-Sébastien, Place Colbert
17. Rue des Fantasques, Saint Bernard's Church
18. PLACE DE LA CROIX-ROUSSE
19. PLACE SATHONAY
20. Botanical Gardens (and street of same name)
21. Rue Burdeau
22. Rue des Tables Claudiennes
23. Cour des Voraces (9, pl. Colbert)
24. Intersection of several streets, among them the Rue de l'Alma where Mme C. lived

Detailed map of the neighborhood studied

*[On the map that appears in the two French editions of volume 2, this location is erroneously referred to as the "Magasins de Roger." It actually refers to the one and only "magasin" of "Robert" — Robert's Store. — *Trans.*]

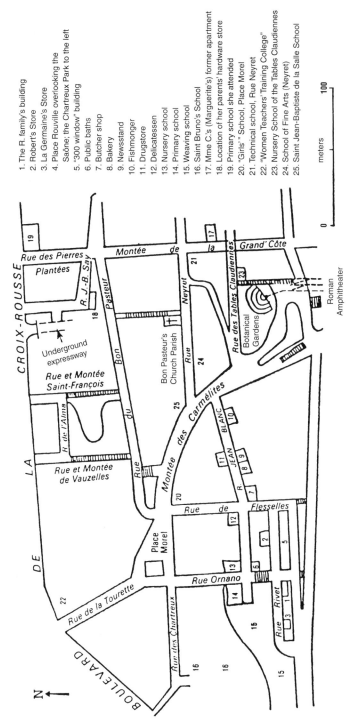

1. The R. family's building
2. Robert's Store
3. La Germaine's Store
4. Place Rouville overlooking the Saône; the Chartreux Park to the left
5. "300 window" building
6. Public baths
7. Butcher shop
8. Bakery
9. Newsstand
10. Fishmonger
11. Drugstore
12. Delicatessen
13. Nursery school
14. Primary school
15. Weaving school
16. Saint Bruno's School
17. Mme C.'s (Marguerite's) former apartment
18. Location of her parents' hardware store
19. Primary school she attended
20. "Girls'" School, Place Morel
21. Technical school, Rue Neyret
22. "Women Teachers' Training College"
23. Nursery School of the Tables Claudiennes
24. School of Fine Arts (Neyret)
25. Saint Jean-Baptiste de la Salle School

The vicinity of the Rue Rivet

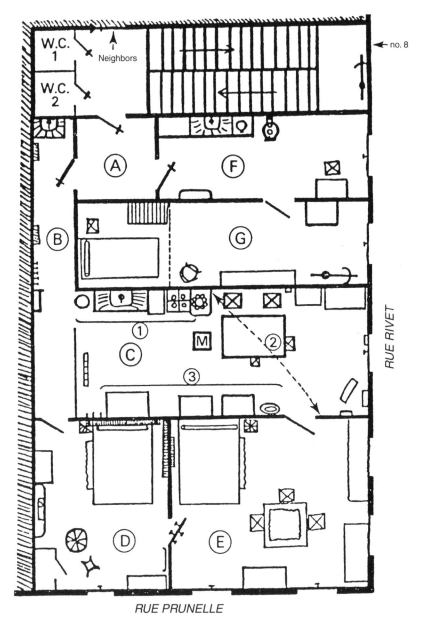

Floor plan of the R. family's double apartment

apartment (about 325 square feet) made up of spaces F and G. Joseph keeps his personal belongings in this second apartment.

Corridor (B)

Behind the door is a "white porcelain" sink installed as part of various renovations done by Joseph in 1960. Along the wall is a medicine cabinet fitted with a mirror, a wooden chest hiding the electricity meter, a coatrack, and a chest for shoes. The corridor leads to Madame Marie's bedroom (space D). The partition wall found on the left side while moving toward this room was put up by Joseph; it is more than eight feet high and thus stops at about two-thirds of the total height of the room, which is more than thirteen feet.

Kitchen and Living Room (C)

The R. family most often lives in this room. It involves a large kitchen "à la lyonnaise" that also serves as a living room. It is the only room in the cold season that has continuous heating available: a gas heater whose burner is located on the right when entering, along the partition wall erected by Joseph.

In subspace 1, a variety of furniture and objects is gathered together. On the left-hand side when moving from B to C is a small plastic trash can. Next to it is a large porcelain sink with a water heater installed by Joseph during the major renovations in the apartment in 1960; a washing machine installed in 1962; a gas cooker that dates from 1958 (in the past, cooking was done on a coal-burning stove: the current gas heater was installed in the space this formerly occupied); a big refrigerator dating from 1956: on top of this is a small cloth doily on which a fruit bowl permanently rests.

Subspace 2 contains several elements. First, there is a red Formica "expandable" kitchen table, surrounded by assorted chairs. The chair marked with an M on the floor plan is that of Madame Marie: it is across from the refrigerator and near all the kitchen appliances. During meals, the seating arrangement remains stable: on Madame Marie's right, Joseph, then Jean if he is there; on her left, Maurice when he is there. The guest or guests usually take a place between Madame Marie and Maurice. Various objects are attached to the wall: a music box in the form of a mandolin, a barometer singing the praises of the aperitif drink Cinzano, postcards from Corsica. There is also a wooden tool rack, strangely painted over in pale mauve by Joseph, on which rests a 1950s-era radio, a bit rounded the way people liked them back then. It no longer works, but its integrated turntable for 78s has played all the tangos in the world. It is topped with a rectangular antenna, decorated with the photo of a mountain landscape. In the corner, there is a piece of furniture from Beaujolais, purchased by Madame R. in 1930 from a person living in Villé-Morgon. It most likely dates from the first half of the nineteenth century; it is divided into two parts: a chest lying on the bare floor (more than three feet high) that opens with two doors and a series of shelves on whose uprights are sculpted bunches of fruits. Various souvenirs are placed on these shelves, along with some postcards, a tiny Savoyard chalet serving as a "piggy bank" with an opening roof, and finally an old round thermometer.

Under the window, on the floor, is a small child's stool on which Madame Marie perches when she wants to look out the window, because she is short. On the right, when looking at the window and slightly in front on its wheeled stand is a color television, bought in 1973 with Joseph's "thirty-five years of service" bonus. On the wall near the window there is an old "weighted" clock. It often breaks down, defying the patience of Joseph, who is otherwise an excellent handyman. Near the door opening onto room E there is a medicine chest with mirror attached to the wall. This is where Madame Marie keeps her "little beauty things": a tortoiseshell powder case, with its pink, puffy, and sweet-smelling blotter; violet and lavender water, various elixirs (among them, of course, that of the "great Chartreuse") "for stomach pains," and so on.

Here are the contents of subspace 3: to the right of the door opening onto room E, symbolized on the floor plan by an oval, is an old Singer sewing machine from 1903: "My mother gave it to me for my tenth birthday so that I would begin to have a trade when I left school." Marie worked her whole life on this finely wrought, venerable machine, whose mechanism is rather fascinating: pedal, wheels, belts, needle mechanism, and so on. Next, there are two identical Formica kitchen counters. Further on down is a vast, old wooden cupboard "for the housework," that contains brooms hanging from nails, rags, and cleaning supplies. Between the open space of this big cupboard and the two Formica counters is the bread bin, and next to it are stored the bottles of "everyday" wine. Between the big cupboard and the gas heater is the "kitchen towel and napkin" corner.

This room also contains a clothes-drying rack not represented on the floor plan: it involves a rectangular wooden frame to which are attached parallel cords on which to hang the laundry to dry. This frame is attached to the ceiling through a system of pulleys that allow it to be pulled up and brought down at will. On "laundry" days, Madame Marie spreads out newspapers on the floor in the space on the floor plan be-tween the letter C and the table in order to soak up the water dripping down from the drying rack.

Madame Marie's Bedroom (D)

One enters here by following the corridor to the left from the door of space C. There is a large bed with a nightstand. On the wall there are bookshelves whose supports are gilded metal and on which are placed Madame Marie's favorite books (a collection of poems, etc.) and family mementos (photos of Madame Marie's parents, her husband Barthélemy, who died in 1949, her sons and grandsons), as well as various knick-knacks. Across from the bed, behind the door is a large modern writing desk (for the "paperwork," as Joseph calls it) whose upper glass portion also contains family photos. Next to it is a fireplace with a record player. Finally, in the right-hand corner, looking at the window, one finds a large storage closet where a part of Joseph's very impressive record col-lection is located. On the other side of the window, there is another bookshelf with books and knickknacks. On one of the shelves is the tele-phone installed in 1972. Next to it, near the door opening onto room E, is a full-length swing mirror. In the middle of the room is a small, low, round table, always bedecked with flowers, and an easy chair. On both sides of the door opening onto room E, there are coat hooks.

Dining Room and Joseph's Bedroom (E)

Although it is called a "dining room," this room is very rarely used for this purpose. It is undoubtedly the nicest room; it is large and very well ventilated. From the two windows that look out onto rue Prunelle, one has a beautiful view of the banks of the Saône, which can also be seen from the window in room D. On the left, coming from room D, there is a large bed; above it are bookshelves where the collection of the journal *Constellation*, bound together by year, is found. Next to the bed is Joseph's nightstand; on the floor, a bedside rug. Between the two windows is a beautiful armoire with a mirror; it contains the sheets, fine linens, and table cloths, and so on, for the family. In a drawer below, Madame Marie sees to keeping her funeral clothing, along with a small bottle of holy water and a branch of boxwood, renewed each Palm Sunday by her very devout cousin Amélie. In the corner, a handsome dresser containing "the silver." On the intermediate shelf separating the lower cabinet from the upper one are various objects, among them a beautiful bowl. Then, to-ward the wall of room C, is the large family wardrobe, topped with a compartment especially designed for storing records, the jackets of which, facing out, serve as decorations. Thus, one can see the photo of Mistinguett, that of Jean Lumière, or of Fyodor Chaliapin as Boris Godunov, and so on. In the middle of the room there is a beautiful square table with four chairs. Behind the dresser and the wardrobe there used to be two windows, currently walled over, that looked out on the rue Rivet.

Second Apartment

Vestibule A, shared with the first apartment, gives onto the kitchen (F), where access is gained into bedroom G.

Kitchen (F)

Upon entering, one finds immediately on the left a large, extremely tall cupboard (it takes a ladder to reach the top), then a "white porcelain" sink, and a dish cabinet on which rests a single-burner modern gas cooker. Next to this is an old coal-burning stove that is no longer used. Across from these items is a folding table with its canvas chair. Against the wall on the same side beyond the door opening onto bedroom G is an unspecified corner where Madame R. piles up boxes.

Bedroom (G)

Immediately on the left upon entering is a small glassed-in bookshelf containing children's books and a few toys; across from it is Joseph's bike: to get to work, Joseph uses an old bike that he usually keeps outside on the half-story landing. Next to it is a walled bookshelf containing Joseph's books, especially his "nice collections" purchased on the installment plan through correspondence with specialized organizations. There are about six hundred books here (novels, poetry, history books, etc.). On one of the shelves there are a few old cameras, cleaned and carefully maintained: Joseph is a photographer, a fan and devotee of everything to do with photography. Below, a piggy bank in the shape of a 1955 automobile, the Renault Frégate: moreover, this model was the first vehicle bought by Joseph "for the family." This room is remarkable in the sense that it includes a "cubbyhole" above the bed, a sort of interior balcony obtained from the height of the ceiling (more than thirteen feet) that served as a bedroom when the weaving loom occupied the center of the room. One gains access to it by a very steep and narrow flight of stairs. Above that, there now are some old books and a storage closet. In front of the curtain, represented by a dotted line on the floor plan, at the base of the cubbyhole is a small armchair.

Chapter 4
The Street Trade

The rue Rivet

The rue Rivet is neither very long nor very lively: two hundred and twenty yards, perhaps a bit more, cut in half by a small cross street (rue Prunelle) that is the extension of a climbing staircase and that ends in another staircase (rue Ornano). This crossroads is a sort of border: for all the inhabitants, the rue Rivet is divided into two "sides," clearly opposed to each other. The R.'s live in one of the buildings on the corner of this crossroads and thus are located right on the boundary dividing the street.

One of the sides, on the left going out from the "alley,"[1] is only crossed on a few occasions: in order to get to Joseph's car when he parks it on the square at the end of the street; to take the trolley bus, number 13, when elderly people wish to "go up to the plateau"; to go for a walk in the Chartreux Park. Symbolically, this portion of the street is inert; one does not stop off there; one only passes by: only one grocery store, antiquated and archaic (gone by the end of 1978), known by the name "La Germaine," was a "holdout" in this sort of desert for which it was a frontier post; beyond that, there is not a single shop for hundreds of yards: the square that closes off the rue Rivet opens on to the cours du Général-Giraud, which only offers strollers the bleak block of the weaving school, followed by interminable fences with, across the way on the other sidewalk, the Chartreux Park bordering the cours along its entire length. The aesthetic impression plays a big role in the pejorative appreciation brought to bear on the left side of the rue Rivet: no store window gives it life (except for the one, just as dark as the walls, of La Germaine); garage doors made of more or less rusted, dented, corrugated sheet metal accentuate the bleakness of the *canut* buildings' grand, naked facades. At the end of the street, the square is surrounded by a retaining wall as high as an apartment building, blind and black. It is truly the "cold" part of the street that no lights brighten up at night, where a terrible wind blows in winter, summoned by the open space of the square from where it rushes into the narrow gully of the street.

It is toward the right, when leaving their place, that the R.'s spontaneously move toward social life: there, the street shops are located on the rue Rivet, and also on the neighboring streets (rue de Flesselles, rue Pierre-Blanc). One store, called "Robert's," is painted in bright colors: its wide display windows radiate a bright light at nightfall: at Christmastime, they are decorated with Chinese lanterns and artificial snow; two cafés that face it are also lit up late at night. The right side of the street is its active side: there are a lot of people, noise, voices; it is human. It also opens onto the park of the Saint Charles clinic, which, at the end of the street, offers the view of its flower beds, its copses, and its trees. It is also in that direction that the R.'s make their way downtown or to various customary walking places.[2]

Robert the Greengrocer

Besides the two cafés (or *canis*, as they are called), the rue Rivet includes most notably a shopkeeper endowed with great symbolic value in this little neighborhood. Everyone knows him and calls him by his first name, Robert; the expression "I'm going by Robert's" is standard here; his store is a rallying place that enjoys the fidelity of almost all the riverside residents of the street, fidelity all the more vigorous and unanimous in that "Robert's" is the only well-stocked grocery store in a relatively important area in relation to the density of the neighborhood. As Madame Marie says, "he's nice with everyone, everyone likes him a lot, he's the *universal Robert* of the neighborhood." Robert certainly owes this "universality" to his "good-natured character," but it has also grown with the disappearance of the neighborhood's shops beginning in the 1960s.

Madame Marie remembers the time when there was a profusion of shops, both big and small, on her street and neighboring ones some fifteen years ago. She recites the names of those that have gone like a litany: there used to be a milkman on the corner of the rue Pierre-Blanc ("well, that's gone!"); there used to be a Bon Lait [a dairy store] at the end of the rue de l'Annonciade across from the Saint Charles clinic, ("well, that's gone!"); Old Durand disappeared from the rue de Flesselles; a baker, a butcher, and a grocer shut their doors on the rue Rivet; there also used to be the delicatessen of Madame Solier (people called her "Madame" deferentially because "she was very distinguished"), who made such a tasty *choucroute* that people came down from the plateau to buy some from her. The register of the *past* is deployed here, a word that assumes a mythical function by emphasizing the fading of a past henceforth gone by but overloaded with symbolic references. In this manner of talking about it, the past becomes the measure of present time, always guilty of a *forgetting*, or of a putting to death.

In the past, then, the social porousness of the neighborhood founded a space that made possible a multiplicity of little shops or of small trades (grinders, glaziers, locksmiths, olive merchants, retail wine merchants, etc.) living in perfect osmosis with the surroundings: people took knives down to the grinder less to have them sharpened than "to give him some business." This intention, "to give him some business," was the origin of numerous purchasing steps in the neighborhood. Thus, Madame Marie used to go to "Old Durand's" once a week just "to give him some business": Old Durand was a small greengrocer in a neighboring street, relatively alcoholic, with a neglected shop, but the people liked him a lot because "he was not mean." Joseph used to go to an old barber, in the rue de l'Annonciade, explicitly in order "to give him some business." On Saturday nights, he used to see two or three regulars there (I was going to say "supporters"), who, to say the least, would not be bothered by a random haircut. This old barber worked until the end of his days in spite of a growing, and worrisome, blindness. An implicit contract for a subtle benefit underlines this move. One could formulate it as such: on the whole, it is better to maintain competition between shopkeepers rather than to fall under the monopoly of just one; flirtation and "infidelities" ("I've been unfaithful to you," says the customer to her shopkeeper when she has produce in her bag purchased elsewhere) are better than marriage "for better or for worse" (in any case, always "arranged") with *only one* shopkeeper. This maintains a gap between supply and demand, a coexistence of several trajectories between each of these terms, a potential game increasing the freedom of choice.

In these "little neighborhoods" of modest incomes, competition is intense; the slightest economic surcharge (operating costs, an increase in trade dues, taxes, considerable growth of "middlemen" monopolizing distribution) destroys an abundant but precarious commercial equilibrium. The great structural reforms in consumer consumption have "cleaned up" these neighborhoods of all kinds of little storekeepers who could not or would not adapt to new requirements. *Robert* is an exception: his business succeeded in maintaining itself by modernizing, without losing anything of the commercial practice belonging to the old system of strongly individualized sociability. Robert owes this exceptionally strong position to two things: his long-standing establishment and his taste for modernity.

Robert's family occupied this grocery store at about the time when the R. family was settling into the rue Rivet (around 1930). He himself was about ten years old and he is now much older than fifty. He took over from his mother ("a rather strict woman," says Madame Marie), after having been the delivery boy for a long time; he took wine and milk up to upper floors, "took the shopping" to sick people, the elderly, pregnant women, and so on.

Joseph, Maurice, and he found themselves growing up together, and had the same problems during the war, the same difficulties "getting established" after the war; and what is true for the R.'s is also true for many other families in the neighborhood. Robert thus has an "internalized" knowledge of *his* street (he told me he "loved" the rue Rivet and was incapable of ever living elsewhere, at least for as long as he worked), of individuals, families, tragedies, an exceptional, fabulous knowledge of everyone. Endowed with a prodigious memory, he forgets nothing, records everything, knows the preferences of each and every person, calls almost all his customers by their first name, is still on intimate terms with all those he knew in childhood,[3] and knows all their children. A rather handsome man ("he is very pleasing," says Madame Marie), with a relaxed gait, intelligent, and good-natured, he managed to impose himself as the center of attraction in the neighborhood, and without him, the rue Rivet would not be what it is; as Jean told me, "He's one hell of a character in the neighborhood. When his son got married in the spring, the entire street was at the windows to wave to the bride. We had never seen such a thing in the rue Rivet!"

Before, his shop resembled any other neighborhood grocery: a large, somber room where crates of vegetables were piled up on the floor and canned goods up on high with, in the back, across from the door with tiny bells on it, a wide refrigerator case (not so long ago, he still had blocks of ice delivered each morning) for the dairy products and cured meats; one pathetic lightbulb flickered over these somber riches. About fifteen years ago, he joined a chain of stores in order to "hold out" and adapt to the new structures of consumer consumption. He went from the level of "shop" to that of "store," designed as a tiny self-service store whose horseshoe floor plan organized the stock on either side of a "one-way path"; to get out, one passes in front of the register where Robert stands. He comes and goes, discusses with this person and that, scolds one child, gives another some candy, serves a customer, and asks how things are going.

Madame Marie once feared that the notion of self-service was incompatible with what she knew of the decay of her neighborhood; it disrupted something in her habits: "In the beginning, it really bothered me, but then I got used to it. It's nice and clean and it's just as good as before." Modernization always brings along a certain number of suspicions with it about the quality of products; standardization, prewrapping, all the modern procedures in food presentation worry people. Robert's strength was precisely to take things into account equitably: he did not abandon "old" products, now presented in a new decor, so there was no symbolic rupture; the main stream of consumption was able to be maintained by simultaneously emphasizing "the past" and "the here and now." This explains the current success of "Robert's Store," which appeals to a large clientele from a broad section of the neighborhood.

Robert's customers experience an equilibrium between the permanence of the past (because he has been the same grocer for forty years) and the "necessities of progress" (because his store is "modern"). Robert's store achieves a compromise that can be accepted by various age levels: the "young" people feel just as well served there as the older people because they find a self-service technique that they have integrated into their *practice* as consumers; and the older people do not feel swindled, rejected by modernization, because Robert continues, under a redesigned market format, to make use of an ancient practice of consumption, in other words, a *speaking* practice: discussions, information, help in choosing, credit, and so on. For Madame Marie, this translates into a small ironic arrogance: having a store on *her* street whose structure has no reason to envy a modern "supermarket," but without having lost the advantage of benefits acquired through long habituation. For the inhabitants who have been established in the relational fabric of the same neighborhood for a long time, the absolute obsessive fear is the anonymity of the "supermarkets." For that, Madame Marie has an evocative expression: "It spoils my appetite!"

La Germaine

In contrast to Robert's store, La Germaine's grocery, at the other end of the street, belonged to another world. In the past, Madame Marie used to go there willingly "to give La Germaine some business," but for obscure reasons, she has lately ceased going there. Before Robert's was modernized, La Germaine's shop, though it was already felt to be "antiquated," was nevertheless able to stand up to it; they were comparable.

Since then, the rupture has been total; it has consecrated the abyss separating the tiny little shop condemned to disappear from the store that managed to insert itself into a modern network of management and distribution. Entering La Germaine's shop was truly like discovering a grocery from the beginning of the century (another in the same genre exists on the rue du Bœuf in the Saint-Jean neighborhood): a somber, dull blue, almost navy blue universe where La Germaine sat enthroned, gray and slow, behind her counter. Fantastic odors were attached to the walls: smells of spices and cured meats in conflict with dairy products and cheese; smells of wine casks, coffee, olive oil, vegetables. On the left upon entering was a tiny counter on a bean-shaped stand on which La Germaine served *canons* (wine by the glass) to a few regulars.

In this room, one experienced the passage of one time period to another, in the same way that a body is expelled from one liquid to another as a result of their different densities; all of a sudden, one left behind the deafening and anonymous rumbling of the city to enter into an extremely heavy social density, transforming habitual gestures into ritualized conventions: one spoke in a hushed voice and she replied in a whisper from her closed, ahistorical universe, completely folded back on itself. Observing the consumers coming to be served there confirmed the strangeness of this feeling: they were especially men and, among them, bachelors or elderly men. La Germaine's "patrons" (one talks about "patronizing" a shopkeeper when one goes there regularly) were the poorest on the street, the "marginalized": retirees in poverty, old alcoholics, semitramps and, along with them, the category always represented as the abomination of desolation, the lushes and women drunkards (old alcoholic women). Some female "clients" (a word indicating an upper rank in the social hierarchy)[4] also came there sometimes, either for convenience in an emergency (its proximity) or to respect the sacrosanct principle of "giving La Germaine some business" before her inevitable disappearance.

The practice of stores thus implies a difference of social status *on* the street; there is no equivalence between Robert's customers and La Germaine's. To go to one or the other implies a social transparency; this is why, fundamentally, Madame Marie's decision to stop going to La Germaine's is less the result of an obscure quarrel than a question of "propriety." This propriety obviously does not come into play in an explicit way; it would not occur to anyone to say that "it is not proper" to go there. It is at play on a deeper level of taking sides with a style of commerce that implies a style of relationship to the city and, through it, by an extension of scale, to the entire society. This taking sides with a "tempered" modernity excludes La Germaine's archaic commercial practice because, from all points of view, the latter stems from a regressive attachment to the past.

Robert the Confidant

One can only understand Robert's "neighborhood function" well if one attaches to his professional role that of a *confidant*. He is a confidant of a particular type: a specialist not at all in confession, but in coded discourse. The utterance of confidences at the grocer's rests on allusion, ellipsis, understatement, euphemism, all the figures of speech that erase, minimize, or reverse the meaning that they explicitly utter. Why this economy of discourse? Robert's is the terminus of everyday trajectories, and very precise operations unfold there during a period of time that, in any case, is limited. It is possible to prolong the conversation for a few minutes after having paid, but propriety does not allow a woman to habitually settle in at Robert's register for a long period of time: the people in the street "would get ideas"; and for Robert, it would be better to lose this customer, "by putting her back in her place," than to allow the slightest misunderstanding to persist. He is expected by propriety, always more puritanical for someone who is prosperous and highly respected, to "remain correct."

An objective constraint at the grocer's forbids a specific time from being devoted to confidential talk. One must seek a status of intimacy that makes it sufficiently possible in order to be perceived as such, but by masking it in its presentation. Confidences have no right to be unveiled as such; they do not use direct discourse; they will latch onto the functional discourse of the purchase and slip through in some way attached to it, just as Ulysses and his companions did in sheep's clothing to escape the Cyclops's vigilance. Confidences are transferred in the chain of commonplaces, of proverbial expressions that match up functional language with the choice of objects. These stock phrases, which are commentary on the actions being carried out, are also the *literary space* in which the confidence arises. The suprasegmental (gesture, intonation) "speaks volumes" in the discernible language that the grocer decodes in order to enter into the proposed complicity. We are within the phatic function of language here ("Is the code working?"), but a phatic function that knows itself to be so: "Have you understood what I mean?" "Yes." "Good, then I can continue..." This is what intonation and gestures (or any other suprasegmental intervention) express in order to ensure that the message has been decoded at its correct level by the receiver.

The following is the summary of a dialogue heard at Robert's between him and one of his customers, Madame X. I have shortened it considerably:

R: So, Madame X, what would you like from me today? You'll want to take a look at my apples, they're splendid.

Mme X: Yes, they'll be fine for me; but let me have some oranges too because, you know, Paul and apples!...

R: And so how is he anyway? We hardly see him anymore.

Mme X: Oh, so-so! Not much new... He's been getting into it with the young one pretty much all the time. But, anyway, *that's the way life is*...

R: Oh, yes, it is (*in an approving tone, then silence*).

Mme X: And so what do you have in the way of cheese?

R: Take a look at that one, it's first-rate!

Mme X: Oh, no! Not for me... I don't like that kind too much:[5] (*in a tone raised little by little and looking Robert straight in the eye*) you know very well, there's no accounting for taste. Can't do anything about it!... Let me have a little of that chèvre there instead, and some *onze* [wine], as usual.[6]

R: And Aline, how is *she* doing?

Mme X: Ah, well,... it's still the same. There's nothing anyone can do to make up her mind; it makes her father furious; what do you want me to do about it, especially at my age?... (*In a tone of obviousness*) Well, anyway, *youth must have its fling! These kids won't be twenty forever!* (*Then she takes her full shopping bag, rests it for a second on the cash register ledge, and, very quickly, in almost hushed tones, as if to finish up, or to "let the cat out of the bag."*) But anyway, let me tell you, they're quite right *not to worry too much*, worries will come along soon enough. If *I* had had such freedom at their age, I would not have deprived myself. Don't you agree? Well, alrighty then, good-bye, Robert, see you tomorrow! Good-bye, sir [to me].

R: That's the way! Alrighty then, Madame X, good-bye.

What does this short conversation tell us? Some raw facts: Madame X likes apples and she also buys oranges, some cheese, and some wine (some *onze*). They talk about Paul and about a girl named Aline who is having quarrels with her father about a problem we are unaware of, but that most likely concerns "morality." What is she giving away to Robert that he alone is able to understand? Let us go back to this text, in which one can distinguish four levels:

1. The functional level of the purchase, which corresponds to the preceding paragraph. It involves the choice of fruits, wine, and so on.

2. An allusive level that refers to a contextual knowledge at Robert's disposal. Robert knows who Paul is, knows his tastes, asks how he is doing. Madame X does without a whole series of pieces of information: "because, you know, Paul and apples"; "not *much new*"; "he's been getting into it with the young one *all the time*." This is thus an informative level that aims at confirming Robert's knowledge about problems that Madame X knows he is aware of.

3. A first level of proverbial expressions: "that's the way life is," "there's no accounting for taste"; this latter expression is absolutely remarkable in the context because it is a transfer in which what seems to be said about cheese is *at the same time* said about another situation that Robert is very well aware of, because he feels authorized to respond with a nominal question: "And Aline, how is she doing?"

4. A second level of proverbial expressions or of commonplaces, all centered on the notion of carpe diem: "youth must have its fling"; "they won't be twenty forever"; in short: "they are right to take advantage of it." Here, Madame X gives her own opinion ("But anyway, let me tell you") about this situation, but without describing it, still hiding behind stock phrases. Having gone this far in voicing her conviction, she seeks approval; she engaged herself in this confidence as far as she could with Robert and she leaves quickly, certain that she was understood.

By reconstructing the "story," we learn that Madame X is Paul's mother and Aline's grandmother. She lives in an apartment near that of her son and her daughter-in-law, and does their shopping because they both work. Aline, barely twenty years old, lives with a boyfriend and refuses to get married, which scandalizes her father. It is a crisis situation that has been dragging on for several months. Madame X does not know which side to take; or rather, she does not dare to openly take her granddaughter's side. This is why the stereotypes brought out in the third level ("that's the way life is," "no accounting for taste") tend to minimize the crisis, to *normalize* it by relativizing it with "popular wisdom." What follows tells of her own position on this crisis: she wants to be "understanding" ("They are twenty years old = they are right"); this is thus a way of telling Robert that she finds Paul to be too harsh and that she does not agree with his severity. By means of a few sentences, and in a relatively short lapse of time, the confidence has gone rather far, thanks to the discursive economy made possible by allusions, quick references to a past known only by Robert, and without anything clear having been revealed to the other customers.[7]

On several occasions, Madame Marie insists on the role of confidant that Robert plays in his practice of the neighborhood. In the example that I retain here, it is she who asks him about his brother, with whom, she tells me, he has had a falling out: "He has fallen out with his brother, he doesn't know what he's been up to, where he's gone. Is Michel married? He doesn't know. I ask him: 'And Michel?'; *we sometimes chat like that, just the two of us*, and so I go: 'And Michel?'; well, 'we don't know where he is' . . ."

The small phrase I have emphasized by itself contains all the conditions on which the register of the confidence relies. It is an exceptional act that cuts through the continuum of habits ("sometimes"); the actors drop their theatricalized "customer/shopkeeper" roles for a moment in order to allow another level of language to come forth on which they can rest for a moment; "we chat like that" means that they talk face to face, "like I'm talking to you right now," as one would talk to a close friend, privately ("just the two of us"), without another interlocutor, at an off-peak time of the day. "And so I go: 'And Michel?'"; the use of the verb *to go* instead of the verb *to say* indicates, I believe, the exact level of language that is used: the performative, that is, in this instance, the awareness of having established a contract that one can say is intensely provisional, in which speech has a price because it binds, even if it is for a short time.

More superficially, Robert's role as confidant is constantly reassured by the manifestations of kindness that burst forth during exceptional events, returns from vacation, holidays, and so on:

> "They married off their youngest son and he sent us the announcement, and for all four of their children, he always let me know in advance, and he would give me my party favor, every time."

And, more generally:

> "If you could just see how he jokes around with all the nice ladies there; the young, the old, he makes compliments, he is . . . he's really chic. But his little woman, she takes it all in stride, you know: she doesn't make a scene . . ."

This last sentence about Robert's wife shows us very exactly what is possible *within the limits of propriety*. If Madame Marie took care to tell me that "Madame Robert" is not jealous of her husband's "liberties," it is less to exalt her virtue than to make it known to me, to me as a listener, that there was no cause for his wife to become angry. We are within the domain of what is not only tolerated, but almost required by propriety. This is inscribed in the social game of the neighborhood that, in its theatricality, wants the shopkeeper to be more than a paid distributor of consumable goods. The space in which he is enthroned must constantly maintain a possibility for speech, the very speech of the street, which finds an opportunity to manifest itself there.

It is at the grocer's that the neighborhood awareness is sharpened much more so than on the sidewalk or on the stairs. Why? Because buying is a public action that binds, not only by the price it costs, but because one is seen by others in the midst of choosing what will become a meal. One thus reveals something about oneself, about one's secret; this creates a permanent availability for speech that, starting from the example of a comment on the quality of various products, takes off from the foundation on which it began rolling in order to rise up into a more general discourse on neighborhood events. Madame Marie often told me that each time an event took place in the neighborhood (an accident, a death, a birth, a police patrol, etc.), all she had to do was stop by Robert's to get the commentary on it. *That is where the neighborhood speaks.*

Robert is the neighborhood's coryphaeus; he receives the rumor of events and gives it a universally communicable form, acceptable by everyone: he changes into news the fragmentary bits of information that come to him from all sides. The oral activity in his store recalls the structure of ancient tragedy: the chorus of women exclaim, question, comment, and amplify before the soloist's words: "It happened just like I'm telling you!" No one would dream of challenging his role as soloist, which invests him with sovereign authority, and which he is the only one able to play in view of the position of information synthesizer that he occupies in the neighborhood: he can add words to the rumor, organize it into utterances, and interpret it through satisfying "lessons." Robert, after all, is essentially a public man. He will thus utilize — and receive — public language, the very language that we were describing earlier: proverbs, commonplaces, stereotypes. For there lies the acuity with which he detects, beneath the universality of this public speech, private and even intimate, secret information. But, in a broader sense, his speech belongs to everyone, and everyone collects it because it gives a universal meaning to neighborhood events so that the greatest number of people can share in the information and excitement.

Finally, the relationship with Robert implies a very elaborate practice of time, linked to both proximity and habituation. The conjunction of these two conditions shows through in verbal expressions such as "With Robert, you can allow yourself to..." That is an announcement of a benefit relating not only to provisions (being well served...) but to time: being able to bother Robert even outside his official working hours. Madame Marie has, for example, the rare privilege—along with a few other people on the street—of being able to knock "on the back door," after eight o'clock, when Robert has already closed. This involves not only tolerance and politeness, but a permission resulting from long habituation. It is a pact that must be used from time to time, two or three times a year, to verify the solidity of the relation established over time. A privilege and gesture that a newcomer would not dare to ask for, it is up to the R.'s to reactivate it regularly, in order to see, in short, if everything is functioning well: a routine. This little rite celebrated a few times a year has a function of *reassurance*, for the R.'s as well as for Robert: it serves to verify that one still has "space" in relations, that one has some "leeway" in everyday relationships, that one can thus count on the other. The two customer/shopkeeper awarenesses tighten the bonds of their recognition by rendering themselves indispensable to each other, to the point of the transgression of business hours that marks this after-hours request.

In a more general way, the structure unique to the grocery store favors the intensity of communication. At the baker's or the butcher's, the choice of foods is relatively simple. They involve only one "moment" in the meal, only one class of objects (bread, meat). One only really chooses one kind of meat for a meal. At the grocer's, the range of goods offered to customers involves a much more complex gastronomic discourse. All by itself, it is a syntagma to be constituted on the spot: vegetables, canned goods, fruits, dairy products, cheese, cookies, desserts, drinks, cleaning products. Consequently, one spends more time there than anywhere else, at the same time revealing one's capacity to master the complexity of this overabundant universe. The "presentation of self" is much more implicated there: one does not really choose the bread one buys, but one can always hesitate before the quality of lettuce or cheese; the savoir faire required is important. From this, I believe, comes the high symbolic value of neighborhood grocery stores: they are, in a certain way and in both traditional and popular urban neighborhoods, the sitting rooms of the street, the public sphere in which it is always possible to "waste a little time," that is, to gain a benefit from recognition.

I remember the extraordinary place held in neighborhood life many years ago by two grocery stores that were very different from one another. The first was run by "Old Michel," whom everyone knew; a decent man, rough and taciturn, he found himself cast in the ambiguous role of bogeyman by various mothers. One often heard yelled in the street, in the public park, the fateful threat: "I've had enough, I'm going go get Old Michel!" He himself went along with the game and rolled his terrifying eyes. The second store occupied an exactly opposite symmetrical position to the first. It was a dairy and grocery store run by a couple and their two children. The wife was a sort of mother for all the neighborhood children; people used to leave her keys to the apartment so she could go to take care of flu-stricken children who stayed home alone during the day while their parents were working. It was thus less a service she provided than a privilege she granted herself and that she undoubtedly believed legitimately involved part of her duties as dairywoman in the neighborhood.

Thus, Old Michel and Madame Carli, each in their own way, were inscribed in the neighborhood, going well beyond the purely functional duties of their roles as shopkeepers. One could not just remain in a simple relationship of consumption with them because that relationship became — it had to become — the support for another discourse that here, in a generic fashion, I call *confidence*.

In order to understand this process well, one must look in the direction of honor: the pure relationship of consumption is insufficient, too brief, to express what it secretly involves on the level of relations. Propriety takes over from the strict economic exchange and creates a linguistic space in which a more complete recognition of these relations becomes thinkable and thus able to be articulated. Submission to this pact remains the essential condition for a good relationship with the neighborhood, that is, the possibility for any subject to take his or her place in the social functioning of the street. Robert's role as confidant consists of producing this space within which the neighborhood can recognize itself by becoming aware of itself through the multiplication of exchanges that it *authorizes*.

Chapter 5
Bread and Wine

I would like now to enter further into the relationship that the R. family maintains with what it consumes at home during family meals. More precisely, it seems to me important to analyze the philosophical function that bread and wine occupy in their gastronomy, because, without these two elements, a meal becomes not only inconsistent, but even unthinkable. Foods bought from the shopkeeper remain within a random distribution as long as they have not been ordered by the organization of the meal. They have been chosen (or rather, their class of objects: vegetables, meat, cheese, fruits), but it is in the kitchen that they become a succession unfolding according to a preexisting canonical order: appetizer [*entrée*], main course (meat or fish with vegetables), salad, cheese, dessert. Culinary preparation imposes a coercive series inside of which the various elements can no longer be rearranged: in France, one does not begin the meal by what is served as dessert, one does not serve the cheese before the meat, and so on. Otherwise, the meal would be perceived as disordered, "improper," and in any case, as something "not to be repeated," in short, a sort of obscenity.

Only two foods "accompany" the meal from beginning to end and are adapted to each moment in the series: bread and wine. They function as two ramparts that maintain the unfolding of the meal. They are thus at the foundation of cuisine, what must be thought about in first place, before any other gastronomic decision. Let us suppose that Madame Marie had planned to cook a rabbit for a nice meal and that at the moment of buying it the poultry shop no longer had any available. She could fall back on a chicken or any other meat without a problem. She could substitute. This is impossible for both bread and wine: neither is replaceable by anything that might take its place. They are the concrete a prioris of every gastronomic practice, its unchallengeable necessity: this is not up for debate; if they disappear, nothing has flavor anymore, everything falls apart. To make a comparison in the outdated linguistics of the eighteenth century, bread and wine (and the category of condiments) are the consonants of the meal, its fixed points, its substantial toughness; the menu is on the side of the vowels, of accidental value. Alone, bread and wine do not constitute a true meal, but both are hierarchically more indispensable than the remainder of the menu.

Within their structural solidarity, bread and wine are irreducible to each other. The connotations evoked by both are antagonistic, as if bread and wine were two opposite poles, creating a tension in which the meal takes place. They do not occupy the same position at all in gastronomic semantics; they are two sides of a same philosophy that is constructed based on a violent antithesis that it forever dominates: drama, work, seriousness, opposed to laughter, alcohol, drama. Drama is at both ends of the chain: in the sweat of a troubled brow and in the delirium of an alcoholic who causes the trouble. Fundamentally, bread and wine exchange terrible cultural provocations, the strength of good, the lure of evil, an archetypal dualism that is seen right up to the common image of the alcoholic who drinks his paycheck, rips the bread right out of the mouths of his children, beats his wife, and destroys his family. The alcoholic is a man who has forgotten bread along the way and who sets his house on fire: this, I think, is the fundamental obsessive fear. One might wonder if, among all these functions attributed to the menu (celebration, nutrition, diversity), one of them, not perceived because it is central, is to maintain a bridge between bread and wine so that the fundamental relationship can be stabilized and the threat of wine by itself averted.

Bread

Bread is the symbol of the hardships of life and work; it is the memory of a better standard of living acquired the hard way over the course of previous generations. Through its royal presence (the R.'s most often buy *couronnes* [crown-shaped loaves]) on the table where it is enthroned, it shows that there is nothing to fear, for the moment, from the deprivations of the past. Even though living conditions have changed considerably in twenty or thirty years, it remains the indelible witness of a "gastronomy of poverty"; it is less a basic food than a basic "cultural symbol," a monument constantly restored in order to avert suffering and hunger. It remains "what we would have really liked to have during the war" (Madame Marie's father nearly died from hunger in 1943: "all we had were tiny slices of bread like that, which we had to share with everybody. Grandpa was old and weak; that was not enough food for him"). Bread arouses the most archaic respect, nearly sacred; to throw it out, to trample over it is a matter of sacrilege; the scene of bread thrown in the trash arouses indignation; it cannot be separated from the working-class condition: to throw bread in the trash means to forget the story of poverty. It is a *memorial*.

Since the baker on the street closed down his shop, Robert also sells bread so that his customers do not have to run too far to buy some. The purchase is often preceded by a very simple ritual, consisting of "putting aside": every morning, Robert puts aside a few *couronnes* for his female customers; he knows the preferences of each one. This gesture implies an understated phrase that accompanies it, which belongs to the oral code actualizing the intrinsic qualities of the bread's substance: "well done," "not overdone," "light," "crunchy," or "floury" according to the customer's taste.

At home, the bread is placed on its breadboard at the end of the table, enveloped in its tissue paper, as soon as one gets back from shopping. One only rarely starts on it before the meal. When the latter begins, the head of the household stands up at the end of the table and cuts as many slices as there are table companions. Then the service continues as long as there are requests for more. Rarely are more than one or two slices cut "in advance": this is done out of precaution so one does not risk having to throw them out. Moreover, bread is never thrown out; when it is too old, one makes pudding out of it, or, in the winter, soup. Or else Madame Marie puts it in a cloth bag that she regularly gives to her cousin Amélie, who knows a "country woman" who has chickens. Bread is constantly the object of an almost unconscious precaution: after the meal, it is carefully put away in a sack placed in the back of the cupboard "so it doesn't dry out."

Sometimes bread almost has the value of a test that allows a guest's social origin to be uncovered. If he or she wastes bread in such a way that impacts the seriousness that bread represents, this guest risks losing all credit: "He never went without, that guy, it's obvious." Bread, very indirectly, allows one to know if someone is "with or against us." It bears a social writing: it is implicitly required to know how to read it correctly. Because one does not joke around with bread: it condenses into a very tight bundle much ardent and painful effort that had to be maintained throughout history so that it would not be lacking. The strange paradox about bread is that this accompanying food (it is unusual to eat bread by itself) is still perceived as the necessary foundation for all food, however festive, because of the force of social representation of which it continues to be the support. When this necessity is ensured (when bread is present on the table), it is the sign that one can legitimately enjoy oneself within the gratuitousness of the menu, because "nothing is lacking," in other words, because there is no urgency about suffering or hunger. As long as there is bread . . .[1]

Wine

Temperance. The discourse on bread is always at the limits of pathos, above all suspicion. That on wine is much more nuanced, as if weighed down from the inside by an indelible ambivalence: the pleasure of drinking well always tends toward the boundary of drinking too much. Bread is stable, a fixed point; wine intrinsically contains the possibility of drift, of a setback; it can be the origin of a journey from which one does not return; the abuse of drinking logically leads to sickness, destruction, death. This reprehensible, pessimistic vision of wine goes back to elementary school discourse on alcoholism. In the Croix-Rousse like everywhere else, everyone has in mind the social image of the alcoholic, angel of misfortune, drunk husband beating his wife, a man whose black and shriveled liver is put on display ("here's a normal liver, and over here is an alcoholic's liver"). Because of this "work" of the cultural representations inculcated in school, one does not go toward wine the way one goes straight toward bread; a detour must be made, which precisely allows us to avoid drinking too much in order to authorize intelligent drinking, always "sober."

This strategy, aiming at turning aside every possible suspicion weighing on the drinker, rests on the claim for a *drinking savoir faire* [*savoir-boire*]. To the repressive discourse, another discourse is opposed that exalts temperance as the savoir faire of qualitative and quantitative tasting. Here too, there is no lack of scholastic references. Everyone knows by heart Pasteur's phrase: "Wine, consumed in reasonable quantities . . ."; everyone knows the official scales for healthy drinking: less than a quart for manual laborers, less than a pint for sedentary workers, and so on. To that are added many opinions reinforcing the legitimacy of drinking: a natural wine can do no harm; drinking during the meal does less harm than drinking on an empty stomach; wine aids in digestion; it is dangerous to drink water with fruit because it causes stomachaches, but a small drop of wine helps everything along; cheese without wine tastes like plaster, it is like a day without sunshine, and so on. It is a question here of a reinforcing discourse aiming to limit the strength of the antialcoholic discourse, which takes the form of a "not guilty" defense speech, in the face of the attacks of which wine is a victim.

Neighborhood checks. The neighborhood has an implicit but important legislative role: it operates like a regulatory authority tempering the consumption of wine. The purchase of wine is in essence a visible act, if not by everyone, at least by the grocer. It suffices for one person in the neighborhood to know that there has been an abuse of alcoholic consumption, thus a transgression of propriety's boundaries, for it to serve as a brake. Propriety thus requires the drinker to situate himself on the threshold immediately below the foreboding signs of reprobation, in the plausible "not too much" category that does not cast a slur on an individual's or a family's reputation. Just as everyone more or less knows the number of members in each family allowed to drink wine, everyone also knows the scales cited earlier; it is thus not difficult to divide the quantity of wine purchased by the number of people and to deduce from this the rate of alcohol intake for a family. It is on this point that neighborhood checks operate and in this way that, in all likelihood, they slow down the consumption of wine and tend to bring it back within what are considered "sensible" or "proper" limits. By holding to this implicit system, one can let oneself be watched without risk by others, all the while procuring the means to "properly wash down" each meal of the week.

If one were to see only repression here, one would misunderstand the checks exercised by the neighborhood. In the deepest sense, "the neighborhood" seeks to preserve *itself*, by preserving the capital of human relations on which it is based through the imposition of implicit limits for alcohol consumption. It tends to disassociate from itself the transgressions that it considers excessive. Having said that, the tolerance thresholds within this normality are quite elastic and adapted to individual cases. More precisely, it involves a self-regulation in which each person knows, more or less clearly, what he or she has a right to. The criteria for this tolerance and the manner in which they can be combined create an equal number of scenarios such as age, gender, profession, sickness, suffering, worries, mental stability, sadness, joy, each according to his or her limits, according to whether it involves an elderly man having greatly suffered (extreme tolerance) or a happy woman in the prime of her life (reduced tolerance). Nowhere do there exist stone tablets of the Law; the only limit is, and always remains, to avert destruction or scandal in the neighborhood: beyond this limit, there is no salvation; within it, everything is possible.[2]

Temperance is maintained as the ideal to which it is recommended to submit as much by "scholastic" discourse on wine as by the public act of the purchase, which are joined in order to exalt it. The street is a glance that constantly interprets the adherence to this submission in order to evaluate the degree of conformity to propriety. A too-prolonged stay beyond this limit, a too-often repeated journey into the magic spell of the bottle involve a progressive social isolation of the individual or group whose too frequent "debauches" arouse the obsessive fear of alcoholism. The neighborhood fights against this monster that constantly reemerges in its womb. A social segregation induces a social zoning of the neighborhood. This now explains the isolation of La Germaine's clientele; her shop is the only public space in the neighborhood in which the few "lushes" around can gather together. This is why it had become so "improper" for Madame Marie to go there.

Wine and celebration: a social landmark. "Mr. Pompidou said that those who drink water were sad people. That's the most intelligent thing he ever said" (Joseph). Two elements, converging toward the same goal, can be drawn from this comment. The first is the reference to Georges Pompidou: his phrase is an authorized remark; it is linked to a position of power, as that of Pasteur, quoted earlier, is linked to knowledge. The opinion of a [former] president of the republic—even if his politics are otherwise contested by the R.'s—reinforces the positive discourse on wine; it comes exactly as a reinforcement against the detractors of the drink: "If even the president says so, then..."

The second element is the sadness of water drinkers, and thus, by way of antiphrasis, the joy of wine drinkers. In one blow, this jest points out the cultural function of wine: it is the symbolic antisadness element, the festive face of the meal, while bread is its laborious face (and water, its penitential one: being sentenced to "bread and water"). Wine is the condition sine qua non of every celebration: it is that for which it is possible to spend more to honor someone (a guest) or something (an event, a celebration). This is to say that wine contains, as a result of the unique virtues attributed to it through a social consensus, a motivating social force that bread does not have: the latter is shared, wine is offered. On the one hand, we are within a calculating economy (don't waste the bread), and, on the other, a spending economy (let the wine flow freely!). Wine is thus par excellence the center of an exchange, the pontiff for the speech of recognition, especially when there are guests.

Thus, at a festive meal at the R.'s home, when the main course comes out, Joseph ducks into his room, where he will have earlier uncorked a nice bottle of wine. If he is a few moments late or slightly distracted at this point, his mother elbows him or mumbles some sibylline phrases in hushed tones: "Hey, haven't you forgotten something?" "My heavens, you're right, there's something still waiting for us ..." He brings out the bottle, sniffs it, "taste-tests" it, and serves his guests. The inevitable round-table discussion ensues ("What do you think? It's good, huh?"), the orality of gustatory judgment (speaking and tasting at the same time) whose function is entirely celebratory. A glass cannot remain empty without becoming indecent: "it's pitiful," "it hurts to look at," "it makes no sense at all," "what's that all about?" As little as it may be, there must be some wine in all the glasses, because this gives a bearing to the table, to the conversation; wine silently gives the assurance that a "plenitude" of being together is possible. If it is lacking, it means that somewhere not enough attention is being paid to the other, a lack of propriety; a duty has not been accomplished: "Hey, boss, you're not doing your work, you're letting us dry out!" "Excuse me, it got away from me." Sometimes, a playful overstatement is added to the game of offering: "Give me a little bit more, then ..." "More!" "Oh, now he's gonna mete it out to me, this guy; come on, pour!" Wine escapes calculation, and is even opposed to it. Proverbs and witticisms burst forth at almost every meal: "Once a drunkard, always a drunkard"; "When my glass is empty I complain about it, when it is full, I empty it,"[3] and so on.

Like bread, wine is a social separator. One fears the "water drinkers": "He's not very cheerful; he don't drink like the rest of us. That bothers us, you feel constrained"; or, on the contrary: "For feast days, we like to go out with the Denises. They eat, drink, and laugh, they're really funny! We get along well because we have the same tastes!" Madame Marie often wondered, in my presence, if the "bourgeois" in the boulevard des Belges or the Presqu'île had wine on the table: "I don't know if they do that at their place ... Surely less so than here!" A naive question where memory of the cleavage between "the people" and "the others" shows through, without wishing to, without even realizing it. Madame Marie has internalized this moralizing ponderousness, but she knows how to turn it against her adversaries, "the others," in a form of contempt, and this contempt can be expressed in the following canonical form: to know how to appreciate wine is to know how to enjoy oneself; one can only enjoy oneself after having worked hard; thus, only workers know how to taste wine properly. This is because wine is the blood of workers, what gives them the strength and courage to accomplish their task; it is the compensation for a miserable life, the celebration they have a right to.

Wine traces out a social borderline because it indicates where social "sadness" begins, that is, the inaptitude for enjoyment; this is why the category of water drinkers corners less the so-called teetotalers than the contemptible class of "fussy," "stuck-up," "sophisticated," "upstart" people, and so on—in short, all those who represent for the R.'s the sadness of life, and whom they assimilate outright to the "bourgeois."

An abrupt social shortcut? In fact, the custom for wine consumption currently in force in Lyons proves Madame Marie right. We know that there exists, in this city and the surrounding region, a quantity of wine called *the pitcher* [*le pot*]: it contains just under a pint of wine, that is, enough to serve about three *shots* [*canons*] (a glass containing about six ounces). Indeed, to order a pitcher is to sign one's social belonging; a bourgeois in Lyons would never risk it; it is an action specific to popular neighborhoods and strata. Without being too far off, one can suppose that this custom becomes more intense as soon as one enters into the Croix-Rousse from below. In a café on the place des Terreaux, "down below," one sees few men at tables surrounding one or more pitchers. As soon as one arrives on the place Sathonay, the look of the tables already changes considerably: people are drinking pitchers and playing cards. Finally, in certain boulevard cafés or on various streets leading up to the plateau, pitchers are almost exclusively served (with white wine in the morning and red in the afternoon.)[4]

Cultural sources: Gnaffron. Lyons folklore provides other, very strong, references to the conviviality of wine. The relationship to wine there is experienced as a regional specificity, a claim of identity. It is the city of "three rivers": the Rhône, the Saône, and the Beaujolais. The popular local theater, the Guignol (which has nothing to do with its Parisian homonym), presents a key character who comes straight into our analysis.[5] He is Gnaffron, the incorrigible friend of Guignol, the friendly drunkard with a glowing red face, always armed with his bottle: his blazon, his coat of arms, his title of nobility, his insolence. "Gnaffron, well, he always has his jug of wine with him, he always had his jug of wine!" Madame Marie says, while evoking her memories as a child spectator. Gnaffron is a cultural hero who occupies a complex place: he stands in the very place of ambivalence that characterizes all discourse on wine—attractive and dangerous, dangerously attractive.

He is attractive because, come hell or high water, he justifies drinking with all his mocking strength: he thunders in its honor. It is the absolute weapon against sadness and boredom, it swallows down all worries into forgetfulness, and it is the sweet, nocturnal river on which one can slide right out of history. Gnaffron proclaims what all drinking songs proclaim: "Drink, good Lord! Don't allow yourself to measure how much!" "Drink, drink, it's drinking we should be doing." In his raspy gullet is held "the horrible cry uttered by [Gargantua], as he first saw the light of this world, bellowing out, 'Drink, drink, drink!'"[6] Gnaffron is an avatar of Bacchus. Popular iconography, found here and there in the cafés of Fourvière or the Croix-Rousse, depicts him asleep under vine branches with enormous clusters of grapes, with vine leaves encircling his old black felt hat; in the distance, among the vines, men and women dance or frolic cheerfully, with a glass of wine in their hand. Gnaffron is a sort of nostalgic proliferation that emerged from the land of milk and honey and entered into popular imagination by the back door.

More profoundly still, Gnaffron arouses a social adherence: he is the "ideal" for the man of the people; within his drunkenness, the subversive speech of the lowest echelons of society dares to speak. He is a carnivalesque character who turns social, family, and political values head over heels. The policeman has law and order on his side; Guignol has cunning and the stick ("And then he smacks the policeman, always! The policeman sure gets what he deserves!"); Gnaffron has his bottle and forthrightness of speech: a coarse, anarchic, rebellious speech. He is Guignol's eternal second in command, his complementary associate (as in comic books with Tintin and Captain Haddock, Astérix and Obélix). Moreover, he plays the role of the valet: he has a lucid but impotent gaze, with no power over society, whose abysmal dysfunction he reveals with his sarcasm. He moons the owner (the horrible Canezou), the policeman, and the priests. He is a form of speech, a social "talk" [un "dire"] that bores deep enough to bring up the latent desire for disorder and drunkenness beneath all social order.

But the theatrical form of this talk forbids him from becoming an "action" [un "faire"] effectively working on the historical thickness of society. This theatrical form is the fantasy-life presentation of the ambivalence that "works" the concept of wine and the social images attached to it, right up to the source of the celebration it invites. At the same time, such theater says that there is an incompatibility between drunkenness and social revolution or transformation. The former is on the side of nostalgia: its way of being an invitation to the spasms of complete joy goes back to the great social archaisms (nudity, dance, sleep). Drunkenness remains, fundamentally, a pathos for the ego. Revolution, on the contrary, assumes a belief, an uprising, a rigor, an assortment of competing forces, and even more, an insertion into the social thickness that it is a question of transforming. Indeed, Gnaffron the libertarian cannot be a revolutionary because of the drink of which he is the active symbol. Beside the fragments of dreams that he arouses deep down — or, more exactly, above them — is inscribed in fiery letters the evil side of wine, the social exclusion of which it is the logical end in the case of drinking too much. Wine brings the subversive dreams about the social to a halt because, in its extreme manifestation, it is a dismissal of History. On the rue Rivet, Gnaffron would undoubtedly have been one of La Germaine's customers, a nice pariah, but a pariah all the same.

Popular wisdom is not mistaken about it. It takes charge of this ambivalence in Gnaffron's character whose connotations are always *doubtful*, simultaneously positive and negative. By extension, it calls the neighborhood drunk "Gnaffron." To a child surprised in the process of drinking the last "drop" from a bottle or a glass, one says, "Look at the little Gnaffron!" — which is a way at once to excuse the gesture (considered to be funny) and to accuse it (because it is dangerous). More generally still, one sometimes says, for example, about a group of politicians famous for their incompetence: "What a bunch of Gnaffrons!" in the same way that one would say, "What a bunch of clowns!"

In short, the relationship to wine, as opposed to the relationship to bread, is not simple. The festivity that it is in charge of assuming is cleaved by a danger correlated to it. A "not too much" always comes along to temper wine, to thwart the logic of the drink that cries: "More! More!" Wine is an invitation to a journey toward a festival, but one cannot go all the way, up to the central, mortal intoxication whose initial exchange, symbolized by the filling of glasses, their clinking, and the wine tasting, is, nevertheless, the premonition. The fantasy of absolute disorder, the abolition of all the personal, sexual, and cultural differences presented by the celebration of wine — the feast of fools — is nowhere currently attainable in social life; propriety requires us to stop in time in order, very precisely, to remain within time.[7]

Giving and Receiving

The R.'s buy wine for everyday consumption at Robert's. This operation is the occasion for a little game whose insignificant appearance hides unsuspected ramifications, as much in relation to the family mechanism as in relation to the integration of the latter in the neighborhood. If the R. family joins in this game, it is because it very exactly matches some constitutive elements of its "vision" of the world. Among these elements, two seem to me particularly distinguished: the giving-receiving relationship (here formed with Robert), and a specific practice of temporality that one might call the taste for waiting.

What does this involve? The cap on every bottle contains a small sticker that one must attach to a card divided into thirty boxes; when one has finished filling up this card (thus, after having consumed thirty bottles of everyday table wine), one exchanges it at Robert's for a bottle of superior quality wine (VDQS), generally a Côtes-du-Rhône. The R. family thus maintains a sort of small, permanent wine-cellar with about two bottles per month, allowing them to celebrate, in a dignified way and freely, at one or another Sunday meal, or to honor a certain friend's or family member's visit. This game can be reduced to two extremely simple acts: filling up the card with thirty boxes (thus *waiting*) and exchanging it for a bottle (thus *giving* in expectation of *receiving* in return). The game of stickers is only thinkable, and thus practiced, when inserted in the logic of the relationship to Robert, with whom it strengthens the ties. It adds to the rhythm of daily comings and goings a scansion measured by each VDQS bottle "earned." Around it is constructed the performative language of reward. The filled-in card is, in essence, proof of goodwill, a record of good conduct; it is a pledge integrated into the text of a contract of which Robert is the representative; it insists on the tie that binds the buyer and the seller in consumer activity. We are at the heart of the practice of exchange. The very idea of a contract assumes that there exists a reappropriation of the market exchange for the consolidation of a social benefit that cannot be reduced to the purchase act alone.

The performativity of language here is formally inscribed in obedience (the *obsequium*, that Spinoza spoke of) to a common will (that of "consuming well," just as propriety is an obedience to "behaving well" in the conventional system of the neighborhood as a social space of recognition), whose game is at once the motive [*mobile*] and the grounds, the rhythm and the visible mark in a network of signs known equally by all. We find the following in this sign: the process of recognition must be invigorated, symbolically comforted, through the legibility of the acquired benefit by both partners in the contract. The card filled with stickers quite obviously signifies (as everybody knows; whether or not there are a lot of people, spectators, at the moment of exchange matters little; the only thing that counts here is the public nature of the place) *Madame Marie's faithfulness, to which Robert himself, in one way or another, is indebted,* because she occupies for him, at this moment and in this particular circumstance, the place of partner-consumer without which his place of partner-seller would have no meaning. The public nature of the place is worthy of publication, a quasi-official, visible manifestation of the contract that underlies it from beginning to end. The "fee" that Robert must pay (what goes back to his partner-consumer as a symbolic supplemental credit added to the mechanical accounting of the purchase) must be spoken too, publicly revealed somewhere in the syntax of the commercial exchange, because the latter is, all things considered, the support for a social exchange (a contract in the language of recognition). In a certain way, one might say that we are witnessing here the substitution of buying (which is only commercial, accountable) with exchanging (a symbolic, beneficial surplus); the practice of the neighborhood goes without an important number of middlemen (for example, the advertising campaign of the company organizing this game) in order to retain only what is proper for the good functioning of the system of relations. Robert thus offers the bottle of good wine ("Here's your little gift"), much less as a stimulus for higher consumption of wine than as the sign of a reiterated alliance, continuing to seal the pact that ties him to his partners-actors, here his buyers, within the space of the neighborhood.

That explains why this "gift" can only be a "good bottle." Supposing that the offer of reward was more everyday table wine—two or three bottles as a free gift for so many bottles consumed, for example—the effect would be completely different; we would be moving from the domain of the exchange to that of equivalence, percentage. There would certainly be a growth in assets, but one would not find this same symbolic tension perceptible from beginning to end in the game of stickers. To be maintained, this tension requires a qualitative rupture that transgresses the continuum of the purchase; it must have access to a superior threshold of consumption. The gap between ordinary table wine and "good wine" is a highly significant gap: it is not the return of the same, as the system of equivalence requires, but an active, symbolic differential, producing motivation where before only plain necessity had prevailed. The "old wine" tears apart the habit-like homogeneity of ordinary wine by backing it up with a promise that leads up to another desire: that of a real feast (a good bottle of wine for a good meal) resulting from a faithfulness maintained within the space of the neighborhood, that is, suitable to propriety.

But if there is a qualitative rupture between the two categories of wine, the rupture is not substantial. We find here again the logic of the drink, the ambivalence of wine mentioned earlier. The strength of this logic constrains ordinary table wine to not be sufficient in and of itself;

it is in some way an economic stopgap, an everyday accompaniment, unsatisfying in making real the feast, for which it nevertheless carries inside it the program (because it is wine). This goes back to saying, conversely, that this insufficiency and this festive inadequacy contain a dynamism that tends to erase ordinary wine in order to assume the festive program, at the level of "superior quality." Wine tends to become abolished as ordinary in order to be realized as "of superior quality." This is exactly what is produced within the internal logic unique to the game of stickers. The ideal for a wine drinker is always on the side of a quality and quantity increase. But, just like all the imperatives of temperance advocated by the implicit neighborhood checks, ordinary wine economically controls a quantitative expenditure that cannot, without endangering a family's economic equilibrium, be squandered in the race for quality.

Here again appears the symbolic gulf that separates wine from bread. One would have difficulty imagining the ideal for the bread eater; there exists no game of stickers at the bakery offering a pie after having consumed so many loaves of bread. Bread is a static nutritional symbol from the point of view of practical cultural experience. Wine, right up to its ambivalence, is a socializing dynamic. It opens up itineraries in the thickness of the neighborhood, weaves an implicit contract between factual partners, and establishes them within a system of giving and receiving whose signs link together the private space of family life and the public space of the social environment. We can perhaps find in this activity the social essence of the *game*, which is immediately to establish the subject in his or her collective dimension as a partner.[8]

Wine and Time

The game of stickers also reveals another side of the R. family's practical cultural experience, just as fundamental as that of exchange (giving/receiving), although it largely surpasses the actual practice of the neighborhood. It involves the relationship that this game has with time and that I earlier called the "taste for waiting." It is always delicate work to commit oneself, to attempt to interpret within the interiority of what "others" experience, and to work on the reverse side of their conscious representations, without at the same time holding on to the certitude of a possible verification of the proposals made. I believe, however, that it is proper to consider this game from the perspective of the study the way a diver puts on a transparent mask in order to contemplate what the surface of the water hides: this modest auxiliary suffices to reveal in one stroke the sumptuous nature of the marine depths.

The game of stickers is somewhat the equivalent of this mask: placed on the visible accumulation of the R. family's habits and customs, it allows us to understand the internal, and secret, functioning of their everyday life; as such, it is the analyzer (the object onto which are transferred conflictual forces that it does not engender, but which are expressed thanks to it) of a particular model of temporal mastery, that is, of a relationship to time that makes one say, or think, that one dominates it from the point of view of everyday practical experience. It seems possible to me to draw out two moments of this mastery, one concerning the visibility of time and the other its availability.

1. The rhythmic progression of the number of stickers increasing from bottle to bottle, occupying a surface area on the card exactly proportionate to the consumption of ordinary wine, and whose internal logic tends to blossom in the promised VDQS, is very precisely the *analogon* of a time accumulator. It marks the stages of the desire that leads to good wine in the same way that other "time instruments" (a savings plan, a wall calendar, etc.) trace a path, counterbalanced by waiting, toward the objects (a car, a family feast, etc.) that will be their end point. From beginning to end, this game is the pattern for waiting, but a concrete, active one whose accumulation of signs (the stickers) holds the desire at a distance from its object until its fulfillment. Thus, it is located within the reality principle's logic: an active patience for the delay that defers—places at the end of a period of time to be covered—the desirable object whose possession only then will be allowed. It actively signposts this delay by deferring the moment of taking hold, with the single goal of rendering the latter real.

After time has become as if thickened by the wait, it is instantly abolished in the expected denouement of the exchange by conferring on the latter a cultural and social consistency by virtue of this dialectic evacuation of time through its own fulfillment. The game is thus a medium of which at least one function is *to make the "time of desire" visible*.[9] It is constituted as an apprenticeship in waiting, whose contradictory polar tensions it balances by inserting in them the promise of its disappearance. As a result, this game also says, following temperance and economy: "Not so fast! I am the realization of your wait. By shortening the stages that constitute me, you risk shortening your life and tricking your desire by giving it an object other than that which it was expecting, in other words, nothing! Because you don't get anything without the wait. It alone makes real the objects you desire, the good wine you hope for. Without it, more or less, it means death."

2. This visibility of time possesses another characteristic that is logically linked to it, even though it is difficult to bring it to the fore in all its vastness. The fact that the accumulation of the wait is an exhibitor of desire almost necessarily entails its access to the interior of a collective, here the R. family, but also other people close to them, and then through the steps of the purchase, to the entire neighborhood, metonymically present behind its "representative," Robert. The visibility of time also signifies that time is not, in itself, the occasion for a private practice "for oneself," but only takes on meaning because it is put at the disposal of others who share the same delaying activity, the same desiring process. Within the framework of its internal interfamilial relations, the sticker card constantly offers the R. family an "open book" reading of its collective time; through it, one knows where one is on the journey, a journey at the end of which takes place the exchange substituting the symbol of the wait (the sticker card) with the good bottle of wine (the reward for the wait).

No privatization comes along to take away this legibility from the collectivity. In that, this game is revealing of something other than itself; it is the analyzer of other types of relationship to time among which it takes up a position. The collectivization of time can also be found in the upkeep of the wall calendar that Madame Marie gets for herself each year, but under another form. It is there that Madame Marie records her own appointments, that she records the minute events in the family. Each person refers to it as to a bulletin board, even adding corrections, if necessary. Conversely, the custom of the personal calendar (with all the rights of "privacy" that it includes) does not exist, or rather it is reduced to the embryonic stage of a customary beginning practice that will take time to become independent. In the same way, the purchase of a car, for example, assumes a very intense, collective preparation, and the reiterated sharing out of hopes contained in the wait. At the R. family's place, the date of the first car purchase (April 1956) and the name of this car (a Renault Frégate) have maintained to this day an extraordinary symbolic value (since then, Joseph has bought another car — a Peugeot 204, in 1968 — but no one remembers exactly when: the wait for the object had become banalized).

This leads us back to thinking time as the formality for a recognition of self, where the self discovers itself concerned in a series of events that is recognizable by others, members of the same family or of the same neighborhood. The game of stickers, like the wall calendar, like the "memory" of the Frégate, thus signifies, fundamentally, formal integration into the field of public, interfamilial recognition: it is the totality of this relational package, mediated through the consumption of wine, on which time transfers the assent of the family's identity, which is offered to Robert's view under the modest appearance of the sticker card. And the return gift of the good wine attests to the reality of this identity, inasmuch as Robert is the third party, the "public witness" of this reality.

Chapter 6

The End of the Week

Saturday and Sunday

On Saturdays and Sundays, the neighborhood dwellers can experience various arrangements of their leisure time. Saturdays are preferentially centered on individual leisure time, with Sundays traditionally remaining mobilized by family-type activities. In the working-class milieu where Joseph works, the day off on Saturday is a relatively recent conquest if measured against the span of his professional "career." This liberation of an unoccupied period of time was the source of a festive reorganization of the week that divides it in a significant way. In Joseph's work crew, all of whose members have experienced the different stages of this conquest, the true beginning of the weekend festivities is on Friday. On that day, the workers share a snack lunch [*mâchon*], a clear improvement on the traditional lunch. Moreover, after work, custom requires them to get together for a longer time in their usual café, almost up until dinnertime. It is a way of symbolizing that one is truly entering into *the* period of peace and quiet. Furthermore, it frequently happens that a few of them, freed from their family obligations, continue the evening in a restaurant or bar. This rite and its diverse ramifications were unthinkable in the previous system (because of work on Saturday morning) and not easily transposable to Saturday night because of the shortness of the weekend, which concentrated it almost exclusively on family activities. The increase in free time remodeled the organization of the week by allowing an authentic *individualization* of weekly time.

The phenomenon is particularly remarkable concerning the appropriation of urban space. Before, Joseph and his colleagues had only a "dead" city at their disposal (closed on Sundays), with the exception of summer vacations. They carried out the majority of their purchases through catalogs, or their wives did it for them. Except for the rarest of exceptions, they never benefited from a direct and prolonged contact with consumption goods and were for the most part unaware of the "aesthetic" experience of this contact (sight, touch, smell). From now on, having Saturdays off allows them to profit greatly from their participation in the commercial life of the city, not only as consumers, but also, and perhaps more so, as *spectators.* On Saturdays, Joseph "has a field day," because this day belongs to him as something he has a right to.[1] Some more general considerations corroborate these observations: the significant presence of men in shops and stores on Saturdays, the development of commercial services capable of interesting them (tools, gardening, car mechanics, etc.), and even the transformation of clothing fashion — the abandonment of the "Sunday best" outfit so characteristic among workers fifteen years ago, in favor of a "younger" and more varied style.

These tiny social events, difficult to analyze in their banality, whose memory is eroding with the years, emphasize, however, the extraordinary accumulation of the desire for the practice of the city, a desire repressed as long as the freedom on Saturdays did not give it a space-time in which to be deployed. In short, consumption has passed from the stage of in vitro (choices in a catalog) to that of in vivo (direct contact with objects). For example, Joseph had once purchased a photo camera as well as a movie camera (with all the accompanying materials: screen, viewer, etc.) based only on the information in a catalog. In May 1975, I went with him to several stores before he made up his mind on the camera of his dreams; but, so he told me, he had been hesitating for several weeks and, every time he could, on Saturdays he would go downtown to look at the window displays and ask for information. Never in the past would he have been able to "allow himself this luxury," he said, meaning to say: "I have never had so much pleasure in choosing, looking, and buying."

Through the increase of weekly days off, "window-shopping" has become a masculine activity: the city offers itself as a spectacle to dreamers. The "urban being" of both Joseph and his colleagues changed nature when they acquired the leisure of actively going through a town that was *awake* and no longer dulled by Sunday dreariness. Now that this benefit has passed into custom, one has difficulty imagining the revolution it introduced into everyday life: the city has veritably become an opened city, a profusion of symbols, a poetical place. Beyond consumption strategies, Saturday leisure time has made possible the appropriation of urban space through the desire of an itinerant subject who, discovering it in the vitality of its living strength, has truly begun to love it because one can finally find one's way there as a consumer and no longer just as a producer.

Department Stores and Supermarkets

Between the neighborhood and downtown, relationships of all kinds are established, both complementary and contradictory ones. In the practical urban experience of the R.'s, this corresponds roughly to two models of consumption that have their topographical equivalent in the city: on the one hand, there are the department stores themselves (traditionally situated in the heart of the city, which is the case in Lyons — on the place des Cordeliers and the rue de la République, where the *Galeries Lafayette*, the *Grand Bazar*, the *Printemps*, etc., are located); on the other hand, there are the "supermarkets" established on the outskirts (the *Carrefour* in Vénissieux and Écully, and the *Mammouth* in Caluire).

The Galeries Lafayette — and when the R.'s talk about it, one must understand that they are referring to all department stores — is inserted in an urban environment of a very high commercial density and with which it is in perfect osmosis. This porousness renders the store infinitely traversable; it is a continuation of the street and one can stroll through it just as one does through sidewalk stalls. The relationship to the Galeries Lafayette is poetic: the stroll that leads there brings sensations into play (crowds, noises, smells); it favors the active work of sensitivity. The relationship to downtown is always accompanied by a secret feeling of beauty linked less to the architecture as such than to the profusion of beautiful objects that are displayed there. This engenders a thematics of expenditure: "Oh, it's so beautiful! I'd so like to have it!"

Downtown is the permission to always dream more about an other life, an *elsewhere*. A momentary forgetfulness of real life is at the heart of the practical urban experience of department stores. The Galeries Lafayette is the medium for a participation in the collective, festive being of downtown. Like all other expenditures, this one too is exhausting. When she comes back from shopping, Madame Marie talks about "whirlwinds": "people step on your feet," "it makes my head spin." But these assessments, always subsequent to the act of displacement itself, must be understood as sports commentary; it is one way of saying that "it had a certain ambiance." This stroll is always accompanied by a stop in a large downtown café, generally at the Bar Américain. The activity engaged in the movement toward downtown buckles up on itself; the Galeries Lafayette is in complementarity with the neighborhood because it offers the festive supplement of which the latter, through its very organization and relative dilapidation, is deprived.

By more closely analyzing the relationship to downtown, one perceives that it is the place for an impressive number of trajectories that, although in large part intersecting with each other (because of the relatively limited surface area of downtown, which, in Lyons, is narrowly hemmed in between the banks of the Saône and the Rhône), nevertheless keep a relative autonomy in relation to each other. Returning home is not "the same" if one takes the rue de la République instead of the rue Édouard-Herriot. The first trip lies completely within the pure pleasure of walking, or even better, of "slowly sauntering along" [*lentibardanner*] (according to Lyons slang); the R.'s have a language appropriate to this style of walking according to which "the return home by the rue de la Ré [publique]" is undoubtedly the most elaborate urban model, especially since the time when this main road became an entirely pedestrian zone: "We came back nice and easy like," "I was just chug-chuggin' along," "I really like droolin' all over the pretty window displays," "we're checkin' out all the changes—it's educational," all of these expressions signifying a temporal gratuitousness in which the pleasure of walking is rooted.

Returning home by the rue Édouard-Herriot integrates some functional steps parallel to the stroll: "I had an errand to run so I took advantage of coming back that way" (generally followed by the name of a store on this street). An explicit or secret justification underscores each itinerary, bores pathways into the somber maze from perpendicular alleys to a few main roads: the rue Mercière occupies a considerable place in Madame Marie's imagination because of specific memories (this is where she began to work in a sewing workshop in 1906), but she is no longer familiar with the name of an alley found a few dozen yards further on. In the perception of space, there are blind spots, whether through moral censorship (the streets with prostitutes, numerous in this neighborhood) or through unfamiliarity as a result of not using this portion of the public streets. "Going downtown" means abandoning oneself to an operation made up of multiple logics: consumption, spectacle, strolling, exploration...Downtown maintains its role of attraction through the orchestration of urban sensations that it spontaneously hands over to the dweller. It is one of the organizing poles of tension for life in the neighborhood, in actual fact, its most extreme outer limit, but the latter remains linked to it in a strongly significant relation.[2]

The relationship to the supermarket, Carrefour, is of an economic type. Based on the distance (one must take the car) and the material conditions of the surrounding area (enormous parking lots to cross, burning hot in the summer and slippery with ice in the winter), "going to Carrefour" cannot be synonymous with "taking a stroll." The R.'s go there only *to buy*. Or rather, they used to go there, because, from a certain moment on, this task, felt to be thankless, was generally entrusted to Joseph, or the head of the household. He buys work clothes there, "sport" shirts, or sometimes food products that, curiously, he would not think of buying near home, such as whiskey ("for friends who sometimes like that sort of thing!"), even though Robert sells it as well. This "extra" is truly the synonym for an extraterritoriality. Whiskey, one might say, seems unable to be inscribed, at least at the beginning, within the neighborhood system: it was truly a strange item that he would have "felt funny" asking of Robert, but that it was thus suitable to go looking for elsewhere, in these distant frontiers of consumption represented by "supermarkets"; for these latter are an "abstraction," an "idea" of consumption almost entirely foreign to the custom of the R. family's consumption, which, profoundly linked to their traditional urban environment, includes proximity and language. One recalls Madame Marie's reflection: "it spoils my appetite"; this "break" synthesizes everything that the supermarkets lack in order to be integrated into her desire as a consumer, notably smells and the contact with shopkeepers. The subjective impression of being exposed to the great rush of objects, to their organized stocking, in these gigantic cathedrals that are the halls of "supermarkets," is frightening because intimacy and confidence are extinguished in favor of a purchasing system whose benefits the R.'s understand poorly.

Joseph heads to Carrefour in the same way that he sometimes visits the building sites of the large ZUPs [Zone à Urbaniser par Priorité, urban development zone] in the suburbs. For him, it is an occasion for a spectacle (he takes pictures), for an experience of radical foreignness, for a manipulation of space exactly the opposite of his own. More brutally, on the part of Madame Marie there is a categorical rejection, without appeals. Let us listen to her tell of an excursion to a restaurant with friends:

> But besides all that, my, my! I tell you! It's true that I'm old, you have to take age into consideration, but when I see those big housing projects, like the other day when we went out to eat in Tramoilles…with the Giovannis, well, when we went through Rilleux, well, I almost got sick! It's a—what do you call it?—a ZUP, that's it. Well, well, I tell you, if I had to live in that, well, it's just frightful! Huge houses, everything chained up, and then there are the streets, wide streets, squares, tiny garden plots…I could never live in that, oh no! Even, I don't know, even if I had been…well, anyway, you never can say, because when you're young, you obviously don't have the same mentality. Ah no! Even if it's pretty, you know. I see, even at Marcel's, pretty entryways everywhere, all that; absolutely not, no! I could not take it. Amélie [her cousin], she would do rather well there: "Oh, anything just to be comfortable at home, a shower room; me, I've still got my little, my old metal sink." Yes, so she, *she* would change. Well, there are five years between us. One changes with age.

(We should remember that Madame Marie is eighty-three and her cousin Amélie is seventy-eight.)[3]

For Joseph, the situation is a little different. Carrefour, supermarkets, the big housing projects, the new cities proliferating in the Lyons region are for him a space of compromise where he can play the "modern citizen" without too much risk, because he knows that, behind him, he still has his cherished Croix-Rousse. For him, these places are an exotic land where he can spend a few nice moments, or "learn" about aspects of modernity, but places from which it is still possible to withdraw in order to return to a social space more in keeping with his practical urban experience. He finds, one might say, an interest as a "decent man" in contemplating the expansion of a consumer society from which he has received so little over so many years, about which his "wisdom" has taught him to demand little, without absolutely mistrusting it either, following the solidly shared argument that "there is something good to be found in everything."

When he returns from there to his neighborhood, it is as if into a space carrying the words of recognition, known by heart, as surprising as the things one likes, a poem, "a music." The return trip from the "modern" parts of the city is marked by the clearing of certain stages leading progressively "toward home": "you start to breathe again," "it does you some good," "the car starts to smell like home." The most precise borderline is situated after the place des Terreaux, at the initial section of streets that head up to the plateau. As of that moment, without fail, Madame Marie is already in her kitchen ("Ah, let's see, what am I going to make for my dinner?") and Joseph, no less without fail, proposes first to go "have an aperitif" in a boulevard café, generally at one called the À la soierie in the place des Tapis. The excursion out into modernity requires this sort of expiatory ceremony; the café is a place of reconciliation with the neighborhood, whose qualities one then celebrates. It is a purification formulated as such: one says that "the air is good here," after the "pollution" of the big housing projects. Moreover, this formula remains typically Croix-Roussian: it aims at rediscovering a specific, secret "charm" appreciated only by connoisseurs, in a neighborhood that all the same remains marked by the bleakness of its housing. One then abandons oneself to the great evening stillness, especially in summer, when the shade of the trees preserves and amplifies the coolness. A strange charm can actually be drawn out of the boulevard, suspended on the border with nighttime, as if abandoned by the rest of the city, whose silence is barely disturbed by the passage of cars or the plaintive siren characteristic of the trolleybuses.

The practice of the neighborhood is thus entirely dependent on the "rest" of the city, downtown or modern suburbs. It is just that the neighborhood is too small to take on the totality of urban desire; propriety as well is too pregnant there to integrate every kind of consumer behavior. Thus, there must be "elsewheres" at the dwellers' disposal in order to enrich their mastery of urban space in general. But it is also from this difference of practice that the neighborhood draws a surplus of identity; the "journey" will only have been a lapse of time, an excess, taken back to its place of origin, to the very place where the pleasure of living in the city surges forth, to the neighborhood. Once the curtain is closed on the exteriority of the rest of the city, the neighborhood itself, far from becoming numb to the grasp of its identity, finds an internal dynamic satisfying the recognition of its dwellers. It is here that the practice of the market conveys all its social force.

The Market

The market is traditionally an important sociological landmark for the understanding of human relations within the practice of the neighborhood. No city or village is without one. At the same time as it is a place of business, it is a place of festival (in small provincial towns, the "pompom of music" frequently accompanies the weekly markets), halfway between the small shops on the street and the department store, or the supermarket, without the elements that constitute it being reabsorbed in one or the other of these terms. It offers a profusion of consumer goods surpassing what a shopkeeper offers, but without falling into the "distributionalism" of supermarkets (the division of consumer goods into categories, which are called "departments": the lingerie department, the children's department, etc.).

The market is unfamiliar with this rational division of space; the stalls follow one another according to seniority, establishment, or the vendor's trade license, but not according to the order of objects. Finally, the relationship to vendors obeys precise laws there. There is an inversion of the recognition system in relation to shopkeepers on the street; vendors' customers are much more anonymous and the relationship is generally less close than that inside the store; conversely, the shopkeeper is valued and regains something from what can be anguishing for customers in an anonymous relationship; the "market vendor," through the "oral" struc-

ture characteristic of the market—the "auction," the friendly heckling—
is always more or less considered as somewhat stentorian, whose "advertising" correlates to an increased social distance.

In the R. family, as in many others in the rue Rivet neighborhood,
"going to the market" is a task generally entrusted to the men. Territorial
reasons account for much of this: in relation to the neighborhood, the
market is "high up" on the boulevard and one gains access to it by going
up steep slopes or long banistered stairs; it is a tiring operation that demands a certain physical effort. When Joseph leaves for the market, he
is, in short, doing his duty, following the example of his neighbors—and
he goes there preferably on Sunday morning, a day primarily devoted to
family-type activities.

An analysis of this process reveals its own "secret": beginning as
something "for the family," it becomes transformed into a practice of
the neighborhood unique to Joseph, in the same way that Madame Marie
"makes a practice of" Robert according to a relational dynamic that is
equally unique to her. The primary home–market trajectory produces
complementary subtrajectories; to the "necessary time" of the market,
Joseph tacks on a "free" time, a personal modification that he links to
familial necessity. The market is the occasion for unique rites, typically
masculine ones, which are condensed in the "aperitif" drunk "with the
guys," in a Croix-Rousse café.

On his way, Joseph makes a complete circle whose beginning and
end points are not home/market, but home/café. He "heads up" to the
market by the most direct route: rue Ornano, then montée de la Tourette;
there he takes a right on the boulevard de la Croix-Rousse and meets up
with the "lower end" of the market three hundred and thirty yards further on. The first pass is a time for the observation and evaluation of
prices; Joseph goes through slowly until he feels he has a correct idea of
the good prices. Then he leaves the crowded alleyway hemmed in by
the market stalls and continues to "head up" the market along the outside, at once to escape the very dense crowd and to continue his little
inquiry into prices based on the indications furnished by the stores par-
alleling the market. He always buys at "the top" of the market. This is
because he leaves his hesitations behind one by one as he advances: he
can henceforth make a decision and so buys very quickly, "as men do."

There he encounters a grocer who in the past used to run a shop on
his street, next to Robert's. People in the R. family know him by the name
of the "little grocer." The "little grocer," recognizing Joseph's "faithfulness" each Sunday, "always looks the other way a bit in the right direc-

tion" (he always adds a little extra to the amount requested). I was able to witness this sign of favor, even though the "little grocer" was a bit bothered by my presence: he was weighing out a kilo of cherries and then began to shout for the benefit of a female customer with the sole purpose of diverting her attention so as to no longer be in her field of vision, and then "quite naturally," added a generous handful of cherries to Joseph's bag, giving him a wonderful wink while he continued to shout himself hoarse. "It's a favor he does for me every time, I find it very nice. Besides, you know, it's always accepted . . ." This favor, which manifests itself explicitly in the theatrical form of the aside, rapidly murmured amid the brouhaha of the crowd, designates Joseph as an "old friend" from the neighborhood.

Even at the market, Joseph meets up with people from his neighborhood with whom a pact, so secret it is unconscious by dint of being automatic, is drawn up as if it involved a common history. The category of "old friend from the neighborhood," which comes out so often when one evokes neighborhood life ("Oh, yes, we know each other by sight like that, he's an old friend from the neighborhood. In the past, he used to live at number 6. We used to see him, at Robert's or on the square when we had our aperitif"), is an additive that colors the inhabitant's identity (last name, first name, age, "old friend" from . . .). The "top" of the market is more than a topographical reality; it is also the place where the effectiveness of the recognition process is the "highest," because it is there that Joseph discovers something from his neighborhood every time.

Once the market and its concomitant activities are finished, Joseph continues to progress toward the "top" of the boulevard, walks along the place de la Croix-Rousse, and enters a street beginning a descent toward the "Rhône" side of the plateau. At the bottom of this street, more than two hundred yards long, rather wide and bordered with trees, one finds a café called À la crèche (there is a nursery school nearby).[4] The practice of the market is unthinkable without this detour. The most curious thing is the distance. Even though the market square abounds with cafés (big, little, "chic," "popular"), Joseph heads to this café, which is far from the market and makes him take a significant detour from his route home. Joseph explains:

> It's because of the name. You wouldn't usually think of calling a place "À la crèche." I myself find it rather amusing, especially for having a drink on Sunday morning. And then, they have a Mâcon wine like no other in the neighborhood. Their wine works along with the seasons, with the weather.

They must have appointed purveyors. Sometimes it's fizzy, you might even say sparkling, and then other times, it's very dry. It varies, you see . . .

The fact that Sunday morning white wine, whose function is to "open up" the meal (it is the Sunday "aperitif"), is formally contained within the word *crèche* makes its tasting an almost religious act: Joseph goes to the *crèche* just as others go to "eleven o'clock Mass," with the same regularity, in order to take part in a collective well-being (meeting his group of guys) whose function is to signify the immutable rest of Sunday morning. The café serves to compensate the sacrificial side of the market as "service to be rendered": "virtue rewarded" is the real justification for this detour.

It is also a reunion among *men*. "In the past," it was spoken of by word of mouth, and among the workers in Joseph's factory, which, however, is on the other side of the city (in the southern suburbs of Lyons). Joseph clarifies:

> It was an old retired guy from the factory who gave us the address. He died since then. But we still meet there with whomever wants to. It's mostly the guys from the factory who live in Croix-Rousse. There are a few of us. Each person comes and waits for the others. Sometimes, I'm all alone with my carafe. But that's rare. It's pretty rare when there's no Léon X. or Robert Y. coming to have a round. And then also, sometimes someone brings a friend, you get to meet people. There are even some young people . . . [He is interrupted by a question] No! Women are rare. At 11:30, they're in the kitchen. Well, yes, of course, sometimes, when they don't live too far away, they come and have a drop with us. But it's not part of the custom. Well, here, let me explain: when they come with their family, it's not a problem . . . But it's when there are only men, it's not the same, I don't know how to say it; Sundays are for us! . . .

The absence of women also indicates the profound meaning of the process: meeting with other men, at À la crèche, is to take oneself "aside," for a time (that of the Sunday morning celebration) before confronting the familial necessities equally unique to Sundays. The *crèche*, the totally arbitrary name of this café, found itself being the symbol, through the polysemy that it connotes (Christmas, childhood, gifts), of the intensity with which the ultimate availability of the last hour on Sunday morning is lived. À la crèche is the corner of the neighborhood that escapes from the authority of the family; it is its *vanishing point*, "the clear vista," toward which converge the itineraries of men.

A symbolic selection of the wine's color links it to the stages of the day: white wine in the morning, for specific dietetic reasons, is considered a stimulant; "it wakes you up in the morning," "it gives you a kick start," it opens up the appetite; when it is too dry, you drink it *cassé*, that is, with a tiny drop of crème de cassis (much less of it than in the famous *kir* from the people of Dijon); it is drunk chilled and it is this cool sensation that corroborates its relationship to the morning. White wine fits within a very precise temporality for this group of "guys": never before ten thirty, and more generally after eleven. The café owners know this very well: after ten o'clock (after the coffee hour), they line up all their available carafes in their cold room and then everything is ready for the eleven o'clock rush. "I never have any until morning's end. I still have the taste of coffee in my mouth. That ruins the wine." Above all, Sunday morning white wine "rinses" — which is said with no other predicate, in an intransitive manner. It is an internal ablution that cleanses, that liquidates the worries of the week, and stimulates the gastric juices for the generally festive Sunday family meal. It is thus a sort of magic act that looks forward to the bounty of the table.

The carafes are subject to a rigorous and *obligatory* sharing. It does not exactly follow the principle of a round of drinks, which rests on a diachronic organization — after Jean's round, it is Joseph's round — where finally each one is a successive game of soloists, in turn masters of the exchange. Rather, their sharing in Joseph's group is simultaneous: the number of carafes ordered corresponds exactly to the number of table companions, and they are brought to the table at the same time. But each person, with his carafe, serves the others and is then served by one of his colleagues. Thus, through this synchrony, reciprocity is immediate and allows one to do without successive precedences (as with rounds), because the giving and the receiving are contemporaneous to each other; consequently, this process allows them to abolish competition in favor of a simplicity that cancels allegiances. At the moment of departure, each person pays for his carafe (or rather, pays for one carafe, because, shared entirely together, they no longer belong to anyone), a ritual that the owner knows so well that she brings along tons of change to respond to the various ways of paying. This apparent pettiness, which has the appearance of an "everyone for himself" attitude, is a way, for the group, to preserve its unity by canceling the reciprocal debits of each member every time.

For Joseph, as for his friends, Sunday morning is a slow progression that becomes more and more intense, right up to the after-meal drop into the torpor of Sunday afternoon. Sunday is truly split into two parts, one of which bears the birth of the feast prepared since Friday night and the other of which is already a downhill slope toward sinister Monday.

Seen from the morning, Sunday afternoon is still masked by the grand finale of the meal. Seen from the afternoon, the morning is already "the day before," another marvelously nostalgic time whose return one awaits the following Saturday.

The slow progression described in Joseph's movement reflects one of the primary worries of the group he represents: to protect for one-self, aside from family "obligations," a pocket, a reserve, a *crèche* where one can meet for no other reason than that of celebrating *every* Sunday morning. This retreat is not imposed but chosen according to symbolic criteria (the *crèche*) that come from the unique organization of this group: a tradition ("an old guy told us about it"), a localization ("we're from the Croix-Rousse), a complicity ("we work in the same place"), the hidden alliance, the exchange of blood (wine).

By following Joseph in this authentic peregrination, one witnesses the putting into place of a neighborhood trajectory fraught with socio-logical meanings. There is first of all the obvious accomplishment of a family duty. But this latter is also a springboard for a subtrajectory that, tacked onto the first, nevertheless pushes in an autonomous direction by swinging from duty to pleasure. One crosses the watershed of the fam-ily horizon to follow "familiar" paths again. The café of the *crèche* is the magnet that attracts this pleasure to itself in order to organize it into a highly typical relational schema: a group of men, almost all of them work-ing for the same company, brought together for a spell around a few carafes of white wine, in a repeated fashion according to a rite that is unique to them (the reciprocal offering of wine). The passage from the market to the café is thus the passage from one social system to another, from interfamilial relations to extrafamilial ones. Once again, one per-ceives how the structure of the neighborhood satisfies apparently con-tradictory requirements. Starting from a single initial action, it diversi-fies meeting places right up to the point of accepting certain blind spots, certain secrets in personal practices, at least as long as they do not threaten friend and family cohesions.

The social structure of the neighborhood thus reveals its extreme complexity: it resists every "all-encompassing" approach. A veritable im-plicit social contract is at the origin of the neighborhood's social effec-tiveness: no one entirely possesses its text, but all participate in it in one way or another. No table of the law displays the articles of this contract; rather, it is inscribed, on the one hand, in an oral tradition transmitted through education, and, on the other hand, in the stereotyped game of behaviors (signs of politeness, tone of voice, glances). Its anthropological function is to mobilize, but also to temper, everyday social interests competing for the same goal. The practice of the neighborhood—the effort that it requires of its dwellers so that the equilibrium is not disrupted—rests entirely on this founding hypothesis: the neighborhood cannot not be beneficial for the dweller if he or she plays the social game supposed by the contract. We have seen in the preceding discussion the extreme diversity of expected benefits at the level of social relationships on which the process of recognition rests (neighborliness, deference, politeness).

The tension that shores up neighborhood life from the inside thus rests on two poles, at once complementary and contradictory: on the one hand, the *respect for propriety*, a regulatory instance tacitly recommending laws of obligation for the benefit of the commonwealth (Spinoza's *obsequium*), and which one might call, more generally, something possible for everyone—that by which each person can abide without harm to himself or herself so that the social cohesion of the neighborhood is protected; on the other hand, the progressive *singularization* of this social space through the everyday practice of the dweller who thus reinforces his or her identity as a social partner. The upholding, in the same place, of this public system of propriety and of the appropriation of space, of its privatization, is the definitional core of the urban neighborhood insofar as a cultural activity is deployed there.

More profoundly still, undoubtedly more elusive, beneath the harangues of politicians and statistical data, to an even further extent than what I have attempted in these pages, the urban neighborhood is the place for a decisive social apprenticeship that, in the same way as family, school, or professional life, introduces one, in a particularly powerful way, to the apprenticeship of everyday life.

Chapter 7
"And So for Shopping, There's Always Robert?"

The following excerpts come from the double series of interviews conducted in Lyons with two elderly women inhabitants of that city.[1] Madame Marie was eighty-three at the time; a corset maker by trade, first in a high-quality firm downtown and then self-employed at home, she worked until the age of seventy after the death of her husband and continued to live alone in her apartment in the Croix-Rousse. Madame Marguerite was seventy-seven at the time of these interviews and passed away before the completion of this study. Employed in an import-export firm, where she ended up in a managerial position, she also worked until the age of seventy. In later years, she lived alone in her own apartment in spite of great difficulty getting around because of a bad fall, complicated by phlebitis, that occurred in 1945. At the request of her interviewer, struck by the vividness and precision of her memory, she had begun to note down for him — in spite of a certain shyness about writing — her memories of Lyons and life in her neighborhood: a few passages have been taken from her writings, which nicely complement one or another point in the interviews.

Madame Marie

Pierre: And so for shopping, there's always Robert?

Mme Marie: Yes, I go to Robert's and to the bakery. Oh, sometimes I buy my bread at Robert's because he sells bread too.[2]

Pierre: Robert is rather practical, for a shopkeeper?

Mme Marie: Oh, he's real nice, he is! I tell you, when I left for a few days in the Midi; well, you know, without, I mean, as if it were you, he grabbed me by the shoulders and kissed me. I came back Saturday morning: "Ah, Madame Marie!" and there he goes again, kiss, kiss, kiss (*onomatopoeia imitating the French greeting embrace: she laughs*). You see, they married off their youngest son and he sent us the announcement, and for all four of their children. They didn't do it for their daughter because she was pregnant: well, they did have a marriage of sorts anyway, but ...

Pierre: They were embarrassed?

Mme Marie: Yes, they were embarrassed. But for all the others, yes, the oldest, he got married in September, he'd been living with the young woman for seven years and he finally got married. Everyone told him: "Well, why don't you get married?" They got along well and loved each other quite a bit but he didn't want to get married because he was a race-car driver and so he was afraid of having an accident; well, in short, he quit. So, they got married. But he[3] always let me know in advance and gave me wedding favors there every time.

Pierre: Really?

Mme Marie: Yes. Oh, shopkeepers like that...I saw him when he was so young! Well, no, he came here when he was twelve. Now he's forty-nine. Yes, his son is twenty-seven. They had him right away and they both got married at twenty. They were both twenty. So it's a good marriage. However, he jokes around; if you could just see how he jokes around with all the nice ladies there; the young, the old, he makes compliments, he is...he's really chic. But his little woman, she takes it all in stride, you know: she doesn't make a scene...

Pierre: Is she nice, his wife?

Mme Marie: She's really nice, oh, yes. There's only one thing about him I don't understand; he had a falling out with his brother and doesn't know what happened to him or where he disappeared to. Is Michel married? He doesn't know. I ask him: "And Michel?"; we sometimes chat like that, just the two of us, and so I go: "And Michel?"; well, "we don't know where he is..." Aside from that, he's very likable, he's very nice with everyone, everyone really likes him. *He's the universal Robert of the neighborhood!* (*Her intonation emphasizes the phrase.*)

Pierre: Where do Robert's customers come from?

Mme Marie: Oh, from all over the neighborhood; oh, yes. The little milkman, there on the corner, he closed down, so everyone comes to Robert's place, oh, yes, from the rue de Flesselles, from the rue Pierre-Blanc...

Pierre: And from the rue de l'Annonciade, I imagine?

Mme Marie: What's there? There's nothing on the rue de l'Annonciade anymore! The milkman shut down, across from the entrance to the clinic. It was a Bon Lait there. There still is a Bon Lait there. But I don't know if it's open. I rarely go by the rue Pierre-Blanc, just to buy my meat and fish from time to time. I have to ask if there's any fresh tuna, after all! I would have to cook some if there was any. Oh, I will more than likely find it at the Halles [large covered market] because there, you see, on Thursdays...There is only frozen fish. If you go on a Monday, Tuesday, Wednesday, or a Sunday, there is only frozen fish. You get fresh fish only on Thursdays or Fridays.

Pierre: Living where you do, how far does the neighborhood extend?

Mme Marie: Oh, for me, the neighborhood is the rue Rivet, the rue de Flesselles, the rue Pierre-Blanc, but otherwise, that's it . . . It's still not the same as in the Saint-Jean neighborhood. It's true that in Saint-Jean, when people are young, they don't have the same way of . . . Well, in the past, for example, the children in little neighborhoods like that, I used to go down there on Sundays, on New Year's Day, for example, all pretty, like that, because we always went out on days like that; I got a little present everywhere; now people don't give things out anymore, huh; I got my little bag of chocolate, a handful of sweets, an orange from the grocer, at the dairy store, everywhere.

Pierre: The shopkeepers used to give all the children little gifts?

Mme Marie: Yes, yes. Now, though, it's not done anymore. Robert always gives me a nice calendar, but sometimes I don't hang it up because I don't know where to put it! Yes. Oh, it's not really the same atmosphere as in the past, but, well, everything has changed so much! Where did I live in Saint-Jean? With my parents,[4] and after that rue de la Baleine, rue du Bœuf, and we then came here. But Saint-Jean is really all about attachment, because it's the neighborhood for all of my . . . all of my kin, after all! So, not long ago I used to go back there, and take a nice, long tour, sort of nostalgic, passing through the streets, the rue des Trois-Maries, well, I saw again my childhood friends who are now both dead, my schoolmates who lived at 11, rue des Trois-Maries, I could see them again, you know, as if we were leaving school . . . with their black smocks, bows in their hair, Jeanne and Adelia, no, Jeanne and *Adélaïde*, Adé, we called her, yes, they used to live at number 11, I looked in the windows. Well, I saw Old Tomet again, the principal at Jean, Maurice, and Joseph's school;[5] he always passed through the rue des Trois-Maries, but he lived on the place des Jacobins. We would meet on the rue des Trois-Maries when I was going to work, and he used to come along with a big tip of the hat. You know, well, I don't know . . . The place de la Baleine, the place du . . . Memories keep us attached to that place. The place de la Mairie, where I used to wait for the kids to get out of school, all that, the, all of them, every-thing . . . Why? Because I had all my kin there. My godfather lived on the montée de, my mother was born at number 7 in the rue, montée du Garrillan, my godfather lived at number 1, number 1 bis, on the lower part of the street, so these are really personal memories. Just like what's his name used to say, I heard. Georges Simenon. Well, he spoke about, he said that he no longer wrote, but someone told me: "Well, yes, he still writes," but anyway, in short, he was there in his garden, he was being interviewed by Yves Mourousi. So, he was saying that he didn't write anymore, he no longer had a typewriter, nothing anymore, he didn't care, all he had left was his tape player, so the other guy goes: "But why a tape player?" . . . "Well, when I get some ideas just like that, memories, I, I," well, he . . . notes, how would you say that? He inscribes?

Pierre: He records?

Mme Marie: He records, yes, immediately. He said: "Perhaps it's..." How did he say it? "It's perhaps..." You know, with old people? How they become...?

Pierre: Gaga?

Mme Marie: Yes, yes. Yes, that's it, he said: "Perhaps it's becoming gaga. But anyway, it makes me happy. I record the ideas that come to mind, or the memories." Yes, you see. So, it's, it's something like that, memories, but it's, it's personal; nobody would be interested, but in the end it still sort of makes up—how can I explain?—the spirit of the neighborhood, really. There are lots of people like me. Yes, yes, Amélie is less..., she's less attaching, attached to her memories, because she is too—how can I explain?—she is too, she has too many things to worry about otherwise, about her children, but not to the point of depression...But she sometimes has worries like that about...She is less attached than I. But I have always been very attached to memories. (*Silence.*)

Mme Marie: But besides all that, my, my! I tell you! It's true that I'm old, you have to take age into consideration, but when I see those big housing projects, like the other day when we went out to eat in Tramoilles with the, for Easter, with the Giovannis, well, when we went through Rilleux, well, I almost got sick, I tell ya: it's Rilleux-la-Pape, you know, it's one of those—what do you call it?—a ZUP [an urban development zone]. Oh, well, I tell you, if I had to live in that, well, it's just frightful! Huge houses, everything chained up, and then there are the streets, wide streets, squares, ga..., tiny garden plots...I could never live in that, oh no! Even, I don't know, even if I had been...well, anyway, you never can say, because when you're young, you obviously don't have the same mentality. Ah no! Even if it's pretty, you know. I see, even at Marcel's, pretty entryways everywhere, all that; absolutely not, no! I could not take it. Amélie [her cousin], she would do rather well there: "Oh, anything just to be comfortable at home, a shower room; me, I've still got my little, my old metal sink." Yes, so she, *she* would change. Well, there are five years between us. In five years, you don't at all..., one changes with age. The more time goes by, the more one goes back to one's...Well, I'm not one of them anyway, like Monsieur Claude, because if I was like that, there would be no white porcelain sink, no washing machine, no fridge, nothing! But anyway, I could not live in those new housing projects, *no. Impossible.*

Madame Marguerite

Mme Marguerite [MM]: On Sunday afternoons, in the summer, we used to go to Montessuy.

Pierre: How did you get there? On foot? By bus?

MM: On foot, or by streetcar. There was an old one, there was a streetcar on a small set of tracks, listen, if only you had seen it, I really wonder when I think about it now! It went vroom-vroom-vroom-vroom-vroom, it made a racket all the way down the line, it did, boy, it was on tracks much more narrow than the ones from . . . here; and then the streetcar itself was more narrow, but it sure did made a racket, let me tell you!

Pierre: And where did you catch it?

MM: Well, we always used to catch it at the same place, at the square, there on the boulevard.[6] It zoomed right up the main street and went all the way to Sathonay.

Pierre: The same as the number 33?

MM: That's it. But when you saw this streetcar, which zoomed by fast, well, in my mind anyway, I still see it, it zoomed by, it zoomed by quick, but it rankled . . . , ran . . . , rattled all the way down the line.

Pierre: You went to Montessuy every Sunday?

MM: My father didn't want to go anywhere else: *it was Montessuy*! (*She emphasizes the words as they are pronounced.*) So we used to leave at three o'clock. Sometimes we would bring something to eat for that night, so my father allowed us the grace of eating alfresco over there at night, so it was nice.

Pierre: At a bistro?

MM: Yes, because there used to be a bistro, it was . . . in the past, Montessuy, it was only meadows. There were meadows everywhere, everywhere you looked, there were no houses. So, we used to have fun in the afternoons there, on the grass; then it was on the road, there at the roadside, there was a café with an enormous number of tables outside, in the open air; if you wanted to eat there at night, there were some bowers, a few, where you could sit under.

Pierre: There were no shows in the Croix-Rousse?

MM: Ah, there were movie theaters that came. There was the Cinéma Dular and then the Cinéma La Croix in the place de la Croix-Rousse. They were the beginnings of cinema, and silent films no less!

Pierre: Lyons used to be a city for cinema.

MM: And then in the place de Chantecler,[7] there used to be a brasserie, the Brasserie Dupuy, that was very pretty. There was a large dining room where you could be very comfortable, where you could eat lunch or dinner, and so it was a kind of restaurant. But then everything was paintings, all around in a sort of Puvis de Chavannes style, you know, the paintings.[8] I'm not even sure if it wasn't him. There was a large courtyard with trees, with plane trees and tables. Then, there was an orchestra with musicians and singers.

Pierre: And you went there for dinner occasionally?

MM: No, no! Because, for my father, it was a bit expensive, you see, for four.[9] But I did eat there, with a friend, Mademoiselle Vincent, who was a schoolteacher. She bought us dinner there once, I remember; and so on Sundays we used to go there, all right, to the Brasserie Dupuy, like that, at night.

Pierre: Just for a drink?

MM: A drink at six o'clock, if you like, or at five. I remember, there used to be a woman, an old woman, well, old, I guess, yes, it's true that she dressed like an old woman, because in the past, at forty, a woman was... Anyway, she had a small cask from which she sold olives; she would dip them out with a slotted spoon, just like that, olives in a bit of paper that she'd give us and she sold them for so much, and it was good like that with our aperitif.

Pierre: Then, there are the *canuts*, the "voracious ones."[10] Who are they?

MM: Oh, there were always *canuts*, much more then than there are now: in all the streets, you could hear the click-clack-wham-bam of the...

Pierre: The what?

MM: Click-clack-wham-bam! It's the movement of the batten on the weaving loom. Well, it was always, we called it the click-clack-wham-bam. It's an onomatopoeia that represents the sound of the loom. The Croix-Rousse was the "laboring" hill, it was all about work, yes. Oh, yes, yes! People worked a lot. But I myself did not live in the *canut* milieu because my father was a shopkeeper.[11]

Pierre: But you had customers who were *canuts*?

MM: Yes, of course, but around the rue Jean-Baptiste Say there were not a lot of weaving looms. They were further along on the boulevard, the rue Gigodot, streets like that, the rue d'Austerlitz, the cross streets, the Grande-Rue. But the life of the *canuts* in the past was a life of... it was something horrible! They used to get up at nearly four in the morning to work. Then there were the young kids that, well, they, someone would put them to work on, uh, I no longer remember what they had to pull, either the shuttle, or I don't know what, so they became hunchbacked, they became... it was just horrible, their life!

Pierre: But they also used to go to their workshop upstairs?

MM: Oh, of course!

Pierre: That's why the apartments are so high?

MM: The ceilings are so high, yes. And then the rooms are very large too, like I had in the rue de l'Alma: I had a room that was more than thirteen feet by fifteen feet, with four windows and thirteen-foot ceilings — it was a real cube. (*She laughs.*) And then it wasn't very warm there, boy o' boy! It was enormous in terms of cubic footage. Moreover, at the Denis' place, it's the same type of apartment, also on montée Saint-Sébastien. Well, they were all *canuts* who lived around there. And then there were old tiles on the floor that were a bit like this (*she pivots her hands as a sign of instability*), so watch out for your ankles! And so then they put their weaving looms inside. They slept in the cubbyholes, the *cub's holes*, as Madame Émilie used to say: I myself never understood why she called them cub's holes, like it was Guignol (*laughter*), saying cub's holes![12]

Pierre: And did you used to go to the Guignol?

MM: Oh, yes, yes, of course.

Pierre: You had to go into the city for that, no?

MM: Ah yes, that's true. Yes, well, we used to go there; sometimes my father would take us; he liked it a lot, it really amused him, so he would take us. But my mother was not really happy because there were really *two* Guignols: there was one that was "nice," for children, for everyone, really, and then another that was . . . they performed plays, but they, what do you call it, when you turn something around, when you change the, there's a name for it, it begins with a "p."

Pierre: Parody?

MM: Parody, that's it. They parodied operas, so it was more or less risqué; we perhaps did not understand much, my sister and I, but my mother was furious, she didn't like us to be taken there . . . But my father only liked that kind of Guignol, because it made him laugh; he didn't like the other one that was for the nuns, well, for children anyway! I always remember the one with Mignon, when she wants to find her father, then she says that she has a beauty mark: "But where?" So she lifts up her dress to show the beauty mark she has on one buttock. (*Laughter.*) Oh, the Guignol was funny!

Pierre: The Guignol was still a very much alive tradition then?

MM: "Oh, yes, it's old, it was old. It dates all the way back to Mourguet, he's the one who created it. No, it was very funny and plus the little theater on the quai Saint-Antoine was very pretty. Back then, we used to go especially to a theater that was in the passage de l'Argue; so when you came out, all the hookers from the rue Thomassin[13] were there. (*She laughs.*) So it ended up appropriately! You were not supposed to look at the hookers or listen to what was being said. My mother was furious, but my father loved it, it amused him. Plus, he was convinced that we didn't understand anything; I don't know if we understood much, I myself am not sure. And there were political parodies. The Guignol was very "red," politically. But I don't remember very much, except for the classic, *Moving Day*, the funny ones, but that one in particular.

Pierre: With Madelon and Gnaffron?

MM: And then he smacks the policeman, always! The policeman sure gets what he deserves! (*She laughs.*)

Pierre: What did Guignol look like?

MM: Well, he had a sort of black hat and then a bunch of hair behind it and so when he moved like that, the bunch of hair would rise straight up. Well, he also had a sort of small brown vest...

Pierre: Whose hat was it? Was it the kind *canuts* wore?

MM: Oh, no, I don't think so. I never saw *canuts* with that kind of hat, unless perhaps at home, perhaps they wore it at home?

Pierre: And was it Lyons speech?

MM: Well, now there, he had the accent, he really had the Lyons accent, *really, really!*

Pierre: With the patois, with Lyons slang?

MM: Oh, the words too, yes! Yes, when he said "you're pawing me" or something like that.

Pierre: What does "pawing" mean?

MM: When you grope someone like that, "you're pawing me"[14]...In the past, I used to have a lot of words like that, I knew them.

Pierre: He's the one who used to say: "See the wolf farting on the wooden stone"?[15]

MM: Oh, well, it could have been he who said it, yes, yes. There was Madelon, Gnaffron, well, he always has his jug of wine with him, he always had his jug of wine! We went to the Guignols in Paris; there, it wasn't like that at all!

MM: There were quite a few spiritualists in Lyons. There was—what's his name?—Philippe a k a Allan Kardec. There's Bouvier, who was a healer. They used to congregate in the rue Longue, in the center of town, near Saint Nizier's Church. I used to go there too, with my husband, he used to give oral presentations, he was really interested in it. But I never knew if he believed in it or not. I think he was proud to give his oral presentations to them, but I never did talk to him about it because it got on my nerves. I sometimes went there, but it wasn't in the rue Longue; we used to have séances; they would summon Cartouche, no, uh, Mandrin. We used to go to the people's house whose name was...oh, darn, darn, all the names, my goodness, they're all gone! Quai Saint-Antoine, they must have lived there, oh, it was a splendid apartment, immense, it was really beautiful! And there was a table that took up the whole dining room, but a huge oak thing, you know, with big legs, the whole bit; when someone said that Mandrin was coming, you heard a broom, broom, broom, broom...It was his horse! But then, you couldn't really deny that it was his horse. I went there often! But in the end, I got scared, so I never went back.

Pierre: There was no trickery?

MM: Ah, I don't think so! There, really... And those people who didn't work, no one worked, well, they ate pretty well. They used to have, he used to say, Mister so-and-so, what was his name now? It begins with a "p," it's always that way with me. I know the first, the first letter of a name, but I don't know the second. Well, anyway, he used to say that it was all about the "contributions" that he received. And I think it really exists, these guys who are very good hypnotists, because for all that, they end up getting contributions.

Pierre: What do you mean by "contributions"?

MM: Well all of a sudden, there would be a pâté right under their noses or other things they hadn't purchased, but that ended up at their house! They used to say so. And then there was Mr. Palud, a lawyer who used to turn up then. He used to get drunk, he really lived in the fast lane, this guy. Well, the table told all sorts of things about him. So he got up, half drunk, you know, and because it had influenced him so, he opened the window, and was going to jump right out!

Pierre: What did the table say to him!

MM: I don't remember anymore, perhaps that he had been behaving badly, you know, all kinds of things like that, it bawled him out! And so he wanted to throw himself out the window! We held him back, though. There were men there, my husband, a man who was the president of the Chamber of Commerce: it was really a rather select milieu, where we used to go (*said in an ironic tone*).

Pierre: So, how did the table speak!

MM: The table? Oh, I don't know, it spoke letter by letter with knocks on the table, A B C D, like that, yes. But there were moments when it was, where they cheated. Once they turned off all the lights and there was a calling card, if I remember correctly, and we asked the table to sign this calling card. It seems that it happened sometimes, things like that! That day, my husband had put the card on the table and he had made a mark on it, you know, but after, it was no longer the same card that had been on the table. He said nothing at the time, but then to me, he said: "No, that wasn't the card." Then after, there was Peyre Jr., who used to talk everywhere that he had found Mandrin's treasure, didn't I tell you about that?

Pierre: No.

MM: He said that he'd found Mandrin's treasure. So he found two old people and totally cleaned them out, all their money, you know! He said that he had to do research, that he needed this and that, and these people coughed it all up and he ended up in prison afterward, Peyre Jr.

Pierre: There were also Black Masses?

MM: Oh, at their place, there must have been some, but I myself never went. They must have done things like that.

Pierre: So it's not a legend, it really existed in Lyons.

MM: Oh, yes, yes, yes! There was a table, a round table at their place; it was all painted, there were the zodiac signs all around it, there were all kinds of...Oh, no, no! Then they wanted to summon up ghosts, but I myself was very much against that sort of thing, and there was one man who was against it too. It frightened me: seeing the table and all that did not frighten me, but seeing a ghost, I didn't want to see that at all.

Pierre: Did they make contact with the dead as well?

MM: Yes, and those who appeared at the table were dead, they were not alive! But anyway, I often had, we used to do a séance, at our house, after, with Madame Lucie, who used to live in the house, and we did things like that. Well, everything that they used to tell you, like such and such a thing will happen, well it never happened, never, never, *never!* Because, even if some spirits come, they are inferior spirits who are, who are at ground level, if you like; a superior spirit does not stick around with us.

Pierre: So, in any case, these were bad visitations?

MM: Oh, yes! I understand very well that you are not supposed to do that; it can only surround you with an evil aura. But my husband had done a lot of it in Holland; he had a professor, Salverda de Grave (*she emphasizes the name while speaking*), I will always remember the name of this professor, Salverda de Grave, that he had at Groningen, I believe. It seems he had actually photographed real ghosts, you understand? They were the doubles of people who were dead. My husband really liked those sorts of things.

Pierre: And now, does it still go on?

MM: Oh, yes, well, I don't know anymore...Oh, no, I didn't want to continue with it; after my husband's death, it was finished. I had other things to do, taking care of the children was already enough. I never again...but then, at that time, Madame Lucie would sometimes come over, then there was another lady too who used to come, and she, this other lady, was a medium; she could be put herself to sleep in five seconds; you didn't need to, all she had to do was sit down at the table and she would be asleep. So then it was she who spoke, so it was no longer the table, but she who was talking. But she was never right either.

Pierre: What did she say? Could she tell the future?

MM: Oh, well, I don't really remember. The future, yes, she could tell it: "You will say such and such, you will do such and such"; I no longer remember, you know, really, that's a long time ago, almost fifty years... I realized that it was all false, you know, everything they used to say...

Pierre: And on the rue Jean-Baptiste Say, did they believe in all this business?

MM: Oh, well, not my father, absolutely not. But my mother, she was completely nuts about it! Oh, yes! Because back then, she had too much, she believed so much, uh, in reincarnation—which can sometimes be very true, we don't know anything about what happens on the other side when it comes right down to it; and in her cat, she saw a future man, you understand! All the same, she didn't have a metempsychosis, but she must have thought that this cat, in another life, would be someone better. But she was just horrible about animals! For example, if we sat down at the table, the cat was the first served and so he became mean, horrible, that little beast. They had him put to sleep by the vet, he started being bad, he clawed at us, he bit, it was a nasty beast, this cat. And so for her, she loved animals, everything was done for the animals, the animals above all else, and so she believed in it blindly.

Madame Marguerite's Notebooks

Why did the people of Croix-Rousse like their neighborhood? I say "did like" in the past tense because the population of our hill is rather mixed today. New houses have brought in people who have never stepped foot in the Croix-Rousse and they cannot assimilate the mentality of the natives. In the past, our neighborhood resembled a village; everyone knew everyone else, you were faithful to your shopkeepers, you had your favorite bistro, hairdresser, and milliner. Now, for example, people change hairdressers ten times a year.

When you got off the *ficelle*[16] [a railway car] on the boulevard, which is beautiful, wide, with a lot of trees, you breathed much better air than in downtown. That is an absolutely truthful and verified statement. The air was purer there, and you immediately felt it at home. There are certain streets, such as the rue de Cuire, where many houses still have farmhouse shutters. Sixty or seventy years ago, it was the country. The houses have a shabby, dilapidated aspect to them, but if you take the trouble to go down the "alley" [a Lyons term], all the way to the end, you are going to find a beautiful garden and often another stylish and pretty little house. There are many individual gardens in the Croix-Rousse and it would just be vandalism to destroy them.

Nowadays, the hill no longer has its big village aspect. As I've said, a lot of "foreigners" have come and moved in. Some of them undoubtedly scorn the conservative character of the old Croix-Roussians, but these big houses, these towers,[17] destroy our view and we certainly miss the warmth of our old neighborhood. I speak lovingly about Croix-Rousse because I was born here and have grown old here. I reckon that I have lived all my life in this neighborhood, except for around five years. . . .

I think that we, in Croix-Rousse, we like well enough what does not change the aspect of the city and life too much. Our neighborhood closely resembled a village where everyone knew one another and met on the *ficelle*. You lived fairly well there because the air was always purer than in the city. But the stores became more attractive, little by little the old houses disappeared....

I have known some very crude shops, display windows of dubious taste, but the shopkeepers knew their customers, there was an exchange of politeness and kindness. Then, little by little, the transformations took place, the shops and the display windows became modernized, and, except for a few holdouts, the overall impression is rather bizarre; in fact, if you take the main street, the Grande-Rue, you notice that some pretty shops have opened on the ground floor of old and often ugly houses, having barely more than two or three floors. But, as for the rue de Cuire, follow the alley and, to your great surprise, you will very often find a pretty garden at the end.... The shopkeepers are unfortunately no longer authentic Croix-Roussians. They have constructed more modern shops, but they have not acquired the native mentality. There are no more friendly conversations, no one knows anyone anymore....

There were a few curiosities in the Croix-Rousse. For a long time, the Lyons–Bourg train used to cross the boulevard de la Croix-Rousse, because the station was on the right side of the boulevard.[18] When the train used to slowly come in with the locomotive in front, you had to hurry to cross the tracks, because, in the morning, the market was on the other side of the train. This train perturbed, bothered traffic for years and shortly before 1914 it was decided to create another station located before the intersection with the boulevard. This other station was never built, the war halted its construction, but there was a provisional one for years. Now the Lyons–Bourg train no longer exists in the Croix-Rousse.

Two funiculars had been installed to go up from the city. Both functioned the same way, with a large cable to pull them and with the coming and going of the two cars, one going to and one coming back. The Croix-Roussians very quickly christened these funiculars with the name *ficelle*, a name that stuck until their disappearance. There was the one-penny *ficelle*, the oldest, which served the silk mill neighborhood, the Croix-Paquet, and then the two-penny *ficelle* linking the rue Terme with the boulevard de la Croix-Rousse.[19] Each car was connected to a flatbed with chains around it (the wagon) where they used to put the horse-drawn carriages, the handcarts, and bikes, and, at quitting time, the wagon was reserved for people, because the car itself was not large enough at such times. The mayor thought he had to deprive us of both *ficelles* at the same time! One of them, the two-penny one, was replaced by a tunnel for automobiles. We, the old Croix-Roussians, wept for our *ficelle* that used to take us near the Terreaux in a few minutes, and the result was not pleasant at all. As for our old one-penny *ficelle*, it was replaced by the metro! I doubt that the Croix-Roussians were enthusiastic about the metro.

As for the *canuts*, some of them were very poor, living meagerly in apartments without modern conveniences. I have never seen a *canut* revolt. The entire Croix-Rousse vibrated in the past with the ticktock of their weaving looms. Moreover, you would see three-quarters of the houses or apartments with very high ceilings to respond to the space needs of the looms. Little by little, all these *canuts* working for silk trade firms disappeared. The weaving was then done in the country or in factories.... Tulle and ribbons were a big development in Lyons, but now there are no more than a few artisans who produce these articles. When a workshop or a factory modernized by buying new looms, the old ones left for Syria, Egypt, and Algeria. Men from these countries came to do internships in Lyons to learn how to weave; then they returned home, where, with our old looms and with much less expensive manual labor than in France, they made their own fabrics, and that's how, little by little, the textile industry in Lyons disappeared....

In the streets you heard the noise of the weaving looms throughout the day. At that time, weaving was done for the most part in people's homes, whether in the city or in the country. I knew a weaver who specialized in top-quality weaving work. He made portraits of the great men of the day. He worked behind closed doors and was forbidden from having anyone visit him because his work was a secret.

The *canuts'* apartments, which still exist, had very high ceilings and so they were very hard to heat... A *canut's* apartment: one large room with a very high ceiling so as to set up the looms (more than thirteen feet high), a kitchen separated from this room by a glass partition that brought in light from the workshop. In general, it had one small window or none at all. This kitchen was divided in two horizontally. The upper part or cubbyhole served as a bedroom. There could be a second room. In the past, in all the streets of the Croix-Rousse, you could hear the ticktock of the looms. There also used to be winding and weaving workshops.... There was so little hygiene in the *canuts'* apartments. The large, well-lit room, with a very high ceiling, was reserved for the looms. What was left was often very dark; certain rooms, especially the kitchen, were divided in two horizontally. The upper part was the cubbyhole, the "cub's hole," as the old *canuts* used to say, and Guignol too!

Every year at back-to-school time, the *fair* came to town. It was a distraction for families that has currently lost all its quaint charm. You used to find many more stands than at present: shooting galleries, lotteries, a glass maker, the freaks: the bearded woman, the half-woman (a trick done by way of a mirror effect), the dwarfs, and so on, lots of rides, marshmallow and Lyons taffy vendors. For many years, there was Raymond "Trembling-Hand," who engraved napkin rings, goblets, and so on. He had a cowboy look: boots, a big hat, and he was very popular in the Croix-Rousse. At the big October Fair, there is still, just like more than a hundred years ago, the sale of roasted chestnuts and sweet white wine.[20] There was quite a bit of "rolling around drunk" at that time.

I used to like — I still do — marshmallows and taffy. I think you can only find this kind of taffy in Lyons. In the past, as I remember, the candy stands set up a cogwheel with the numbers one through ten. For two pennies, you could spin the wheel and you won as many sticks of marshmallow as the number it stopped on. Ten sticks was a godsend!...

I should not forget to say that the first cinemas were itinerant ones and that we saw them at the fair. The fairground stands must have made a fortune. There was especially the Cinéma Dular, which never went very far from Lyons. (There was an annual fair in many Lyons neighborhoods.) Then the cinema settled in the place de la Croix-Rousse in a building where it stayed for many years.

Let me come back to our Sundays. So, in the summer, we used to go to Montessuy, which at that time included on the right and on the left Vauban-like fortifications. There was a lot of grass and the children had a good time. We would sometimes have a cold supper and we would eat under a bower. Those were the days of grand luxury!

In the winter, Mom used to take me to the two o'clock show at the small cinema near our house. In the past, it was a cinema that followed the "fair," the first cinema that we had seen. These were serial films such as *Judex* [a serial created by Louis Feuillade beginning in 1916]. One thing that used to make me angry would really amuse the young people of today: on the screen, when a man and woman kissed on the mouth, I was not supposed to look! My mother would glare at me. And I have retained this sort of guiltiness because even now I don't like to look at two lovers kissing on the screen!

A lot of Croix-Roussians used to go for picnics in the Lyons Mountains. Whole families left together on foot, carrying provisions that one cheerfully hauled up to the top of Mounts Cindre, Thou, Verdun... These were days full of songs and gaiety that I never knew personally. Perhaps in the evening, while returning home, the men slightly lost their sense of how to stand upright! But it was a stock of fresh air for the week....

My Sundays in the winter were rather sad. We stayed in the back of the shop where the lamp was lit only when we really couldn't see anything at all.[21] To mark Sunday, my father would give my sister and me two pennies. We used to get Russian marshmallow at a grocer's down the street, who wasn't closed either.[22] I loved that marshmallow; even though it was seventy years ago, I can still taste it in my mouth. I don't know if it still exists. I don't remember having felt the impression of being frustrated by my parents. Those two pennies were a gold mine, a reward, and I never envisioned getting more. What would the children of today think of that?...

There was also, once a year, a trip to Île-Barbe, where we would dine on fried fish. It was pleasant to sit on the banks of the Saône when night fell. To return to Lyons, we used to take an old streetcar, more like a small train consisting of a locomotive and several cars poorly attached to each other that "hammered along" at twenty-five miles an hour, I think, dragging along the noises of the rails and the chains, all of that on a set of tracks where the cars rocked from left to right. They called this train "the Guillotine," because so many poor guys got smashed by it! But it was really something picturesque about which the old people of Lyons still talk laughingly.[23]

Intermezzo

Michel de Certeau and Luce Giard

Chapter 8
Ghosts in the City

An Uncanniness of the "Already There"

The strategy that, yesterday, aimed at a development of new urban spaces has been little by little transformed into a rehabilitation of national heritage. After having considered the city in the future, does one begin to consider it in the past, like a space for journeys in itself, a deepening of its histories? A city henceforth haunted by its strangeness—Paris—rather than taken to extremes that reduce the present to nothing more than scraps from which a future escapes—New York.

In Paris, this reversal was not sudden. Already, within the grid pattern of functionalist planners, obstacles sprang up, "resistances" from a stubborn past. But the technicians were supposed to make a tabula rasa of the opacities that disrupted the plans for a city of glass. The watchword: "I don't want to know about it." The remnants had to be eliminated in order to be replaced. This urban planning destroyed even more than war had. Yet, some old buildings survived, even if they were caught in its nets. These seemingly sleepy, old-fashioned things, defaced houses, closed-down factories, the debris of shipwrecked histories still today raise up the ruins of an unknown, strange city. They burst forth within the modernist, massive, homogeneous city like slips of the tongue from an unknown, perhaps unconscious, language. They surprise. Better and better defended by devoted groups, these islets create exotic effects within. They alternately worry a productivist order and seduce the nostalgia attached to a world on its way toward disappearing. Heterogeneous references, ancient scars, they create bumps on the smooth utopias of the new Paris. Ancient things become remarkable. An uncanniness lurks there, in the everyday life of the city. It is a ghost that henceforth haunts urban planning.

Naturally, this uncanniness did not come back all by itself. It was brought back by the protectionist economy that is always reinforced in periods of recession. It is also made the object of fruitful operations led by developers of lofts, or of renovated neighborhoods. It allows for an economic development of lands and a transformation of shops. Thus, in the renovated Saint Paul block, the trade is henceforth reduced to antique stores and book shops. Restoration in Paris takes up a position on the international art market. It multiplies profitable investments.

This ghost is exorcised under the name of "national heritage." Its strangeness is converted into legitimacy. Moreover, the care accorded to blocks or to deteriorated neighborhoods prolongs a policy going back to the Malraux law (1962) concerning the safeguarding (still timely) of ancient, civil, and everyday architecture, and even further back to the May 2, 1930, law about sites to be protected (housing developments already), or even that of 1913, which involved only monuments. A tradition becomes amplified whose origin would be the speech of Abbé Grégoire against vandalism (1794): this tradition articulates the protection of selected monuments that have a "national" interest over the necessary destruction of a bygone past. First placed under the sign of "treasures" to be extracted from a body doomed to die, this museumesque policy already takes on, with Malraux, the character of an aesthetics. Today it encounters the point of view of urban planners who notice the premature aging of modern buildings rapidly changed into obsolete and outmoded constructions.[1] Must we then renew our buildings every twenty years? For economic as well as national and cultural reasons, one comes back to this past that has often aged less than that which is new. Therefore, renovation is preferred to innovation, rehabilitation to development, and protection to creation.

But something insinuates itself here that no longer obeys the "conservative" ideology of national heritage. This past is generally looked on as imaginary. A stranger is already there, in residence. This gothic novel scenario agrees with the research of architectural schools, such as Site in the United States, that aim at giving city dwellers the possibility of imagining the city, dreaming it, and thus living it. More than its utilitarian and technocratic transparency, it is the opaque ambivalence of its oddities that makes the city livable. A new baroque seems to be taking the place of the rational geometries that repeated the same forms everywhere and that geographically clarified the distinction of functions (commerce, leisure, schools, housing, etc.). Indeed, the "old stones" already offer this baroque everywhere. It is useless, as in Berlin, to invent a country landscape at the end of grand avenues onto which they would open out, like rivers, onto the sea. The remains of waning pasts open up, in the streets, vistas on another world. At the quai des Célestins, on the Saint Paul block, and in so many other places, facades, courtyards, cobblestones, relics from ravaged universes are enshrined in the modern like oriental precious stones.[2]

Quite far from aligning itself with the historian pedagogy that still often organizes the museum into a *vaterländische Museum* of a small or a big "fatherland," the new renovation distances itself from educational or state-controlled perspectives that inspired the protection of a treasure "in the public interest."[3] It is less interested in monuments than in ordinary housing, less in the circumscriptions of national legitimacies than in the exogenous historicities of local communities, less in a privileged cultural period (the Middle Ages, the age of Louis XIV, the Revolution) than in the "collages" produced through the successive reuses of the same buildings. The new renovation still undertakes to "save" things, but now this involves complex debris that it is impossible to classify within a pedagogical linearity or to lodge within a referential ideology, and that is disseminated throughout the city like traces of other worlds.

A Population of "Legendary" Objects

In the urban imaginary world, there are first of all things that spell it out. They impose themselves. They are there, closed in on themselves, silent forces. They have character. Or, even better, they are "characters" on the urban stage. Secret personas. The docks on the Seine, Paleolithic monsters washed up on the riverbanks. The Saint Martin canal, a misty quotation of a Nordic landscape. The derelict houses [in 1982] of the rue Vercingétorix or the rue de l'Ouest, teeming with the survivors of an invisible catastrophe... By eluding the law of the present, these inanimate objects acquire a certain autonomy. They are actors, legendary heroes. They organize around them the city saga. The pointed stem of a corner house, a roof open-worked with windows like a Gothic cathedral, the elegance of a well in the shadow of a seedy-looking courtyard: these personas lead their own lives. They take responsibility for the mysterious role that traditional societies accorded to great age, which comes from regions exceeding knowledge. They are witnesses to a history that, unlike that of museums or books, no longer has a language. Actually, they function as history, which consists in opening a certain depth within the present, but they no longer have the contents that tame the strangeness of the past with meaning. Their histories cease to be pedagogical; they are no longer "pacified," nor colonized by semantics — as if returned to their existence, wild, delinquent.

These wild objects, stemming from indecipherable pasts, are for us the equivalent of what the gods of antiquity were, the "spirits" of the place. Like their divine ancestors, these objects play the roles of actors in the city, not because of what they do or say but because their strangeness is silent, as well as their existence, concealed from actuality. Their withdrawal makes people speak—it generates narratives—and it allows action; through its ambiguity, it "authorizes" spaces of operations. Moreover, these inanimate objects occupy today, in painting, the place of ancient gods: a church, a house in the paintings by van Gogh; a square, a street, a factory in those by Chirico. The painter knows how to "see" these local powers. He only precedes, once again, a public recognition. To rehabilitate an old concrete gas factory, the mayor of Tours, Mr. Royer, and Mr. Claude Mollard, from the Ministry of Culture, honor a "spirit" of the place,[4] as did Lina Bo Bardi in São Paulo for the Fábrica da Pompei (which became the Centro de Lazer), or as did many other "ministers" from these local cults.

But where does one stop, how does one demarcate the population from these things that are "spirits"? Trees too are a part of them; they are the "sole, true monuments"—"the majestic hundred-year-old plane trees that warehouse speculation protected because they were useful and sheltered the wine and spirit storehouses from the heat of the sun."[5] But also a fountain, the detail of a facade, the corn or ham hung from the ceiling of a small café, a barrel organ or an Edison phonograph in the shadows of a boutique, the curved shape of a table leg, toys, family photos, the wayfaring fragments of a song...This population spreads out its ramifications, penetrating the entire network of our everyday life, descending into the labyrinths of housing, silently colonizing its depths. Thus, there is the linen shirt that opens, like a Muse, *Le cheval d'orgueil*:[6] it passes from generation to generation, worn successively by members of the family, washed and decorated twice a year the way statues of patronymic saints were long ago, a silent goddess, the subject of a story for which human beings only make up circumstances and adjectives in turn. Along with the watch, the wardrobe, the spade, or the *bigouden* costume embroidered in green and yellow, this population traverses time, survives the wearing away of human existences, and articulates a space.[7] A peasant experience? No. The urban rationality undoubtedly eclipses it in the name of city-dweller ideology—"bourgeois" or technocratic—of a voluntarist rupture of rural "resistances," but, in fact, this experience is the very one that the city amplifies and makes more complex by creating the pantheon where the "spirits" in so many heterogeneous places cross paths and compose the interlacings of our memories.

Michelet was right.[8] If the great ancient gods are dead, the "little ones"—those of forests and houses—have survived the upheavals of history; they teem, transforming our streets into forests and our buildings into haunted houses; they extend beyond the dogmatic borders of a supposed "national heritage"; they possess places even though we believe to have shut them in, stuffed, stamped, and set them under glass in the hospitals for popular arts and traditions. Some of them undoubtedly died in these museumesque zoos. But after all, they represent only a minuscule proportion among the population of ghosts that teem within the city and that make up the strange and immense silent vitality of an urban symbolics.

The promoters of urban renovation are thus rightly suspicious. They should be even more suspicious when they open up the city and accord legitimacy to these unknown immigrants. Still, they proceed carefully. From all these ancient things, they only admit what can be tenured as "national heritage." According to which criteria? This remains unclear. Its size, age, (economic) value, and especially the (social or electoral) importance of its "supporters" or of its inhabitants can earn for an "old-fashioned thing" its incorporation in the national heritage. It thus becomes restored. The objects ennobled in this way see themselves recognized with a place and a sort of insurance on life, but, as with all things tenured, in return for conforming to the law of renovation. They become modernized. These histories corrupted by time, or wild ones from who knows where, are trained in the present. Certainly, the pedagogical processes of which they are the object include an internal contradiction: they must at once protect and civilize that which is old, make new that which is old. The products that come out of restoration are thus compromises. That is already a great deal. The renovated "old stones" become places for transit between the ghosts of the past and the imperatives of the present. They are passageways on the multiple frontiers that separate periods, groups, and practices. In the same way as public squares which lead many different streets, renovated buildings constitute, in a historical and no longer geographic mode, interchanges between foreign memories. These shifters ensure a circulation of collective or individual experiences. They play an important role in the urban polyphony. In this respect, they respond to the ideology that underlies rehabilitation and that associates the "status" of the city with the safeguarding of aging buildings. Whatever the framework in which this "salvational" will is inscribed, it is true that restored buildings, mixed habitats belonging to several worlds, already deliver the city from its imprisonment in an imperialistic univocity. However enamel-painted they may be, they maintain there the heterodoxies of the past. They safeguard an essential aspect of the city: its multiplicity.

A Policy of Authors: Inhabitants

Restoration nevertheless tends to transform these heterodoxies into a new cultural orthodoxy. There is a logic to conservation. Even distributed outside the patrimonial temples of memory and placed at the inhabitants' disposal, restored objects turn into museum pieces. Their dissemination works yet again at extending the museum outside of its walls, at museifying [*muséifier*] the city. It is not that the museum is a plague or that it can be transformed into a scarecrow or a scapegoat. The museum often exercises the role of laboratory, ahead of urban planning.[9] But it functions in its own way. It conceals from users what it presents to observers. It stems from a theatrical, pedagogical, and/or scientific operation that pulls objects away from their everyday use (from yesterday or today), objects that it offers up to curiosity, information, or analysis. The museum forces them to move from one system of practices (and from one network of those who practice) to another. Used for urban planners' ends, the apparatus continues to produce this substitution of addressees: it takes away from their usual dwellers the buildings that, through their renovation, it destines to another clientele and to other uses. The question no longer involves renovated objects, but the beneficiaries of the renovation.

If one refuses to accept the logic of conservation, what other hypothesis will take over? When the museum pulls back, what wins? The *law of the market.* Such is the alternative presented to the interventions of the state and Paris city hall: they must either uphold the institutions of preservation (more or less pedagogical), both public (museums) and private (associations and hobbies of all sorts), or enter into the production-consumption system (real-estate agencies, project developers, architectural firms). In the second hypothesis, the museumesque "subtraction" (buildings taken away from private housing in order to be transformed into public theatrical institutions) is replaced by an economic misappropriation (buildings taken from disadvantaged inhabitants in order to be improved and sold to better-off buyers). Twenty or so examples from the past few years demonstrate this: the Marais neighborhood, the rue Mouffetard, the Halles neighborhood, and so on. This urbanistic restoration is a social "restoration." It brings bourgeois and professional classes back to a damaged and repaired terrain. Rents are going up. The population is changing. The renovated blocks form ghettos for well-off people, and the real-estate curettages are thus becoming "segregative operations."[10]

A politics of renovation seeks to play between the "conservationists" and the "merchants." Some rules aim at limiting or controlling one group by the other. Certain intermediary powers insinuate themselves into these power relationships. The highway department [Le Corps des Ponts et Chaussées], in particular, has slowly carved out an empire in this jungle in the name of a technical position and of technocrats escaping at once from the ideological narrowness of conservation and from the incoherent pragmatism of the market. But the first "intermediaries" to be promoted should be the people who practice these places to be restored.

Through its own movement, the restoration economy tends to separate places from their practitioners. A misappropriation of subjects accompanies the renovation of objects. More than from malicious intentions, this movement results from the very logic of an apparatus (technical and scientific) that is constituted by isolating the treatment of objects from the subjects' consideration. In this particular case, it is not surprising that technical administrations are so interested in buildings and so little in the inhabitants, or that, for example, in a time of recession that requires a struggle against the degradation of existing buildings, they grant things capable of resisting time a value that they refuse to elderly people. They select and manage what they are equipped for—which concerns a production or a restoration of objects.

They obey this rule precisely as therapeutic institutions. Renovation participates in the medicalization of power, a process that has not ceased to develop for two centuries. This power is becoming more and more a "nursing" power. It takes responsibility for the health of the social body and thus for its mental, biological, or urban illnesses. It gives itself the task, and the right, to cure, protect, and educate. Passing from the individual body to the urban body, this therapeutic power does not change its methods. It treats organs and circulatory systems by not taking people into account. A broken-down block is simply substituted for an ailing liver. In this widened medical administration, the misappropriation of subjects remains the prerequisite for a restoration of the body. Thus, the affected urban parts are placed under supervision, taken away from inhabitants, and entrusted to preservation, real-estate, or highway department specialists. This is the hospital system.

Just as the therapeutic relation is reintroduced, still very marginally, within the field of a medical technocracy, the dynamic of relations be-

tween inhabitants and specialists must be restored. It puts power relationships into play between citizens who are supposed to be equal before the law. A policy is involved here that goes beyond and controls any
economic management. Many projects and achievements demonstrate
how inhabitants can be informed and consulted through the mediation
of local authorities; how neighborhood associations (for example, in the
Guilleminot neighborhood) are able to participate in decisions; or how
the [French] state or the city can protect tenants against the exclusion that
threatens them because of renovation. In 1979, concerning the Sainte-
Marthe block, Mr. Léon Cros, Paris councilman, declared that "owners,
in order to benefit from city or state subsidies, must sign an agreement
that will shelter tenants from too high of an increase" in rent and that
"the tenants involved will benefit from personalized housing aid."[11] Certainly, no such measure is completely satisfactory. Beyond the fact that
this plan leads us to ask about the taxpayers imposed on to finance such
subsidies (who pays and for whom?), it pushes owners into Malthusian
renting practices. A political debate is imperative in order to come up
with better solutions.

Inasmuch as a policy takes its inspiration from the principle that
"national heritage," as J.-P. Lecat said, must "become the business of all
French people,"[12] a particular but fundamental form of it must be un-
derscored, the right to creation, in other words, an autonomy in relation to the draconian regulations fixed by certain specialists. The inhabitants, especially the disadvantaged ones, not only have, according to the
laws, a right to stay on the premises, but they have a right to select their
own aesthetics. In fact, though, their "taste" is systematically denigrated
and that of the technicians is privileged. "Popular" art is no less praised
to the heavens, but only when it involves a past or a background transformed into an object of curiosity.[13] Why does this esteem collapse as soon
as it involves living workers or shopkeepers, as if they were less creative
than in the past, or as if the developers or civil servants of today demonstrate an overwhelming inventiveness? From Albert Demard's peasant museum in Champlitte[14] to Michel Thevoz's museum of *art brut* in Lausanne,
everything, on the contrary, proves the unusual poetic talents of these
inhabitant-artists disdained by the engineer-therapists of the city.

Among many other reasons, urban futurology itself requires these
unrecognized artists to regain their authorship in the city. From TV to
electronics, the rapid expansion of the media will put at the individual's
disposal the means that a paleotechnique reserves for an elite. A democratization of artistic expression must correspond to this democratization

of techniques. How can one expand the latter if one censors the former? Can a cultural conservatism be allied with a technological progressivism? This contradictory hodgepodge is unfortunately quite frequent (a general law: cultural traditionalism compensates for economic advancement in a society). But this wastes the true capital of a nation or a city because its national heritage is not made up of objects it has created but of creative capacities and of the inventive style that articulates, as in a spoken language, the subtle and multiple practice of a vast ensemble of things that are manipulated and personalized, reused and "poeticized." In the end, national heritage is made up of all of these "ways of operating."[15]

Today, art is made up of these and recognizes in them one of its sources, just as African or Tahitian creations were for it in the past. The everyday artists of ways of speaking, dressing, and living are ghosts in officially recognized contemporary art. It is high time that an urban planning still seeking an aesthetics recognize the same value in them. The city is already their permanent and portable exposition. A thousand ways of dressing, moving around, decorating, and imagining trace out the inventions born of unknown memories. A fascinating theater. It is composed of innumerable gestures that use the lexicon of consumer products in order to give a language to strange and fragmentary pasts. As gestural "idiolects," the practice of inhabitants creates, on the same urban space, a multitude of possible combinations between ancient places (the secrets of which childhoods or which deaths?) and new situations. They turn the city into an immense memory where many poetics proliferate.

Mythical Texts of the City

Within the perspective of a democratization, a condition for a new urban aesthetics, two networks in particular hold our attention: *gestures* and *narratives*. They are both characterized as chains of *operations* done on and with the lexicon of things. In two distinct modes, one tactical and the other linguistic, gestures and narratives manipulate objects, displace them, and modify both their distributions and their uses. These are "bricolages" in accordance with the model that Lévi-Strauss recognized in myths. They invent collages by marrying references from various pasts to excerpts from presents in order to make them into series (gestural processes, narrative itineraries) where opposites come across.

Gestures are the true archives of the city, if one understands by "archives" the past that is selected and reused according to present custom. They remake the urban landscape every day. They sculpt a thousand pasts that are perhaps no longer namable and that structure no less their experience of the city. Ways in which a North African moves into an HLM [Habitation à Loyer Modéré, public housing], in which a man from Rodez runs his bistro, in which a native of Malakoff [a Paris suburb] walks in the subway, in which a girl from the sixteenth arrondissement wears her jeans, or in which a passerby marks with graffiti his or her way of reading a poster. All of these practices of "making do," polysemic customs of places and things, should be maintained by "renovation." How can the square, street, or building be offered up more to their inventions? This is a program for a renovation policy. Too often, such a policy takes the life away from concerned blocks that it then transforms into "tombs" for well-off families.

The wordless histories of walking, dress, housing, or cooking shape neighborhoods on behalf of absences; they trace out memories that no longer have a place—childhoods, genealogical traditions, timeless events. Such is the "work" of urban narratives as well. They insinuate different spaces into cafés, offices, and buildings. To the visible city they add those "invisible cities" about which Calvino wrote. With the vocabulary of objects and well-known words, they create another dimension, in turn fantastical and delinquent, fearful and legitimating. For this reason, they render the city "believable," affect it with unknown depth to be inventoried, and open it up to journeys. They are the keys to the city; they give access to what it is: mythical.

These narratives also constitute powerful instruments whose political use can organize a totalitarianism. Even without having been the object of the first systematic exploitation that Nazism made of them,[16] they make people believe and do things: narratives of crimes or feasts, racist and jingoistic narratives, urban myths, suburban fantasies, the humor or perversity of human-interest stories…They require a democratic management of urban credibility. Political power has known for a long time already how to produce narratives for its own use. The media has done even better. Urban planners themselves have tried to produce them artificially in new housing projects such as La Défense or Le Vaudreuil. Rightly so. Without them, these brand-new neighborhoods remain deserted. Through stories about places, they become inhabitable. Living is narrativizing. Stirring up or restoring this narrativizing is thus also among the tasks of any renovation. One must awaken the stories that sleep in the streets and that sometimes lie within a simple name, folded up inside this thimble like the silk dress of a fairy.

Narratives are certainly not lacking in the city. Advertising, for example, multiplies the myths of our desires and our memories by recounting them with the vocabulary of objects of consumption. It unfurls through the streets and in the underground of the subway the interminable discourse of our epics. Its posters open up dreamscapes in the walls. Perhaps never has one society benefited from as rich a mythology. But the city is the stage for a war of narratives, as the Greek city was the arena for wars among the gods. For us, the grand narratives from television or advertising stamp out or atomize the small narratives of streets or neighborhoods. Renovation should come to the aid of these latter. It does so already by recording and distributing the memories that are recounted in the bakery, the café, or at home. But this is done so by uprooting them from their spaces. Festivals, contests, the development of "speaking places" in neighborhoods or buildings would return to narratives the soil from which they grow. If "an event is what one recounts,"[17] the city only has a story, only lives by preserving all of its memories.

The architect Grumbach said recently that the new city that he would like to build would be "the ruins of a city that had existed before the new one." These would be the ruins of a city that had never been, the traces of a memory that has no specific place. Every true city corresponds in fact to this project. It is mythical. Paris, someone has said, is a "uchronia." Using various methods, Anne Cauquelin, Alain Médam, and many others have paid attention to this source of strangeness within urban reality. This means that renovation does not, ultimately, know what it is "bringing back"—or what it is destroying—when it restores the references and fragments of elusive memories. For these ghosts that haunt urban works, renovation can only provide a laying out of already marked stones, like words for it.

Chapter 9
Private Spaces

The territory where the basic gestures of "ways of operating" are deployed and repeated from day to day is first of all domestic space, this abode to which one longs to "withdraw," because once there, "one can have peace." One "returns to one's home," to one's own place, which, by definition, cannot be the place of others. Here every visitor is an intruder unless he or she has been explicitly and freely invited to enter. Even in this case, the guest must know how to "remain in his or her place," not to allow himself or herself to circulate from room to room; he or she must especially know how to cut short a visit or risk being thrown into the (feared) category of "pests," those who must be "reminded" about the "discretion" of correct behavior or, worse still, those who must be avoided at all costs because they do not know how to follow the rules of propriety, to maintain an "appropriate distance."

Envisioning One's Living Conditions

This private territory must be protected from indiscreet glances, for everyone knows that even the most modest home reveals the personality of its occupant. Even an anonymous hotel room speaks volumes of its transient guest after only a few hours. A place inhabited by the same person for a certain duration draws a portrait that resembles this person based on objects (present or absent) and the habits that they imply. The game of exclusions and preferences, the arrangement of the furniture, the choice of materials, the range of forms and colors, the light sources, the reflection of a mirror, an open book, a newspaper lying around, a racquet, ashtrays, order and disorder, visible and invisible, harmony and discord, austerity or elegance, care or negligence, the reign of convention, a few exotic touches, and even more so the manner of organizing the available space, however cramped it may be, and distributing throughout the different daily functions (meals, dressing, receiving guests, cleaning, study, leisure, rest) — all of this already composes a "life narrative" before the master of the house has said the slightest word. The informed glance recognizes pell-mell fragments from the "family saga," the trace of a production destined to give a certain image of the dweller, but also the involuntary confession of a more intimate way of living and dreaming. In one's own place, it floats like a secret perfume, which speaks of a lost time, of time that will never be regained, which speaks also of another time yet to come, one day, perhaps.

Indiscreet, the home openly confesses the income level and social ambitions of its occupants. Everything about it always speaks too much: its location in the city, the building's architecture, the layout of the rooms, the creature comforts, the good or bad care taken of it. Here, then, is the faithful and talkative indicator about which all inquisitors dream, from administration to the social sciences, such as this judge for children who established a model questionnaire for families having a brush with the law, which detailed several distinctive housing types: "Private home or farm, classic rental apartment building, old public-housing block, modern public-housing block, self-built housing, garden city, boarding house or hotel or furnished room, questionable hotel or café, hobo camp, truck, fixed trailer or barge, mobile homes."[1]

The diversity of places and appearances is nothing compared to the multiplicity of functions and practices of which private space is at once the effective decor and the theater of operation. The gesture sequences that are indispensable to the rhythms of daily activity are repeated here in indefinite number through their minute variations. The body has at its disposal here a closed shelter, where, to its liking, it can stretch out, sleep, hide from the noise, looks, and presence of others, and so ensure its most intimate functions and upkeep. Living by oneself, outside of collective places, means having a *protected place* at one's disposal where the pressure of the social body on the individual does not prevail, where the plurality of stimuli is filtered, or, in any case, ideally ought to be. Hence, the growing intolerance in the contemporary city to the noise of neighbors, the odor of their cooking. Hence, even more so, the profound physical emotion experienced by a person who discovers, upon returning from a brief absence, that his or her apartment had been "paid a visit," burglarized. The stories match; the suffering does not come from the "loss" of stolen goods, but from the upheaval that this intrusion into one's home produces: a male friend said to me that "it felt like I had been raped; I dreamed about it fearfully, trembling for several days."

A Place for the Body, a Place for Life

As a general rule, in this private space one rarely works, except at that indispensable work of nourishment, of cleaning, and of conviviality that gives a human form to the succession of days and to the presence of others. Here bodies are washed, adorned, perfumed, and take the time to live and dream. Here people hug, embrace, and then separate. Here the sick body finds refuge and care, for the time being exempted from its obligations of work and representation on the social stage. Here custom allows one to hang around "doing nothing," even if one knows very well that "there is always something to be done in the house." Here the child grows up and stores away in memory a thousand fragments of knowledge and discourse that later will determine his or her way of behaving, suffering, and desiring.

Here one invites one's friends and neighbors and avoids one's enemies or boss, as long as the society's power respects the fragile symbolic barrier between public and private, between an obliged sociality imposed by the authorities and elective conviviality regulated by individuals. Here families gather together to celebrate the rhythms of time, to confront the experience of generations, to welcome new births, to solemnize marriages, to go through hard times—all of this long work of joy and mourning that can only be accomplished "with one's kin," all of this slow patience that flows from life to death along the river of time.

The more exterior space is made uniform in the contemporary city, and restricting through the length of daily trips, with its injunctive erection of signs, its nuisances, its real or imagined fears, the more one's own space becomes smaller and valued as the place where one can finally feel secure, a personalized private territory where are invented "ways of operating" that gain a defining value: "For me, this is how I do it...In my family, we always do it this way..." The strange thing is that the more one's own space becomes cramped, the more it becomes encumbered with appliances and objects. It seems necessary for this personal place to become denser, materially and emotionally, in order to become the territory in which the familial microcosm is rooted, the most private and dearest place, the one to which one enjoys coming back at night, after work, at back-to-school time after vacation, after a stay in a hospital or the military. When the public sphere no longer offers a place for political investment, men turn into "hermits" in the grotto of the private living space. They hibernate in their abode, seeking to limit themselves to tiny individual pleasures. Perhaps certain ones are already dreaming in silence about other spaces for action, invention, and movements. On a neighborhood wall in June 1968, an anonymous hand wrote these words:

"Order in the streets makes for disorder in our minds." Reciprocally, social despair restores imagination to power within solitary dreams.

The Enclosed Garden Peopled with Dreams

Oppression makes no mistake about it, the oppression that tears citizens away from their private happiness in order to stack them up in its prisons or camps by imposing on them the torture of a public life with the most intimate functions: from then on, the horde is reconstituted where every man becomes a wolf. Utopia makes no more of a mistake about it, the utopia that extends its panoptic surveillance to the most private gestures of the individual body in order to run the whole show and control everything in "the perfect city"[2]...Ordinary memory knows it so well that it sings, in all languages, of the sweetness of one's "home, sweet home." Yet, the enclosed garden where the body hides its pains and joys is not a "forbidden city." If it does not want to become a synonym for a terrible house arrest, separated from the living, the private space must know how to open itself up to the flow of people coming in and out, to be the passageway for a continual circulation, where objects, people, words, and ideas cross paths; for life is also about mobility, impatience for change, and relation to a plurality of others.

Only a dead language no longer changes; only the absence of all residents respects the immovable order of things. Life maintains and displaces; it wears out, breaks, and reworks; it creates new configurations of beings and objects across the everyday practices of the living, always similar and different. Private space is this ideal city in which all the passersby have beloved faces, whose streets are familiar and safe, whose interior architecture is changeable almost at will.

Our successive living spaces never disappear completely; we leave them without leaving them because they live in turn, invisible and present, in our memories and in our dreams. They journey with us. In the center of these dreams there is often the kitchen, this "warm room" where the family gathers, a theater of operations for the "practical arts," and for the most necessary among them, the "nourishing art."

Part II

Doing-Cooking[1]

Luce Giard

Chapter 10
The Nourishing Arts

What follows very much involves the (privileged?) role of women in the preparation of meals eaten at home. But this is not to say that I believe in an immanent and stable feminine nature that dooms women to housework and gives them a monopoly over both the kitchen and the tasks of interior organization.[1] Since the time when Europe left its geographic borders in the sixteenth century and discovered the difference of other cultures, history and anthropology have taught us that the sharing of work between the sexes, initiation rites, and diets, or what Mauss calls "body techniques,"[2] are reliant on the local cultural order and, like it, are changeable. Within a certain culture, a change of material conditions or of political organization can be enough to modify the way of conceiving or dividing a particular kind of everyday task, just as the hierarchy of different kinds of housework can be transformed.

The fact that there are still *women* in France who in general carry out the everyday work of doing-cooking stems from a social and cultural condition and from the history of mentalities; I do not see the manifestation of a feminine essence here. If, in this study, we judged it necessary to become interested in this example of cultural practice rather than another, it is because of the central role it plays in the everyday life of the majority of people, independent of their social situation and their relationship to "high culture" or to mass industrial culture. Moreover, alimentary habits constitute a domain where tradition and innovation matter equally, where past and present are mixed to serve the needs of the hour, to furnish the joy of the moment, and to suit the circumstance. With their high degree of ritualization and their strong affective investment, culinary activities are for many women of all ages a place of happiness, pleasure, and discovery. Such life activities demand as much intelligence, imagination, and memory as those traditionally held as superior, such as music and weaving. In this sense, they rightly make up one of the strong aspects of ordinary culture.

Entrée

As a child, I refused to surrender to my mother's suggestions to come and learn how to cook by her side. I refused this women's work because no one ever offered it to my brother. I had already chosen, determined my fate: one day, I would have a "real profession"; I would do math or I would write. These two paths seemed closely linked to me, as if they called out to one another. Age, travel, and books seemed to guarantee that one day, by dint of work and practice, it would be possible for me to attain these writings of words and numbers that were destined to fill my life.

Having left home early on, I did, as did many others, an apprenticeship in communal meals, in institutional food lacking both taste and identity, and in noisy, depressing cafeterias. My only memory is of the omnipresence of potatoes, sticky rice, and meats that could not be named, which, to my mind, perpetuated the survival of ancient animal species: only their great genetic age seemed to justify their degree of toughness. I thus discovered, *a contrario*, that up to that point, I had been very well fed, that no one had ever measured out the amount of fruits and cheeses I received, and that the prosperity of a family was expressed first in its daily diet. But for a long time, I still regarded as elementary, conventional, and pedestrian (and therefore a bit stupid) the feminine savoir faire that presided over buying food, preparing it, and organizing meals.

One day finally, when I was twenty, I got my own small apartment, apart from school barracks, that included a rudimentary but sufficient facility in which to prepare my meals. I discovered myself invested with the care of preparing my own food, delighted with being able to escape from the noise and crowds of college cafeterias and from the shuttling back and forth to face preordained menus. But how was I to proceed? I did not know how to do anything. It was not a question of waiting for or asking advice from the women in the family because that would have implied returning to the maternal hearth and agreeing to slip back into that discarded feminine model. The solution seemed obvious: just like everything else, these sorts of things could be learned in books. All I had to do was find in a bookstore a source of information that was "simple," "quick," "modern," and "inexpensive," according to my then naive vocabulary. And in order to secure the means to do so (at least, so I thought), I undertook the close study of a paperback cookbook devoid of both illustrations and "feminine" flourishes. To my mind, this absence endowed the book with eminent practical value and sure efficiency.

From the groping experience of my initial gestures, my trials and errors, there remains this one surprise: I thought that I had never learned or observed anything, having obstinately wanted to escape from the contagion of a young girl's education and because I had always preferred my room, my books, and my silent games to the kitchen where my mother busied herself. Yet, my childhood gaze had seen and memorized certain gestures, and my sense memory had kept track of certain tastes, smells, and colors. I already knew all the sounds: the gentle hiss of simmering water, the sputtering of melting meat drippings, and the dull thud of the kneading hand. A recipe or an inductive word sufficed to arouse a strange anamnesis whereby ancient knowledge and primitive experiences were reactivated in fragments of which I was the heiress and guardian without wanting to be. I had to admit that I too had been provided with a woman's knowledge and that it had crept into me, slipping past my mind's surveillance. It was something that came to me from my body and that integrated me into the great corps of women of my lineage, incorporating me into their anonymous ranks.

I discovered bit by bit not the pleasure of eating good meals (I am seldom drawn to solitary delights), but that of manipulating raw material, of organizing, combining, modifying, and inventing. I learned the tranquil joy of anticipated hospitality, when one prepares a meal to share with friends in the same way in which one composes a party tune or draws: with moving hands, careful fingers, the whole body inhabited with the rhythm of working, and the mind awakening, freed from its own ponderousness, flitting from idea to memory, finally seizing on a certain chain of thought, and then modulating this tattered writing once again. Thus, surreptitiously and without suspecting it, I had been invested with the secret, tenacious pleasure of *doing-cooking*.

When this became clear in my mind, it was already too late; the enemy was on the inside. It then became necessary to try to explain its nature, meaning, and manner to myself in the hopes of understanding why that particular pleasure seems so close to the "pleasure of the text," why I twine such tight kinship ties between the writing of gestures and that of words, and if one is free to establish, as I do, a kind of reciprocity between their respective productions. Why seek to satisfy, with one as with the other, the same central need to *spend* [*dépenser*], to dedicate a part of one's lifetime to that of which the trace must be erased? Why be so avid and concerned about inscribing in gestures and words the same fidelity to the women of my lineage?

There have been women ceaselessly doomed to both housework and the creation of life, women excluded from public life and the communication of knowledge, and women educated at the time of my grandmothers' generation, of whom I would like to retain a living and true memory. Following in their footsteps, I have dreamed of practicing an impoverished writing, that of a *public writer* who has no claim to words, whose name is erased. Such writing targets its own destruction and repeats, in its own way, that humble service to others for whom these non-illustrious women (no one knows their names, strength, or courage anymore) represented for generations basic gestures always strung together and necessitated by the interminable repetition of household tasks performed in the succession of meals and days, with attention given to the body of others.

Perhaps that is exactly what I am seeking in my culinary joys: the reconstruction, through gestures, tastes, and combinations, of a *silent legend* as if, by dint of merely living in it with my hands and body, I would succeed in restoring the alchemy of such a history, in meriting its secret of language, as if, from this stubborn stomping around on Mother Earth, the truth of the word would come back to me one day. Or rather, a writing of words, reborn, that would finally achieve the expression of its wonderful debt and the impossible task of being able to return its favor. Women bereft of writing who came before me, you who passed on to me the shape of your hands or the color of your eyes, you whose wish anticipated my birth, you who carried me, and fed me like my great-grandmother blinded with age who would await my birth before succumbing to death, you whose names I mumbled in my childhood dreams, you whose beliefs and servitudes I have not preserved, I would like the slow remembrance of your gestures in the kitchen to prompt me with words that will remain faithful to you; I would like the poetry of words to translate that of gestures; I would like a writing of words and letters to correspond to your writing of recipes and tastes. As long as one of us preserves your nourishing knowledge, as long as the recipes of your tender patience are transmitted from hand to hand and from generation to generation, a fragmentary yet tenacious memory of your life itself will live on. The sophisticated ritualization of basic gestures has thus become more dear to me than the persistence of words and texts, because body techniques seem better protected from the superficiality of fashion, and also, a more profound and heavier material faithfulness is at play there, a way of being-in-the-world and making it one's home.

Innumerable Anonymous Women

I began with a few very precise images of my childhood: seeing my mother next to the kitchen sink, my mother carrying packages. I did not want to do a kind of naturalism, but rather, with a very stylized image, to attain the very essence of reality.[3]

When all is said and done, *Jeanne Dielman* is a hyperrealistic film about the use of time in the life of a woman bound to her home, subjected to the imposed conformity of everyday gestures...I thus revalued all these gestures by giving back to them their actual duration, by filming in sequence and static shots, with the camera always facing the character, whatever the character's position. I wanted to show the right value of women's everyday life. I find it more fascinating to see a woman—who could represent all women—making her bed for three minutes than a car chase that lasts twenty.[4]

But with regard to my cinema, it seems to me that the most appropriate word for it is *phenomenological*: it is always a sequence of events, of tiny actions described in a precise way. And what interests me precisely is this relationship with the immediate glance, the way one looks at those tiny actions that are going on. It is also a relationship with strangeness. Everything is strange to me; everything that does not surface is strange. It is a strangeness linked to a knowledge, linked to something that you have always seen, which is always around you. This is what produces a certain meaning.[5]

These sharp-edged sentences and effective images of Chantal Akerman translate almost too well the intention of this study on the Kitchen Women Nation [*le peuple féminin des cuisines*]. In this voice, in its gentleness and its violence, I recognized the same necessity of returning to triviality in order to break through the entrapment. It represents the same will to learn how to detach one's view from that of "high culture," this inherited background, much praised among the residents of good neighborhoods. It also represents the same distance with regard to the "popular culture" whose naive praises one sings all the better while one is burying or despising those people who gave birth to it. It represents the same refusal to denigrate a "mass culture" of which one deplores the mediocrity produced on the industrial scale, all the while sharing in the advantages that this industry provides. Thus, a will to turn one's eyes toward contemporary people and things, toward ordinary life and its indeterminate differentiation. A wish to rediscover the "taste for the anonymous and innumerable germination"[6] and everything that constitutes the *heart* of it. A will to see the fragile frost of habits, the shifting soil of biases in which social and user circulations are inserted and where shortcuts are to be guessed at. A will to accept as worthy of interest, analysis, and recording the ordinary practices so often regarded as insignificant. A will to learn to consider the fleeting and unpretentious ways of operating that are often the only place of inventiveness available to the subject: they represent precarious inventions without anything to consolidate them, without a language to articulate them, without the acknowledgment to raise them up; they are bricolages subject to the weight of economic constraints, inscribed in the network of concrete determinations.

At this level of social invisibility, at this degree of cultural nonrecognition, a place for women has been granted, and continues to be, as if by birthright, because no one generally pays any attention to their everyday work: "these things" must be done, someone has to take care of them; this someone will preferably be a woman, whereas in the past it was an "all-purpose maid," whose title alone best describes her status and function. These jobs, deprived as they are of visible completion, never seem likely to get done: the upkeep of household goods and the maintenance of family bodies seem to fall outside the bounds of a valuable production; only their absence garners attention, but then it is a matter of reprobation. As the healthy verve of the Quebec women sings it, "Mom don't work 'cause she got too much to do!"[7]

Like all human action, these female tasks are a product of a cultural order: from one society to another, their internal hierarchy and processes differ; from one generation to the next in the same society, and from one social class to another, the techniques that preside over these tasks, like rules of action and models for behavior that touch on them, are transformed. In a sense, each operator can create her *own style* according to how she accents a certain element of a practice, how she applies herself to one or another, how she creates her personal way of navigating through accepted, allowed, and ready-made techniques. From thus drawing on common savoir faire, each perfect homemaker ends up giving herself a manner suitable for playing one chronological sequence on top of another and for composing, on given themes, *ne varietur*, music of variations that are never determined in a stable form.

Culinary practices situate themselves at the most rudimentary level, at the most necessary and the most unrespected level. Traditionally in France, the responsibility for them falls almost exclusively on women and these tasks are the object of ambivalent feelings: the value of French cuisine is enhanced when compared to that of neighboring countries; the importance of diet in raising children and care for the family is emphasized in the media; the responsibility and role of the housewife as primary buyer and supplier for the household are stressed. At the same time, people judge this work to be repetitive and monotonous, devoid of intelligence and imagination; people exclude it from the field of knowledge by neglecting dietary education in school programs. Yet, except for residents from certain communities (convents, hospitals, prisons), almost all women are responsible for cooking, either for their own needs or in order to feed family members or their occasional guests.

In each case, *doing-cooking* is the medium for a basic, humble, and persistent practice that is repeated in time and space, rooted in the fabric of relationships to others and to one's self, marked by the "family saga" and the history of each, bound to childhood memory just like rhythms and seasons. This women's work has them proliferate into "gesture trees" (Rilke), into Shiva goddesses with a hundred arms who are both clever and thrifty: the rapid and jerky back and forth movement of the whisk whipping egg whites, hands that slowly knead pastry dough with a symmetrical movement, a sort of restrained tenderness. A woman's worry: "Will the cake be moist enough?"; a woman's observation: "These tomatoes are not very juicy, I'll have to add some water while they cook." A transmission of knowledge: "My mother (or aunt or grandmother) always told me to add a drop of vinegar to grilled pork ribs." A series of techniques [*tours de main*] that one must observe before being able to imitate them: "To loosen a crêpe, you give the pan a sharp rap, like this." These are multifaceted activities that people consider very simple or even a little stupid, except in the rare cases where they are carried out with a certain degree of excellence, with extreme refinement—but then it becomes the business of *great chefs*, who, of course, are men.

Yet, from the moment one becomes interested in the process of culinary production, one notices that it requires a multiple memory: a memory of apprenticeship, of witnessed gestures, and of consistencies, in order, for example, to identify the exact moment when the custard has begun to coat the back of a spoon and thus must be taken off the stove to prevent it from separating. It also calls for a programming mind: one must astutely calculate both preparation and cooking time, insert the various sequences of actions among one another, and set up the order of dishes in order to attain the desired temperature at the right moment; there is, after all, no point in the apple fritters being just right when the guests have barely started on the hors d'oeuvres. Sensory perception intervenes as well: more so than the theoretical cooking time indicated in the recipe, it is the smell coming from the oven that lets one know if the cooking is coming along and whether it might help to turn up the temperature. The creative ingenuity of cleverness also finds its place in culinary production: how can one make the most out of leftovers in a way that makes everyone believe that it is a completely new dish? Each meal demands the invention of an alternative ministrategy when one ingredient or the appropriate utensil is lacking. And when friends make a sudden, unexpected appearance right at dinnertime, one must improvise without a score and exercise one's combinatory capacities. Thus, entering into the vocation of cooking and manipulating ordinary things make one use intelligence, a subtle intelligence full of nuances and strokes of genius, a light and lively intelligence that can be perceived without exhibiting itself, in short, *a very ordinary intelligence.*

These days, when the job one has or seeks in vain is often no longer what provides social identity, when for so many people nothing remains at the end of the day except for the bitter wear and tear of so many dull hours, the preparation of a meal furnishes that rare joy of producing something oneself, of fashioning a fragment of reality, of knowing the joys of a demiurgic miniaturization, all the while securing the gratitude of those who will consume it by way of pleasant and innocent seductions. This culinary work is alleged to be devoid of mystery and grandeur, but it unfurls in a complex montage of things to be done according to a pre-determined chronological sequence: planning, organizing, and shopping; preparing and serving; clearing, putting away, and tidying up. It haunts the memories of novelists, from the fabulous excesses of Rabelais's heroes, all busy eating, digesting, and relieving themselves,[8] to the "long lists of mounds of food" of Jules Verne,[9] passing through the "bourgeois cuisine" of Balzac's creatures,[10] the recipes of Zola, and the tasty simmering dishes of Simenon's concierges.[11]

Listen to these men's voices describing women's cooking, like Pierre Bonte's simple people, whose hearty accents [on an early morning radio talk show] used to populate city mornings with good savages:

> You see, this soup, made with beans, is what we call, of course, a bean soup, but you shouldn't think there are only beans in it. My wife made it this morning. Well, she got up at seven o'clock, her pot of water was on the wood-burning stove—she put her beans on to soak last night—then she added two leeks chopped very fine and some nice potatoes; she put all that together, and when it started boiling, she put her salt pork in. An hour before serving it to us, after three and a half to four hours of cooking, she made a fricassee for it. A fricassee is made in a pan with bacon drippings. She browns an onion in it, and when the onion is nice and golden, she makes up a nice flour roux and then puts it all in the soup.[12]

I will admit it myself: I still dream about the rice croquettes and the fritters that nice children in the Comtesse de Ségur's books used to eat for dinner as a reward for good behavior; I was less well behaved than them and these unknown dishes, which seemed to me adorned with exotic flavors, were never served at our family table. But, taken out of its literary dressing and stripped of its fleeting ennoblement, culinary work finds itself once again in dreary reality. This women's work, without schedule or salary (except to be paid off through service to others), work without added value or productivity (men have more important things to calculate), work whose success is always experienced for a limited duration (the way a soufflé just out of the oven, balancing in a subtle equilibrium, in this glorious peak, is already wavering well before it finally collapses). Yes, women's work is slow and interminable. Women are extremely patient and repeat the same gestures indefinitely:

> Women, they peel potatoes, carrots, turnips, pears, cabbages, and oranges. Women know how to peel anything that can be peeled. It's not hard to do. You learn when you're very young, from mother to daughter: "Come and help peel some potatoes for dinner, dear."...Women peel potatoes every day, noon and night; carrots and leeks too. They do it without complaining to themselves or to their husbands. Potatoes, they're a woman's problem.... Women's domain is that of the table, food, and the potato. It's a basic vegetable, the least expensive; it's the one about which you say little but that you peel and prepare in a thousand ways. How am I going to serve the potatoes tonight? That's what you call a domestic problem. Supply. How much importance should we give supply...? "You do everything so well, honey. I love your potatoes," says the man. "Will you make me French fries tomorrow?" And the woman makes fries. The stakes are high, higher than the discussion itself: not to make him unhappy so that he'll still want me, as much as he wants my fries. And the next day, she peels again, vegetable after vegetable; she chops and slices them into small, patient, meticulous, and identical pieces. She does this so that everything is good and also pretty, well presented. Something that is well presented makes you hungry. Then you'll want to feed yourself, to feed off of me. "I'm hungry for you," says the man. "You're pretty enough to eat. I want to munch on you—one day," says the man. "I'm hungry for the food you give me."[13]

Women's Voices

In order to better grasp the modes of these culinary practices, all readings, experiences, and personal memories have been supplemented with a series of rather long, individual interviews conducted in a flexible format. They had as a goal neither to record opinion frequencies nor to constitute a representative statistical sample, but rather to allow us to hear women's voices: they talk about their way of doing-cooking, of organizing this work, of living and experiencing it—this will give us a way of knowing their own language, their words, and even the inflections in their voices, even the rhythm of their speech. These interviews aimed neither to sort out underlying images nor to reveal unconscious roots, nor to define and classify attitude types. Their sole intention was *to hear women speak*: to talk about the very activity that is generally accorded no attention. Thus, we can learn from them, and them alone, how they represent their role and ability, if they take an interest in their savoir faire, and what secret pride they take in finding a personal way to fulfill an imposed task.

These interviews were done rather freely and thanks to the friendly goodwill of certain friends and relatives of mine or of Marie Ferrier, who collected the data. We excluded our mothers, sisters, and sisters-in-law from this group: the all-too-strong emotional effects or the trace of family conflicts might have distorted the dialogue. For similar reasons, we appealed to no woman whose profession was in psychology, psychoanalysis, medicine, or university education: their professional experience, cultural domain, and training in communication would have introduced a definite bias into our inquiry. The women whom Marie Ferrier met and questioned at length (about two hours for each interview conducted at the home of the person interviewed) belong to the lower-middle class and the middle class. They have various ages, status, and professions; their education is in general literary or turned toward administrative work, which corresponds to an old practice in the schooling of young girls who were excluded from the techniques of industrial manufacture and professions linked to the hard sciences. They do not all have children, but they know that a teenager or an adult male does not ask for the same kind of food as a woman. Finally, we did not question teenage or young women still living with their parents: they would have had a tendency to provide a discourse repetitive of their mother's practices or in reaction against her, or even a description of an imagined and unrealized practice.

Each interview took place according to a rather loose framework that left a great deal of freedom to the spontaneity of the interviewee and the movement of her associations. Throughout the discussion, Marie Ferrier proposed a limited series of themes in order to make possible a comparative analysis of contents and to avoid a total drifting of the conversation. These themes included the following points and more or less followed this order:

1. Planning meals and choosing a menu
2. Shopping and organizing purchases
3. Recipe sources and the mode of culinary apprenticeship
4. Preparation and the role of personal invention

5. The use of industrial food products (canned goods, frozen foods, and ready-made meals, including the practice of home freezing) and electrical appliances (beaters, mixers, etc.)
6. The role of the man of the house and his interventions in the kitchen

In these interviews, there was neither a fixed form of questions, nor a battery of questions to be asked in strict order, nor a ready-made questionnaire to be filled out. Our methodological option was completely different:[14] Marie Ferrier recorded in full long, informal conversations with friends or with women who might have become so. She then listened to the recordings over and over again to peruse and transcribe them. We decided to include in this volume the entire transcript of one interview, with Irène, to allow one of these voices its freedom and fullness.[15] These voices, whose faces will remain unknown to us, make up a melodious polyphony. They are diverse, living voices that approve of, are moved, and remember themselves; voices that regret, answer, and contradict themselves. They are voices that talk simply about ordinary practices with everyday words, women's voices that talk about the life of people and things. Voices.

Our procedure has privileged the voice of women accustomed to handling French and capable of talking about themselves without too much difficulty or timidity; to avoid these types of difficulties, we abandoned questioning women we did not know or those from more modest backgrounds. In this sense, our small sample is hardly representative of the average condition of women, of their alienation with regard to language, and of their discomfort in speaking a word in public that directly concerns them. Nevertheless, if these interviews were conducted in a face-to-face format, at the interviewee's home, at times in the presence of a husband or a child, it was always stipulated that these conversations would be published in some form with the ongoing research.

During the course of the inquiry, we realized too late that it would have been worthwhile to plan a second discussion with each interlocutor a few days after the first: many of them manifested such a desire after the fact, saying that they had continued to think about the discussion after Marie Ferrier had left and regretted not being able either to bring out further information or nuances, or not being able to continue a dialogue that had barely gotten going. The time limits assigned to this part of the research and the geographic distances between interviewees only allowed second interviews in the case of number 5 (Élisabeth), which Marie Ferrier conducted in my presence. Here, then, under fictitious names (which are designed to protect, as they wished, the anonymity of their voices), is the list of the collected interviews:

1. Agnès, college student
2. Beatrice, college student
3. Colette, teacher
4. Denise, assistant editor in a research consultant office
5. Élisabeth, supply attaché in a large junior high school
6. Françoise, librarian
7. Geneviève, professional
8. Henriette, artist
9. Irène, private secretary
10. Jeanne, housewife
11. Karen, housewife
12. Laurence, housewife

The alphabetical order of names corresponds to their increasing age: the first four at the time of the interviews (1978) were between 25 and 30, the next four between 31 and 40, Irène between 41 and 50, Jeanne between 51 and 60, and finally the last two between 61 and 70. A third of them had not yet had children (which mostly concerns the younger ones); the others had one child (three cases), two (one case), three (two cases), and seven (one case), respectively. They lived in Paris and its suburbs (seven cases, but half of them spent their childhood and adolescence in the provinces), in another large city (one case in France and one abroad), in an agglomeration of ten thousand inhabitants (one case), or in a rural community (two cases), all of them spread throughout various regions of France. Two are French citizens born to foreigners, one from a country bordering France and the other from a European country much farther from France. Both still have family in these countries. All of these details, along with other characteristics, will not be reported in a summary table in order to preserve the anonymity of the various voices.

One of the recordings proved unusable because of material conditions in its collection and it was impossible to repeat the meeting (case 4, Denise). We have, however, used certain elements stemming from this discussion because Marie Ferrier had noted down certain points during the interview. As for Élisabeth, it was possible to record a second discussion at my home two weeks after the first, so that the material of usable inquiry in total consists of twelve discussions with eleven different people. Subsequently, what I borrow from these voices is always specified by the speaker's name and the quotations faithfully reproduce the words spoken, as the word-for-word tape transcription by Marie Ferrier reconstructed them. Through this procedure, I hope to have readers perceive the particular quality of these voices, a sometimes rough and bitter movement, a quavering due to emotion or memory. It represents a texture of true and living voices that gives density to ordinary speech.

Other Sources

This limited collection of direct and personal information was increased through recourse to sources of facts and data that come from the work of the INSEE [Institut National de la Statistique et des Études Économiques] and that of the INSERM [Institut National de la Santé et de la Recherche Médicale]. The INSEE makes regular studies of French consumption according to a precise method; at the time of writing this part of our study (in 1979), the most recently published installments dealt with alimentary consumption in 1972 by category of purchase (including individual self-production, evaluated when it occurred) and the distribution of meals in 1971 (at home or out).[16] The technique of the study is well defined: it is based on the selection of a representative sample of around ten thousand ordinary households (as opposed to what the sorting of data calls "collective households," indicating the residents of retirement homes, convents, student hostels, prisons, etc.); a "household" is made up of a group of people who belong to the same household, whatever their family ties or legal status.

The INSEE sample is made up in such a way as to be representative, for the whole of France, according to (1) the division of heads of household into socioprofessional categories; (2) the geographic region of residence; (3) the size of the commune of residence; (4) the number of people living in this household. The study consists of consulting each household during the course of a week (a preliminary interview, a very precise recording of all the household purchases in a notebook, a verification of the validity of the furnished information with the help of a written form, etc.); the study is spread out over an entire year (except for the first half of August and the second half of December, vacation or holiday periods during which the information gathered would be partial or heterogeneous compared to ordinary weeks) in order to compensate for seasonal variations and to constitute data series that are as homogeneous as possible. This clear methodology and the size of the sample thus make possible a statistical processing of the collected information.[17]

As for the INSERM, works concerning the nutrition section were consulted thanks to the kindness of its members. It constituted a rather large study, focused on 1,367 families living in four departments (Bouches-du-Rhône, Loire, Rhône, Meurthe-et-Moselle) and in three types of zones (county seat, midsize town, and rural region).[18] As the researchers indicate, the sample is not representative with regard to the division into socioprofessional categories; moreover, the Paris region is completely absent and the size of the families questioned (21 percent have four or more children) is larger than the national average. But the partial publication of the results, even without refined statistical processing, furnishes precious indications about the alimentary behavior of these 6,196 people between 1965 and 1966, each family having been observed for three days. The method used consisted in having the mother of the family fill out a long and detailed written questionnaire: three-quarters of these women were housewives, which contradicts the general statistics on women's employment, but is explained here by the high birthrate among the families surveyed. This questionnaire was then followed up orally with supplemental questions from the researcher; finally, there were group discussions in the cities on certain themes.[19]

We should notice that the work of the INSERM was in part financed by the United States Department of Agriculture. If one wonders why the latter was interested in the alimentary behavior of the French, in their opinions on mass-produced food products, and in their desires to increase their food purchases, I remind the reader that at this time:

1. The American food industry was starting the second phase of its penetration into the European market, often in the guise of former British firms that came under the control of American financial groups;
2. American agriculture was in the midst of reorganization: the size of cereal fields to be replaced by grass or feed-grain production or other crops oriented toward cattle food products was tied to estimations on the consumption of meat in the years to come, and so on.

Whatever the interests of its sponsor, the study done by the INSERM provides precious information about familial consumption habits, likes and dislikes, the aspirations to change these habits, and the composition and atmosphere of meals, and all that information is being grasped through the image supplied by the women who prepare the meals, because they were the only ones consulted.

Earthly Foods

Why do we eat? The primary reason: to satisfy the energy needs of a living organism. Like other animal species, humans must submit to this necessity throughout life; but they distinguish themselves from other animals by their practice of elected periods of abstinence (voluntarily, or to save money, or in periods of shortage) that can go so far as the observance of a rigorous and prolonged fast (Ramadan in Islam or African rites of initiatory purification) or as far as a steadfast refusal of all food (anorexic behavior or hunger strikes driven by a political will that consists of opposing the symbolic and tangible counterviolence of torture of one's own body as a response to the violence of power or of the established order).

This daily intake of food is not undifferentiated. In quality as well as quantity, it must satisfy certain imperatives (the makeup of intake and the relative proportions of various nutrients) at the risk of not being able to ensure the maintenance of good health for the individual, protection against cold or infectious agents, and the capacity to sustain steady physical activity.[20] Below a certain quantitative threshold, a paltry *subsistence intake* ensures the temporary survival of a weakened organism, which reabsorbs in part its own tissues to feed itself, loses strength and resistance and, if this situation persists, enters a state of undernourishment.[21]

Similarly, a diet unbalanced in both quality and diversity leads to malnutrition. Daily intake must provide a sufficient supply of proteins, a quantity proportionate to the weight, age, and physical activity of the individual; the makeup of this supply (proteins from both animal and plant sources) also enters into the equation. In addition to the three classes of nutrients (proteins, fats, and carbohydrates), alimentary intake must also provide certain indispensable elements (vitamins, minerals, and both amino and fatty acids), but according to a system of subtle proportions and interrelations: thus, the same nutrient "can represent the gain of one vitamin at the loss of another";[22] likewise, mineral needs cannot be isolated from each other because their metabolism is interdependent; certain elements must be combined in order to allow assimilation, and so on.

The history of medicine itemizes an entire list of illnesses caused by deficiency or resulting from the poor quality of absorbed foods, such as the *mal des ardents*, common during the Middle Ages and the Renaissance, whose descriptive name concerns ergotic poisoning from ergoticized rye flour, that is, rye flour that contains a parasitic fungus; the *new plague* of the Crusades, which was the vitamin deficiency associated with scurvy; *Saint Quentin's grand mal* during the Hundred Years' War, an edema of famine caused by the lack of proteins; pellagra caused by a lack of vitamin B$_3$, common in rural areas where corn provides the food base (though certain local practices, such as the liming of corn in Mexico, have avoided it in Latin America), and so on.[23]

There does not exist one precise description of alimentary intake that is always appropriate for human beings; the needs for proteins, minerals, and vitamins vary according to the size, weight, sex, and climatic life conditions of individuals (living conditions, clothing, protection from inclement weather), as well as the intensity of their activity and the stage of life (growth, pregnancy, breast-feeding, adulthood, old age). We now know that a state of malnutrition coming at certain periods of life has profound and lasting consequences: thus, the undernourishment of a nursing infant slows brain growth and leads to irreversible disorders of the structure and function of the brain, and hence to effects on mental ability.[24] We know about the temporary sterility in women of childbearing age caused by severe undernourishment (for example, the amenorrhea associated with famines, observed during prolonged sieges in cities such as Leningrad during World War II).[25] The lack of animal proteins considerably increases the risk of toxemia in pregnant women;[26] the nursing period requires a surplus in both quantity and quality of food intake, to protect the mother and the infant.

To all of these traditional illnesses must be added, in the overfed West, the illnesses of abundance or excess that are at the heart of the new *maladies of civilization*. Epidemiology has documented some troubling facts.

1. The growing frequency of cancers and disorders of the intestines seems to be in direct correlation with the impoverishment of diets rich in cellulose and vegetable fiber (resulting from a drop in the consumption of cereals and a taste for white bread and refined flour);[27] this is why bakers have been encouraged to offer "bran bread," which is less refined, and "specialty breads" made from different grains.

2. The extent of cardiovascular diseases appears linked to, among other things, diets too rich in glucides and certain types of fats.[28]

3. The increase in cases of death by cancer in France, from 1950 to 1967, differs depending on the region (the highest rate exists in the

north and the lowest in the Mediterranean region), and seems to correlate to diet (the lowest consumption of fruit is in the north as well as the high use of butter for cooking instead of vegetable oil).[29]

That should suffice to underline what is essentially at stake for health in the composition of an alimentary diet and how many subtle and multiple requirements there are to reconcile with the pleasures of the table—something that at first glance seems simple and natural.[30] If things are much more complicated than they first appear, it is because there is no standard popular wisdom in this field: beyond all economic limitations, certain culinary traditions encourage by choice diets that are deficient or dangerous for certain of their members. Thus, we know about the strange story of the kuru that selectively affects the women and children in the Fore tribe in New Guinea: this always fatal illness is a slow viral attack of the central nervous system, transmitted by the consumption, reserved as a choice gift to warriors' wives, of the brains of killed enemies. A genetic factor is most likely responsible for the persistence of the virus and for the absence of an adapted immune response.[31]

Moreover, there is no innate wisdom in the individual: to be convinced, it suffices to perform a short inquiry among one's family circle; this would allow us to quickly assemble an amazing assortment of stupidity. Even well-educated people, attentive as they are to precise and exact information in other fields, shamelessly talk about foods that are "easily digestible," "light," "fortifying," or "good for kids." Such talk becomes a sundry mix of hearsay, old wives' tales, baseless prejudices, and vague pieces of information gleaned anywhere. Here, what is obvious loses its primary clarity and collides with the absence of man's internal regulation of alimentary behaviors, because human practices are more flexible and adaptable than those of animals, but they also make humans more vulnerable.[32] Through ignorance, lack of concern, cultural habit, material shortage, or personal attitude (if one considers, for example, the complementary behaviors of bulimia and anorexia), people can ruin their health by imposing on themselves deficient or excessive diets, and go as far as to die from what they eat, "digging their graves with their teeth," as it were–not to mention accidental or intentional poisonings (in these cases, success stories often remain anonymous).

No more so than any other elements of material life, food is not presented to humans in a natural state. Even raw or picked from a tree, fruit is already a *cultured foodstuff*, prior to any preparation and by the simple fact that it is regarded as being edible. Nothing is more variable from one human group to another than the notion of what is edible: one has only to think about the dog, spurned in Europe but appreciated in Hong Kong; or grasshoppers, considered disgusting here yet highly prized in the Maghreb; or the worms savored in New Guinea.[33] Closer to home, there is the offal lovingly simmered in Latin countries but despised in the United States, with, moreover, differences of national tradition inside Europe itself: certain cuisines prefer brains and others tripe, but would not eat lamb spleen or *amourettes*, fried spinal marrow.[34] Sometimes the necessity or the contagion of exoticism pushes us to eat elsewhere what we would never consider eating at home, but we have also seen people reduced to famine who allow themselves to die rather than eat unusual foods, such as the African villages in a rural area suffering from a long drought that gave to their animals the powdered milk that international relief organizations distributed among them.[35]

There exist a complex geography and a subtle economy of choices and habits, of likes and dislikes. Food involves a primary need and pleasure, it constitutes an "immediate reality," but "substances, techniques, and customs all enter into a system of significant differences,"[36] a system that is coherent and illogical. Humans do not nourish themselves from natural nutrients, nor from pure dietary principles, but from *cultured* foodstuffs, chosen and prepared according to laws of compatibility and rules of propriety unique to each cultural area (in the Maghreb, for example, poultry is stuffed with dried fruits and in England currant jam is served with a roast, whereas French cuisine practices a strict separation between sweet and savory). Foodstuffs and dishes are arranged in each region according to a detailed code of values, rules, and symbols,[37] around which is organized the alimentary model characteristic of a cultural area in a given period. In this detailed code, more or less well known and followed, the organizer of the family meal will draw on inspiration, on her purchase and preparation possibilities, on her whim and the desires of her "guests." But sometimes lassitude overtakes her in the face of the ephemeral, perishable character of her task. Even her "successes," in the words of her "customers," will not seem to justify the trouble they cost her: "It's such a mess, and then in almost no time, everything disappears. I find that hopeless" (from Marie Ferrier's interview of Irène).

This wavering, a fugitive moment of discouragement, the Kitchen Women Nation knows it all too well, but does its best not to give in to it. Tomorrow will be the day for another meal, another success. Each invention is ephemeral, but the succession of meals and days has a durable value. In the kitchen, *one battles against time*, the time of this life that is always heading toward death. The nourishing art has something to do with the art of loving, thus also with the art of dying. In the past, in the village, a burial was the chance for an extended family reunion around a solid meal, serious and joyful, after the interment. People thus began the work of mourning by sharing earthly foods. In the past, death was a part of life; it seems to me that it was less alarming that way.

Chapter 11
Plat du jour

Every alimentary custom makes up a minuscule crossroads of histories. In the "invisible everyday,"[1] under the silent and repetitive system of everyday servitudes that one carries out by habit, the mind elsewhere, in a series of mechanically executed operations whose sequence follows a traditional design dissimulated under the mask of the obvious, there piles up a subtle montage of gestures, rites, and codes, of rhythms and choices, of received usage and practiced customs. In the private space of domestic life, far from worldly noises, the Kitchen Women Nation's voice murmurs that it is done this way because it has always been done more or less like that; however, it suffices to travel, to go elsewhere to notice that *over there*, with the same calm obviousness, they do it *differently* without seeking to explain further, without noticing the profound meaning of differences and preferences, without putting into question the coherence of a compatibility scale (sweet and savory, sweet and sour, etc.) and the validity of a classification of those things that are inedible, disgusting, edible, delectable, delicious.

Histories

Regarding primitive societies, Mary Douglas has done research on the definition of "dirt," "a relative idea," one element in a symbolic system through which a culture orders the sensible world, and both classifies and organizes matter, so that, dissimulated under this obsession with avoiding stains, of performing sacred purification rites, "reflection on dirt involves reflection on the relation of order to disorder, being to non-being, form to formlessness, life to death."[2] This remark can be applied to the question of food, provided one recognizes in the fabric of this symbolic structuration the presence of parameters linked to a given history and geography.

The first level stems from the *natural history* of a society (the available animal and vegetable species, the nature of cultivated land, the climatic conditions), but this level is not easily distinguished from the *material and technical history* (techniques of clearing, plowing, and irrigating, the improvement of animal and vegetable species, the introduction and acclimatization of species borrowed from other geographic regions, the increase of yields thanks to fertilizers and soil enrichment, the ways of preserving and preparing foodstuffs, etc.). All of that remains inscribed in long-term cycles whose benefits we inherit without realizing it: thus, as of the sixteenth century, French cuisine borrowed vegetables from Italy that were improved by its horticulturists (asparagus, artichokes, cauliflower, etc.) and acclimatized plants that had come from the Americas (peppers, tomatoes, beans, etc.).[3]

The so recent growth of our means in this field has made us quickly forget the worries of the past. With the acceleration of the means of transportation, the multiplication of exchanges from country to country, the monitoring of food preservation conditions, whether raw or cooked (sterilization at high temperature, pasteurization, freeze-drying, freezing and deep-freezing, etc.), the memory of the constant struggles of the peasant, wholesaler, and housewife against heat, humidity, insects, and rodents in order to preserve stored supplies (seeds, fodder, winter provisions) has become blurred within a few generations.

Yet, from antiquity up to our century, all human societies were obsessed with the necessity of protecting their sustenance, of storing away grains and foodstuffs: reserves of grain buried in deep ditches to protect them from fermentation;[4] cured, smoked, or salted meats; milk surpluses made into butter and cheese; fruits and vegetables dried, preserved in oil, vinegar, or alcohol, and so on. Here, inventiveness works wonders, with each culture having its strokes of genius, its tricks, and its knowledge gaps: thus, around 1800, the Nivernais peasants did not know how to preserve summer fruit crops for winter,[5] whereas Poles in the sixteenth century dried fruits, fish, and certain meats (bacon), dried and smoked turnips and onions, cured cabbage, cucumbers, pork, and beef in barrels, and preserved carrots and turnips in sand.[6]

But it is not enough to know about a technique to put it into practice; the necessary resources must still be available; for a modest farmer, for instance, the raising of one or two pigs depends on the available food (leftover grains, fruit and vegetable peelings, beechnuts, acorns) and the price of the salt needed to cure the meat of the slaughtered animals.[7] The introduction of a new plant species had two obstacles to overcome, the mistrust of prejudices and the scope of culinary customs: as of the end of the eighteenth century, the potato could have fed five times more people than ordinary grains planted on the same acreage, but it would take a long delay for it to cease being considered a foodstuff reserved for cattle[8] and for a new cuisine to be invented with learned recipes (around

1820), then bourgeois ones (around 1860), and finally a thousand popular variations so that it could earn its stripes as a basic food, appreciated by everyone.[9]

This aspect of things provides access to the third level, that of a *social and economic history*. The price of food commodities, the fluctuation of the free market, the regularity of supplies, their abundance, and possibly their rationing all make up the appearance of prosperity or shortage in a society. Without evoking the black specter of the great famines, without evoking the dark times of war and the scarcity of food it engenders, one can recall the ordinary misery of average people throughout the centuries. In the eighteenth century in Paris during the riots, people first ransacked the bakeries and stole wheat or bread; the judicial archives show the trace of numerous women, most often ranging in age from twenty-five to thirty-five, and with children, who stole things from market stalls so they could feed them: some meat and a few vegetables. They stole little, modestly, barely enough for a meal: a chunk of bacon, a few leeks, a basket of cherries, almost nothing, barely enough to live on.[10]

But there has been worse. In the nineteenth century, the Parisian bourgeoisie and its providers (caterers and restaurateurs) all did business with their leftovers. A table profusely laden for receptions and the accepted abundance for those who wished to maintain their rank or justify the reputation of their business were costly, and the techniques of preservation were still very basic, hence the widespread practice of reselling leftovers. These leftovers followed an entire circuit trickling down (as their freshness decreased) through the city neighborhoods: every marketplace included stalls reserved for the commerce of "jewels" [*bijoux*], as they were called at the time. Becoming more and more rotten, having lost their identity, refined taste, and specificity, these scraps still ended up finding a taker at the lowest of price.[11] In truth, the poor are not particular—or rather, they cannot be—and that is all there is to it. Hunger exists, the bodies of the poor claim their pittance, and too bad if they have to forfeit their health or lives over it. They used to call this slow poisoning by poverty the "bad fever" or "divine will." People submitted and accepted the blows dealt by fate.

With this obstinacy of the poor, these hungry bodies that do not cease being hungry, indefinitely dreaming of an impossible satiation, of an abundance that might invert the common law of proportions, singing the litanies of fulfillment, drawing pictures of the all-too-full mythical land of plenty in the thousand legends of Cockaigne, replete with the immortal hero of Rabelais's Pantagruel, popular literature never ceases to come back to that which nourishes.[12] The example of the *Bibliothèque bleue* is characteristic: in the approximately 450 titles continuously re-published from the seventeenth to the nineteenth century, one finds a long series of booklets that describe "feasts" and "banquets," give "lists" and "inventories" of mounds of food, and report the "stories" and "exploits" that take place at the table, a festive space par excellence, the legend-cycle of an improbable excess where the archaic pleasures of drinking and eating are joined together.[13]

The age-old experience of these worn-out litanies of words used to evoke food that is lacking is a game taken up again thousands of times in collectives, in high-school cafeterias, in soldiers' barracks, in the prisoner's cell, and here in an internment camp of stateless Jews in Switzerland during World War II:

> With Germaine de T., we invented a very useful game. At each meal — there were ten of us around a table — by whispering, but such that our whole table of women could hear, she and I used to discuss the menu of the day: "I suggest a cheese soufflé for an appetizer. . . . And for the meat dish? What would you think of chicken with tarragon and for the sauce, some slightly dry Moselle wine? . . . And for dessert? A coffee-flavored custard with whipped cream; that's not too heavy. We'll need some strong coffee." . . . And while we talked, the eight other women and ourselves, we swallowed the thin daily cabbage soup and the old boiled potatoes with the celestial taste of culinary marvels on our tongues.[14]

This evocative magic of detailed recipes brings back, for an instant, the happy times of abundance. But this magic assumes that a real experience of culinary happiness had preceded it. The poor, the truly poor, those who have always been so, do not have a cuisine, as studies and memories indicate. Old Mother Denis talks about the Breton world of her childhood near Pontivy at the turn of the century in the following terms: in the morning, they ate boiled buckwheat, at night soup with pancakes. The more copious Sunday meal included salt pork (never any other kind of meat), potatoes, and more pancakes. Monotonous and frugal, lacking in meat, this diet reproduces exactly that of peasant farmers of the Middle Ages, throughout the unchanging history of poor rural areas.[15]

Employed as an all-purpose maid in the home of a merchant from a neighboring town, the young Jeanne, another future Old Mother Denis, discovered the incredible luxury of solid meals served every day; she still remembers her wonderment at the festive meal, "a blowout," that used to conclude, one Sunday every two months, the big laundry day for the whole house. Jeanne learned how to do some cooking at this merchant's house—stews and roasts—a rough apprenticeship where people made fun of her complete ignorance on the subject. But sometimes she recalls the everyday frugality of her parents; for her engagement, they offered the young fiancés a festive meal that was simply a meal made up of pancakes with butter and bacon. At the end of a long and rough life of work, Old Mother Denis—a former railway-crossing guard, on-call maid, and piecework washerwoman—holds on to the customs of her childhood: for lunch every day, there are pancakes and bacon, the latter a sign of enrichment; to honor her interviewer, she prepares a festive meal, the only one she knows: a pot of stewed cabbage with bacon along with nice, hot pancakes.[16]

In another region, in another milieu, at the same time, and in the same state of poverty we find the Avesnois weavers who work at home in the winter and who rent themselves out as agricultural workers in Normandy in the summer. An old woman, with a quiet voice, tells of the same hardships: during her childhood, she never had milk or fruit, except for an orange as a Christmas present; every day they used to eat slices of bread with cream cheese (the father himself made the weekly bread for a long time to save a few pennies), soup, and sometimes a few potatoes. On Sundays, the mother used to buy a little low-grade meat, a small chunk that she used to cook and overcook to render it more tender and that was supposed to give the stew "some flavor" and the children "some strength"; in this case, the smell probably nourished them more than the meat itself; as Kant says: "Smell of food is, so to speak, a foretaste."[17] When their uncle the peddler stopped by on his way, they offered him an extraordinary meal in the eyes of the children: bacon and cabbage. The mother knew about plants and herbs that cured minor health problems, but "there was only one malady, my mother used to say, that she could not control with her plants: that one thing was hunger when there was not a lot around to eat."[18]

Asked by Marie Ferrier about recipes passed down through family tradition, some peasant women from the Jura Mountains replied: our grandmothers did not have culinary customs, we were too poor; they mixed everything together in a big pot that cooked slowly, suspended from the trammel above the fire, and it was imperative not to waste anything. The poor people from East Anglia said the same thing.[19] Choosing, matching, and preparing foods are city gestures for "when you already have enough." As city dwellers in the era of abundance, we dream of healthy foods and natural products and we think that people living in the country are much better off than we are. This is perhaps true today for some rural people, but the phenomenon is recent and one should be careful not to forget that there are nowadays the "new poor" in our cities, jobless and homeless, who sometimes buy the least expensive of foods, those made for cats and dogs.

The history of peasant farmers is a history of poor people who deprive themselves in order to sell the best of their production to people in the cities, and who keep the mediocre subproducts for family consumption. Thus, Alsatian farmers hardly consumed any butter or cheese, products reserved for sale, and for their own use contented themselves with skim milk and buttermilk.[20] Historical inquiries show everywhere the "undeniable alimentary superiority of the city over the country." "The country feeds its population poorly, in spite of or because of self-consumption, and in times of a sustenance crisis, it receives the full brunt of the shock, amplified even more by the total or quasi-total absence of money.... The peasant farmer comes to the city both to work and to consume."[21]

This assessment is still valid today. The study by INSERM, brought to fruition some years ago,[22] allows us to define a "traditional, rural alimentary type," found in Morbihan as well as in the Toulouse region, where soup is the only dish served at every meal, prepared according to a slow-cooking technique whereby the boiled vegetables and meats (the latter in small quantities) make up a mixture that changes little from day to day.[23] In this framework, the more self-consumption is important and money circulation weak, the more the diet is poor in meat products and monotonous, deprived of fruits. We know that the development of elementary schools in the country has had a beneficial impact on children's health, not thanks to the good principles instilled there, but to the creation of school cafeterias where poor children received a well-balanced hot meal for lunch:[24] in 1904, the elementary school inspector from Château-Chinon indicated that the majority of grade-school students (who must walk several miles to school, morning and night) bring as their only provision the "inevitable *grapiau*, a buckwheat pancake that is rather good when hot, but heavy and indigestible when cold."[25]

One last element that corroborates this poverty-stricken image of the peasant diet is the kind of kitchen items mentioned in posthumous inventories: in Auvergne, during the eighteenth century, the essential item for peasants is the *pot* or cooking pot that hung over the fire, plus some copper cauldrons and a few pans; more complex utensils (drip pans and roasting spits) appear only among affluent people.[26] A similar study in the Meaux region notices an increasing appearance of earthenware and glassware after 1750: at the end of the century, one already finds seven or eight plates, one serving dish, and a few bowls per family.[27] These detailed indications seem to confirm commonsense supposition: there is a "diet hierarchy" that overlaps social hierarchy, as Guy Thuillier remarks about the Nivernais of old,[28] and that still remains true today.

From one social group to another, people do not consume the same products, do not prepare them in the same way, and do not ingest them by respecting the same code of table manners. Stated differences are often attributed to a *regional cultural history* with obscure particularities, when it is really a question of material necessities established little by little through tradition, a way of adapting to local agricultural production: when one harvests this fruit or that vegetable in abundance, one must learn to prepare and preserve it. Thus, as of the second half of the eighteenth century, junior-high-school menus presented a rather clear regional aspect: cabbage and sauerkraut in Alsace, white beans and chestnuts in Auch.[29] Similarly, if Alsatian cuisine made a specialty for itself out of sauerkraut and of recourse to turnips, it is because great quantities of these two vegetables were available, that were adapted to the region's soils and climate, and thus ways had been found to preserve them through curing and fermentation.[30]

In each regional cuisine, if a particular "way of operating" has been invented, whose significance or rationale has then subsequently been forgotten, it is generally in order to respond to a necessity, to a local law. In the past, foreign travelers admired the subtleties of southern China, whose cuisine is based on poorly refined rice, peppers, green vegetables, soy, and fish; but the elements in this composition were imposed by the situation: these products were at once the least costly and the most nutritious available in the area.[31] Often, a dish's flavor stems from the unique nature of a local product: prepared with Californian apples, *tarte Tatin* loses the delicate balance of acidity (due to *pommes de reinettes*) and caramelized sugar that gives it its charm, and Mexican *pollo negro* is unfeasible without (unsweetened) cocoa powder.

At present, people and things are transported from one continent to the other. People taste exotic cuisines, experience new flavors in strange combinations, bring back surprising recipes, and the cause and effect link between inexpensive available products and ordinary local cuisine is broken. Local conditions no longer impose the choice of a dish or its way of preparation, but rather the opposite. One decides to prepare a dish that comes from the Maghreb or the Caribbean and then one procures all the ingredients: here, some sweet potatoes, there, some lamb, mangoes, and green bananas. In the end, every regional cuisine loses its internal coherence, this money-saving spirit whose inventive ingenuity and rigor make up all its strength; in their place remains only an insignificant succession of "typical dishes" whose origin and function are longer understood, much like certain well-known picturesque sites that weary tourist groups pace through without being able to understand what they were for. In our cities, a thousand hired cooks fabricate simplified exotic dishes that are adapted to our prior habits and to the laws of the market. Thus, we happily eat shreds of local cultures that are disintegrating, or a material token of a past or future voyage; thus, the West is biting with gusto into the pale copies of these subtle and tender marvels established throughout the slow movement of centuries by generations of anonymous artists.

Other factors can be added to this multiplication of borrowings, born from a society of spectatorship and travel, that concur to uproot a regional cuisine from the tang of its soil [*terroir*]. There is this new phenomenon of regular provisioning throughout the year, with fruits and vegetables being imported out of season or having their ripening slowed by various processes, so that the limitations that once gave birth to certain regional practices now lose their weighty effect. Moreover, the horizon for women who cook has been remarkably expanded in the last one or two generations. In the past, one learned the recipes of one's mother or grandmother. Throughout the years, my mother carefully preserved the manuscript notebook of recipes that her mother had written down for her at the time of her wedding; neither my mother nor I found it useful to continue this when my own wedding day came around. Times had changed and my sources for culinary information were more often in the media (recipes written in women's magazines, or explained on radio or TV shows) or my friends. Each one of us thus turns toward the experience of those in her age group, abandoning in silence the model of preceding generations, with the vague feeling that traditional recipes from the past would be too complicated, too time-consuming to make, unsuitable to our new way of life, and that deep down they referred to an outdated social status for women. I believe that, in my generation, many of us thought that to the refusal of the former status was to be added the refusal of former ways of operating attached it. We also had to change our *cooking style.*

It is true that regional dishes often stem from a rural cuisine, requiring a long, slow, regular cooking that is difficult to ensure in today's urban life: neither people's schedules nor their cooking appliances (types of ovens and heat sources) are suitable for it. In addition, a wide range of regional cuisine involves festive meals and demands both rustic ingredients (wild game, for example), which are costly for city dwellers, and long preparation times. Adding it all together, all of these traits explain the clear deregionalization of culinary practices, as if an entire historical stratum were being erased from our memories. The social and professional mobility of the younger generations, as well as their territorial exogamy, intensify this effect: people choose their spouses less often than before from the tight circle of the neighborhood, cousinship, or the village. The young woman brings many modifications to her mother's cooking that she learned to love as a child, some borrowed from the different tradition of her mother-in-law and others from the advice of office colleagues, or as a memory from a recent vacation abroad.

In a strange way, however, we continue to valorize reference to a regional cuisine that each one of us would know well and from which each would draw her best recipes. Thus, the majority of Marie Ferrier's interviewees, and always the oldest ones, thought a priori at the beginning of the interviews that they were being consulted on the regional cuisine that they were supposed to be currently practicing, and they apologized in advance for having remained in general not very faithful to their regional customs. Of course, this presupposition depended on the usual way of taking into account—or rather, discounting—everyday practices. Our female interlocutors thought that ordinary cuisine and everyday practices could not merit the attention of a researcher "who had come especially from Paris," as one of them from the Midi said (Laurence).

Like the rest of ordinary life, ordinary cuisine constituted for all of them a zone of silence and shadow, hidden within the indefinitely repeated detail of common existence. As the interview progresses, one hears their voices becoming freer, livelier, and happier, liberated from the fear of "not having anything good to say" (Jeanne), or of "not being interesting" (Irène). One hears them rushing to say more, so happy to find "the words to explain," reestablishing quite naturally a dialogue between women in collusion, a complicity in the discourse marked by a multiplicity of phrases such as "you know how we do it, right?" and "you see," "you understand," "I don't need to explain that." It is a matter of pleasure found in breaking the law of public silence, a pleasure in recounting the very thing that concerns the succession of days and hours, a pleasure in recounting one's self, by thus authorizing oneself to be a woman, to take care of household tasks, and to find in them meaning, diversity, interest, and ingenuity. Each one of them was practicing unknowingly, yet all the while desiring to do so, the reversal of Monsieur Teste: "Along with the neglected creations produced every day by commerce, fear, boredom, or poverty, I thought I could make out certain *inner* masterpieces, lost amid the brilliance of published discoveries. It amused me to extinguish known history beneath the annals of anonymity."[32]

Cultures

If one leaves behind the diachronic dimension of histories stacked up in the evidence of culinary practices and tries instead to consider them in the fiction of a pure present, one is at first struck by their teeming diversity from one society to another, by the strange impression that there must be some reason for this and that the food customs from a given society in a given time are linked by internal coherences, invisible but real. Everything happens as if a specific alimentary diet expressed a world order, or rather, postulated in its very act the possible inscription of such an order on the world. With the four volumes of *Introduction to a Science of Mythology* (1964–71), and in the case of the American Indian, Lévi-Strauss has provided a dazzling example of this where one can find an analytic model of determined cuisines, of their choices, prejudices, and prohibitions, and of the explicit social discourse that, through the legendary and mythic mode, renders an account of them.

Lévi-Strauss is interested in all aspects of food: foodstuffs considered edible, ways of preparation, ways of consuming them (along with the rules for compatibility and incompatibility), digestive activities, and functions of elimination. He made the hypothesis that all of these elements, all these networks of diverse information, of minor differences and frank oppositions, have meaning, cuisine forming "a language in which each society codes messages which allow it to signify a part at least of what it is,"[33] that is, "a language through which that society unconsciously reveals its structure."[34] The coherence that inhabits these falsely incoherent appearances, and that does not acknowledge itself as such, unless in a discourse that is itself falsely explanatory, is situated on three levels: a logic of perceptible qualities, a logic of forms, a logic of propositions.[35]

The first involves the initial choice of foodstuffs accepted as edible, to be consumed in the form of *raw food*, or requiring preparation that transforms them into *cooked food*, or having lost through putrefaction their first quality of being edible (*rotten food*). The second logic involves both the authorized mixtures and the recognized ways of preparation, everything not being acceptable in a given social group. The third deals with table manners and the calendar of provisional prohibitions (which dishes at which period of life, or which food prepared in a certain way for initiation rites, etc.).

Each of these logic systems functions beginning with a large number of exclusions and a limited number of valid authorizations within a particular circle of compatibilities, such compatibility concerning not only mixtures of ingredients, but also the appropriateness of a certain food to social status or for a particular age. One wonders what is more surprising, the limitation theorem operating at each level, the inventiveness that presides at the formation of compatibility lists, or even the ruses of discourse that serve to render an account of them.

These are all things to be taken seriously, as the social discourse repeats more clearly perhaps on this point in societies with no written language: "The violation of food taboos, the failure to use table utensils or toilet accessories, the carrying out of forbidden actions, all these things pollute the world, ruin harvests, frighten away game and expose *others* to sickness and famine."[36] For the stakes are the respect for a world order, and good table manners or faithfulness to food prohibitions manifests a necessary "deference toward the world."[37] This anthropological reading of food practices seduces all the more in that it allows us to give meaning to prohibitions that cannot be explained, as in the case of Judaism and its minute prescriptions.

Taking up Mary Douglas's theses and completing them through a patient consideration of details, Francis Martens has explained the (quasi-)inexplicable recommendation of the Pentateuch, "you shall not boil a kid in its mother's milk" (Exodus 23:19), as linked to the prohibition of mother-son incest, particularly fearsome in a ritual universe where the maternal figure plays such a preponderant role.[38] If it is difficult to reveal the coherence of the system of prohibitions that gives meaning to each of them and the necessity that gives rise to the detail of alimentary prescriptions, it is because the efficiency of symbolic processes seems to guarantee their unconscious character, maintained by a defensive justification and a refusal to pursue the discussion further, as certain currently received explanations announce in their own way: "it has always been this way" or "in any case, it's healthier."[39]

To this kind of reading, one might substitute or juxtapose another, it too established at the synchronic level, for example, in the sociological mode. Bourdieu proposes a model of it in *Distinction* by treating preference behaviors (food, clothing, furniture, music, etc.), ordinarily referred to individual taste, but at the same time acknowledged as being linked to social stratification, if only in the judgments of common language: the lower class has "vulgar" tastes, while the bourgeois have "distinguished" tastes. Bourdieu's central thesis, already present in his earlier works, is clear:

> Thus, the spaces defined by preferences in food, clothing or cosmetics are organized according to the same fundamental structure, that of the social space determined by volume and composition of capital. Fully to construct the space of life-styles within which cultural practices are defined, one would first have to establish, for each class and class fraction, that is, for each of the configurations of capital, the generative formula of the habitus which retranslates the necessities and facilities characteristic of that class of (relatively) homogeneous conditions of existence into a particular life-style.[40]

In this hypothesis, which seems to receive a dogmatic value for Bourdieu, each individual is, at the starting point, assigned a class position, characterized by the amount of capital held (real or symbolic), and modifiable in certain proportions (which are limited) by the happy or unhappy result of strategies for social mobility. Everything happens as if society, without any history other than the temporal unfolding of individual trajectories, were immobile, locked in the vise of a stratification into classes and subclasses that are clear-cut and strictly hierarchical. In this overall rigid structure, the only individuals who can move are those prepared to adopt, for the most visible part of their way of life, the ways of operating in use in the social stratum of arrival. But this conformation remains superficial: that which involves clothing, furniture, or food, sectors of social life that are the object of "early learning" and are not taken up again within the educational mold, remains more narrowly and significantly tributary to the class habitus received at the start.[41]

Such an interpretation rests on the postulation of a term-for-term homology between social groups and ways of operating, each social group defined by its class position and its ways of operating stemming from a *necessary* circulation in "a set of ready-made choices, objectively instituted possibles."[42] The inventiveness of the group or the individual is thus challenged in advance, and nothing new that matters can occur, neither a broadening of taste by a chance discovery (an intriguing tune heard on the radio, a publicity poster done in a new eye-catching graphic style), nor a striking encounter with a new interlocutor who introduces you to other cultural practices, nor a personal desire for self-education in a certain aesthetic field. One might say, using the vocabulary of Karl Popper, that Bourdieu's theory is irrefutable because it is not "falsifiable": no "novel" fact can appear that cannot be interpreted within his theory and that can shake its structure.

From Bourdieu's perspective, food practices are just as immobile as others, if not more so, because they are always linked to earliest childhood, to the maternal world.[43] Moreover, the nature of products used seems to him less important than the way of treating them and especially of consuming them, if one includes in their consumption ways of serving, presenting, offering, and sharing:[44] even if the hypothesis is debatable, because a cuisine's quality depends essentially on the quality of those products used and their meticulous choice, it inspires in Bourdieu a keen attention to different styles of table manners from which he pulls out some superb anthological passages on the "working-class meal," a place of "plain eating," whereas with the bourgeoisie, everything works toward eating "with all due form."[45] On the other hand, in spite of its scope, *Distinction* remains silent on ways of doing-cooking: as is often the case with Bourdieu, feminine activities are a place of silence or disinterest that his analysis does not trouble itself to take into account.

Memories

What does one eat? It seems obvious that one eats what one can "get" or what one likes—a proposition full of false clarity and loaded with erroneous simplicity. What one "can" here goes back to what is available for supplies, what is affordable in terms of price, what can be assimilated through digestion, what is authorized by the culture, and what is valorized by the social organization. What one "likes" is just as confusing, linked as it is to the multiple game of likes and dislikes and founded in childhood habits, which are either magnified by memory or counterbalanced by the adult will to be rid of them. "In general, we eat what our mother taught us to eat—or what our wife's mother taught her to eat. We like what she liked, sweet or salty, morning jam or cereal, coffee or tea, olive oil if one is from Provence, *gaffelbitter* if one is Scandinavian," so that "it is more indicative to believe that we eat our most reassuring memories, seasoned with tenderness and ritual, which marked our childhood."[46]

Eating, in fact, serves not only to maintain the biological machinery of the body, but to make concrete one of the specific modes of relation between a person and the world, thus forming one of the fundamental landmarks in space-time. One can see it well among elderly people put into a nursing home, whose complaint obstinately demands the respect of their former food habits. Thus, Amélie, from the Jura, who expected to find the lard she knew from her childhood and the profusion of green vegetables from her rural past, says: "The way we are fed here, we cannot think about . . . , about being well, about being, no, well, no . . . In the country, we only eat green vegetables, in other words: cabbages, lettuce, spinach, cooked lettuce, you know, everything from leeks to asparagus."[47]

Likewise, when political circumstances or the economic situation forces one into exile, what remains the longest as a reference to the culture of origin concerns food, if not for daily meals, at least for festive times—it is a way of inscribing in the withdrawal of the self a sense of belonging to a former land [*terroir*]. It is a multisecular experience, easily verifiable, that has been reproduced by the Maghreb Jews newly arrived in France at the end of the wars for independence: "We do 'our own style' of cooking, 'our' cuisine, the way we used to do 'over there,' in order to remember Algeria and the time before we left. Food thus becomes a veritable discourse of the past and a nostalgic narrative about the country, the region, the city, or the village where one was born."[48] Reserved for the day of the Sabbath and for big events, whether liturgical or stemming from family history (birth, marriage, etc.), traditional food with its meticulous rites of composition (a certain dish for Passover or one for circumcision) and preparation becomes the support and the "narrative of difference, inscribed in the rupture between the alimentary time of the 'self' and the alimentary time of the other."[49]

But we also eat our social representations of health, what we assume to be "good for us." In the study by Claudine Herzlich, the most often mentioned hygiene practice necessary to the maintenance of good health is diet.[50] In the study by INSERM, the concern over a "healthy" and "hygienic" diet increases with the standard of living, the degree of education, and the rate of urbanization of the community in which one lives.[51] In addition, it should be pointed out that these representations depend on social rank or, as Bourdieu rightly states, that there are the "paradoxes of the taste of necessity": popular tastes, by economic necessity and by habit, focus on the "foods that are simultaneously most 'filling' and most economical" because of "the necessity of reproducing labour power at the lowest cost."[52] Thus, there most often exists a close relation between what a family can acquire for ordinary food, what it begins to like, and what it supposes to be beneficial to one's health.

The evolution of the words *diet* and *dietetics* is revealing of the role accorded to the type of food needed to maintain good health. In Greek, *diaita* generally designates the "lifestyle" and, in particular, one that is "prescribed by the doctor"; for Hippocrates, *diaitētikē* is the "science of hygienic prescriptions," a meaning that the word still maintained in French during the Renaissance: "the second part of medicine is called dietetics, which aids the sick through good hygiene in life," says Ambroise Paré.[53] But, in contemporary French, *diète* means the suppression of all solid food and dietetics involves the study and organization of a diet, as if what is essential for good hygiene in life were defined only by the food recommended.

Every food practice directly depends on a network of impulses (likes and dislikes) with respect to smells, colors, and forms, as well as to consistency types; this geography is as strongly culturalized as the representations of health and good table manners and thus is just as historicized. In the long term, of all these exclusions and choices, the food that is reserved, authorized, and preferred is the place of a silent piling up of an entire stratification of orders and counterorders that stem at the same time from an ethnohistory, a biology, a climatology, and a regional economy, from a cultural invention and a personal experience. Its choice depends on an addition of positive and negative factors, themselves dependent on objective determinations of time and space, on the creative diversity of human groups and individuals, on the indecipherable contingency of individual microhistories. Citing the example of America entering into European modernity in order to arouse there "these movements of men, plants, and foods," Fernand Braudel dreamed of "the simultaneous history of these alimentary associations, slow to join together and then to detach from one another, . . . an assemblage to be seized in its parts and its duration, as in its relations with other assemblages."[54]

The inventory of ingredients, of their associations and of their transformations into diverse preparations, provides the elements for an immense *multientry combinatory set* whose univocal inventory should be abandoned for a hundred reasons: animal and vegetable species travel and vary in quality according to their conditions of production (being raised on an industrial or a small scale, types of fodder, the nature of the land or available sunlight, the choice of seed varieties or fertilizers, etc.); flavors are not quantifiable and are distinguished with difficulty, as Jean Anthelme Brillat-Savarin, an expert on the matter, knew: "given the fact that there exists an indefinite series of simple tastes which can change according to the number and variety of their combinations, we should need a whole new language to describe all these effects, and mountains of folio foolscap to define them, and unknown numerical figures for their classification."[55]

All the pleasures of the mouth are twice submitted to the laws of *orality*: as much by absorbing food (the pleasure of swallowing) as by support of a profuse linguistic activity (the pleasure of speaking), which describes, names, distinguishes, nuances, compares, makes iridescent, and doubles. An infant puts everything he or she can grab hold of into his or her mouth, randomly in the exploration of surrounding space, but this is not only by a compulsive desire to incorporate everything: as Michel Tournier rightly recalled, an infant's mouth serves as a second touch organ, allowing him or her to "touch more," to feel things, to experience the coarseness of matter, to know its grain intimately.[56] Much later, in the adult, through the impenetrable game of food behaviors and their minuscule variations from person to person, histories (cultural, social, and familial) and memories superimpose themselves. Together, they inspire habits, customs, and preferences, tributaries of mentalities and sensibilities, marked also by a necessary *inscription in temporality* that intervenes at different levels.

Like cultures, social groups do not live in immobility and their tastes do not remain unchanging. A certain dish valued at a certain period by a certain milieu will later be brushed aside as "too crude," "unrefined," or "heavy." For food, the common custom is also reliant on fashion, as is the choice of clothing or ideas in vogue. Thus, rice figured in the meals of "high style" during the better part of the nineteenth century; in 1870, it was still served more often as a sweetened dessert than as a savory dish to accompany meat; as for cheese, so closely associated today with the image of French customs, it hardly ever appeared on bourgeois tables in the nineteenth century because it had the connotation of a relationship to the land.[57]

Time still imposes the cycle of seasons that has apricots follow strawberries and endives follow butter beans; it requires agreeable and regular permutations whose succession gives rhythm to the months of the year, even if today, thanks to preservation techniques and diversification of supplies, they are less restraining than in the past. Market stalls continue to transform themselves from week to week: the Périgord strawberry gives way to Beurré Hardy pears, the Belle de Boskoop apple appears next to Hamburg muscat grape, and soon comes the return of the unforgettable rennet apple [Reine des reinettes]. With small strokes, a fantasy-like geography of colors, smells, and shapes is drawn, announced in a loud voice by the vendors who, in a firm tone, all hawk their excellent wares, guaranteed by the semantic magic of their attachment to unknown places, whose repetition year after year becomes familiar to you; a silent complicity is woven between you and them, as between a vendor and his potential client, for whom he reactualizes a ritualized repertoire with the same conviction every year; for example, in quince season, one of them proclaims: "To find quinces, ladies, step right this way,"[58] while one of his associates emphasizes with an equivocal sweetness, "Come and get me, come and pick me, I am the prettiest, the sweetest in the market," indicating his marvelous muscat grapes with an inviting gesture.

Linked to the age scale, time still manages to modify, at different stages of life, both biological needs and food preferences, the great old-timer quite naturally rediscovering childhood tastes, dairy products, sweet desserts, pureed vegetable soup, and unctuous fruit compotes. But there is also the time of the calendar year, the scansions of the calendar with the alternation of workdays and weekends, then the arrival of liturgical holidays whose culinary rites bravely survive the erosion of religious practices, and finally family celebrations (birthdays, baptisms, marriages, etc.). Thus, the signs of real time and those of biological, psychological, familial, and social time superimpose themselves, by completing or restricting themselves, on the choice of dishes and the organization of meals.

Certain of these traits have an inexplicably long life. Thus, in the Paris region, which for the most part has become estranged from Catholic practices, Friday remains the day of highest fish consumption.[59] Is it the habit of housewives that is determinant, or community inertia, or the accrued ease of fresh fish supplies on that day, or perhaps the unconscious need to mark the passing of the week with a reference point before the return of the pleasures constituted by the free time of the weekend? If traditional religious prohibitions are erased, new ritualizations come forward to take their place, which come from the marketing sphere, such as "the nouveau Beaujolais has arrived," or "macrobiotic" diets, whether vegetarian or vegan, whose adepts voluntarily impose on themselves a system of exclusions and strict precepts, while others intend to provide themselves only with products harvested from "organic farming" methods (in theory, those that do not use fertilizers or pesticides and that plant out in the open), supposedly less dangerous to one's health than the products of an intensive agriculture eager for high yields.

Split between fear and memory, inhabited by contradictory desires, the heart and mind also vacillate between "what is good" (that is, my personal taste) and "what is good for my health" (that is, what is in my best interests). We thus sail between the Lake of Fondness and the Ocean of Reason, between the adages of tradition and the advice of modern dietics. One insinuates that "nothing is better than Grandma Marie's slow-simmered meals or Aunt Adèle's huge homemade cakes; the other warns that "it's time to learn how to eat healthy,"[60] "one pound too much means getting one year older"[61]; and whereas Bourdieu still judges food practices to be outside of educational discourse, the National Committee on Health Education offers to teachers, as an early learning activity, a pedagogical package called *Eat Right* [*Mangez juste*] that allows schoolchildren to learn, in a game format, how to organize well-balanced meals and how to use various food products.[62] O unfair fight between greediness and prescriptiveness, of the reasonable against the desirable!

These are memories stubbornly faithful to the marvelous treasure of childhood flavors. The almond cakes, for example, about which my father, an old man already suffering, used to repeat to me the tasty secret that disappeared with his beloved grandmother, who passed away at the beginning of the century, before he was seven. And those *œufs à la neige* that a friend who is getting on in years saw me order in a restaurant, not allowing himself to do so because this dessert held for him the taste of his first school successes, which had been rewarded with this very dish at his family's table. Flavors of lost moments of happiness, sweet flavors of time gone by: "This glass of pale, cool, dry wine marshals my entire life in the Champagne. People may think I am drinking: I am remembering…"[63] This wine, I recognize it, even if it was the product of a whole other soil [*terroir*]; it is the one that my grandfather, a solitary and lofty walker, used to put in a stream to cool, upon coming out of the woods, for the picnic that crowned the long silent walk that he mysteriously knew how to make into an unforgettable festival.

Already destined to the anonymity of death, Gabriel spends his last days in a nursing home and his only memories involve the food prepared by his mother: "I think about her often, my mother, I think about her quite often, she was a nice person. My brothers and sisters, I think they were not unhappy with her, but I was always well received, even being married. When she invited us over, she used to make some nice little meals"; or the meal provided by his grandmother: "Every Sunday, Grandma prepared chocolate soup, and then we had a meal of ham omelettes, salad, butter, and potted pork [*rillettes*]; at the end of the meal, just about everything was on the table."[64] It is as if talking about these meals from the past that were offered and shared were his only way, meager and modest, to repeat the sweetness of the past and the tenderness of well-loved faces.

Bodies

In food behaviors, so deeply inserted into everyday life that they appear overly simple, two relational modes, which begin to define and structure themselves as of the first moment of life, are actualized, entangled, and act against each other. One involves the first relationship with the nourishing mother, or whoever takes her place; the other designates the relationship that the individual fosters with his or her own body as a living body, subject to being worn away by time, destined to die, and as a sexualized body, destined to take either a feminine or a masculine form.

A child is nourished by its mother and receives from her hand what she has prepared for its benefit; later on, she will consult the child on his or her preferences, but will always consider, as a last resort, that she knows better what is "good for the child." Many family meals are a forum for a fierce power struggle, the power of the mother and the father over the body of the child, who is forced to "finish his or her plate" and to "eat all the meat if he or she wants to have dessert."

It is true that there is no natural wisdom in humans, young or old, and that if only a child's preferences were entertained, the result would often be an unbalanced diet, rich in sweets or starches, poor in animal proteins and fresh vegetables, as the interview with Élisabeth in our study confirms: she reports the disagreements observed a thousand times between the cafeteria staff of her high school who demand menus adapted to children's tastes (rice, pasta, potatoes every day) and the supply director who feels obligated to follow the dietary directives received from the Éducation Nationale and insists on introducing cooked vegetable dishes, fish pâté, and so on, which the children, especially before the ages of eleven or twelve, refuse to eat.

The mother insists, forcing the child to eat, and thus reiterates that the child's body is still hers: "Mother was always concerned that we should eat all the dinner she gave us. I often didn't want it. She would persist in trying to shovel it in. 'Just one more spoonful, one for uncle, two for auntie. Look at all the nice gravy and the greens that Mummy cooked. Make you grow big and strong.'"[65] The child insists on refusing, looking first of all to shield his or her body from maternal law, divining in an obscure sort of way that he or she possesses a major trump card, that, by refusing, he or she can hold the mother in his or her power, resist her, worry her, "kill her with grief, with worry," as is sometimes said by the plaintive cook whose food is not appreciated.

It is a body-to-body struggle that is engaged by small spoonfuls and big words around the family dinner table: the child wants to be free immediately and will grow up later; the mother asks him or her to eat first, that is, to obey now in order to be big, strong, and free later on, but the child becomes impatient and cannot wait. He or she thus invents a thousand ruses—he or she is never hungry at home, but devours anything and everything when out. Soon he or she discovers other sneaky kinds of vengeance, speaks highly of other people's food, and wounds the mother's exclusive affection:

> Once when Father took us out we had Welsh Rarebit, cheese on toast, in a teashop. Enthusiastically I told Mother about this delicious food that she didn't make. . . . Mother was very cross. I couldn't understand why or how it was. I felt 'naughty,' ashamed. Now I see how Mother sensed our eating other people's food as a betrayal of herself.[66]

But this conflict is neither general nor continuous. Everything depends on how the mother experiences the refusal, on her capacity to yield partially to the child's demands, or on her stubborn determination to engage the entire weight of her authority in the battle. Geneviève, speaking of her ten-year-old son, says: "He doesn't like anything. He would prefer me to make kebabs, or fries, or a pizza every day. *He doesn't like anything*, that's the way he is, just like his father" (the parents are separated). "With him, everything revolves around ham and cheese, eggs, mashed potatoes, French fries, noodles, spaghetti, hamburgers, roast chicken, and then even that . . . You see, he just revolves around these ten particular things." Geneviève evokes her past efforts, useless, unrecognized, and it is the complaint of a rejected offer of love:

> When he was little, I made an effort, you know, to vary his meals, to never give him the same thing twice. I made imaginative efforts: I gave him some green beans with half a potato and half a carrot, and I mixed it up with some chicken. I made him his meals, but I would get so upset—he didn't want anything! I made so much effort without results that I let go of everything, well, I abandoned many things.

Her voice lowers on this last sentence as if to add: "He abandoned me, he didn't love me—just like his father."

Often, if the mother is happy, reassured by the affection of those around her, the meal will be a marvelous festive moment for the baby, the occasion for an intense exchange of laughter, caresses, inarticulate speech, and a thousand signs addressed to the mother to get her attention, to attract her looks, to make her the child's own. Much later, still walking clumsily, the child will come to hide electively in the kitchen or under the table, playing at her mother's feet, rummaging among the treasure of the cupboards, licking the mixing bowl, becoming intoxicated by the smell of melting chocolate or the sticky scents that rise from the fruit preserve pan.

The child looks, observing the mother's movements, admiring the strength of kneading hands; the mystery of the sourdough ball that rises in its glass container is fascinating; he or she silently appreciates the cleverness of the small knife that nimbly slices off the extra pie dough from the rim of the pie pan; he or she learns to accomplish simple tasks (cracking open nuts without smashing them, pitting apricots, peeling apples); he or she learns the names of dishes and utensils, to differentiate action verbs or degrees of doneness. In the kitchen, the child does an essential part of his or her sensory and motor apprenticeship: "To keep a child out of the kitchen," says Bachelard, "is to condemn him to an exile that distances him from dreams he will never know. The dreamlike qualities of foods are activated by observing their preparation.... Happy is the man who, as a young child, 'hung around' the woman of the house."[67]

The kitchen can be the blessed place of a sweet intimacy, of rambling chatter pursued without having to be spelled out with the mother who pirouettes from the table to the sink, her hands busy but her mind available and her speech quick to explain, discuss, or comfort. Later, as an artist in his or her own kitchen or a visitor in someone else's, the adult sighs: "But I receive so much pleasure going into the kitchen. Every time, I feel like I'm going back to my childhood."[68] Sometimes the call of the past is so strong that one decorates one's kitchen in an old-fashioned style or one chooses to install an appliance from the past:

> As of yesterday, I have a stove, one that you heat up, one where you have to light a fire, a real one that gets your hands dirty, that burns, and that I have to tame, one that requires some time. I have dreamed about this stove for a long time; I like to make a fire in the morning, the wee small hours, and then at night, when it gets colder, I like to watch over it.... I just find a forgotten happiness in it, a childhood memory. And what if our entire life was just a search for these moments of happiness? What if we passed them by unnoticed? I feel good, my hands, my feet, and my heart are warm...[69]

The relationship that one maintains with one's own body and with others is read, translated into visible acts, across the interest and care given to meals, in the range of pleasures that are authorized or the restrictions that are imposed. Studying the theme of food among adolescents and young adults, *Le Monde* concluded that these new generations, eager to try drugs or alcohol, showed little interest in food itself. The majority of them answered that, yes, they voluntarily skipped one meal if not two in a row, to save time and money, wanting to save themselves for other leisure activities, and that they hated the slowness of the family meal and hardly ever put aside time for an occasional preparation of a more elaborate meal to share with friends. This same study recalled other information of the same kind: in 1975, in the university cafeteria at Rennes, out of a thousand students observed, more than a third dispatched their meal in less than twenty-five minutes; in Paris, in a large Social Security dining hall of which half the two thousand daily diners were young adults, the duration of the meal was on average twenty minutes.[70] We should not, however, accord an absolute value to these numerical figures; in France, a collective dining hall is rarely a nice place that is sound-proofed, well ventilated, and tastefully decorated, and so people frequent it only out of necessity and only spend the least amount of time possible there.

Perhaps one must be reconciled with one's body in order to take the trouble to nourish it appropriately, or one has to have already known the fullness of a lasting love tie in order to find pleasure in preparing a meal destined for others. One can analyze these issues by posing them within the quadrilateral of their excesses, which runs from bulimia to obesity, and then to the weight-loss cure, before ending up with anorexia nervosa. If I make reference here to these extreme behaviors, it is because they seem to intensify and take to the extreme, to theatricalize and reveal what, at other moments, insidiously tempts us all and takes shape in ourselves in a minor way. It is a kind of internal distress, a threatening possibility between the death-wish excess of eating or drinking too much with no limitation and the just as excessive renunciation of eating and drinking, symmetrical behaviors through which the individual proclaims her hate for her own body and the failure to ensure its autonomous survival.

The first of these excesses, *bulimia*, continually pushes the person who suffers from it toward food, any food, no matter what, and in the largest quantity possible. It is not a question of choosing, of simmering some nice little gourmet meal, but of finding something as quickly as possible to swallow, in order to stuff oneself, to fill one's body, to fill its emptiness, to make it swell, to stretch it, to deform it, to take away its recognizable form.

I have to eat, eat, very substantial things, bread, mashed potatoes diluted with water, even flour... with my fingers so I can eat faster... until it starts to hurt. I am bloated, swollen everywhere, I have a stomach like a woman who is five months pregnant; I can't walk anymore because it pushes on my stomach. When I look at myself in the mirror, I say to myself: it's not possible, it's not me. Someone has changed me. I stop when I truly can go no further.[71]

After such a force-feeding session, often the young girl (a category from which the majority of bulimia sufferers come) forces herself to vomit, and then, feeling relieved, begins the same process again, as if she felt forced to repeat a stereotyped sequence of compulsive acts. As with anorexia, but in a less transparent way, a battle to the death is engaged with her own body: the individual cannot spare the body and crams it with food the way a boxer pummels his adversary with punches. The body becomes the "place of mortal combat," with the alternation of periods where, without falling into anorexia as such, one starves the body in order to prevent it from taking on a feminine form, to not change into a woman like one's mother, to not look like her, then one wolfs down food with all speed, as if the body were nothing more than a big bag with undifferentiated regions, a bottomless waterskin to be urgently refilled, as if to escape through this irrational violence from the law, from the previous glance of the mother who said what was reasonable, who chose and prepared the child's meal, and measured out her share. "Bulimia thus masks a conflict that concerns gender." It appears after puberty when the young girl, trapped within the family constellation and in an overinvested relationship with her mother, can neither break this privileged tie to render herself "separate," autonomous, nor identify herself as a sexually defined body in order to experience the impulses that are linked to it.[72]

Obesity is distinguished from bulimia in that the excess weight is the object of constant care, is maintained by regular overeating—even though it seems to depend, in certain cases, on metabolic disturbances that are still poorly understood. The classic obese person likes to eat and eat well, in quality as well as quantity; he or she often has a preference for sweets and desserts.[73] He or she appears to dream of a return to young childhood, to the trembling happiness of first steps risked under the vigilant gaze of a protective mother, to the time of first successes rewarded with a kiss and a small treat. He or she wants to avoid blows, quirks of fate, life's hardships, both big and small, and thus constructs a symbolic shell, a plump and fat enclosure that increases the distance between fragile self and the aggression of others; in his or her own way, he or she seeks to soften the blows, to diminish the risks. In industrialized countries, as the standard of living rises, one sees the number of obese people increase: this is not because more money becomes available to buy more food, but because the social system increases at once the demand for security by the citizen and the pressure exerted by a hundred constraints, hence an accrued anguish over meeting the insidious and menacing norm requirements. With their hypertrophied body, with goodwill that runs from diet to relapse, obese people ask the people around them, and their doctor, to "listen to them," to answer first their "demand to be taken care of globally, to protect them from the pain of everyday living.[74]

Already obese or only "a little plump," "stout," "well padded," "full-figured," as popular language has it, our contemporary will quickly become easy prey to misleading temptations and false promises offered with a lot of advertising through innumerable *weight-loss plans* as diverse as they are ineffective. Some magic procedures promise—for money, of course—marvelous results, effortlessly obtained thanks to a miracle cure, with no diets, with no difficulty, or thanks to the imposition of a selective fast, both severe and dangerous, pushed to absurdity.[75] In this rapidly expanding market, one can find a gold mine; charlatans and con artists, sometimes with medical degrees, do not hesitate to get involved, and reasonable and honest counterinformation has difficulty opposing them.[76] In truth, one is stupefied by the credulity that sensible people display in this field. One can see here the sign of an emotional overinvestment for which food is the site, so that food behaviors find themselves, naturally as it were, outside the field of the rational or even of the reasonable.

The role of fashion and of collective representations simply adds to the weight of other factors: the general cult of youth and beauty, the fright inspired by old age and death, the imposition of models of beauty to which only a small number of people can conform without difficulty, the contradiction between the celebrated ideal of beauty (muscled thinness) and the reality of lifestyles (sedentary process, comfort, absence of physical exercise, disdain for manual labor)—all this prevents the great number of people from feeling at ease with their body and accepting its imperfect image. Hence, a puerile belief in the idea that their *ennui de vivre* or their frustration is essentially caused by a few too many pounds. Accustomed by received education and by all social discourse to believing that their "beauty capital," according to magazine and advertising vocabulary, constitutes their entire stock of assets, women overinvest more than others in the narcissistic image of their bodies: they have thus provided the most sensitive public for questions of appearance and the most credulous in matters of weight-loss plans or aging cures. At present, advertising and social stereotypes are attempting to persuade men too of the need to look after their appearance. Drifting from alimentary aberration to the abuse of diuretics and laxatives, with the obsession of "losing weight," too many people often forfeit their health, and always their money. In truth, food behaviors and their accessories constitute one of the primary markets for money and profit in our society.

As for *anorexia nervosa*, this voluntary diet so severe that it can end up in death through malnutrition, it is generally not the outcome of a prolonged weight-loss plan. This refusal to eat most often appears amongst teenage girls between fifteen and twenty; however, certain similar transitory behaviors can already manifest themselves in a nursing baby or a young child. For teenage girls, it involves a type of sadistic relationship with their own body, at once hated at the moment of its transformation into a sexually defined body and experienced as a fantasy-like representation of a "body-tube" to be continually emptied of all contents, either by induced vomiting or excessive use of laxatives. The anorexic tries desperately to empty the same body that the bulimic vainly tries to completely fill up. A self-starver, thus lightened, hyperactive, and triumphant, the anorexic defies those around her and common law; she deifies her self by placing her body outside this law and, through food and sleep deprivation, obtains a masochistic pleasure from this triumphant march toward death. It is a question of hatred and death every inch of the way in this struggle, which is confirmed by the suicide attempts that occur when the anorexic is force-fed in the setting of a hospital.[77]

The last element whose importance in food behaviors I would like to point out, or rather, the aspect that plays a fundamental role, is of course their intimate proximity, both corporally and emotionally, to love practices. Let us start with this obvious concrete fact: we eat with our mouth, a corporal orifice whose parts (lips, tongue, teeth, mucous membranes) and functions (tasting, touching, licking, caressing, salivating, chewing, swallowing) intervene par excellence in a love relationship. One acts to nourish one's body, to develop it, build it, or transform it according to one's image and desire: one defines one's own alimentary diet to embellish, to purify, to prepare one's self to be pleasing; one chooses a companion's food to conform his body to our desire for it, to render it stronger, softer, or fatter, tender or well muscled. By cooking, one "prepares for oneself" a partner cooked "just right" and, when this partner comes home at night, one tells him with false innocence: "I (lovingly) made you some chicken, just the way you like it, with grapes and apples." O seductive maneuvers that obtain their objective: the flesh becomes tender; the title of a seventies Brazilian movie formulates this secular experience marvelously: *Como era gostoso o meu Francês*, yes, how good he tasted and how nicely he let himself be tenderly devoured.

Love is inhabited by a devouring fantasy, by a cannibalistic assimilation of the other by oneself, a nostalgia for an impossible, identifying fusion. "Loving another, desiring him or her, involves gorging oneself and at the same time assuaging one's hunger, a symbolic hunger to which real or biological hunger has given up its seat."[78] Everyday common language is not wrong when it says about a plan for seduction that he (or she) is going to "make himself (herself) up" just like one "makes up" a nice steak with vegetables au jus. The love exchange at times transforms the partner into a delectable morsel, decks him or her out with pet names taken from culinary vocabulary ("my honey bun," "my little lamb," "my little chickadee"), devours him or her "with a glance, with caresses, with kisses." The vow of separated lovers remains in the same vein: "I miss you, I'm hungry for you, I could just eat you all up."

Lévi-Strauss refers to an African myth where doing-cooking is compared to making love, with a word-for-word correspondence in which "the hearthstones are the posteriors; the cooking pot is the vagina; the pot ladle is the penis."[79] Without sinking down into this literalism, one might consider that the table and the bed often seem to serve a common purpose. Picnics, luncheons on the grass, accentuate the resemblance. By representing the peak of such a luncheon, Édouard Manet stirred up the prudish indignation of the Second Empire bourgeois, but he only foregrounded an image of what is well known: the luncheon on the grass, with its softly stretched-out bodies that allow themselves to be seen under the seductive veil of clothes, with its guests who allow themselves double entendres that would be unacceptable in an austere dining room, this meal encourages one, through the rural sweetness of its absence of decorum, to consider the possibility of another kind of intimacy. It is already rather cleverly lascivious — it speaks to the guests of something else, another proximity, another feast.

Customs are strict around a table. Everyone must hide the lower half of his or her body under the table or the fringes of the tablecloth. Only one's bust is presented to onlookers, held vertically, with both wrists lightly resting on either side of the plate. As opposed to British etiquette, the French code of good manners finds any hand hidden under the table, and thus concealed from the vigilant glance of those around, to be inappropriate; one quickly suspects the worst of intentions, perhaps because the tablecloth masks it from view, whereas in England the table is often set with individual place mats that do not extend beyond the table itself and thus the edges of and the space below the table are clearly visible. In France, the essential visible fields at the table are the faces of one's neighbors, their glance that flits from place to place or from dish to dish, calculating what will remain when the platter finally reaches them, and their ever-present mouth, always ready to open in order to speak, eat, or laugh. The table first and foremost celebrates the mouth as the center of the ceremony; it is much more interested in the mouth itself than in the instruments that are indispensable in actualizing the convivial rite, meaning the fork and spoon that are necessary for carrying food to the mouth. But language clearly marks off the hierarchy of values: the phrase "to wave a mean fork" manifests a hearty appetite, a pleasant and contagious drive to eat with gusto; "to have a refined palate" designates the superior discernment available to connoisseurs in matters of fine cuisine.

The table is a social machinery as complicated as it is effective: it makes one talk, one "lays everything on the table" to confess what one wanted to keep quiet, one gets "grilled" by a skillful neighbor, one yields to a momentary excitement, to a fit of vanity, to the velvet smoothness of a red wine, and one hears oneself tell all about what one had sworn the day before to hide from everyone. There is nothing quite like a fine dinner, face to face, to help promote money matters and those of the heart. One admires the splendor of a complexion enlivened by the pleasure of good food, the brilliancy of a glance enhanced by candlelight. One maintains the conversation, one talks, nicely and caustically, and underneath this explicit discourse, one communicates without having to spell it all out: "I like you, you are tempting. Maybe one day, if you wanted to . . ." The tablecloth is also, already, the bedsheet; its wine or fruit stains make one think of other marks left behind.[80] The accentuated smell of warm food, the proximity of your guest's body, and his or her perfume wake up the sense of smell, stimulate its perceptions and associations, and make one imagine other seductive smells, secret scents of a naked body, finally becoming up close and personal. The guest dreams, muses, and is already hoping. He turns to his table companion, slips her a funny remark, fixes her a moment longer with his glance, letting her divine the silent compliment that rules of discretion and seemliness still forbid him to pronounce, and then he turns to Mrs. So-and-so to thank her for the melt-in-your-mouth *filet en brioche* and compliments Mr. So-and-so for the perfect match between the *filet* and his Saint-Émilion 1976. The host replies, delighted yet modest: "A minor estate, my dear friend, but a great year." The table is a place of pleasure; this is an ancient discovery, but it holds on to its truth and its secret, because eating is always much more than just eating.

Chapter 12
Gesture Sequences

I am certain that I was able to interpret *Jeanne Dielman* in this way only because it was filmed by a woman who liked the gestures I made. Not my acting but all these gestures: washing the bathtub, knitting, doing the dishes...I knew she loved them....One would have to talk about the compassion of one woman for another who she could have been and yet who she succeeded in not being....One felt that this was [for Chantal Akerman] the world of her childhood, which she did not actually want for herself, but that she looked upon with such respect...And I think that it remains in the memory of all children, little boys as well as little girls. The little boys also loved these loving gestures, those that their mother made.[1]

How can one find the right words, words that are rather simple, ordinary, and precise, to recount these sequences of gestures, bound together over and over again, that weave the indeterminate cloth of culinary practices within the intimacy of kitchens? How can one choose words that are true, natural, and vibrant enough to make felt the weight of the body, the joyfulness or weariness, the tenderness or irritation that takes hold of you in the face of this continually repeated task where the better the result (a stuffed chicken, a pear tart), the faster it is devoured, so that before the meal is completely over, one already has to think about the next.

A succession of gestures and steps, repeated and required. *Inside*: to the kitchen to prepare; from the kitchen to the dining room to serve and eat, getting up constantly to run and check the things on the grill or to fetch the mustard missing from the table; from the dining room to the kitchen to clear away the dishes; once again in the kitchen to wash and put things away. *Outside*: from the house to the market, to the grocery store, the bakery, the butcher shop, the wine shop; then back to the house, arms full of shopping bags. On the way, you pass a young woman even more heavily laden than you and who mumbles to no one in particular: "I'm just the family packhorse. All I do is carry, carry, carry." *Inside*: to the kitchen to empty the bags; put away the groceries; wrap up the things to be put in the refrigerator; note down the expenses, check the change and the receipts. Sit down, finally. Today, tomorrow, and the day after, repeat the same chain of events, engage in the same litany of questions: What's left for tonight? How many people will there be? And what about lunch tomorrow?

> The hardest thing for me is *knowing what to do*! It's not so much in the execution. . . . In fact, the big problem for me is always having to know what to eat. And that just kills me! It's something that Paul, for example, does not understand, the need to *always think about it*. All you can do is think about it. I would like to be able to not think about this place, you know, to be able to do something else. As dinnertime approaches—what are we gonna eat? It's traditionally that way, every day. (Colette)

But the word *gesture* here is misleading; one would have to find a term that could include the movements of the body as well as those of the mind. "Cooking is not complicated—you have to know how to organize yourself and to have a good memory and a little taste. Quite simply, I learned to cook by doing," according to Old Mother Brazier.[2] Yes, in cooking the activity is just as *mental* as it is manual; all the resources of intelligence and memory are thus mobilized. One has to organize, decide, and anticipate. One must memorize, adapt, modify, invent, combine, and take into consideration Aunt Germaine's likes and little François's dislikes, satisfy the prescriptions for Catherine's temporary diet, and vary the menus at the risk of having the whole family cry out in indignation with the ease of those who benefit from the fruit of other people's labor: "'Cauliflower *again*! We just had it on Monday and on the Friday before, too! I don't want anymore! I don't like it!' Me neither, but how can one make them understand that it is the only affordable fresh vegetable available right now? They will arrogantly respond: 'You'll just have to figure somethin' out!'"

In cooking, one always has to *calculate*, both time and money, not go beyond the budget, not overestimate one's own work speed, not make the schoolboy late. One has to *evaluate* in the twinkling of an eye what will be the most cost-effective in terms of price, preparation, and flavor. One has to know how to *improvise* with panache, know what to do when fresh milk "turns" on the stove, when meat, taken out of the package and trimmed of fat, reveals itself to be not enough to feed four guests, or when Mathieu brings a little friend to dinner unannounced and one has to make the leftover stew "go a little farther." One has to *remember* that the Guys already had cabbage *à la saucisse de Morteau* the last time they came to visit and that Béatrice cannot stand chocolate cake, or that the fishmonger, the only one in the neighborhood, will be closed all week, even though he is usually open. With all these details quickly reviewed, the game of exclusion, impossibilities (from lack of time, money, or supplies), and preferences must end in the proposal of a solution to be quickly realized because one has to come up with a menu for tonight, for example, roast beef with oven-baked potatoes. But one also has to choose a wine to *match* and not plan on a dessert made with cream if the proposed appetizer is cornets with béchamel or if one of the guests cannot stand dairy products.

Doing-cooking thus rests atop a complex montage of circumstances and objective data, where necessities and liberties overlap, a confused and constantly changing mixture through which tactics are invented, trajectories are carved out, and ways of operating are individualized. Every cook has her repertoire, her grand operatic arias for extraordinary circumstances and her little ditties for a more familial public, her prejudices and limits, preferences and routine, dreams and phobias. To the extent that experience is acquired, style affirms itself, taste distinguishes itself, imagination frees itself, and the recipe itself loses significance, becoming little more than an occasion for a free invention by analogy or association of ideas, through a subtle game of substitutions, abandonments, additions, and borrowings. By carefully following the same recipe, two experienced cooks will obtain different results because other elements intervene in the preparation: a personal touch, the knowledge or ignorance of tiny secret practices (flouring a pie pan after greasing it so that the bottom of the crust will remain crispy after baking), an entire *relationship to things* that the recipe does not codify and hardly clarifies, and whose manner differs from one individual to another because it is often rooted in a family or regional oral tradition.

The Field of Oblivion

Considered from a bit on high and from afar, the everyday work of cooking seems, in the private sphere, entirely doomed to repetition, a repetition of an archaic structure, a knowledge linked to very ancient social codes, stabilized in old forms of equilibrium, that is, in an obscure and hardly rational medley of preferences, necessities, and received customs. Seen from this angle, by those who "don't lend a hand in the kitchen," the totality of these practices hardly appears capable of evolving, except perhaps on minor points. Yet, examined in their details, current practices reveal themselves to have been considerably modified since the nineteenth century, as a result of a general change in lifestyles.

The elevation of the standard of living and the generalization of education, increased geographic mobility and the multiplication of travel, as well as the practice of exogamy all played their roles in this change.

But the industrialization of objects and the mechanization of basic tasks, and the substitution of electromechanical energy for muscular strength, have also transformed the everyday life of the Kitchen Women Nation. The increased requirements in terms of comfort and hygiene, the corresponding modifications of common representations involving health and food, the large-scale production and distribution of diverse, low-priced appliances—all of this affects the daily work of the cook. Already, many gestures and processes that were commonplace for my grandmothers' generation, ways of operating that were a part of a young girl's normal apprenticeship and of her (average) savoir faire capital, have been erased from common consciousness and no longer subsist except in the childhood memories of certain people, in the incomplete stories of old people, or, thanks to ethnologists, those city people intent on collecting the last marks of a moribund peasant culture, on preserving the memory and the trace of a past that is near and already distant.[3]

"There is a life and a death of gestures," notes the historian who pays attention to the movement of everyday life.[4] If some polished gestures from century to century, almost immobile in the long term, have magically disappeared in one or two generations, it is because the technical gesture only lasts as long as it is inhabited by a necessity (material or symbolic), a meaning, and a belief. The technical gesture, to be distinguished from the expressive gesture that translates a feeling or a reaction, is first defined by its utilitarian aim, its operating intention. Entirely oriented by its purpose, it seeks to attain a realization that will manifest its efficacy as a gesture. Whether it is done with a tool (chopping an onion with a small knife) or with the bare hand (kneading bread dough), the technical gesture calls for an entire mobilization of the body, translated by the moving of the hand, of the arm, sometimes of the entire body swinging in cadence to the rhythm of successive efforts demanded by the task at hand.

The action of the gesture can be divided into an orderly series of basic actions, coordinated in sequences of variable duration according to the intensity of the effort required, organized on a model learned from others through imitation (someone showed me how to do it), reconstituted from memory (I saw it done this way), or established through trial and error based on similar actions (I ended up figuring out how to do it). The skill at adapting the gesture to the conditions of execution and the quality of the obtained result constitute the test for putting a particular savoir faire into practice and foregrounding it. Whether it involves the culinary field or another type of material transformation conducted with a specific intention, the gesture is first of all a *body technique*, according to Mauss's definition, one of the "ways in which from society to society men know how to use their bodies."[5] In the gesture are superimposed invention, tradition, and education to give it a form of efficacy that suits the physical makeup and practical intelligence of the person who uses it. If the gesture comes to lose its usefulness, either because the term in the operating chain no longer seems worthy of interest or because a process less costly in time, energy, skill, or material appears, it loses both meaning and necessity. Soon, it will no longer exist except in a truncated form, illegible, in a way, before becoming the inarticulated, insignificant witness of a defunct material culture and of a former symbolism, a fragmented, incomplete, deformed gesture that slowly sinks into the obscure ocean of forgotten practices; for the technical gesture really only lives off its concrete or symbolic necessity (in the case of protective practices, rituals, or religious observances), and most often in tight symbiosis with one milieu and its retinue of technical objects. The gesture lasts only as long as its utility function, maintained by the thousands of reactualizations of its practitioners, and only thanks to their consensus. A gesture is only reworked if it is still considered efficient, operating, based on a good return or a just necessity in light of the work it involves. Its life is linked to the belief that is invested in it: it must be judged necessary, convenient, operating, beneficial; one must believe in its possible success in order to continue repeating it.

Ordinary language is unambiguous on this point: one does it that way "because we've always done it that way," besides, "you have to do it that way," and finally, "you have to follow custom." Deserted by the strength of belief, abandoned by necessity, the technical gesture withers and dies: why tire oneself out doing what is no longer useful? In any case, like the articulation of phonemes in language and for the same reasons, the technical gesture obeys the principle of generalized economy and increased simplification. Like them too, it has a unique function, in a sense. But it also consists of its illusions, ostracisms, errors, and prejudices, for it is caught, along with all human action, within the systems of categories and oppositions that characterize every culture in its specificity. Thus, an entire tight fabric of rites and habits, of beliefs and presuppositions, armed with its own unique logic, and making up in its own way a system, determines and models technical gestures practiced as useful, necessary, and credible.[6]

Ancient gestures have not been chased away only by the entry of household appliances into kitchens, but by the transformation of a material culture and of the subsistence economy to which it was linked. When the nature of provisions changes, so do the gestures of culinary preparation: thus, for the peasant farmers of the Cévennes, nourished in the past by chestnuts, today only the memory of the old people who remained there can recite the litany of precise, multiple, complex gestures with which one dried, smoked, shelled, sorted, preserved for winter, or ground these chestnuts into flour.[7] When the gestures vanish, the recipes attached to them disappear as well; soon nothing remains but the internalized memory of very ancient flavors, frozen in the sweetness of lost childhood, clouded over but indestructible, like the *laïssoles* and *pascades* from the Rouergue, intermediaries between thick gruel, a *matefaim*, and a pancake, or like the *fouace* [a type of pastry] from the old days:[8] "Nowadays, they're used to the *fouace* that you can find just about anywhere, and they think it's good because it is good; but when I'm the one who makes the comparison, I prefer the old-fashioned one."[9]

More than anything else, it is the available ingredients that have changed since the last century, and above all in their presentation. In the past, one bought products *in bulk*: olives and pickles from the brine barrel, flour from the baker's sack, oil according to the desired quantity for which one brought one's own empty bottle to the store. Marvels of mixed scents from these darkened shops where a semifrightening atmosphere reigned, this cave of Ali Baba where the grocer sat enthroned in the center of a learned disorder of sacks, casks, and jars whose true nature and secret classification he alone knew, a unique space that he crisscrossed with cautious itineraries, riveting the customer to the spot with an imperious injunction: "Don't move, don't touch anything. I'm the one who does the work here!" A nimble gesture of his hand rolled up a cone of sturdy paper (called "grocer's paper"), whose base he pinched firmly before pouring in the contents of a large, potbellied wooden spoon, pierced with holes, that he had just plunged into the olive barrel. Tiny aluminum shovels, wooden or wicker dippers, were used to weigh out on request sugar, lentils, split peas, or prunes. There was also the Roberval scale with heavy copper pans whose pointer for me never seemed to go back completely to its point of balance: did the grocer cheat or did my childhood glance not know how to judge the relative positions in proper perspective?

Once returned from the store, we used to carefully sift the flour before using it. Wide-open hands held the fragile wooden circle of the sifter at two diametrically opposite points and shook it with a light tapping of the fingers applied alternately on each side. A tender complicity was established with this volatile and precious flour: you could not lose any with too brusque a movement or too wide a shake. This gesture was done gently and in a measured fashion, restrained and silky like the touch of certain pianists.

Everything in the kitchen was arranged according to a subtle geography of hot and cold, wet and dry, well ventilated and closed up "against tiny little creatures," because everything provoked fear, the neighbor's cat, sugar-loving ants, the cockroaches synonymous with filth, and the accursed weevils, objects of much hatred and learned precautions, whose sneaky invasions terrified me. You always had to be on guard and know a parrying gesture: cutting off the "green" parts of potatoes, flattening half-cooked fish in order to remove the deadly bones, slicing apricots in half to avoid swallowing the worm with the fruit.

In this time before the reign of products that are sorted, graded, deboned, carved, prepackaged, and packaged in an anonymous form where only the generic name attests their original nature, everything had flavor because everything was dangerous, surprising on both the good and the bad side. Each purchase was a chance for the buyer to *use trickery with the vendor's trickery.* The visit to the market was the time for a marvelous gestural ballet, for winks and funny faces: the outstretched index finger lightly touched the flesh of fruits to determine their degree of ripeness, the thumb tested the firmness of the radishes, a circumspect glance detected the presence of bruises on the apples, one smelled the scent of melons at length as well as the odor of chèvre cheeses, one muttered comments about the relationship between quality and price. All this involved actualizing a certain competence, proving your judging capacities, and founding on a gestural activity a moral judgment concerning the merchant and the merchandise. One came back home tired and delighted, an innocent theater of the poor in which each person in turn improvised insolent retorts, of which the child perceived the effects without understanding the equivocal meaning or register.

People were also thrifty and organized at that time. Necessity issued its edicts. Announced from afar by the jingling of the little bells on his horse, the milkman stopped by every night with his ramshackle little cart full of heavy milk cans. The child ran toward him, alongside the road, with a large pan in hand, and then came back to the house with measured steps, holding the full pan with both hands, clumsy and proud, careful to keep it horizontal so as not to spill the least drop. One then put the milk on to boil for a long time, an operation accompanied by the monotone clap-clap of the "anti-boil-over device," a heavy, small metal disk riddled with concentric grooves that one placed on the bottom of the pan, but no one explained to you the how and why of it. One then poured the boiled milk into a large shallow stoneware basin that was quickly covered with a large plate and put in a cool place for the next day, after grandma had solemnly removed the "milk skin," this viscous, soft, detestable thing that grandma valued. "It's the cream of the milk, the best part," she used to say. The jar of cream became filled little by little; in time, it was used to make delicious pancakes that one ate hot right out of the oven, and within the space of one mouthful, one felt one's grudge against the "milk skin" melt away.

Checking the quality of ingredients took up a lot of time. One candled the eggs with backlighting, and one subjected them to the truth test by plunging them into a pail of cold water (they settled between the bottom and the surface in order of decreasing freshness). One carefully inspected the chicken's head, the brightness of its eye, the color of its comb, the status of its beak, and one felt the size of its gizzard before killing it. Then dressing the animal required much care: one had to pluck it, singe it to take out the last remaining nubs, gut it — a malodorous operation that made you flee the kitchen screaming until they called you back: "You can come back now — it's clean as a whistle." Half hidden behind the door, the child had seen the cook skillfully remove a flood of entrails, the heart, the gizzard, and the liver, which she nimbly separated from its pocket of gall.

Each week, one had to make a suspicious inspection of the jars of canned goods made at home according to empirical processes whose results were not assured. They were arranged in order, as in a parade, in the food storage cupboard; each one was dated with a small label, written with superb handwriting, with its regular downstrokes and upstrokes, its perfect capitals like those you can still see in old city hall registers. One examined each jar closely to detect the beginnings of mold, one tested with a finger the firmness of the paraffin wax that plugged the mouth of the jar, one tightened the paper that closed off the jars of jam. Sometimes, as a glutton, one insinuated that the jar of orange marmalade had flecks of green in it; grandma would turn it around and around, take it out into the clear sunlight of the terrace to examine it better, ask a second opinion of all the inhabitants of the household in order to finally decide in a weary tone: "I don't see anything, but you can never be too careful — we better open it right away before it's completely spoiled!" There was a strange illogical nature to these successive proceedings. In spite of indignant complaints, grandma persisted in oversalting to preserve things and then to soak them to remove the salt before eating them.

But the worst involved salted cod that was purchased elsewhere: you had to soak it for an entire day in a bath of slightly vinegared water, which was changed often; the fish was kept in a footed colander, which was then placed in the basin containing the liquid. Thus, so they used to say, "the salt falls to the bottom" and the child imagined immense mountains of salt hidden at the bottom of the oceans. For ham, one proceeded in the same way, but the last soak was made with water cut with milk "to make the taste milder" and this alliance of contrasts left one perplexed. Today, filets of frozen or barely salted semipreserved fish have rendered all of these manipulations obsolete. The necessity of preserving provisions for later, fruits and vegetables for winter, was the cause of a thousand ingenious practices. Certain fruits (apples, plums, apricots) were dried. One subjected some vegetables (peppers, tomatoes) to a refined treatment: a light roasting after being seeded, sun-drying, quick-frying in oil, storing them in earthenware jars full of oil (a part of this process is still used for certain small-size cheeses). Other vegetables, broken into pieces and sliced (cauliflower, artichokes, carrots), were preserved through maceration in oil scented with a variety of spices and lemon slices. Pickles were preserved in vinegar. Certain fruits, peeled and slightly poached, were kept in a light syrup (this especially involved pears and apricots); others were put in brandy (cherries and various berries).

One also made jams and fruit jellies, macerations, and various liqueurs. One had to take advantage of the abundance of the brief harvests in order to appear provident and industrious. Through their diversity, through the multiplicity of the gestures and implied savoir faire involved, all of this work was accomplished with a certain exhilaration, in the midst of joyous bustling activity. For the child, all of these tasks gave a certain rhythm to the wondrous summer, far from the constraints of school. In the large bustling house, one had scarcely the time or the inclination to get bored. Sometimes one would share skills with the neighbors: one was renowned for her jams, another admired for her pickles, so one went alternately to another's house to accomplish what one excelled in, and then she came to help you with another task, "for payback," as people used to say. And these words retain the sticky smell of jams stirred for a long time in a big copper pan where the mass of fruit and sugar bubbled, agitated by worrisome convulsive movements, before calming down in a homogeneous mixture with a beautiful amber tint, nice and thick, as if weighed down with the pleasures to come.

To all these practices that were possible in a house of a market town, the farmers added the essential: the pig, slaughtered and cured according to a well-established ritual of recipes, gestures, and prohibitions in which empirical knowledge and symbolic structuration were inextricably mixed.[10] For a long time, the presence of the hearth allowed certain pieces to be smoked. Even having disappeared from modern kitchens, which are arranged and heated differently, the hearth imposes its memory in language through the gestures that it aroused: even if the trammel where one hung the "communal pot" no longer exists, people continue to celebrate at each move to a new house with the "hanging of the trammel," the outdated symbol of a family's settling down. When gestures die out, when objects disappear or become immobilized in the darkness of an attic, or in the display window of a museum, words sometimes still subsist, in memory of the bygone past.

New Knowledge

Henceforth, one buys one's provisions in diverse packaging that calls for an entire range of gestures prior to every culinary preparation. To do one's shopping, one really has *to love reading* and know how to decipher labels. For example, for meat prepackaged in tiny trays placed in a refrigerator case, one has to find the date and grasp its meaning. Does it mean the day the animal was slaughtered (to be flavorful, meat must be a little aged), the packaging date, the "sell-by" date (which still allows forty-eight hours for potential consumption), or the recommended expiration date? One must read and mentally calculate in order to determine which of the two chickens is a better bargain. But how does one choose between a "free-range" one (what wonderful happiness) and one that is "corn-fed for seventy days" (o brief destiny), between the wearer of the "France High Quality Certified" label and a "Grade A free-range chicken"? To interpret this information exactly, one has to know how to read fluently, to go over a daily newspaper of quality with a fine-tooth comb, and especially to memorize. Thus, one will know that the date written on egg cartons corresponds neither to the egg-laying date nor to the packaging date, but derives from a learned computation that quite legally and according to the regulations enacted by the EEC [European Economic Community] (where there is little taste for jokes) allows for a date later than the actual laying of the egg to be indicated.

Buying food has become a skilled work that requires several years of schooling. One has to love the rhetoric of figures, to have a taste for deciphering minuscule inscriptions, a certain aptitude for hermeneutics (the science of interpretations valued by Aristotle), and certain notions about linguistics (which are always useful for making one's way in society). Thus endowed, you will know how to interpret, and therefore to take advantage of the information generously "placed at the consumer's disposal," as the producers say. It is thus necessary to read, examine, and compare in order to avoid the fruit jellies with suspicious coloring and fruit drinks especially rich in water and sugar. One has to know how to guard against the seductive whiteness that a preserving agent makes in certain shredded potatoes and celery. One must not use the zest of citrus fruits that have been injected with chemical substances in order to prolong their beautiful appearance. One must know how to tilt a "brick" of pasteurized milk in low-angled light in order to reveal the freshness expiration date. One must especially know how to combine all these fragments of knowledge and be able to mobilize them in an instant, almost effortlessly.

Thus, the gestures and practices of the buying woman have had to be transformed in order to adapt to new market habits. In the past, one had to learn how to look at things, to not be distracted by the vendor's stream of words, to estimate the quality of a cut of meat in the wink of an eye, to smell the almost too-strong odor of cheese, and to notice the yellow color of butter past its prime. Today, one must know how to read and trust no longer in a personal and empirical savoir faire that comes from a traditional structure, acquired through long apprenticeship, within the familiarity of an elder, but in a collective scientific knowledge, codified in regulatory statements and transmitted anonymously. You have to believe in the wisdom of state-controlled regulations whose how and why escapes you, in the vigor and efficiency of inspections that ensure their observance.[11] Each person must *support through belief* the entire edifice, must *believe* the norms to be in accordance with one's own interest and the indications placed on packaging to be truthful.

Once back in her kitchen with her purchases, the cook has an entire display of materials (plastic wrap, aluminum foil, waxed, grease-proof, and cellophane paper) and airtight containers to hold her provisions and to store them in her refrigerator, cupboards, or freezer. For grocery products, she will have to solve the problem of opening boxes, cans, and jars. The cardboard box will cede under the pressure of a finger or the tip of scissors along a perforated line. For certain cans, a toothed can opener will suffice; for others, one has to pull, without breaking, on a metal tab that will then bring with it an entire circle of metal, thus separating the body of the can from its lid. For cans of fish, the metal tab must generally be introduced in the slot made at the base of a special key that must then be turned on itself with a supple movement of the wrist in order to roll up the remainder of the lid around the handle. For jars with airtight metal lids, a strong hand is needed to force the lid to turn or else a new instrument, the jar opener, whose double arch of metal, jointed at the top, can be adapted to the circumference of jars of various dimensions and whose two little handles are held with both hands to ensure the hold and to facilitate the necessary effort.

There are also the fruit juices packaged in cardboard "bricks": to open them one has to pierce two diagonally opposite holes on the top. The most fearful remains the ground coffee stored in airtight metal cans: on the edge of the lid, one has to detach a thin metal tab with a quick gesture that then brings off the entire top part of the can. Too bad for clumsy people: the cutting edge of this metal opening is sharper than a butcher knife and deeply cuts the palm of the hand if one does not carefully calculate the angle of attack or the trajectory.

Then comes the time to prepare the meal. There again the gestures of tradition withdraw before those imposed by new tools. There is the electric mixer to beat egg whites, the blender that mixes almost everything, the fruit juicer, the pineapple or apple corer. A series of tiny metal instruments have come along to help the housewife, or rather, to give "professional" perfection to the presentation of her dishes, and that is a pity because it is as if she has to mimic the production of a caterer or an industrial cookie factory in order to please her guests. The addition of these tools and appliances, born of an intensive use of work in metals, plastic materials, and electric energy, has transformed the interior landscape of the family kitchen.

Certain of these new tools limit themselves to perfecting and standardizing the old gesture of the bare hand, this "tool of tools" that Aristotle made into the symbol of human superiority,[12] or that of the hand armed with a rudimentary instrument (rasp, knife, spoon). Others make possible stereotyped repetition, at a more brisk pace, of a gesture whose result they codify: one can thus increase the quantities of materials involved and lessen the operating time as well as the intensity of the effort necessary. Still others have arisen to accomplish new tasks, created by the industrialization process itself (the electric knife to slice frozen food products), or made necessary by this industrialization and by the evolution of an aging population (the electric can opener). Finally, others, superfluous ones, play on the desire for novelty and the infatuation with the electromechanization of basic tasks, and make one hope to save time and energy. But they hide the fragility of the instrument or the difficulty of its use, its limits (the electric meat grinder shreds meat or grinds it

into a pulp) and its heaviness, its noisy character and its cumbersome-
ness, and finally the length of cleaning tasks, so that after three valiant
tries the appliance is found silently relegated to the rank of useless object.

To measure the importance of the changes that have taken place in
fifteen or twenty years, it suffices to refer to the list of technical objects
(appliances, utensils, containers) that make up the normal equipment of
a particular kitchen. In the past there was the trammel and its various
cooking pots, the earthenware vinegar cruet, the mortar and pestle, the
copper casserole dish tin-plated on the inside, earthenware jars, the glazed
earthenware colander, the cheese draining board, wooden spoons, and
so on.[13] Today they have been replaced by Pyrex baking dishes, pressure
cookers, stainless steel pots, pans with nonstick coatings, and the polyvalent food processor that shreds, chops, mashes, mixes, and beats.[14] The
spread of microwave ovens has added its battery of dishes (those for re-
heating or browning). An entire series of industrial objects henceforth
reigns in the kitchen. Their shapes are new, their materials diversified.[15]
One part of these utensils has been adapted to new cooking methods: in
fifty years, simple gas or electric stoves have been succeeded by hot plates
with sensors, inductive heating surfaces, sequential burners, and microwave ovens.[16] In the same way, simple operations have become more complex and autonomous and henceforth demand special equipment. This
is so for making coffee, which, in one or two generations, has gone from
the grandmothers' "sock" filter to the dual-body Italian coffeemaker,
then on to the electric coffeemaker, and next to the reduced model, pump-
or steam-operated, of the professional machines in cafés that allow one
to obtain at home "a good strong frothy espresso" as in the neighborhood bistro—and here one sees the separation between the private space
of the kitchen and public space become blurred.

The Past-Present

The change involves not only the utensil or tool and the gesture that
uses it, but the *instrumentation relationship* that is established between the
user and the object used. In the past, the cook used a simple tool, of a
primary kind, that also fulfilled simple functions; her hand furnished the
kinetic energy, she directed the progress of the operation, supervised
the succession of action sequences, and could mentally represent the
process for herself. Today, she employs an elaborate tool, of a secondary
kind, that requires complicated handling; she truly understands neither
its principle nor the way it works. She feeds this technical object with
ingredients to be transformed, then unleashes the movement by push-

ing on a button, and collects the transformed matter without having controlled the intervening steps in the operation. In the past, the cook applied her savoir faire each time, she could perfect her dexterity, and display her ingenuity. At present, just about anyone can use an industrial object as well as her, and so she has become the *unskilled spectator* who watches the machine function in her place. She finds herself doubly deprived: deprived of her empirical savoir faire (compared to the past) and of the theoretical or technological knowledge that produced the tool (in relation to the present). Along with the complexity of her task, with the qualification acquired through experience, the diversity of gestures for doing things and the joy of knowing how to distinguish them and make them succeed have disappeared. Within the work of doing-cooking there also used to be the skill of the artisan, proud of his or her work, in love with the worked matter, and attached to perfecting his or her method or varying the products, careful to put circumstances to good use.

Industrialization (of products, tools, and transforming operations) has come along to destroy within domestic space — as it had done first in the working-class space — the regime of this labor. It introduced there the same schema of parceling, of standardization, and of the repetition of tasks. Certainly, it allowed people to save time and decrease one type of fatigue, but this was done in order to give rise to gray, homogeneous, empty time, the time of effortless and joyless boredom. Of course, industrialization and the progress that accompanied it have had beneficial effects. The removal of coal or wood stoves eliminated the handling of a heavy, dirty fuel that required regular and tiring maintenance. The distribution of hot running water sinks improved comfort and hygiene conditions;[17] it has been the same for the low-priced production of efficient cleaning products.[18] The fastidious process of "doing the dishes" has been considerably lightened because of it. The generalization of electric fryers and the installation of range hoods have made the stench of cold grease disappear. A number of repetitive and daily tasks have been lightened or simplified — for which one is thankful. But all of that has *had its price* and broken the ancient balances in the transmission of savoir faire and the management of time.

Can one retain the advantages of a material culture without being subjected to its inconveniences? Is there the possibility for a happy marriage between the old and the new? To this question, which is central to us today, we do not have an answer to offer. But I do not believe in the happiness of a humanity deprived of all physical activity, of all manual labor, subject to the seizure of power by industrial machinery. There is a profound pleasure in achieving by oneself what one offers to one's guests, in practicing a modest inventiveness, in ephemeral results, but whose subtle combination silently defines a *lifestyle*, circumscribes one's *own space*. The multiplicity of practices and technical gestures gives shape to ordinary life and the richness of the social fabric depends on it. This is why I judge more perspicacious than ridiculous the aficionados of workshops for relearning how to make the gestures of the past.[19] I find them naive as well: the past cannot be reborn from its ashes; a culture that stops moving decrees its own death. In the cacophony of social exchanges, one can also lend an ear to newer notes and remark on the proliferation of microexperiences, hidden in the anonymity of local networks of friends in which several people try modestly to invent other behaviors, to define a lifestyle straddling the two cultures and their two temporalities. If, at the same time, one becomes conscious here and there of the importance of the symbolic and technical capital placed within the "ways of operating" that furnish ordinary life, and if one becomes attached to grasping the combinatory rules that associate concrete intelligence, do-it-yourself ingenuity, and creative cunning in the undefined whirlwind of everyday practices, this would already be a good sign.

Between the symmetrical errors of archaistic nostalgia and frenetic overmodernization, room remains for microinventions, for the practice of *reasoned differences*, to resist with a sweet obstinance the contagion of conformism, to reinforce the network of exchanges and relations, to learn how to make one's own choice among the tools and commodities produced by the industrial era. Each of us has the power to *seize power* over one part of oneself. This is why the gestures, objects, and words that live in the ordinary nature of a simple kitchen also have so much importance.

Chapter 13
The Rules of the Art

Knowing how, learning how, and telling about how to do things: the fade-in and fade-out of gestures, the skillfulness of certain knacks, these things too need words and text in order to circulate within the Kitchen Women Nation. These people have their own language and corpus of reference, as well as their own secrets and complicities — an "implicit, well-known" knowledge that the most detailed of recipes will not communicate to you.

A Four-Entry Dictionary

The language used in talking about cooking involves four distinct domains of objects or actions: the ingredients that serve as raw materials; the utensils and pots and pans, as well as cooking appliances, beaters, mixers, and so on; the performance, action words, and descriptions of skillful knacks; the finished products and the naming of obtained results. These four registers in the same lexicon are found in the shortest of recipes; they are necessary in order to write a description in the command form that gives rise to and accompanies the movement toward the act, and then to engender the promised result within the required delay by the methods indicated. I will leave aside the linguistic level that involves the consumption of the finished product, in spite of the semantic and linguistic richness of the often "savory" expressions that rightly serve to express the flavor of dishes, the pleasure of tasting, and the stages of bliss involved in eating and drinking well. By placing myself resolutely on the side of the makers, I will be interested only in the production process.

Wittgenstein asked himself:

> Why don't I call cookery rules arbitrary, and why am I tempted to call the rules of grammar arbitrary? Because 'cookery' is defined by its end, whereas 'speaking' is not. That is why the use of language is in a certain sense autonomous, as cooking and washing are not. You cook badly if you are guided in your cooking by rules other than the right ones; but if you follow other rules than those of chess you are *playing another game*; and if you follow grammatical rules other than such-and-such ones, that does not mean you say something wrong, no, you are speaking of something else.[1]

215

But the culinary recipe complicates the matter, because through it, it is a question of "speaking in tongues" about actions, of saying only what is strictly necessary without forgetting indispensable information, of describing without ambiguity by not skipping any stages, in essence of expressing without equivocation. Here, men take back the podium: between the rules of grammar and those of the kitchen, between saying something well and doing it well, only the second level is important for a woman — "Who cares if she offends some grammar book / So long as she doesn't offend us as a cook?"[2]

In every language, culinary recipes make up a kind of *minimalist text*, through their internal economy, their conciseness, and their minor degree of equivocation, aside from technical terms such as "to blanch," "to brown," "to line a baking pan," and "to deglaze," of which one must have a prior knowledge. As a (future) classic of French cuisine already stressed in the eighteenth century, at a time when regional tradition was moving in France from oral to written transmission: "I have made use of simple dishes, new and good, of which I have offered explanations that are intelligible and within reach in terms of understanding by those who themselves do not know anything about it [cooking]."[3] In fact, cookbooks constitute a very old and always fruitful publishing backlist. There are many of these in France, traditionally a country of fine dining, often as shameless plagiarism of a previous best-seller success, but this is not the place for such a discussion.[4] Innumerable movie actors, television presenters, or heiresses endowed with famous noble family names publish their "collections of recipes." Many of these volumes sell well, but old favorites still remain intact, such as *Authentic Family Cooking, Including 1,000 Recipes and 500 Meal Plans* [*La véritable cuisine des familles, comprenant 1000 recettes et 500 menus*], by Aunt Marie, one of the first editions of which appeared in 1913 and is regularly reissued.[5]

In this type of classic volume for families not belonging to the upper class, the signature takes on an anonymous form, both familiar and reassuring, that spreads Aunt Marie's relationship to the frontiers of the French-speaking world and allows her to directly transmit to everyone the family treasure of tradition, without the presence of a patronymic name to impose the brand of a proprietor or to claim a certain originality. Thus, many cookbooks are, even today, signed with a simple feminine first name, often embellished with a mythical familial title — "Cousin Adèle," "Aunt Aurora," "Mother Jean," "Grandma Madeleine" — as if to initiate the process of reconstituting the world of childhood when the child learned about culinary activities by watching his or her mother or grandmother.

On the other hand, books written by men include their full name under the title, the author thus proudly affirming his creative capacity and his property rights: Raymond Oliver, Paul Bocuse, Michel Guérard. Women with quaint first names spoke of and for family intimacy, took care of the everyday, and talked about private life; such books are neither the springboard to a publishing career nor the way to achieve the status of gastronomy expert. Men describe the cuisine of great moments and great chefs, complicated and costly refinements, the festival, the feasts that one comes to savor religiously from beyond the borders; their recipes are attached to public life, to the visible circulation of money, to expense, profit, success, and power. To the humble vestal virgins go anonymity, the ordinary everyday that has no market value, that brings neither profit nor glory, the art of making use of leftovers and "feeding the family on a shoestring budget." To the high priests go the puffs of incense, the television cameras, the broadcast interviews, the propaganda trips to Japan or the United States to "sell French taste," the *urbi et orbi* publicity, the notoriety, the profit, and the complementary claim to being the only ones with know-how and inventiveness (your share of the pie diminishes the more you share, as any child will tell you). Moreover, the great chefs long wanted to forbid women restaurateurs-cooks from wearing the chef's hat, the symbol of the profession (a phallic one?). An example of this position is held by the famous Paul Bocuse: "I intend to repeat my conviction here that women are certainly good cooks for so-called traditional cooking.... Such cooking, in my opinion, is not at all inventive, which I deplore."[6] *Et hop, passez muscade!*[7] One will recall, for the record, that people have similarly and successively tried to prevent women from obtaining a high-school diploma, university *agrégation*, medical degrees, and so on, and that the Third Republic obstinately denied them the right to vote—this right was not granted until 1945 by the Fourth Republic.

Let us allow Valéry to respond for the obscure Kitchen Women Nation:

> If someone offers me a tasty dish, I do not worry, while enjoying this delicate food, if the person who prepared it invented the recipe. What does the original inventor have to do with me? The trouble he took is not what touches me. I do not feed myself from his name and I receive no enjoyment from his pride. I am consuming a perfect moment.[8]

But this does not address the heart of the problem.

This role sharing among men and women is in fact ancient. At the end of the eighteenth century in France, cooking becomes an object of discourse, gastronomy comes forward as a theoretical code of culinary practice, and, under the decisive influence of Grimod de La Reynière, as "gourmet eloquence," an exercise of style that sorts, classifies, and names the riches of fine dining;[9] the popular press and literature from that moment on accord increased attention to food behaviors, but without worrying further about the word-for-word account of ways of operating or about gathering recipes. In this movement toward elaborating a culture of the culinary and toward *legitimating* dishes (this term also comes from Grimod), women have no part. They are virtually excluded from the great restaurants where the good connoisseurs meet to educate themselves in taste and to develop their judgment capacities; the great artist-cooks whose excellence is appreciated are all men; no one supposed then that a woman could contribute to a written work that explains, refines, and theorizes. Gastronomy will thus be exclusively an affair of men: "Women, who, everywhere else, make up society's charm, find themselves out of place at a dinner of gourmets, where the attention, far from wanting to be shared, is based entirely on what garnishes the table and not on what surrounds it."[10] Nineteenth-century bourgeois society, which continued this gastronomic enterprise and thus dreamed of gaining access to the former aristocratic refined style, regarded these food practices as a male social activity, founded on this exclusionary decision with regard to women, judging them "too weak" physically to absorb so much strong, spicy, seasoned food in a single meal, and "too stupid" to take part in the theoretical and scriptural side of the ongoing work.[11]

The situation still has not changed much in this field. It is men who write the food columns in large newspapers, who head the annual guides that draw up restaurant ratings, who make up the various tasting juries. The stakes, of course, are high: taking away the market of the pen and the "gourmet," and earning notoriety and this power that allows one to cause the rise or fall of a restaurant according to whether one exalts or belittles its business, all this is worth a lot and, as usual, the best sources of profit and the jobs with authority and social legitimacy go by birthright to men. On the other hand, the monotonous tasks, the inferior work, or the nonaccountable housework is willingly left to women.

Things continue to present the same facet in the intimacy of households. Our study confirms it: in couples under forty-five, men enjoy cooking more often than their elders did, but *from time to time*, for a festive meal more elaborate and costly than an ordinary everyday one. "I'm not interested enough in the question to spend an entire day on it. There are some who really like it, real refined people, I see it especially in men," says Henriette. And Françoise tells us:

> A weekend rarely goes by that he [her husband] doesn't make an entrée or a cake, something hard to make... and he cooks the way men usually do, that is, he has to use an inordinate amount of space and an unbelievable number of pots and pans, and I mean unbelievable! And he is also much more careful than me with what he does; if he cuts carrots into rounds, he will cut them all the same thickness, consistently, by applying himself... It's also perhaps that this is not an everyday thing, so he can spend more time on it.

And he can stop playing this game as soon as it no longer amuses him; he is not tied to this kitchen work by an implicit contract.

The Language of Recipes

For women, in the modest collections that they read for doing day-to-day cooking, the language of recipes is simple, with some archaic features. It constitutes the place of preservation and the means of circulation for an ancient technical vocabulary, because it is also a conservatory of earlier fabrication processes, like these anonymous recipes, expressed in kitchen language and referring back to a previous practical knowledge, that the eighteenth-century *Encyclopedia* collected to mark the movement in cuisine from a regional oral tradition to its written recording.[12] Finally, culinary language appears to be rather stable, not because it has no use, but because it was fixed rather early by collections of recipes: for almost three centuries, it hardly had need of transformation, because it described ways of operating that changed little. The big revolution came here with the entrance of industrial innovation into household tasks, with, successively, the refrigerator, then the freezer in rural areas, stoves with adjustable heat and perfected ovens, and today with the mastery of the "frozen food chain" and the distribution of frozen food products, whose consumption is enhanced by the spread of the microwave oven, which considerably shortens defrosting times.

Most kitchens have been equipped with these innovations since 1945, more or less completely, with certain women resisting the contagious movement because of the noise and the cost of the appliances or their encumbrance and upkeep: "In the end, all the time you save using them, you lose in the cleanup" (Irène). Others appreciate the saving of time and effort that they allow:

I purée my vegetable soup with a blender. Oh, no, I don't do it like before anymore, with a hand mill, oh, ouch, ouch, it takes forever. And, of course, I no longer have the strength: with the blender, it goes fast. It takes no effort. But when you had to turn and turn and turn . . . oh, now I don't think I could do it like that anymore! Keep in mind, though, that I still have it, the hand mill, I keep it, I can't throw anything away. (Laurence)

With electric kitchen appliances, masculine mechanization, its technical organization, its machines, and its logic have entered women's kitchens, without really allowing them to adapt these machines to their time-honored body techniques, by authoritatively imposing on them a new relationship to things, other modes of organization, and thus new ways of reasoning. Yet, nowhere does one receive a systematic initiation into the use of these domestic robots, so that, according to their makers and repairmen, families do not take advantage of all the possibilities of their equipment; in the first months following the purchase, the frequent cause for warranty claims is not a malfunction or a manufacturing defect, but a misunderstanding of how the appliance works. It is true that reading the operating instructions is often no help: they are often obscure texts, inaccurate, badly translated from a foreign language, written according to a logic better adapted to a repair technician than to an average woman user, in other words, comprehensible if one has a minimum knowledge of electromechanics and unresponsive to practical questions posed by a user keen on obtaining a particular result or of carrying out a particular operation.[13]

The entrance of these appliances into kitchens has changed the procedures of preparation, cooking, and preserving; it has thus had a direct effect on the language of recipes. It has introduced the quantification and unification of measures (weight and volume), as well as the precision of cooking times and temperatures. Hence, a certain impoverishment of vocabulary and the erasing of numerous small procedures (how to know how hot an oven is, how to avoid having mayonnaise turn, how to successfully make whipped cream) whose secret will disappear along with the memory of the older generation. By the same token, the recent custom of finding an exact indication of proportions and cooking times in recipes renders many manuscript recipes, written as synopses with a loose sense of proportions, difficult to understand (often there are only the names of ingredients as in the following: "take some butter, flour, and eggs and make a rather flexible dough by watering it down with some milk, then . . . , etc."), recipes that were passed down from generation to generation, witnesses of a period when apprenticeship was done by ob-

serving a relative or a neighbor. The generalization of a written transmission in place of oral communication entails a profound reworking of
culinary knowledge, a distancing of tradition, just as pronounced as the
movement from the soup pot in a hearth or on the wood stove to electric or gas appliances.

The Imposition of the Name

As for the naming of dishes, the fourth entry in our multiple dictionary,
it presents a double configuration according to its place of origin. In the
current collections of recipes aimed at housewives, the name of the dish
is descriptive: "saddle of rabbit with mustard," "low-fat stuffed tomatoes," "chocolate cake." In her private sphere, the cook acts accordingly
and proposes "sautéed veal with carrots" or "eggplant with chickpeas"
to her guests. Her language becomes even more modest when she offers
one of her own dishes: "Oh, I just made do with what I had on hand.
No, it doesn't have a name, it's just some celeriac and red cabbage with
cubed bacon." Her analytic title tells how and with what the preparation is made, in direct relation to an action, but not specifying a unique
way of operating. The essential remains silenced, hidden in the anonymity
of the author, who does not claim status as inventor or creator — no, she
simply "made do with a few things" — and who does not believe for an
instant that her idea could possibly be known about outside the closed
circle of her family. Cuisine that is not baptized is found in the private
life of ordinary people.

In restaurants, on the contrary, the higher their status, the more the
menu proposes mysterious dishes with pompous names whose reading
generally provides no information; one must humbly resort to the help
of a maître d', who is a trifle condescending, to get an explanation of
what "veal Orloff" or "Ruy Blas cake" is. Here the name is used to veil
or theatricalize, thus to intrigue and cloud, and the customer must blindly
order unknown words that will become dishes filling him or her with
satisfaction.

This remains a heritage of the two previous centuries: the end of
the ancien régime brought with it the end of the table of princes and
nobles; their cooks turned toward the new clientele made up of the bourgeoisie and flattered its palate with noble names and princely terms ("veal
supreme à la Grand-Condé," "turbot à la royale"), to raise its common
rank to these semantic heights.[14] The gastronomic discourse of Grimod
de La Reynière and other followers then takes over and assumes the power
of naming, based on false historical references or through allusion to the

contemporary world of artists and theater:[15] thus, "pears Belle Hélène" and "peach Melba" will come down to us without our knowing for certain the circumstances of the dish's creation or those of its naming. For certain of these names, there was soon a movement, as a ransom of success, toward becoming common nouns: béchamel, charlotte, and so on. Alongside this naming process still subsists that of geographic borrowing, or regional references, halfway between the pretentious and savant lexicon of gastronomy and that, both modest and descriptive, of ordinary practices. This type of name — "chicken basquaise," "Norwegian omelette" — indicates a place of origin, whether real or fictitious; unlike the discourse of gastronomy, it does not use names of people, and unlike ordinary cuisine, it is not strictly analytic and explanatory. It designates someplace other than here without offering a Jacob's ladder leading to social heights.

On March 8, 1941, twenty days[16] before committing suicide by drowning herself in a nearby river, Virginia Woolf wrote in her journal: "Occupation is essential. And now with some pleasure I find that its seven; & must cook dinner. Haddock & sausage meat. I think it is true that one gains a certain hold on sausage & haddock by writing them down." These words constitute the last entry in her diary.[17] It is perhaps from having received this final position, at the end of a life of internal suffering and writing, that these stripped sentences gain their force. They do not seek to explain the fundamental link (in our cultural universe) between a woman, cooking, and her language. They record it.

The nourishing arts have come down to us from the depths of the past, immobile in appearance in the short term, but profoundly reworked in reality over the long term. Provisions, preparation, cooking, and compatibility rules may very well change from one generation to another, or from one society to another. But the everyday work in kitchens remains a way of unifying matter and memory, life and tenderness, the present moment and the abolished past, invention and necessity, imagination and tradition — tastes, smells, colors, flavors, shapes, consistencies, actions, gestures, movements, people and things, heat, savorings, spices, and condiments. Good cooks are never sad or idle — they work at fashioning the world, at giving birth to the joy of the ephemeral; they are never finished celebrating festivals for the adults and the kids, the wise and the foolish, the marvelous reunions of men and women who share room (in the world) and board (around the table). Women's gestures and women's voices that make the earth livable.

Chapter 14
"When It Comes Down to It, Cooking Worries Me..."

The following is the complete text of one of the interviews solicited on feminine culinary practices. Marie Ferrier collected and transcribed this discussion with Irène, who was forty-four at the time. Born and raised in a Francophone country, Irène has lived in Paris for more than twenty years. She has always worked full-time and is currently a private secretary in a publishing company. She is married to Jean, a writer and translator. Their daughter Sarah was ten at the time of the interview. Jean has two sons from a previous marriage, Emmanuel and Pierre, who were eighteen and sixteen at the time and lived with their mother's family.[1]

Marie: Do you cook every day?

Irène: Every night.

Marie: For three people?

Irène: For three people. Well, it depends. We haven't had much company over lately. I guess it depends on the time of year.

Marie: For instance?

Irène: There are times when it's easier to have friends over. At one point, for example, we had some neighbors over. The young woman worked and was going back to school and, very often, when I returned home at night, her husband would be over here with the children and we would decide to share in making an impromptu dinner together, but that's all over. Now it's often only the three of us. We don't have time for visits, except maybe on Saturdays, when one or the other of Jean's sons comes over for dinner.

Marie: Well, how does it work out? In other words, on a day when, if you like, there are only the three of you, or one when people come for an impromptu meal, your neighbors, or even the day when you have friends over, do you do things very differently?

Irène: Well, first, it's Jean who does the shopping. So when it's just the three of us, we make vague plans: he'll buy some meat, some fish, and a vegetable. We make vague plans as to what he will get. And then, when we're expecting guests, I...we make more precise plans: I make a list so as not to forget anything because, more often than not, when I get back at night, there's a surprise waiting for me: I make do with what Jean has bought. Besides, it's very convenient for me to find the shopping done because, in the past, I used to leave work late and then all the stores would be closed, so I had to manage with almost nothing.

Marie: I see.

Irène: Now, it's much easier...

Marie: You didn't have it [the shopping] organized on a weekly basis or something along those lines...?

Irène: Not at all! I always just took it one day at a time. Well, on Saturdays and Sundays, when I'm home, I would often do something more elaborate, for example, a pot-au-feu or a dish that would last through Monday and Tuesday. So, at the beginning of the week, I very often had some leftovers, or I would make soup that would last two or three days. A few years ago, I used to make soup practically every other day... We would get up everyday at the same time, 7:00 A.M., and I would always make soup in the morning, well, every other morning, in any case. Now, we're much lazier; we get up at 7:30, so I never make soup anymore in the morning, and at night, I have to manage with what's here.

Marie: But, it's you who cooks, though, Jean does the shopping, but...

Irène: He does the shopping, but the cooking, no.

Jean: I've done it once, I think.

Irène: You once made an extraordinary soup that everyone still remembers, really! (*She laughs.*)

Jean: A tomato soup!

Irène: Yes, but it's about the only time that you did any real cooking. Well, when I have meetings after work and I get home late at night, he manages well enough to feed himself and Sarah. Then it's the *classic* sort of meal: mashed potatoes and fried eggs. Besides, it's the meal Sarah prefers. She's completely delighted!

Marie: Yes, that's amazing, we've had many reactions just like that. When people evoke the days when they stayed home all alone with their fathers, they said it ended up being a celebration. The kind of family hierarchy that is established when the whole family is together, with the father, mother, and children, such a hierarchy falls apart the day when only the father is there, and so it becomes a kind of celebration.

Jean: Well, for me, I kind of, I hate instant mashed potatoes! But (*he laughs*) Sarah loves it, it's no problem!

Irène: Yes; in the end, you make these kinds of meals when there's a strike going on, during a teachers' strike, for example, very often when there's a school strike.

Jean: Yeah, but the other day, I wanted to make something else, but Sarah didn't want to!

Irène: On Wednesdays, when it so happens that she's here, and during teachers' strikes, very often you pick up one of Sarah's friends, whose parents both work, so they can have more fun together.

Jean: But then, I at least go so far as to make some pasta!

Irène: Yes, you go so far as to make pasta! Very nice! (*She laughs.*)

Marie: Do you make instant mashed potatoes, too?

Irène: No. Given that they already eat quite a bit, I avoid making any. Unless I really...

Marie: Unless by accident?

Jean: I hate instant mashed potatoes!

Irène: (*She laughs.*) No, but I make a very simple and fast cuisine. I don't spend more than half an hour. In any case, I have a pressure cooker that I use a lot; for vegetables, it's very practical, well, vegetables are really good made in it, then... I use it daily and I arrange it so that I can make things that get done quickly. I can't have any fun making very elaborate dishes. In the end, even when there are guests, I make a cuisine that does not take too much time. On Saturdays, I sometimes tell myself that I'm going to take more care, but that...

Jean: But it's perfectly fine that way!

Irène: When I make things that are too complicated, I worry and I ruin everything, so it's to my advantage to make simple things. When it comes down to it, cooking worries me, I don't know why.

Marie: In the end, I think it's much more a question of being accustomed to making complicated things, more elaborate things, in any case.

Irène: Yes and also I feel sort of inhibited: I'm absolutely incapable of cooking without a cookbook, except for very, very simple things. On Saturdays, I still sometimes take the trouble, especially when Jean's kids are coming to eat, because they are very hearty eaters. They're big boys, eighteen and sixteen, so you have to give them something solid to eat, and there's no question of skipping a meal. And then, we take our time a little bit more on Saturdays. On Saturday nights, it's almost a celebration when one of them comes over. Afterwards, we spend the night playing games; or we discuss things together. At times like this, I make a little more effort, but I never make very complicated things.

Marie: I see.

Irène: What I really like about having company over is having guests who are no bother, who can stop by unexpectedly; that way, you can serve whatever and you manage with what you find in the fridge. If I have guests whose visit makes me worry, for whom I have to think already in the morning about a meal I'm going to make that night, that really bothers me. I don't know, when it comes down to it, I don't really feel very much at ease in the kitchen. Like nowhere else, really. However, I do quite a few things; I sew and knit, but always with patterns. In the end, I'm not very inventive.

Marie: And it's the same thing in the kitchen? You follow the cookbook faithfully?

Irène: Yes, yes, I follow the cookbook. I have more of a tendency to simplify rather than to complicate things! It's very rare that...I would really like to have more freedom, to be able in fact to improvise, to feel at ease. When it comes down to it, it's a domain that I don't have much of a mastery over! I have never done much cooking for the simple reason that when you come home at 8:15 P.M., you're not going to start preparing a complicated menu! And on Sundays, we're often not at home, we go on a picnic, or we go to see my stepfather, so there are relatively few occasions to make truly refined meals.

Jean: When we go camping, you don't take your cookbook!

Irène: You're right! But there, we really make an ultrasimple cuisine! When you go camping, the advantage is that everything tastes good, even the mashed potatoes!

Jean: That's true!

Irène: And so there you don't mind eating a soup mix, which you would never do at home! (*She laughs.*)

Marie: So, what happened? I mean, didn't you learn, when you were young, how to cook?

Irène: No, I didn't learn when I was young. We went to a home economics school for a few years, but you don't learn a whole lot in such a school. At home, my mother did the cooking. Or my sister. There was sort of a division of labor; she did the cooking and I did the dishes and those sorts of things.

Marie: But why? Because you didn't like it or your sister liked it more, or for some other reason? (*A long silence follows.*)

Irène: I feel it's because that was the way the roles had been assigned to us. It had been decided—which seems very dangerous now, in retrospect—that *she* had more imagination, *she* had more creativity, so she fulfilled this kind of role, and that I fulfilled other kinds that were more organizational roles and that sort of thing. (*Irène emphasizes the pronoun* she *here in her speech.*)

Jean: It's the same thing with my sons, isn't it? Pierre cooks. Emmanuel is younger![2]

Irène: Yes, but Pierre is a bit of a hearty eating gourmet, while Emmanuel will eat just about anything.

Jean: Yes, but I assume it comes from the same motivation.

Irène: Yes, I don't know if it could be the same source! In the end, very, very often, I think that parents give a role, assign a fixed role to their children. When you have a family with two or three children, you assign a well-defined role to each one; afterwards, they have a lot of trouble trying to break out of it. It's something that I've discovered very recently: when it comes down to it, I had been completely trapped in a certain role.

Marie: You were the youngest?

Irène: No! I was the oldest! I was the oldest![3] But I don't know, in the end, my . . . my sister, who is two years younger than I, fulfilled more of a leadership role, if you like, in this kind of domain.

Jean: And then she's a housewife too!

Irène: She got her freedom more than I did, and earlier. Me, I got my freedom very, very late; I remained for a very, very long time subject to my mother's authority, while my sister, she rebelled and left home much earlier! She got married earlier too, and had children; she got her housewife life and she has a certain mistress-of-the-house authority that I myself do not have. I have the impression, though, that, for me, the role of the mistress of the house has always been a secondary role, because in the end, I never stopped working full-time.

Marie: Well, yes . . .

Irène: When it comes down to it, I never stopped working! My longest vacation was my maternity leave. I would have really liked to have had a second child in order to have a second maternity leave! It's true, to have a long, long vacation, that was something. It's a nostalgia that lasts a long time and becomes more and more pronounced. Now, if only I could take three months of vacation in a row. I would really be very, very happy.

Marie: And what did you do during this long vacation? Did you lead the life of a housewife, did you cook?

Irène: It happened to me just once and it passed very, very quickly because, at that time, Jean wasn't working, he didn't have a book in progress, so we used to go for strolls and we walked a lot during that period. It was very nice, but I never really led the life of a housewife.

Marie: OK. Hold on, about what you were saying earlier: "in the end, he cooks because he is a hearty eater." Is it, well, aren't being a hearty eater and liking to cook in fact linked? Are you a hearty eater yourself?

Jean: That's very strange. (*Jean and Marie spoke at the same time.*)

Irène: What did you mean?

Jean: For Pierre, it's strange because, when he was very young, very little, he abhorred eating. It was a devil of a job to get him to swallow something. He was as thin as a rail. (*Here there was an inaudible sentence on the tape.*) Afterwards, it was the exact opposite; he became enormous and he started eating like a pig. He had a fear of not getting enough, which was absolutely pathetic when you saw him. He always had his hands in the pot.

Irène: It was really unpleasant because his worry and his greed…

Jean: And he became a real *gourmand.*[4] Now he's a real gourmet.

Irène: The least thing we brought to the table, he was all over it. He was always afraid of not getting enough, he always wanted to have more than everyone else. It's Jean's second son, Pierre, who is sixteen.

Marie: Yes.

Irène: Well, *gourmandise,* you know, I've always thought that it was considered a sin. That's perhaps too strong, but in the end, eating well was judged as something secondary. It's part of this whole Protestant and puritan tradition in my family: we ate because we had to, but *gourmandise* was frowned upon.

Marie: I see. So your family is Protestant?

Irène: Yes, yes, yes. But for Sarah, when she likes something, I'm really happy, I'm ecstatic, you see! But at home, that's something that wasn't given much support. And my mother was always in a big, big hurry; she had a busy, busy life because my father had his own small business and she helped him a lot. She never had very much time to cook; meals were rather speedy affairs! When it comes down to it, meals here are a bit more relaxed. We have long, drawn-out meals! In the morning, for breakfast, all three of us eat together; since Sarah likes to take her time, we get up at 7:30; she leaves for school at 8:15, so we have plenty of time to eat together. At night, we dine peacefully: of course, I do the cooking rather quickly because, in my heart of hearts, I'm a rather practical and speed-oriented woman. I don't get weighed down in the details, I'm very expedient; whatever I do, I do it quickly. Then, at the table, we take our time. When it comes down to it, we have a rather rich family life from this point of view. We spend quite a bit of time together in proportion to other people. We see each other for quite a while in the morning and again at night, even more so now that Sarah is older and goes to bed at 9:30 P.M.; so that leaves us a little more freedom. Last year or two years ago, she had to go to bed earlier and that cut down the amount of time that we could spend together.

Marie: Yes, that's often the problem with children.

Irène: But from that point of view, I think Sarah has been relatively lucky: you see children already in day care right after birth, but she was already three months old when we put her in. In the end, I was always able to spend a good bit of time with her. For example, she stayed on the bottle for a very long time. I even had friends who made fun of me because I still gave her a bottle when she could have drunk very well from a cup; but it was a moment when we were together, when I really did nothing else but take care of her. Since I usually have a tendency to be in a hurry and to rush things, it forced me to remain seated, to take care of her at length, and I think that has been very, very beneficial for her.

Jean: Oh, the bath, too, that always lasted a long time.

Irène: Yes. And then Sarah also benefited from the fact that you were home a lot, compared to other children whose mother works, because it can be a serious problem when children come home from school and no one is there. When it comes down to it, when Sarah comes home, you are generally there, or, if you're not, it's because of special circumstances.[5] (*Silence.*)

Marie: And in terms of the preparation of food itself, how do you feel about it? Is cooking pleasurable?

Irène: It is only recently that I am taking pleasure in cooking. I'm rather anxious, if you like, anxious not to mess up what I'm making. For example, for a very, very long time, I never made desserts. It's only been since Sarah started liking them that we make any, because Jean, you didn't like them very much and before, when I was by myself, it was not really worth the trouble to make desserts. So it was really something barred from my experience . . . I really have trouble taking pleasure in cooking, because when it comes down to it, I'm not relaxed enough or sure enough of myself. Maybe later on I will be less worrisome and calm enough, in fact, to invent some things and to do it with pleasure. But, for the moment, this is not the case, because it's a domain where I do not feel at all at ease. So I just cook, that's all. There are some things I do rather well—soup, for example. I make some soups that are pretty good.

Jean: Oh, they're very good. Your green vegetable soups are delicious.

Irène: Yes, but for other things . . . Well, when we eat something good, something that is a success, I get the impression it's just by chance. It's just lucky.

Jean: No, you're kidding. You make s simple cuisine, but it's very good. Just go into a few restaurants and you'll see!

Irène: Oh, you're just too nice! (*Silence.*)

Jean: No. I like either very simple cuisine or very elaborate cuisine.

Marie: Really?

Jean: When I say very elaborate, I mean dishes made in a wood stove, with sauces, with bay leaves, a court bouillon that takes forty-five minutes to make . . . The day I made my famous tomato soup, I spent three hours on it. I dirtied up the whole kitchen, I stained all sorts of things, the ingredients were all over the place, I mixed a little of this with a little of that, and it was delicious, but now that I think of it, you didn't like it very much.

Irène: Oh, that's not true!

Marie: That must be why he never tried it again!

Irène: Oh, come on, we still talk about it! Your soup has become legendary!

Jean: Paul didn't even notice it.[6]

Irène: Why, was Paul even there?

Jean: Yes! You see?

Irène: I don't remember who we ate with anymore, but I remember that we all found it delicious. (*Silence.*)

Marie: If I understand it right, when you have a lot of people over, people who you don't know well, or at least several unexpected people, it's a problem?

Irène: Yes, it makes me a little anxious.

Jean: That's changed because you used to get really nervous two or three years ago.

Irène: You think so?

Jean: Well, yes! Before, you used to be trembling two hours ahead of time.

Irène: I don't know. I guess it's something I got from my mother: she gets horrible anxiety when she wants to do something well.

Marie: I think when you do something you're not used to doing, something you don't do every day, you're always a little afraid of not succeeding. I know I'm the same way when I cook.

Irène: Really?

Marie: I usually don't cook.[7] Sometimes, when I invite friends over, I would like to, I really would, but I get anxious. In reality, you mess things up much more easily when you get anxious. I think it's very much a question of habit. (*Silence.*) In other words, when you do something regularly, or something close to it, you become accustomed to it and you can occasionally add a minor ingredient to it, to improve on it or just to modify it slightly. But I don't think you can do it when you don't have enough regular practice.

Irène: Yes, perhaps. Sarah really likes chocolate mousse, and she begs me to make it very, very often, so my chocolate mousse ends up not being too bad after all.

Jean: It's actually quite good.

Irène: He doesn't even like it! Too bad for me! (*She laughs.*)

Marie: Do you make other desserts?

Irène: Pretty rarely. On weekends, you know, I make custards, or chocolate mousses and things like that. But cakes, I never make them!

Marie: And the custards, you make them all by yourself, or . . . ?

Irène: Oh yes! Yes, yes, yes, all by myself! There I at least have my sister's recipes! We spent some spring vacations in the country with my sister; there were many children who loved custard, so she used to make them every day. We had fresh milk from a farmer next door, so it was really nice. She used to make about five pints of custard every day, either caramel, or vanilla, or chocolate, and I started to make some too. Sometimes they're not bad at all.

Jean: Yes, I managed to get some down!

Irène: Yes, you did manage to, that's it. But otherwise, with cakes, I absolutely never make them. It's so happened that I've made some pies too, but pretty rarely, because there too, you don't really like them...

Jean: No, I have to have basic ingredients like durum wheat, for a pie crust [*pâte brisée*], that's all.

Irène: A pie crust isn't too complicated to make... (*then, in a hesitating tone*) that might be within my reach.

Jean: Me, I'm too difficult, if you like, to appreciate a "half-and-half" cuisine. I prefer simple cuisine, at least there are no snags. Just like with wine. I prefer to have a mediocre table wine rather than a Burgundy that only resembles a real Burgundy.

Marie: Who takes care of the wine?

Jean: Well, we don't take care of it! I gave up! I gave up because, in order to have real smooth ones, you have to go directly to a wine co-op or I don't know where...

Irène: In the past, there was a wine cellarman on our street who was...

Jean: Oh, he went bankrupt!

Irène: No, that's not true! He did not go bankrupt.

Jean: He sold his stock.

Irène: That's not the same thing at all! He couldn't find a way of training someone else to replace him, which happens often around here and it's very sad. Shops close and no one comes in to take their place.[8] Since then, anyway, we buy wine, but most of the time we just drink ordinary table wine...

Jean: Yes, because in Paris, buying a good bottle does not depend first of all on the price: you can have a fifteen-dollar bottle of wine[9] that is utterly revolting and an inexpensive one that is excellent! To buy really good wine, you have to know the producers. It's not the case with me, because I don't know any.

Irène: Yes, our friends who buy good wine most often buy it directly from the producer.

Jean: Well, the Denis' wine is not excellent!

Irène: But it was good, the wine we had there.

Marie: What you often get buying directly from the producer is a wine that is "sincere."

Irène: Yes, yes.

Marie: But you know wines all the same?

Irène: I know them a little; you can't say I know them very well, but I appreciate wine. In any case, with the cuisine I make, I don't appreciate it very often. It's very rare that I find that it's good, especially if there are guests! When it's just the three of us, I can judge whether it's good or bad. Otherwise...

Marie: You're too nervous to do so?

Irène: Oh, I don't know. But in terms of wine, especially when it's not me who chooses them, I can appreciate it, appreciate it even more.

Marie: When you dine at a friend's house, someone who cooks well, let's say, you can appreciate it?

Irène: Oh, yes, yes!

Marie: Thus, in terms of food, you're not all that interested?

Irène: No, that's not it. In fact, I can be somewhat of a hearty eater!

Marie: OK, it's just that you are not really sure about yourself in terms of cooking.

Irène: Yes, that's it.

Marie: So, for making dinner, I suppose you decide what you will eat every day more or less based on what Jean buys.

Irène: Yes, in the morning we see what provisions we have left and then decide to buy some type of vegetable, for example. But Jean has the freedom to buy the meat, fish, or vegetable that he wants, based also on what he finds, and at night I just make do with what he has brought back.

Marie: Doesn't he ever bring back some kind of meat that you don't know how to cook?

Irène: Oh, yes, but I just dive into my recipes and rush to my cookbooks. (*She laughs.*) I ask myself: what can we make with this?

Jean: Ah, but one day, I bought squid and it was I who prepared it... (*Silence.*) Don't you remember?

Irène: No!

Jean: So it's no use taking the trouble to cook! (*He laughs.*)

Irène: It's just to discourage you!

Marie: So, after the tomato soup that was not justly appreciated, we have the squid that left no trace!

Irène: The other day you brought back some stingray, so, to make stingray in brown butter sauce, I first looked in a cookbook. You had to make a court bouillon and that would have taken a long time. Finally, I found a recipe that was much faster and it was delicious! The risk of having Jean do the shopping according to his mood of the moment is that he brings back things that don't go well together, so you still have to have certain provisions on hand that allow you to match things, season well, and supplement too. For example, you have to have enough onions, garlic, tomatoes, and things like that to make do very quickly.

Marie: Is there a great variety in what you make, or is it always pretty much the same things over and over?

Irène: I try to vary things a little, but when it comes down to it, my cooking is pretty monotonous, after all.

Jean: It starts getting expensive to buy other vegetables or other meats, such as mutton or leg of lamb, or a beef filet.

Irène: Yes, we do too buy mutton! But we buy neck meat or cuts like that. We do tend to buy inexpensive meats. We never buy veal. When we buy pork, it's generally a loin, but we very rarely make roast beef, all the more so since we get the chance to eat good meat when we're invited here or there! (*She laughs.*) That allows us to save money at home. And besides, we don't eat meat every day! For example, when I make a meat dish on Saturdays, and when I make enough, it so happens that we have it for three days even. If I make neck of mutton or a pot-au-feu or something like that, we can have it for three days, but interspersed with other things: for example, we eat it on Saturday, but not on Sunday, then on Monday and then again on Wednesday. At least there's some alternation! But you can't say we have an extremely varied menu.

Jean: No.

Irène: We eat a good deal of potatoes, rice, pasta, beans, split peas, lentils, or things like that . . .

Marie: When you have a dish like that you say that you "eat it for three days." Is it exactly the same dish? You put it in the fridge, and you reheat it, or do you change it along the way?

Irène: That depends! There are things that are just fine reheated; for instance, we had made—I had made—some beans, a cassoulet. Well, I heated them up the first time, and it was a little dry; the second time, I heated them up in a tomato sauce that I'd made beforehand, and it was much better! Or, when we have roast pork, the first time, we eat it just as a roast; the second time, we have it cold or heated up in a sauce; and finally, I make a shepherd's pie with what's left or something like that with ground meat; I add onions and garlic, things like that.

Marie: Even so, you have basic recipes that you know well: for instance to add a tomato sauce to the beans, you don't have to look in your cookbook.

Irène: No, that's just something I invented: of course, I didn't need to look in my cookbook. And, for example, with leftover fish, I can make a soufflé. You see, we really use every last bit.

Marie: What kind of cookbook do you use?

Irène: I have a little book by Mapie Toulouse-Lautrec that is very well done, with recipes that are fast, with menus you can make in thirty or forty or fifty minutes. I find a lot of things in it. Then I get recipes from *Elle*, which we get a little late in my office. The magazines come under the name of a guy who left for Canada a long time ago. We get them two or three months late: there, I generally get knitting patterns and I take the recipes that interest me, simple recipes that might be useful to me. On Saturdays or Sundays, before Jean goes shopping, I often take a look at these recipes just to try to vary things and make something new. That way, I try to make something different.

Marie: And do you jump right into something new easily, something you've never done? With pleasure?

Irène: Yes! I have a lot of fun! Yes, I like it. (*Silence.*)

Marie: So you have that one particular cookbook; do you have any others?

Irène: Yes, I have a book called *The Recipes of Aunt Marie*, or something like that: it's the classic hardback where I can find, for example, hints on cooking times that are not always given or that are given incorrectly in the other book.

Marie: This title, *The Recipes of Aunt Marie*, for me, it evokes recipes that would be rather complicated.

Irène: Oh, no, they're really quite easy, dead simple!

Marie: And the clippings from *Elle*, are they usable?

Jean: Well, they're not great! It's mostly for show.

Irène: Jean, that's not true at all! You're just joking around. I don't agree!

Jean: Just some nice pictures!

Irène: No! Sometimes there are some rather astute things, and other times some very, very simple things, too!

Jean: And the sea bream with oranges, where did you find that?

Irène: That was Mapie Toulouse-Lautrec. But, for example, I also have the book they give out with pressure cookers; when you buy an SEB cooker, you also get this book.[10]

Marie: Yes, and it's very practical.

Irène: There are a lot of things in it, a lot of very simple things that you can play around with. Mapie's recipes, for example, I cook with them, but

I make them in a pressure cooker, and so I adapt the cooking times, things like that. I once had a bad time with the pressure cooker book: I had cooked some dried beans (*she laughs*) and the cooking time was too short—there was a printer's error for the cooking time, so stupidly... (*she laughs*).[11] So we had two cousins eating with us that night, two very, very nice boys, and they had some trouble eating their beans! It was really touching.

Jean: One of them even asked for more! I don't know how he did it! (*Laughter.*)

Irène: So I've had a few misadventures. Another time, I made a dessert with kirsch, but I put ten times too much kirsch in it. The result was horrible. And the same cousins were there!

Marie: They have no luck!

Irène: Those guys are really very, very nice, and asked for more again, saying it was very good.

Marie: Maybe they like kirsch!

Irène: Maybe they do like kirsch!... (*Silence, followed by an interruption while turning the cassette over.*)

Marie: What were we talking about? Oh, yes, with the women at your office?

Irène: Yes, it so happens that we talk a little about cooking or things like that. But in the end, I have never asked them for recipes; I've gotten recipes from a cousin or my sister: in fact, for the custards, I imitated my sister's recipe, and since then they turn out much better than following the recipe from *Elle* or from other books.

Marie: Yes, I think that, generally, recipes we receive like that are often better than cookbook recipes.

Irène: Yes, perhaps; in the end, they're probably better adapted to our situation.

Marie: Perhaps that too, yes. (*Silence.*)

Irène: We eat well pretty often. I have a friend who is a very, very good cook. It's a real pleasure to go to her place! And she never pays attention to the price of meat, so she always buys high-quality things, very, very good wines...

Jean: Two incomes, no children—it's only natural!

Marie: Yes.

Irène: Yes. But when we're treating ourselves at her house, I never note down recipes because I'm thinking of something else, or we're doing something else together! I could ask her afterwards, because we see her fairly often! But when it comes down to it, I have never asked her for a recipe: cuisine, that's her domain, if you like.

Marie: Perhaps you feel a bit that these are the kinds of things that you'd never succeed in making?

Irène: Perhaps a little, yes.

Jean: It's just that she uses the most expensive things!

Irène: No, that's not it, she likes to...

Jean: The day you were all ecstatic about her salad, what was in it? Some nuts, some bean sprouts, nothing original!

Irène: I don't know. In any case, it was a recipe that she got somewhere, she didn't invent it either.

Jean: How could you get a salad recipe? You take raw vegetables, you put them in a bowl, you add a little vinegar, and then you toss it.

Irène: Of course not! That's not true! There are things that...

Marie: No, there's a way to do it, after all, and certain things go together better with others.

Irène: Absolutely!

Marie: Variations in the sauce...

Irène: You who think you're so smart, you don't seem to know anything at all! You should just try to do it yourself!

Jean: No, because I didn't think her salad was all that extraordinary, precisely because I found there were some things that didn't go well together. (*Laughter.*)

Marie: That's another story!

Irène: Yes, but generally, she makes really good cuisine. She makes desserts and then again, she takes the trouble, and she likes to have people over a lot, and she does it all well.

Marie: Yes. And does she work too?

Irène: Yes, she works. They're people who have no kids so they really enjoy having friends over! I really like to have friends over, but, in the end, during the time when our neighbors used to come over like that, unexpectedly, I liked it quite a bit because I was faced with the task of having to feed six people and of getting by with what I had on hand. So I didn't worry in advance over the menu that I was going to make, over the things I didn't have when I got home; there, I just managed, and if it was a flop, it was because a certain number of things were lacking. So it was OK. In the end, it was very pleasant. When we have friends who stay with us for a week, I end up liking that too! We make a slightly more elaborate cuisine, but we don't go to too much trouble; if it's one of my sisters, she chips in a little too to lend a helping hand.

Marie: How do you decide when you have guests over, well, people who come by, how do you choose what you're going to make? In other words, depending on the people who are coming, do you think about...

Irène: There are some people who I know don't like certain things, so I pay attention to that.

Marie: You manage to remember all of that?

Irène: Yes, yes, yes! Even so, I try to remember a little what I made the last time they came over. There are some people who we don't have over very often, so we end up remembering what we made for them. Those I like to have over almost the most are your sons (*she says, turning toward Jean*), because it's a real pleasure to indulge them; we really get the impression that they appreciate it, these big boys with their big appetites, so for them, I will take the trouble; I will try to make something that's a little better than usual.

Marie: But for someone whom you don't know, or not very well, how do you decide?

Irène: Oh, I don't know, I flip through my clippings from *Elle*, and I let myself get carried away with inspiration. Then, in the end, I usually like to make something new. I'm not really afraid of throwing myself into something new, even for strangers, because, when all is said and done, I don't feel that I do any better with things I have already done than with new things. So, you see, I don't feel that I'm taking many risks!

Marie: One question that we have asked ourselves is when, for example, a woman so often says to herself, "What am I going to do for dinner? What am I going to make? Hey, I know, I'll make this — they'll surely like it!" How can one guess, or well, what happens in this choice, this way of deciding? Does it happen to you that way, to have a sort of intuition into what a certain kind of person will like?

(*Silence.*)

Irène: For people who are close, it's rather easy because we know them well.

Marie: That is to say, even if you make something new, you know in advance that they will like it?

Irène: Yes! I think so, anyway.

Jean: In other words, when it comes down to it, we don't have any friends who are gourmets.

Irène: No! *Gourmands* like Claire and François, it's better to get invited to their house, precisely because they make a very good meal, rather than inviting them over here!

Marie: Yes, if they come to your house, they know they're not coming to "eat well," after all. They come for something else!

Irène: Yes, yes. Moreover, it's very funny, because actually, my friend Claire was in the hospital for a time, and it so happened that François came to dinner three times. It was really unexpected, because I would be at her bedside at the same time as he; and, leaving the hospital, instead of him going back to his place to eat alone, I would tell him: "Why don't you come over to our house for dinner?" And it was exactly on days when there was nothing to offer him, the poor guy, who was used to eating well! This being said, with Claire in the hospital, he had to eat noodles almost every day because he wouldn't cook much more than Jean! So everything I made was a little bit better than what he usually ate all by himself. Finally, François practically only came here to eat during Claire's illness. Afterwards, to see them, we took up the old habit of going to their house; they already have more free time to make things, and we know we will eat well when we go there, so it makes us happy! I have to say that I appreciate going to someone else's house to eat, not having to worry about cooking.[12]

Marie: Right, in other words, for you it's really...

Irène: For me, it's a worry all the same!

Marie: From the point of view of the utensils you use, you have the pressure cooker you use a lot. And do you use any electric appliances, things like that?

Irène: No. We don't have any electric appliances, except for the coffee grinder that we got as a gift.

Marie: Why?

Irène: Because, first of all, I abhor noisy things and I prefer using elbow grease than listening to the noise of a motor! So I prefer beating my egg whites with a hand whisk rather than having an electric gadget. And these kinds of appliances are often annoying to clean afterwards, whereas manual ones are very simple. In the end, all the time you save using them, you lose in the cleanup. And it's also very cumbersome. We have space concerns here, after all; it's not very big, so it would be horrible to be encumbered with a ton of stuff.

Jean: You wouldn't mind having a Moulinex [brand of household appliance], though!

Irène: I thought that I might buy a Moulinex to beat egg whites or things like that, but the issue of noises from the motor held me back. You see, I find that kind of noise even more tiring than doing things by hand. There's one thing that's annoying to do, and that's grinding meat, because I'm poorly equipped for that. When there's some leftover pork, for example, that you have to grind to make minced meat or stuffing, it really takes an incredible amount of effort! But it wouldn't really be worth it, because I don't often make these kinds of things. So I would have an appliance that takes up an inordinate amount of space, and what would it be good for? Darn! I'm really not tempted to buy a ton of kitchen appliances. Perhaps it's linked to the small amount of time I spend there?

Marie: Yes, that's possible...

Irène: I manage very well with what I have. In the end, what I really like is when we go camping and have to make do with really a minimum of utensils. So you have to invent little tricks, because you don't have thirty-six pots and pans; you only have two of them, so you have to combine things together so that all your cooking can be done in just two, you see. You have to manage in the end with insufficient means; I have a sort of poverty ethic—which surely comes down to me from my Protestant childhood. When it comes down to it, austerity is something that has never frightened me, on the contrary.

Jean: Well, there, I'm just like you!

Irène: The camping life, that pleases me enormously: you see, you spend a minimum amount of time doing things, or not at all! It's not even a question of time, because there, you really have the time to peel your potatoes! But you don't mind spending three hours peeling vegetables: in any case, you do it outside, under the trees, and you can look at the landscape at the same time.

Marie: Yes, that's it, there are other pleasures...

Irène: There are other pleasures! You do everything in a more relaxed way: you have to invent things to do the dishes too, because you have only one container to wash in, and then you have to conserve water because you have to walk a mile to get more; things like that, it's really something that pleases me. What displeases me about all these modern appliances is perhaps the impression of waste. In the end, we practically throw away nothing, you see. We have a friend who always makes fun of us because we have such a tiny trash can: her trash can is twice as large and she always says to us: "How do you get by with such a small trash can?" Well, first off, we only have one meal a day here, and also we throw out very little!

Marie: Yes.

Irène: Waste is something that has always profoundly shocked me.

Jean: That's sort of the reason why I don't do any real cuisine: you have to have all kinds of things, pots and pans, it never ends.

Irène: You're the one who should wash them if you used them.

Jean: So I have to wash them too, huh?

(*Silence.*)

Marie: Yes, that's one aspect of cooking that discourages me too. I say to myself: it's such a mess, and then in almost no time, everything disappears. I find that hopeless. (*Silence.*) And in terms of shopping? Where do you shop, whether it's you or Jean? Do you prefer to go to little shops with shopkeepers who are always the same, or do you change a lot by frequenting open-air markets or big supermarkets, and so on?

Irène: There are a certain number of things that I buy at a Monoprix [a large, widespread supermarket in France] that's near my office, because, afterwards, even if I have a very heavy bag, I take the bus right there and I get home quickly. So, for a certain number of things, for economic reasons, even though I have never calculated what I could save—for pasta, coffee, rice, and things like that, sugar, I buy at Monoprix. I go there regularly. Jean never counts on what I buy because, in the end, if I get out of work late, the Monoprix is closed. I know that I'll find what's needed at home, though, you see; so what I buy at Monoprix, it's mostly basic provisions. We used to have a greengrocer a couple of paces from here who was really extraordinary, the little neighborhood grocer who had good-quality vegetables, no more expensive than at the open-air market, and he also had very good-quality fruit; he gave us quite a bit of good advice on cheeses—he was really marvelous! Then they closed this summer; we found the door closed at back-to-school time in September, and we looked out the window every morning to see if anyone had delivered any milk, but no! He sold out, like all the people in that neighborhood, to a clothing vendor! So now Jean goes to an outdoor market a bit farther away.

Jean: No! I don't go to the market, I go to . . .

Irène: You go to Félix Potin [a small grocery store], for groceries, huh?

Jean: Yes, not for vegetables.

Irène: For vegetables, you go down to the rue Ducrot? We each have our habits, after all. When I go shopping, *I* go to the rue Saint-Louis or the big market on boulevard Davila, where I sometimes go on Sundays. That's a real market. I really like that a lot!

Marie: It's a pleasure, the market, yes . . .

Irène: Yes, it's really delicious! I do bring back plenty of things, but when it comes down to it, I rarely go.

Marie: I think the market is really a pleasure for the eyes.

Irène: Yes . . . and also a pleasure for other reasons: there are the smells, and then the atmosphere, and the choice too. You have ten kinds of potatoes all next to each other, you have a lot of greens, there's a sort of marvelous abundance. It's not like a big supermarket where everything is spread out and offered in a provocative way; at the market, it's proposed in a much more natural way, much less ostentatious, you see. To get you to buy, the people at the market have to make a much greater effort, they have to call you over, and shout and make an unbelievable sales pitch, whereas at Monoprix, everything is offered just as it is, immobile, without movement. However, I find Monoprix to be very practical to do your shopping very quickly. There are a certain number of things that I do better buying at Monoprix; corn flakes, for example, if you buy them at Félix Potin next door, you have little boxes like this; at Monoprix, I bring back huge boxes like this (*she makes hand gestures to illustrate*). That's important, after all!

Marie: Yes. And why Félix Potin, then?

Jean: Why Félix Potin? Oh, because I get a little lost in all the stores on rue Ducrot. You have to go to one for cheese, another for eggs, a third for milk, and a fourth for vegetables. So there, I get vegetables from the vendor, never the same ones, either, it depends on their quality. The price, I never pay attention to it, it's always more or less the same price!

Irène: That's not true! You should, you could pay more attention!

Jean: Pffhh! You know very well that one pound of carrots is enough. Listen, there's only the two of us![13] What's the point? What's the point in saving a dime on a two-pound bag of carrots that only costs ninety-nine cents?

Irène: No, but when it adds up every day, that...

Jean: Since I change vendors, the prices always change!

Irène: (*She laughs.*) Yeah, right! I don't think that's very rational, but it's no big deal!

Jean: It's not rational, but I consider that, based on our lifestyle, our income, and the price of vegetables, it's not worth the effort to choose the least expensive vegetables!

Irène: Humph...OK...

Jean: One day I ran into Philippe,[14] who said to me: "Hey, I was at the other end of the market and it's less expensive!" Fine, then, if it's cheaper at the other end, OK; I went to see: it was less expensive for two days, and then it was no longer the case. It depends on availability, there's no set rule.

Irène: You just go to Félix Potin because it's the closest!

Jean: It is the closest!

Irène: It's the closest and it's rather convenient; you're familiar with it and you know where to find things.

Jean: Yes, that's it, I know where everything is. But I don't buy a whole lot at Félix Potin, wine, always the same, milk, yogurt, bread, but I don't like their bread because they don't have *bâtards* [short baguettes]: they're much better than a baguette. My bread, I buy it a bit farther away.

Marie: And for meat?

Jean: Oh, for meat, I have a butcher I go to. Always the same. I changed butchers because the one at the end of the street was bad. And I didn't like him either, whereas over there, at the other place, there's a charming woman. I have always found that meat is always better according to the kind of person who sells it, and I have never been wrong. When the butchers are nice, male or female—it depends—the meat is good; when the butchers are disgusting, their meat is bad!

Marie: (*laughing*) You'd have to verify that!

Irène: (*She laughs too.*) Yes!

Jean: (*overly serious*) Just try it and you'll see!

Marie: (*still laughing*) No, but I have the same sort of reactions!

Jean: In restaurants, well, now I don't eat in restaurants anymore, I don't really know what they're like anymore; but ten years ago or more,[15] when I often ate in restaurants, I by chance noticed that in those that had red-and-white tablecloths, the food was very good! You know, the classic rustic tablecloths.

Irène: Yes, yes.

Marie: In fact, it's also perhaps a psychological effect: I, too, like to eat on these tablecloths a lot, and I'll go into a restaurant more easily if there are red-and-white checkerboard tablecloths.

Jean: Well, for me, it's not psychological! I have very fine taste, I'm sure that the food is better: it's traditional cuisine, blanquettes, pot-au-feu, anything "meunière," those kinds of things.

Marie: Exactly. It's really just saying that the decor has to be adapted to the style of cuisine.

Irène: Yes.

Jean: Now, it's no longer valid, with all the Borel and other restaurant chains...[16] In the past, "Chez Whomever" was good; as if the person who did the cooking had his honor at stake and wanted absolutely to maintain the reputation of "Whomever." (*He emphasizes the words "Chez Whomever" each time.*)

Marie: Yes...

Jean: Or Gérard, or Jean, or...I used to know several restaurants that were called "Chez So-and-so," and it was delicious, no more expensive than anywhere else. With Borel, though, they don't give a damn! Their cooking is lousy because there is no name to defend: they defend their money, not their name.

Irène: Yes, all he's interested in is earning money!

Jean: Earning money, it's just lousy! The guy with a place called "Chez Gérard," well, it's a question of his grandfather or his father or himself, so he wants to maintain the name!

Marie: That's true.

Jean: I used to know a little restaurant, "Chez Jean," near the ORTF, that was absolutely delicious![17] I used to know one, "Chez..." I don't remember what, on the place Cortot, that was absolutely delicious!

Marie: About this question of checkerboard tablecloths, I was just thinking about the presentation aspect of all this. Is it something that you think about?

Irène: Yes. I haven't a lot—we don't sound the depths of imagination, but we think about it.

Jean: Tonight, for example, I had put the oilcloth on the table and she made me take it off and put on the tablecloth.[18] (*Laughter.*)

Irène: No, but for example, we like to light candles for dinner. Everything looks better under candlelight. We don't make a lot of effort at decoration, but I like it when the table is pretty! In any case, from the point of view of tableware, we have everything we need. Even if I make no effort to buy kitchen gadgets, I still like the dishes we have, I chose them with care, I didn't buy just any old thing! They are simple dishes, because I don't like things that are too ornate, and I like the fact that we can replace them rather easily, replace broken plates, and so on, because I don't like to have a set of dishes that is a complete mishmash either. I like the dishes we have well enough: they are earthenware with simple, somewhat rustic, serving platters. We always take the trouble to see to it that the table is not crowded with a pile of things, so that the leftovers or the vegetable dish are not still there when we're eating dessert. When it comes down to it, I don't like that!

Marie: Yes.

Irène: I find, though, that there is still a certain harmony in the way we live. We don't eat lunch in disorder and we don't eat dinner at high speed, we take our time for meals.[19] Jean generally sets the table while I'm making dinner; there's not a lot of variety from one day to the next, but we still make an effort.

Marie: And the presentation, that counts too, I mean the presentation of dishes.

Irène: Oh, yes! Don't you think so? Yes? (*She speaks, turned toward Jean.*) For example, when I set out the hors d'oeuvres, I have fun making things that are rather pretty.

Jean: Yeah.

Irène: I bought a set of pots and pans, among the most expensive, that you can easily bring to the table: it's practical and attractive at the same time. They match the dishes and it avoids having to use a pan plus a serving dish, and so on, you see. But I wouldn't bring just any old pan to the table![20]

Marie: When you are cooking, do you think about the colors you put together? Do you have preferences for certain colors of foods?

Irène: For a time, I had black dishes and I found them very pretty because the food really comes out well against a black background. We changed these black dishes later because we couldn't find any more to complete the set: it was no longer in fashion! There are only two plates left and we use them for the cat. You have no idea how lucky you are, Mr. Cat!

Marie: He seems to know because he purrs like crazy!

Irène: We bought other kinds of plates, but, for example, I would never use the orange plastic salad spoons with just any salad! I wouldn't use them for beets, for example. That would be very ugly.

Jean: We'll have to change those salad spoons anyway, they are vile!

Irène: Listen, that is not true! (*Silence.*)

Marie: You have earthenware dishes, so I suppose that you have things in wood too; do you like that kind of style?

Irène: Yes, I have things made of wood; we have some Swedish flatware in a style that I find very pretty, and very simple glasses that come from Monoprix but that I find pretty too and that are easily replaceable! Glasses are easily broken so you have to be able to replace them one by one: we don't have one set of dishes for Sundays and another for the rest of the week; we have one set of dishes that are all kept in the kitchen, and there are relatively few of them. We are not equipped to have a large number of guests at the same time. We prefer to receive people a few at a time, rather than having big gatherings or large reunions.

Marie: And while you're cooking, do smells—you were saying earlier that you like the smells at the market—are there smells that bother you, or that you like?

Irène: Yes. Well...in the kitchen, in general, there are usually the smells that one really likes!

Jean: We hesitated a long time before making sardines!

Irène: We did hesitate a long time before having sardines, but we like to eat them a lot, so when we do, we air the place out a bit...

Marie: But why? Was this the problem with French fries earlier?[21] It's for the same reason?

Jean: I'm the one who's opposed to them, because of the smell! Because of the smell and the fact that the oil stays in the fryer indefinitely.

Irène: And also, you're convinced that I'd let them cook too long and that I'd heat the oil too high and that...yes...

Jean: And I'm also convinced that she would let them burn!

Marie: That's not very encouraging!...

Irène: It's not very encouraging for me! (*Laughter.*)

Marie: It's not as hard as all that to make good fries!

Irène: No! But there are a certain number of things that I don't try to do, because…

Jean: No, but I'm used to it! It all comes from my childhood! We had a cook who cooked very poorly, who always cooked poorly, it was too greasy; and for her fries, she used oil that had been around for months and months.[22]

Marie: A bad memory…

Jean: Disgusting! So I've kept a memory of the fries at Saint-André! I'm very sensitive about fries, so I would rather not bawl out my wife every time she'd make some that were bad!

Irène: Maybe I could make them well!

Jean: Maybe, but there's a risk at stake. (*Laughter.*)

Irène: But I still haven't found the courage for the last ten years!

Jean: Before, there was a fellow who sold fries just down the street and they were excellent! When we wanted fries, we bought them there! But he closed down, so you can make them now.

Irène: No, but it's like for cakes or desserts; in the end, you don't really appreciate them that much, so…

Jean: No, I've changed. Now I'm starting again to…

Irène: You're starting to appreciate cakes? So I'm going to have to make some? What a job! (*She laughs.*)

Jean: It's safer to buy them at a bakery![23]

Marie: That, I think, is something that you can easily do better than in a bakery.

Irène: You think?

Marie: Yes, homemade cakes are not the same.

Irène: Homemade cakes, yes, sure, I could easily find recipes that would be good!

Jean: Yes, a pound cake, for example.

Irène: I could certainly ask Thérèse[24] for some: she makes cakes often. It often smells nice in her kitchen when you go by.

Jean: But she buys ready-made pastry dough.

Irène: To make pies, yes.

Jean: I don't know.

Irène: It's not hard to make pies!

Marie: I think frozen pastry dough is practical.

Irène: Yes, it's practical, but it's not hard to make pie dough!

Marie: For pastries, there is obviously the small problem of the oven. You have to know your oven, to know if it cooks fast.

Jean: Since they've changed, since they put in natural gas, there's a pressure problem.

Marie: Ah, natural gas, yes. I've never had a gas oven myself, but I have had problems with the heater, problems with the pilot light.

Irène: Here, when I finally decide to turn on the oven, I haven't been able to use the burners at the same time ever since we got natural gas.

Marie: Yes, so it's also a problem to make pastries, because you generally bake them while you're preparing the rest of the meal.

Irène: Yes...

Jean: You can't use both at the same time, the burners and the oven?

Irène: The burners don't work well at all when the oven is on.

Jean: Well, call them, we have a six-month guarantee.

Irène: But I don't know if we can...

Marie: Coming back to smells, one really nice smell is exactly that, the smell of baked goods.

Irène: But there are also meat smells; it often smells very good when meat is cooking. I really like that. Smells of baked goods, there's not a lot of that here!

Marie: Cold desserts do not have much of a smell.

Irène: They don't have a smell at all!

Jean: Oh, cauliflower is horrible! It will stick in all the rooms, even in the back of the apartment, and it stays there. It's also very strange that these odors move to the most distant rooms in the apartment, but they clearly do! It doesn't smell like cauliflower in here anymore,[25] nor in the kitchen, but it smells in our bedroom...

Marie: That's not pleasant! Another thing too is the act of touching things: is it something you think about, I don't know, are there things that you like to touch, that you like to handle, or, on the other hand, things that disgust you?

Irène: There are not many things that disgust me. The thing that made the strongest impression on me was once when we were camping by the sea and I scaled a fish that was still alive. Well, that made me...

Jean: It was a wrasse.

Irène: It was a wrasse that we had bought from a fisherman who had just caught it. It seemed to be done in and then, when I scaled it, it woke up, and that was really very unpleasant! Otherwise, there are relatively few things that disgust me.

Marie: For example, a young woman told me that she really liked to handle meat. She doesn't like to eat it very much, but she really likes to play with meat when it's raw, to trim off small bits of fat, and so on.

Irène: Really! I wouldn't go so far as to say that: for example, when we have leftover chicken still on the carcass, I make a soup rather easily. Now, with the cat here, we give what's left to the cat—before, I would carefully pick off the small bits of meat from the carcass to put in the soup, and that would end up as a soup with small chunks of chicken in it. When it comes down to it, I really liked touching that meat, but it was raw meat—no, cooked, well-done meat even! I don't really like to touch raw meat.

nvoi

Michel de Certeau and Luce Giard

A Practical Science of the Singular

Considering culture as it is practiced, not in what is most valued by official representation or economic politics, but in what upholds it and organizes it, three priorities stand out: orality, operations, and the ordinary. All three of them come back to us through the detour of a supposed foreign scene, *popular culture*, which has benefited from numerous studies on oral traditions, practical creativity, and the actions of everyday life. One more step is necessary to break down this fictive barrier and recognize that in truth it concerns *our culture*, without our being aware of it. This is because the social sciences have analyzed in terms of "popular culture" certain types of functioning that remained fundamental in our modern urban culture but that were considered illegitimate or negligible by the academic discourses of modernity. Just as sexuality, repressed by bourgeois morality, resurfaced in the dreams of Freud's patients, these functions of human sociality, denied by an unyielding ideology of writing, production, and specialized techniques, made a comeback in the guise of "popular culture," in our social and cultural space, which in fact they had never left.

By progressively ensuring their autonomy, industry and technology of culture detached themselves from these three sectors in order to make them the very object of their conquests. Oral culture became the target that a writing was supposed to educate and inform. Practitioners have been transformed into supposedly passive consumers. Ordinary life has been made into a vast territory offered to the media's colonization. Yet, the elements that were thought to have been eliminated continued to determine social exchanges and to organize the way of "receiving" cultural messages, that is, transforming them through the use made of them.

Orality

Orality demands the recognition of its rights, and rightly so, because we are beginning to grasp more clearly that the oral has a founding role in the relation to the other. The desire to speak comes to the child that the music of voices envelops, names, and calls out to exist for his or her own account. An entire archaeology of voices codifies and makes possible the interpretation of relations based on the recognition of voices that are familiar and quite close.[1] These are musics of sounds and meanings, polyphonies of speakers who seek each other out, listen, interrupt, overlap, and respond to each other. Later on, the oral tradition that he or she will have received will measure the child's reading capacity. Only cultural memory so acquired allows one little by little to enrich the strategies for questioning meaning whose expectations are refined and corrected upon deciphering a text. The child will learn how to read through the expectation and anticipation of meaning, both nourished and coded by the oral information already at his or her disposal.[2] The neglected child, to whom one rarely speaks, in an impoverished language, is caught unprepared by the thickness of a text's meaning: faced with the multiplicity of signals to identify, interpret, and coordinate, such a child remains dazed and disoriented.

Orality also constitutes the essential space of community. In a society, there is no communication without orality, even when this society gives a large place to what is written for the memorizing of tradition or the circulation of knowledge. Social exchange demands a correlation of gestures and bodies, a presence of voices and accents, marks of breathing and passions, an entire hierarchy of complementary information necessary for interpreting a message that goes beyond a simple statement—rituals of address and greeting, chosen registers of expression, nuances added by intonation, facial movements. It must have this *vocal grain* through which the speaker becomes identified and individualized, and this way of making a visceral, fundamental link between sound, meaning, and body.

Telecommunication practices have reorganized the speaking space, but the telephone, which triumphed over the telegraph and diminished the use of the personal letter, presents the voice with redoubled intensity as a *singular voice*. It amplifies its particularities (timbre, delivery, stress, pronunciation), just as radio does. It teaches you to distinguish one voice from every other, for perceptive (auditory) attention is concentrated here on the voice separated from the image (and from visual, tactile perception) of the body to which this voice belongs. Each of us thus becomes a living memory of cherished voices, such as the opera-crazy music lovers who recognize a female singer from the very first notes sung. This concert of voices also involves television, more often "heard" than seen: turned on for a large part of the day, it furnishes a horizon of voices that, from time to time, call out to be seen. Orality thus retains the primary role in our societies of writing and figures; it is more served than thwarted by the media or the resources of electronics. In its favor is listening to recorded music, which has become habitual, a listening whose diversity has widened common perception to include other registers of voices, instrumental timbres, and tonal scales. The voice imposes itself everywhere in its mystery of physical seduction, in its polycultural treatment,[3] to which it is suitable to associate the rapid development of "independent local radio stations," which have contributed to liberating us from rigid models and have given rise to new "sonorous landscapes."

Orality is everywhere, because *conversation* insinuates itself everywhere, organizing both the family and the street, both work in a business and research in a laboratory.[4] Oceans of communication have infiltrated everywhere, and are always determining, even there where the final product of the activity erases all trace of this relationship to orality. Conversation probably takes its inferior theoretical status from being natural and necessary in all places. How can one credit the ruses of so ordinary a practice with intelligence and refined complexity? Yet, the study of cognitive processes shows that new information is received and assimilated, that is, becomes appropriable and memorizable, only when the person acquiring it succeeds in putting it into *his or her own form*, in making it his or her own by inserting it into conversation, into usual language, and into the coherencies that structure his or her previous knowledge.[5] Failing to pass through this stage, new information will remain fragile and at any moment likely to be forgotten, distorted, or contradicted. Its acquisition depends also on the configuration of speaking situations where it comes into play: every speaker occupies a certain social position, and what he or she says is understood and interpreted as a function of this position.[6] School failure and the difficulty of continuing adult education have to do with the lack of understanding about speaking situations, with the erroneous belief in the signifying transparency of statements, outside the process of enunciation.

Priority goes to the illocutory, to that which involves neither words nor phrases, but the identity of speakers, the circumstance, the context, the "sonorous materiality" of exchanged speech. All the inventiveness of "language games" slips in across a staging of conflicts and interests pointed out in half-words: ruses, semantic drift, misunderstanding, sound effects, invented words, and distorted words in the style of Gildas Bourdet's *Saperleau*,[7] dialogues that proliferate and journey afar, with the humor-filled distancing and indexing that ordinary people make use of in order to modify the discomfort of life and to make a laughingstock of the slogans of the day. A city breathes when *places for speech* exist within it, regardless of their official function — the neighborhood café, the marketplace, the line at the post office, the newspaper stand, or the main door of the school at the end of the day.

Operativity

Culture is judged by its operations, not by the possession of products. In art, understanding a painting involves recognizing the gestures that gave birth to it, the painter's "strokes," "brushwork," and "palette." The art of the cook is all about production, based on a limited choice of available ingredients, in a combination of gestures, proportions, utensils, and cooking or transformation methods. Similarly, communication is a *cuisine of gestures and words*, of ideas and information, with its recipes and its subtleties, its auxiliary instruments and its neighboring effects, its distortions and its failures. It is false to believe henceforth that electronic and computerized objects will do away with the activity of users. From the hi-fi stereo to the VCR, the diffusion of these devices multiplies ruses and provokes the inventiveness of users, from the manipulatory jubilations of children faced with buttons, keyboards, and the remote control, to the extraordinary technical virtuosity of "sound chasers" and other impassioned fans of hi-fi. People record fragments of programs, produce montages, and thus become producers of their own little "cultural industry," compilers and managers of a private library of visual and sound archives. In turn, this collection becomes the bartering object in the network of family or friends. A new form of conviviality thus becomes organized within the circle of regulars, and thus perception becomes refined, then the critical judgment of viewers or listeners who return twenty times to an image, a fragment of a melody, who repeat a sequence, dissect it, and end up penetrating its secrets.

By itself, culture is not information, but its treatment by a series of operations as a function of objectives and social relations. The first aspect of these operations is *aesthetic*: an everyday practice opens up a unique space within an imposed order, as does the poetic gesture that bends the use of common language to its own desire in a transforming reuse. The second aspect is *polemical*: the everyday practice is relative to the power relations that structure the social field as well as the field of knowledge. To appropriate information for oneself, to put it in a series, and to bend its montage to one's own taste is to take power over a certain knowledge and thereby overturn the imposing power of the ready-made and preorganized. It is, with barely visible or namable operations, to trace one's own path through the resisting social system. The last aspect is *ethical*: everyday practice patiently and tenaciously restores a space for play, an interval of freedom, a resistance to what is imposed (from a model, a system, or an order). To be able to do something is to establish distance, to defend the autonomy of what comes from one's own personality.

The example of Lorraine Cœur d'Acier (LCA, Longwy), an ephemeral independent local radio station (March 17, 1979–January 20, 1981) has much to teach. In a declining industrial region, the Lorraine Cœur d'Acier station established the bias of live broadcasting, each person being able to have access to the airwaves by coming in to the studio or by calling in. A dynamic was thus created for the appropriation of radio by a working-class population little accustomed to public discourse. The experiment acted as a revelation or a spur: someone astonishingly discovered that his or her coworker secretly wrote poems, and someone else confessed to being an amateur painter. By focusing attention on the local object and ordinary speech, according to its slogan "Listen to Yourself," LCA returned to this object, to this speech, their dignity and equalized them with other objects, other types of speech.[8] A steelworker, overwhelmed by the experience, summed it up beautifully:

> There, on the radio, it was possible to say, you'd say things to yourself, and you wanted to say it. It was possible to send words down into homes and after a while the listener would become the actor and inevitably he or she sent the words back up.... It was a reflection of life — life is a kind of disorder, freedom is a kind of disorder.

And, he concluded marvelously: "Now I have a certain rage inside me. I want to write with an 'I,' and on all subjects, that way no one will stop me anymore. I want to do it."[9] Sometimes a local experience suffices to open up a field of action to the operativity of those who practice, to bring its dynamism to light.

The Ordinary

For about the last fifty years, the ordinary has been the terrain for literary reflection (with Musil, Gombrowicz, or Beckett) and philosophical reflection (with Wittgenstein or Austin), which redoubles the work of anthropology or of psychoanalysis, specified by the upgrading of the most ordinary.[10] Ordinary culture and mass culture are not equivalents; they stem from different problematics. The latter refers to a massive production that simplifies proposed models in order to spread their distribution. The former involves a "consumption" that treats the lexicon of products as a function of particular codes, often the works of those who practice, and in view of their own interests. Mass culture tends toward homogenization, the law of wide-scale production and distribution, even if it hides this fundamental tendency under certain superficial variations destined to establish the fiction of "new products." Ordinary culture hides a fundamental diversity of situations, interests, and contexts under the apparent repetition of objects that it uses. *Pluralization* is born from ordinary usage, from this immense reserve that the number and multiple of differences constitute.

We know poorly the types of operations at stake in ordinary practices, their registers and their combinations, because our instruments of analysis, modeling, and formalization were constructed for other objects and with other aims. The essential of analytic work, which remains to be done, will have to revolve around the subtle combinatory set, of types of operations and registers, that stages and activates a making-do [*faire-avec*], right here and now, which is a singular action linked to one situation, certain circumstances, particular actors. In this sense, ordinary culture is first of all a *practical science of the singular*, which takes in reverse our thinking habits in which scientific rationality is knowledge of the general, an abstraction made from the circumstantial and the accidental. In its humble and tenacious way, ordinary culture thus puts our arsenal of scientific procedures and our epistemological categories on trial, for it does not cease rejoining knowledge to the singular, putting both into a concrete particularizing situation, and selecting its own thinking tools and techniques of use in relation to these criteria.

Our categories of knowledge are still too rustic and our analytic models too little elaborated to allow us to think the inventive proliferation of everyday practices. That is our regret. That there remains so much to understand about the innumerable ruses of the "obscure heroes" of the ephemeral, those walking in the city, inhabitants of neighborhoods, readers and dreamers, the obscure Kitchen Women Nation, fills us with wonder.

Notes

Translator's Note

1. For his translation of *L'Invention du quotidien*, vol. 1, *Arts de faire*, Steven Rendall conflated the general title of the set (*L'Invention du quotidien*) with the title of volume 1 (*Arts de faire*), the result of which in English is *The Practice of Everyday Life*. This conflation makes a translation of the title for volume 2 (*L'Invention du quotidien*, vol. 2, *Habiter, cuisiner*) problematic because, though it shares the general title of the set, it differs in its volume title. I have thus chosen to keep Rendall's translation for the general title but have reestablished a "subtitle" for volume 2 in order to mark out the specificity of *Habiter, cuisiner*.

2. *The Practice of Everyday Life* (Berkeley: University of California Press, 1984; paperback edition in 1988).

3. *Dictionnaire historique de la langue française*, vol. 2 (Paris: Dictionnaires Le Robert, 1992), 2108.

Introduction to Volume 1: History of a Research Project

1. Page references to volume 1 have been integrated parenthetically. [Except where there are differences between the 1980 Union Générale des Éditions version and the 1990 Gallimard edition, these page references come from Steven Rendall's translation, *The Practice of Everyday Life*, paperback edition (Berkeley and Los Angeles: University of California Press, 1988). *Trans.*] *L'Invention du quotidien* is divided between two books and three authors: vol. 1, *Arts de faire*, Michel de Certeau; vol. 2, Luce Giard and Pierre Mayol, *Habiter, cuisiner* (Paris: Union Générale des Éditions, 1980). [In this introduction, Luce Giard refers to each of these works by their respective titles. Because the general title of the set and the title of volume 1 were conflated in Steven Rendall's English translation as *The Practice of Everyday Life*, I will refer to *Arts de faire* as "volume 1" and *Habiter, cuisiner* as "volume 2." *Trans.*]

2. Several fragments of the two books appeared in *Traverses* between 1975 and 1979, and in *Esprit* in 1978 and 1979. The overall research project is presented by Michel de Certeau and Luce Giard in two jointly written articles, "Manières de faire et pratiques quotidiennes" and "Pratiques culinaires: une mémoire," in *Le Progrès scientifique* (review published by the Délégation Générale à la Recherche Scientifique et Technique [DGRST], no. 193 (March–April, 1978): 45–56.

3. Emmanuel Le Roy Ladurie, "Le diable archiviste," *Le Monde*, November 12, 1971, reprinted in his collection *Le Territoire de l'historien* (Paris: Gallimard, Bibliothèque des Histoires, 1973), 404–7. This can be compared to the entirely different analysis of Philippe Boutry, "De l'histoire des mentalités à l'histoire des croyances: *La Possession de Loudun* (1970)," in *Le Débat*, no. 49 (March–April 1988): 85–96. On the place of Certeau among historians, see Dominique Julia, "Une his-

toire en actes," in Luce Giard et al., *Le Voyage mystique: Michel de Certeau* (Paris: Cerf and Recherche de Science Religieuse, 1988), 103–23.

4. On his relationship to Freud and Lacan, see Michel de Certeau, *Histoire et psychanalyse entre science et fiction* (Paris: Gallimard, Folio essais, 1987), chaps. 5–8.

5. These articles, which appeared in *Études* and *Esprit* between June and October 1968, were reprinted in *La Prise de parole* (Paris: Desclée de Brouwer, 1968) (the book's printer's indication gives October 22 as the date of completion) [appeared in English as *The Capture of Speech*, trans. Tom Conley (Minneapolis: University of Minnesota Press, 1997). *Trans.*].

6. Certeau, *The Capture of Speech*, 33.

7. "La rupture instauratrice ou le christianisme dans la culture contemporaine" (1971), reprinted in Michel de Certeau, *La Faiblesse de croire* (Paris: Seuil, Esprit, 1987), 183–226.

8. Certeau, *The Capture of Speech*, 4.

9. Ibid., 10.

10. Ibid., 48.

11. Michel de Certeau, *La Culture au pluriel* (Paris: Union Générale des Éditions, 10–18, 1974); 2d ed. (Paris: Christian Bourgois, 1980); new ed. (Paris: Seuil, Points, 1993) [*Culture in the Plural*, trans. Tom Conley (Minneapolis: University of Minnesota Press, 1997). *Trans.*]. The texts on Arc-et-Senans constitute chapters 9 and 10.

12. Certeau, *Culture in the Plural*, 145.

13. The phrase "the beauty of the dead," serves as the title for a wonderful study written with Dominique Julia and Jacques Revel in 1970 and reprinted in *La Culture au pluriel*, chap. 3. [It appears in English in Michel de Certeau, *Heterologies: Discourse on the Other*, trans. Brian Massumi (Minneapolis: University of Minnesota Press, 1986), 119–36. *Trans.*]

14. Ibid., 140.

15. Ibid., 145–46.

16. The Délégation Générale à la Recherche Scientifique et Technique [General office for science and technology research], directly connected with the prime minister, was then charged with guiding and managing contracted public research.

17. This group was made up of economists (Bernard Guibert, Claude Ménard, Alain Weil) along with Certeau and myself. The work would last a bit less than a year, divided between fascination and exasperation faced with specialized publications about "futurology."

18. *Pratiques culturelles des Français*, 2 vols. (Paris: Secrétariat d'État à la Culture, Service des Études et Recherches, 1974). The same department has published a follow-up to this study with a renewed perspective: *Les Pratiques culturelles des Français, 1973–1989* (Paris: La Découverte et La Documentation Française, 1990).

19. [The last sentence here was added to the 1990 edition and so was not translated by Steven Rendall. The translation is my own. *Trans.*]

20. See Michel de Certeau, *The Writing of History*, trans. Tom Conley (New York: Columbia University Press, 1988), chap. 1, 25–27 (on the religious sociology of Gabriel Le Bras), and chap. 2, 75–79 (on recourse to computers and what François Furet says about quantitative history).

21. Michel Foucault, *Surveiller et punir* (Paris: Gallimard, Bibliothèque des Histoires, 1975) (the book's printer's indication gives February as the month of

completion). [*Discipline and Punish*, trans. Alan Sheridan (New York: Vintage Books, 1979). *Trans.*]

22. Michelle Perrot, "Milles manières de braconner," *Le Débat* 49 (March–April 1988): 118.

23. See the conclusion to Certeau, *Culture in the Plural*. See also "Actions culturelles et stratégies politiques," *La Revue nouvelle* (Brussels) (April 1974): 351–60. Michel de Certeau was fond of this article, to which he refers in volume 1 of *The Practice of Everyday Life* (introduction, n. 18; chap. 2, n. 6).

24. Half of chapter 4 is dedicated to each of them. On the respective references to one or the other, see the index at the end of the book. On the relation to Foucault, see *Histoire et psychanalyse entre science et fiction*, chaps. 1–3 [see *Heterologies*, chaps. 12–14. *Trans.*].

25. Gilles-Gaston Granger, *Essai d'une philosophie du style*, 2d ed. (Paris: Odile Jacob, 1988), and Gerald Holton, *Thematic Origins of Scientific Thought: Kepler to Einstein* (Cambridge: Harvard University Press, 1973) (a work partially translated in *L'imagination scientifique* [Paris: Gallimard, 1981]), have sought, each in his own way, to define these characteristics of a thinking style about which Certeau says: "style, a way of walking through a terrain, a non-textual move or attitude, organizes the text of a thought" (47).

26. Certeau, *Culture in the Plural*, 142.

27. Michel de Certeau, *La Fable mystique*, book 1, 2d ed. (Paris: Gallimard, Tel, 1987), 282 and all of chap. 7. [*The Mystic Fable*, trans. Michael B. Smith (Chicago: University of Chicago Press, 1992). *Trans.*]

28. This text, titled "Actors in Search of a Play (Part II)" and dated July 14, 1974, ends with a bibliography to read during the summer, divided into two parts: one involving "general works about culture" (Pierre Bourdieu, Gérard Althabe, Pierre Legendre, Richard Hoggart, etc.) and the other, "urban space and its culture" (the July 1970 special issue of *Annales ESC*, and Manuel Castells, Claude Soucy, Charles Alexander and Serge Chermayeff, Richard Williams, etc.).

29. Later, a Brazilian student who had frequented the seminar, wrote in a brochure on Paris VII a marvelous portrait of the "master who did not want disciples."

30. [The two preceding quotations are additions to the 1990 edition and so these translations are my own. *Trans.*]

31. On his way of running things, see Michel de Certeau, "Qu'est-ce qu'un séminaire?" *Esprit* (November–December 1978): 176–81.

32. ["Master's thesis" here is only an approximate translation of the French "mémoire de DEA," which is actually a major paper written at the end of one year of graduate work *beyond* the master's degree. *Trans.*] On Certeau in California, see Paul Rabinow, "Un prince de l'exil," and Richard Terdiman, "Une mémoire d'éveilleur," in Luce Giard, ed., *Michel de Certeau* (Paris: Centre Georges Pompidou, Cahiers pour un temps, 1987), 39–43 and 91–96.

33. I hope to bring together these fragments of volume 1 in a small book along with other works published together after 1980 on ordinary culture.

34. See chap. 14 on the kitchen and chap. 7 on the neighborhood in this volume.

35. He thus worked in Italy, each year from 1974 to 1978; in Spain, England, and Denmark in 1975; in Switzerland in 1977 and 1978. Outside of Europe, he was in Quebec in 1974 and 1975, Brazil in 1974, Israel in 1976, the United States in

1977 (in Vermont) and also in 1976 and 1978 (in California). A particular place is to be attributed to regular exchanges with Belgium for which Marie Beaumont and Georges Thill, in Brussels and Namur, were the center; it is particularly to these two — to Marie's unforgettable generosity and the active innovative milieu that surrounded them — that the passage on the widespread practice of the *perruque* refers, spreading from the working-class world to the scientific institution, there where "artistic achievements" and "the graffiti of . . . debts of honor" are inscribed (28).

36. François Hartog, "L'écriture du voyage," in Giard, ed., *Michel de Certeau*, 123–32.

37. Françoise Choay, "Tours et traverses du quotidien," in ibid., 85–90.

38. Perrot, "Mille manières de braconner," 117.

39. Anne-Marie Chartier and Jean Hébrard, "L'invention du quotidien: Une lecture, des usages," *Le Débat*, no. 49 (March–April 1988): 97, 99, 100.

40. On Michel de Certeau, see the three collections dedicated to him by the Centre Georges Pompidou (n. 32 above), in part in an issue of *Le Débat* (n. 39), and under the title *Le Voyage mystique* (n. 3). See also Luce Giard, Hervé Martin, and Jacques Revel, *Histoire, mystique et politique: Michel de Certeau* (Grenoble: Jérôme Millon, 1991). In *Le Voyage mystique*, one will find his "complete bibliography," which I compiled (191–243).

Times and Places

1. Luce Giard, "Histoire d'une recherche," in Michel de Certeau, *L'Invention du quotidien*, vol. 1, *Arts de faire*, new edition (Paris: Gallimard, Folio essais, 1990), i–xxx. [See the translation in the present volume, "Introduction to Volume 1: History of a Research Project." *Trans.*] On Augustin Girard's work and influence, see *Trente ans d'études au service de la vie culturelle* (March 8, 1993, roundtable discussion organized at the time of Augustin Girard's retirement) (Paris: Ministère de la Culture, 1993).

2. I gave the name "first circle" to the young researchers gathered around Certeau in June 1974 (see Giard, "Introduction to Volume 1." Marie Beaumont died in Brussels in August 1984, Marie-Pierre Dupuy in Paris in July 1992.

3. Marc Guillaume, "Vers l'autre," in Luce Giard et al., *Le Voyage mystique: Michel de Certeau* (Paris: Cerf and Recherche de Science Religieuse, 1988), 181–86.

4. Michel de Certeau, *The Writing of History*, trans. Tom Conley (New York: Columbia University Press, 1988), 77. Dominique Julia, "Une histoire en actes," in Giard et al., *Le Voyage mystique*, 103–23.

5. Michel de Certeau, *Histoire et psychanalyse entre science et fiction* (Paris: Gallimard, Folio essais, 1987), chap. 4; *The Writing of History*, chaps. 3, 4, and 9. Luce Giard, Hervé Martin, and Jacques Revel, *Histoire, mystique et politique: Michel de Certeau* (Grenoble: Jérôme Millon, 1991).

6. This is a quarterly review, published by the Society of Jesus, which has done in-depth, sustained work on philosophical activity outside of the Francophone world. Marcel Régnier, S.J., guided it from 1954 to 1990 with as much efficacy as philosophical discernment.

7. Karl Popper, *Logik der Forschung* (Vienna, 1934); *The Logic of Scientific Discovery* (London: Hutchinson, 1959; several expanded editions appeared subsequently); *La logique de la découverte scientifique*, preface by Jacques Monod (Paris:

Payot, 1974). It is possible that Certeau read Popper's article "Conjectural Knowledge," *Revue internationale de philosophie* 25 (1971), reprinted in his work *Objective Knowledge* (Oxford: Clarendon, 1972), chap. 1. On Popper's theses and their slow diffusion in France, see Luce Giard, "L'impossible désir du rationnel," in Imre Lakatos, *Histoire et méthodologie des sciences* (Paris: PUF, Bibliothèque d'Histoire des Sciences, 1994), v–xliii.

8. See the remarks of Pierre Vidal-Naquet, "Lettre," in Luce Giard, ed., *Michel de Certeau* (Paris: Centre Georges Pompidou, Cahiers pour un temps, 1987), 71–74, and Pierre Vidal-Naquet, *Les Assassins de la mémoire* (Paris: La Découverte, 1987), in particular chap. 5, which gives its title to the volume. Lakatos thought that the failing of Popper's thesis led to skepticism and that such had been the case for Paul Feyerabend (see my study cited in the preceding note).

9. Richard H. Popkin, *The History of Skepticism from Erasmus to Spinoza* (1960), 3d ed. (Berkeley: University of California Press, 1979). This edition is dedicated to the memory of Lakatos.

10. Published as a co-edition by Desclée de Brouwer, Aubier, Delachaux and Niestlé, and Éditions du Cerf, this series included works from James Barr, Jean Ladrière, Louis Marin, Georges Thill, and so on.

11. Philippe Boutry, "De l'histoire des mentalités à l'histoire des croyances," *Le Débat*, no. 49 (March–April 1988): 85–96; this article was part of a dossier titled "Michel de Certeau historien."

12. I have explained Certeau's relationship to Hegel in Giard, Martin, and Revel, *Histoire, mystique et politique*, 27–31. On the presence of Hegel in French intellectual life, there is an incomplete but useful analysis: Michael S. Roth, *Knowing and History: Appropriations of Hegel in Twentieth-Century France* (Ithaca, N.Y.: Cornell University Press, 1988).

13. Michel de Certeau, *La Prise de parole (1968) et autres écrits politiques* (Paris: Seuil, Points, 1994). [*The Capture of Speech*, trans. Tom Conley (Minneapolis: University of Minnesota Press, 1997). *Trans.*]

14. The index of the two books maps the geography of our itineraries during our common navigation on the ocean of practices.

15. Pierre Bourdieu et al., *La Misère du monde* (Paris: Seuil, 1992).

16. Blandine Masson, ed., *L'Art d'hériter, Cahiers du Renard*, no. 14 (July 1993).

17. Martine Segalen, *Nanterriens: Les familles dans la ville* (Toulouse: Presses Universitaires du Mirail, 1990); Joël Roman, ed., *Ville, exclusion et citoyenneté* (Entretiens de la ville, II) (Paris: Esprit, 1993).

18. Gérard Althabe et al., eds., *Vers une ethnologie du présent* (Paris: Maison des Sciences de l'Homme et Ministère de la Culture, 1992).

19. Raymond Trampoglieri, *Mémoires d'archives* (Avignon: Archives de la Ville, exposition catalog, July 1993).

20. See Giard, "Introduction to Volume 1."

21. Marc Augé, *Non-lieux* (Paris: Seuil, 1992); Anne-Marie Chartier and Jean Hébrard, *Discours sur la lecture (1880–1980)* (Paris: Centre Georges Pompidou, Bibliothèque d'Information, 1989); Pierre Chambat, ed., *Communication et lien social* (Paris: Descartes et Cité des Sciences de l'Industrie La Villette, 1992); Louis Quéré et al., *Les Formes de la conversation* (Paris: Centre National d'Études des Télécommunications, Réseaux, 1990).

22. Pierre Mayol from his side, and myself from my own, as well as within different networks, continue to receive numerous requests of this nature, often from the provinces, as if, outside of Paris, these texts had the time to make a deep impact.

23. Michel de Certeau, *The Practice of Everyday Life*, trans. Steven Rendall (Berkeley: University of California Press, 1984). Certeau taught full-time at the University of California (San Diego) from 1978 to 1984.

24. Brian Rigby, *Popular Culture in Modern France: A Study of Cultural Discourse* (London: Routledge, 1991), 16–34 in particular; Lawrence Grossberg et al., eds., *Cultural Studies* (New York: Routledge, 1992), notably the chapters by John Fiske, 154–65, and by Meaghan Morris, 450–73; Roger Silverstone, "Let Us Then Return to the Murmuring of Everyday Practices," *Theory, Culture and Society* 6.1 (1989): 77–94.

25. The themes of *The Practice of Everyday Life* were already sketched in *La Prise de parole* (1968) and in *La Culture au pluriel* (1974), new ed. (Paris: Seuil, Points, 1993). The complete bibliography of Michel de Certeau can be found in Giard et al., *Le Voyage mystique*, 191–243.

Entrée

1. [I have kept the French of this title in spite of the fact that *entrée* in English has a different sense than that in French. In English, it refers to the main dish of a meal, whereas in French it refers to the equivalent of an appetizer, that which begins one's "entrance" into the meal. The various connotations suggested by "entrance" in the French word *entrée* are vital to this title and would be erased by recourse to an English translation such as *appetizer. Trans.*]

The Annals of Everyday Life

1. Paul Leuilliot, preface to Guy Thuillier, *Pour une histoire du quotidien au XIXᵉ siècle en Nivernais* (Paris and The Hague: Mouton, 1977), xi–xii.

2. See Michel de Certeau, *The Practice of Everyday Life*, trans. Steven Rendall (Berkeley: University of California Press, 1984; paperback edition, 1988).

3. *Recherches* 19, titled *Histoire de la rue des Caves* (1975), 17.

4. In the first volume [see bibliography in note 1 to the "Introduction to Volume 1" above. *Trans.*], I presented the overall problematic that inspired this work beginning on p. xi. I gratefully acknowledge the financing of the DGRST (research grant 74.7.1043), which made this research possible.

5. Georges Simenon, *Pedigree*, trans. Robert Baldick (London: H. Hamilton, 1962), 363–64.

1. The Neighborhood

1. James Agee and Walker Evans, *Let Us Now Praise Famous Men: Three Tenant Families* (Boston: Houghton Mifflin, 1969).

2. See, among others, Adélaïde Blasquez, *Gaston Lucas serrurier* (Paris: Plon, 1976); Josette Gonthier, *Pierre Joly canut* (Paris: Delarge, 1978); Serge Grafteaux, *Mémé Santerre* (Paris: Delarge, 1975), and *La Mère Denis* (Paris: Delarge, 1976); Jean-Claude Loiseau, *Marthe les mains pleines de terre* (Paris: Belfond, 1977).

3. *[Notes marked with an asterix are those added by Pierre Mayol for the second edition of this volume. *Trans.*] *Cultural practices*: Since the time of three studies (1974, 1982, and 1990) on this topic authored by the Department of Research at the Ministry of Culture, a "cultural practice" means a statistical description of behaviors in relation to an activity predetermined as cultural, for example: "Going to the theater or not and, if so, how many times? Watching television or not, and for how long? Reading or not, and what exactly?" and so on. The questionnaires for these three studies involve all aspects of cultural life, from the most casual to the most "elitist," hence a very complete range of information. The publication of the results: *Les Pratiques culturelles des Français* (Paris: La Documentation Française, 1974); same title (Paris: Dalloz, 1982); Olivier Donnat and Denis Cogneau, *Les Pratiques culturelles des Français, 1973–1989* (Paris: La Découverte et La Documentation Française, 1990). On these studies and their results, see Pierre Mayol, "Culture de tous les jours," *Projet* 229 (spring 1992), and "Introduction à l'enquête sur les pratiques culturelles," in Daniel Dhéret, ed., *Le territoire du créateur* (Lyons: La Condition des Soies, 1992). See also Christian Ruby et al., "La bataille du culturel," *Regards sur l'actualité* 189 (March 1993); the special issue "Culture et société" in *Cahiers français* 260 (March–April 1993); Jean-François Chougnet et al., *La création face aux systèmes de diffusion* (Paris: La Documentation Française, 1993), which is the report written by the group "Création culturelle, compétitivité et cohésion sociale" presided over by Marin Karmitz for preparation of the Eleventh National Plan.

In my text, the expression "cultural practice" is always implicitly taken in the sense of the anthropological tradition (Morgan, Boas, Frazer, Durkheim, Mauss, Lévi-Strauss, etc.): underlying value systems structuring the fundamental stakes of everyday life, unperceived consciously by subjects, but decisive for their individual and group identity. Each time this expression appears, I have added another term to avoid confusion with its current statistical meaning.

4. See the excerpts of interviews with Madame Marie in chapter 7.

5. *From 1975 to 1977, I questioned almost one hundred people. The resemblance of statements about the Croix-Rousse neighborhood, the social values attached to it, professional life, and the similarities in layout of apartments and the evolution in domestic comfort (the "white furnishings" of bathrooms and kitchen appliances, the "black furnishings" of audiovisual items) have helped me to focus the contents of interviews on just one group. This came about through editorial thrift as well as to avoid the dispersal and false realism resulting from the proliferation of quotations and interlocutors. I realize that by focusing my information on just one family group on one street, the rue Rivet, I have respected the first preamble (or prelude) from the First Exercise of *The Spiritual Exercises of St. Ignatius Loyola* about "a contemplation of the place," which fixes the imagination on "the physical location of the object contemplated," or, more humbly, understood and analyzed. [The quotation of *The Spiritual Exercises of St. Ignatius Loyola* comes from Elisabeth Meier Tetlow's translation (Lanham, Md.: University Press of America, 1987). *Trans.*]

6. See especially Bernard Lamy, *L'Intégration du citadin à sa ville et à son quartier*, vol. 3, ed. Paul-Henry Chombart de Lauwe (Paris: Centre de Sociologie Urbaine, 1961); Henri Coing, *Rénovation sociale et urbaine et changement social*, 2d ed.

(Paris: Éditions Ouvrières, 1973), 62; R. Ledrut, *L'espace social de la ville: problèmes de sociologie appliquée à l'aménagement urbain* (Paris: Anthropos, 1968), 147, and *Sociologie urbaine* (Paris: PUF, 1973), 119; Henri Lefebvre, ed., "Le quartier et la ville," *Cahiers de l'Institut d'aménagement et d'urbanisme de la région parisienne* 7 (March 1967); B. Poupard et al., *Le Quartier Saint-Germain-des-Prés* (Paris: FORS, 1972); Reine Vogel, "Caractéristique d'une animation urbaine originale," *Urbanisme*, no. 143 (1973).

7. Jacqueline Palmade et al., *Contribution à une psychosociologie de l'espace urbain: La dialectique du logement et de son environnement* (Paris: Ministère de l'Équipement, 1970), 64.

8. For an in-depth analysis of the practice of neighboring, cf. Jacques Caroux, *Évolution des milieux ouvriers et habitat* (Montrouge: Centre d'Ethnologie Sociale, 1975), 52–58, 96, 136.

2. Propriety

1. [The French words *obligation* and *lien* here do share a common Latin etymology (*ligo, ligare*, etc.), which the original text points out, but their closest English equivalents — *obligation* and *link* (or *bind, tie*) — unfortunately do not. *Trans.*]

2. See Gisela Pankov, *Structure familiale et psychose* (Paris: Aubier, 1977). I will cite the following lines, which elucidate the body: "I have defined the image of the body through two fundamental functions that are *symbolizing functions*, in other words, functions that allow us, first, to recognize a dynamic link between the part and the whole of the body (*the first fundamental function of the body image*) and then, beyond form, to seize the very contents and meaning of such a dynamic link (*the second fundamental function of the body image*). I am talking about symbolizing functions in order to emphasize that each of them, as a 'set of symbolic systems,' aims at 'a reciprocity rule,' an immanent law of the body that is implicitly provided by the fundamental function of the body image" (8–9; see also the reference to Gaston Fessard, 74–75).

3. Pierre Antoine, "Le pouvoir des mots," *Projet*, no. 81 (January 1974): 41–54 and especially 44–45: "In opposition to the information function, the participation function is all the larger if what is said is well known, familiar. It is through the probability of the message, and no longer through its improbability, that one might attempt to define its measure."

4. The word *circumstance* here refers to the very precise meaning given to it by Umberto Eco: "If it is true that signs directly denote real objects, *the circumstance is presented as the overall reality that conditions the choices of codes and subcodes by linking decoding to its own presence*. The communication process, even if it does not point to referents, seems to unfold *within the referent*. The circumstance is this overall material, economic, biological, and physical conditioning at the interior of which we communicate" (*La Structure absente* [Paris: Mercure de France, 1972], 116). [Since this text by Eco has not been translated into English, I am forced into the unenviable position of translating the French translation of the original Italian (*La Struttura assente* [Milan: Bompani, 1968]). Eco explains in the foreword to *A Theory of Semiotics* (Bloomington: Indiana University Press, 1979) that after two unsatisfactory attempts at translating *La Struttura assente* into English, he gave up and rewrote the book directly in English. *Trans.*]

5. Roman Jakobson, "Closing Statement: Linguistics and Poetics," in *Style in Language*, ed. Thomas A. Sebeok (Cambridge: MIT Press, 1960), 350–77. On the "contact" factor and the phatic function that stems from it, see p. 355.

6. Benedict de Spinoza, *Political Treatise*, in *The Chief Works of Benedict de Spinoza*, trans. R. H. M. Elwes (London: George Bell and Sons, 1909), 298.

7. Henri Coing, *Rénovation sociale et changement social* (Paris: Éditions Ouvrières, 1966), 62ff. This work concerns the sociological problems posed by renovation in the thirteenth arrondissement in Paris.

8. Pierre Bourdieu, *Esquisse d'une théorie de la pratique* (Geneva: Droz, 1972), 203; my emphasis. [Because Richard Nice's translation, *Outline of a Theory of Practice* (London: Cambridge University Press, 1977), was based on a subsequent, revised edition of Bourdieu's text, the translation here is my own. This being said, we both independently came up with the phrase "semilearned grammar." *Trans.*]

9. [The play on words here is between the French "femme *de* ménage" and "femme *en* ménage." *Trans.*]

10. [This problematic play on words in French is between *touffes de salade* (mounds of lettuce) and *au ras de la touffe* (a short skirt, for example, described as being "up to the pubic mound"). I have translated the second phrase with a reference to the somewhat dated Almond Joy/Mounds jingle, which contains a less obvious, but still present, sexual play on the word *mound*. Unfortunately, this translation does not duplicate the richness of the original French. *Trans.*]

11. Louis-Jean Calvet, *La Production révolutionnaire* (Paris: Payot, 1976), 18ff., 37ff.

12. *At the beginning of the seventies, Julia Kristeva's concept of a "signifying practice" seemed promising. It was not at all. The mountain of *Séméiotikhé* (1969), *La Révolution du langage poétique* (1974), and *Polylogue* (1977) did not even amount to a molehill. I have thus shortened these final paragraphs to avoid references that have become useless.

13. Julia Kristeva, *Séméiotikhé: Recherche pour une sémanalyse* (Paris: Seuil, 1969), 12–13, 27, 44–45; and Julia Kristeva et al., *La Traversée des signes* (Paris: Seuil, 1975), 11. On the notion of a "signifying practice," one should refer to the synthesis done by G. Namur, *Paragrammatisme et production de sens dans la sémiotique de J. Kristeva* (Université Catholique de Louvain, Institut de Linguistique, "Cours et documents," no. 7, 1974).

14. *"Carnival": this is naturally an allusion to the magnificent book by Mikhail Bakhtin, *Rabelais and His World*, trans. Hélène Iswolsky (Bloomington: Indiana University Press, 1984).

15. Kristeva, *Séméiotikhé*, 160.

16. Ibid.

3. The Croix-Rousse Neighborhood

1. I will not have the opportunity to talk a great deal about the urban area of Lyons in its entirety. I will thus refer to a few works on this subject where one will be able to find any desired information: V.-H. Debidour and M. Lafferrère, *Lyon et ses environs* (Grenoble: Arthaud, 1969); J. Labasse and M. Lafferrère, *La région lyonnaise* (Paris: PUF, 1966); D. Dubreuil, *Rhône* (Paris: Seuil, "Guides," 1970). Historical works: Maurice Garden, *Lyon et les Lyonnais au XVIIIe siècle* (Paris: Flammarion,

"Sciences," 1975); A. Kleinclausz, *Lyon des origines à nos jours* (Lyons: Paul Masson, 1925) and *Histoire de Lyon*, 3 vols. (Lyons: Paul Masson, 1939). A very critical political approach: Jean Lojkine, *La Politique urbaine dans la région lyonnaise, 1945–1972* (Paris: Mouton, 1974).

2. See Maurice Moissonnier, *La Première Internationale et la Commune à Lyon* (Paris: Éditions Sociales, 1972), 20. On the *canut* revolts (1831, 1834, 1848), see, by the same author, *La Révolte des canuts, Lyon novembre 1831*, 2d ed. (Paris: Éditions Sociales, 1975); Fernand Rude, *Le Mouvement ouvrier à Lyon de 1827 à 1832* (Paris: Anthropos, 1969); *C'est nous les canuts* (Paris: Maspero, 1977); *Luttes ouvrières*, "Les dossiers de l'histoire populaire," no. 1 (Meudon: Éditions Floréal, 1977): "les canuts," 32–65.

3. Moissonnier, *La Première Internationale*, 16.

4. Ibid., 17.

5. Ibid., 20.

6. Thus, according to the 1968 census (statistics established by the INSEE [Institut National de la Statistique et des Études Économiques]) in neighborhood 4 of the first district, including the area between the quai André Lassagne on the Rhône, the place Croix-Paquet, and the rue des Fantasques, 100 percent of the buildings date from before 1871.

7. Michel Bonnet, "Étude préliminaire à la restauration des pentes de la Croix-Rousse" (Ph.D. diss., Unité pédagogique d'Architecture de Lyon, June 1975), 21.

8. *In the Croix-Rousse in 1936, there were still six hundred weavers using 2,500 semimechanical looms. In 1969, there remained about one hundred weavers and four hundred looms. The looms were sold, especially in Algeria (almost four hundred in 1968). The president of the weavers union then deplored the fact that "Eastern articles are no longer born in Lyons. Shawls, damask, *bourrichats* [baskets], Arab cloaks constituted excellent backup manufacturing. North Africa was a large importer. Today, it manufactures . . ." He also regretted the disappearance of the Lyons tie, "which represented the glory of Lyons," in favor of those from Italy (source: *Le Progrès de Lyon*, April 1969). In 1975, at the beginning of the study, only thirteen weavers-*canuts* remained (see the interview with Madame Marguerite, chap. 7). Among the numerous associations that have developed since then, several have taken up the *canuts'* heritage through the practice of amateur weaving. A small museum dedicated to the *canuts* is located in the fourth district. A superb mural fresco, impressive in its trompe l'oeil, was painted by certain artists from the Cité de la Création (from Oullins, near Lyons) on the back of a six-story building, boulevard des Canuts, to recall the memory of the neighborhood.

9. *"Traboule," from the etymology *trans ambulare*: to traverse, to walk across. See René Dejean, *Traboules de Lyon: histoire secrète d'une ville*, photos by Bernard Schreier (Lyons: Le Progrès, 1988). It is a repertoire of 315 *traboules* canvased between June 1986 and June 1988, among them 150 found in the Croix-Rousse: 142 in the first district and 8 in the fourth.

10. *We learn from testimonies that between the two wars, young working-class households from the center of Lyons (including the slopes of the Croix-Rousse) were often required to live with the parents of one of the spouses—more often with the young woman's or with the man's if his mother was a widow—

because of the lack of apartments available at reasonable rents. This forced cohabitation could last several years in cramped and inconvenient spaces, which led to a fearfully conflictual lack of privacy—as is testified to by the sarcasm of "mother-in-law stories," which are still fresh in people's memory. Although no general rule can be drawn from this, it seems that young couples finally established themselves in "their place" only after the second, even the third, child was born.

11. Bonnet, "Étude préliminaire," 33ff. According to the INSEE statistics (1968), in the first district, 50 percent of the apartments do not have interior toilets (versus 27.9 percent for Lyons), 70 percent do not have bathrooms (versus 48.9 percent for Lyons), and 10 percent do not have running water (1 percent for Lyons).

12. *The building was purchased in 1985 by a developer who fixed and cleaned it up and put all the apartments up for sale. The R.'s were able to buy theirs. On the landings, an elevator occupies the placement of the bathrooms, henceforth installed inside the apartments, increasing their sanitary comfort and thus participating in the general evolution of real estate. The statistics are eloquent: whereas 50 percent of the lodgings in the Croix-Rousse were deprived of in-home "bathrooms" in 1975, in the 1990 census, this is the case for only 8.3 percent of them in the first district (1,361 lodgings out of 16,354) and 5.5 percent in the fourth (907 out of 16,371).

13. *And the Beatles, the Rolling Stones, and so on. Maurice died in November 1987. Among his things, his family discovered paperback orchestral scores, carefully annotated (a few symphonies; Mozart's and Beethoven's violin concertos, Schumann's piano concerto, that of Tchaikovsky, and even Ravel's "left hand"). He also possessed rock music records that he appreciated for their antiestablishment and pacifist messages. An eclectic musician who won a prize for bassoon at the Lyons Conservatory in the sixties, a singer with a beautiful tenor admired in (secular) choirs, Maurice was a left-wing anarchist, close to the most radical fringes of the postwar PCF [Parti Communiste Français (French Communist Party)], but without ever having been "card-carrying." He voted "for the left, always the left, the furthest left possible," and loved election time: "he would have voted every Sunday," reported those around him.

In my study, I encountered no other "skilled worker" (according to the INSEE terminology) possessed with such a passion for music, or rather, kinds of music. On the other hand, I found, as I indicate in the text, numerous book readers. It is appropriate to add that retirement at age sixty and preretirement have multiplied the numbers of sports fans and "senior" travelers.

14. Michel Bonnet, ed., *Lyon, les pentes de la Croix-Rousse. Résultats de l'enquête, tableaux et commentaires* (UPA and UER sociologie, Lyons). This document is inserted as an appendix in Bonnet, "Étude préliminaire."

15. *See "Supplemental Note: Unemployment among Young People between Fifteen and Twenty-Four" later in this chapter.

16. The INSEE statistics (1968 census) are very revealing about the relationship between the number of foreigners and the rate of demolition in the first district. In essence, the part of the montée de la Grande-Côte actually demolished is the highest part, the area between the rue Neyret and the rue des Pierres-Plantées; this involves, on either side of the Grande-Côte, Blocks 14 and 19 (neighborhood 3, first district in the 1968 INSEE classification), which were entirely leveled. These two blocks were indeed those where the proportion of foreigners was the highest, as table 12 demonstrates.

Table 12

	Total population	Foreigners		
		Total	% in relation to the population	Algerians in the population
Totals from neighborhood 3	13,250	2,159	16	1,144
Totals from Block 14	716	322	43	213
Totals from Block 19	1,130	510	45	437

17. *A series of articles in *Le Progrès de Lyon* (June 17–28, 1982), using the results of the 1975 census to describe the nine districts of the city of Lyons, specified that the first district had, after the ninth (the Vaise neighborhood: 42.3 percent), one of the highest proportions of workers in the agglomeration: 41.1 percent. The fourth district (the "plateau" of the Croix-Rousse), for its part, had 35 percent. The other hill of Lyons, Fourvière, the "mystic hill," had only 4.9 percent.

18. Jacques Caroux, *Évolution des milieux ouvriers et habitat* (Montrouge: Centre d'Ethnologie Sociale, 1975). For a shortened presentation of this research, see Jacques Caroux, "Le monde ouvrier: De l'autonomie à l'atomisation," *Esprit* (May 1978): 25–38; and, by the same author, *Un couple ouvrier traditionnel* (Paris: Anthropos, 1974) and *La Vie d'une famille ouvrière* (Paris: Seuil, 1972).

19. *On gentrification, see Daniel Dhéret, ed., *Le territoire du créateur* (Lyons: La Condition des Soies, 1992), which contains a study on the artists living in the Croix-Rousse (where they are numerous): many of them settled there in precisely the years 1975–80, bringing an intellectual and demographic renewal to the neighborhood (see "Supplemental Note: The Croix-Rousse under Question" later in this chapter). This book is the result of a conference (November 1990) sponsored by the "social development" service of the first district. On the procedure of "social development of neighborhoods" (DSQ), see my article "Radiographie des banlieues," *Esprit* (June 1992). See also Laurence Roulleau-Berger, *La ville intervalle, jeunes entre centre et banlieue* (Paris: Méridiens Klincksieck, 1991), on young artists having difficulty integrating in Lyons, among whom a few reside in the Croix-Rousse.

20. *See Catherine Foret and Pascal Bavoux, *En passant par le centre . . . La rue de la République à Lyon: Anthropologie d'un espace public* (Lyons: Trajectoires, 1990). Curiously, there is no reference to my analysis in this study, even though the research territories are related.

21. This process of segregation is particularly felt in Lyons because of the tortured configuration of this urban site (the hills, the Rhône, the Saône). Cf. Debidour and Lafferrère, *Lyon et ses environs*: "Behind the enormous train stations of Part-Dieu and the Brotteaux on the tracks to Geneva, the neighborhoods of La Villette, Montplaisir, and États-Unis and the Villeurbanne commune have such a difficult access to the many resources of downtown that life has been organized around particularly active secondary centers, where new formulas have been tried out with success: for example, the Theater of the Cité in Villeurbanne, the cultural center of the eighth district, the self-service stores in the Jean-Mermoz neighborhood . . . The suburb itself has proliferated around independent centers. The industries that transformed these former

rural communities were all looking for sites separated from the Lyons urban area itself, either for using vast terrains (railroad material in Oullins, automobile manufacturing in Vénissieux, textiles in Saint-Priest) or for reducing certain kinds of pollution (artificial silk production in Decines, chemical production in Saint-Fons and Neuville-sur-Saône). At different periods, large factories and worker housing developments have thus developed more or less attractive urban areas, but all are separated from Lyons. Today, the empty spaces between the city and the suburbs are being filled in" (18–19).

22. [Sunday dinner here refers to the midday meal. *Trans.*]

23. *One should say "supper" here: in the popular language of the Lyons region, *déjeuner* [lunch] corresponds to breakfast [*petit déjeuner*], *dîner* [dinner] to the midday meal, and *souper* [supper] to the evening meal.

24. On all of this, see chapter 6, the section titled "The Market."

25. *Added to this edition to complete the description of the Croix-Rousse.

26. *This appended section, completely recast, is based on my chapter of the same title in Dhéret, *Le territoire du créateur*, 16–23.

27. [This description of attitudes about "downtown" versus the "suburbs" runs counter to that commonly held in the United States and thus betrays a sharp difference in urban perspectives between France and the United States. *Trans.*]

28. *At the same time, one notices a diversification of the socioprofessional categories of the inhabitants. An almost majority working-class neighborhood for quite some time, the slopes of the Croix-Rousse have integrated employees, managers, intellectual professions (professors, journalists, advertisers), and health professions.

29. *Through phonetic and semantic slippage, *compagnon du devoir* [fellow journeyman] (many *canut*s, adherents of Workmanship, belonged to this guild) becomes *devoireur*, *dévoreur* [devourer], and finally *vorace* [voracious one], terms created after the insurrections of November 1831 and April 1834. By extension, the word *vorace* becomes applied to every popular revolt or demand. Philippe Boutry, *Prêtres et paroisses au pays du Curé d'Ars* (Paris: Cerf, 1986), 79, points out the "struggles of the voracious harvesters" against the landowners of the Dombe, but he omits the etymology. One may read with interest Jacques Perdu, *La révolte des canuts 1831–1834* (Paris: Spartacus/René Léfeuvre, 1974), printed as it should be (44 rue Burdeau) on the slopes of the Croix-Rousse, near the *traboules* where the fighting was quite violent between the *canuts* and the forces of order of the prefect Terme. The rue Burdeau runs along the Botanical Gardens, where the amphitheater of the Three Gauls stood: there, according to tradition, the Lyons martyrs perished. Christian martyrs, revolting *canuts*, anarchist publishers and printers (there has also been a libertarian and anarchist bookstore on the rue Rivet since 1990) live together in the same small perimeter, separated only by the centuries.

30. *See the analyses of Boutry, *Prêtres et paroisses*, a captivating book, and my article on it, "Au pays du Curé d'Ars" (*Esprit* [January 1987]: 51–64), in which I emphasize the *gnostic* tradition of Lyons Catholicism, which, in my opinion, marked Jean-Marie Vianney in his childhood. I think this tradition is still active, even if the erosion of religious practices has marginalized it.

4. The Street Trade

1. *Allée* [alley]: a term from the Lyons region to refer to the entrance of a building.

2. *In this part of the rue Rivet stands the famous "three hundred window" building, which overlooks the place Rouville and which one can see from the riverbanks of the Saône downtown. Impressive for its austere harmony and the height of its facades, it was erected in 1826 by the Savoyard architect Brunet, who wanted to make it into a symbol of time: four portes cocheres for each of the seasons, two times six floors for the months, fifty-six apartments for the weeks, and 360 windows for the days. Moreover, a plaque, affixed in 1990 between the numbers 15 and 17 on the rue Rivet, recalls (something I did not know) the birth of a much more famous architect: "Here Tony Garnier, 1869–1948, was born, architect, 'Premier grand prix de Rome,' precursor of contemporary architecture and urban development."

3. [In other words, he uses the informal *tu* form when addressing these people instead of the more formal *vous* form in French. *Trans.*]

4. [Mayol makes a distinction here between the marginalized regular "patrons" (*pratiquants*) who "patronize" (*pratiquent*) La Germaine's store as opposed to the occasional female "clients" (*clientes*). *Trans.*]

5. [In the original French, the phrase is "J'y aime pas bien" and Mayol explains in a note that the use of *y* in this context is particular to the Rhône-Alpes region. Because this linguistic particularity disappears in English translation, I have chosen to omit the details of this note. *Trans.*]

6. *Onze*, that is, 11 percent alcohol wine in a liter bottle. This detail means that Madame X was buying a family wine more "proper" than the discreditable *douze* [12 percent], "much too heavy," and connoting the strong wine of big drinkers. As for the *dix* [10 percent], too light to be "reinvigorating," it is considered a low-quality wine just right for certain sauces with boiled meats, nicely referred to as *ragougnasses*, a pejorative diminutive of *ragoût* [stew].

7. *Aline shocked her father with a marital behavior that the "good old folks" of the rue Rivet and elsewhere called "shacking up together," but that the demographer Louis Roussel characterized more seriously in 1978, in the review *Population*, as "juvenile cohabitation." At the time, it involved less than 10 percent of young couples. This new behavior was, as one knows, destined for a brilliant future, in all social milieus.

5. Bread and Wine

1. *Since the time of this study, the cultural status of bread has changed greatly. Then a product of necessity ill advised by nutritionists (bad for the figure), it is today an object of ceremony, of "distinction," with recognized dietetic virtues (good for the heart and the intestinal tract). All the same, its place in the meal has not ceased to diminish: people used to consume 84.3 kg per year and per person in 1965; 68.4 kg in 1969; 51.3 kg in 1979 (shortly after the study), and "only" 44.3 kg in 1989 (source: Michèle Bertrand, *Consommation et lieux d'achat des produits alimentaires en 1989* [INSEE, August 1992], 31). As with wine, people consume less, but of better quality (see note 5 below). See the wonderful book by Bernard Dupaigne, *Le Pain* (Paris: Messidor, 1979); as well as Lionel Poilâne, *Guide de l'amateur de pain* (Paris: Robert Laffont, 1981); André Garnier, *Pains et viennoiseries* (Lucerne: Dormarval, 1993), a recipe book that contains a historic and symbolic synthesis on bread.

2. *Doctors underscore that the alcoholic increases purchase points far from the neighborhood in order to cunningly lose the traces of his or her "shame" by diminishing the chances of being "recognized." A shopkeeper recently confided in me that the purchase of wine in plastic bottles, which contain a liter and a half (which, it seems to me, did not exist around 1975), has become the almost indubitable sign that one is dealing with an alcoholic, a real one, a "tippler," because the wine they contain "is really not good." On these ruses and tactics, see Véronique Nahoum-Grappe, *La culture de l'ivresse: essai de phénoménologie historique* (Paris: Quai Voltaire, 1991); Pierre Mayol, "Les seuils de l'alcoolisme," *Esprit* (November–December 1980): 155–63.

3. [Unfortunately, the English translation here of the French proverb, "Quand mon verre est vide je le plains, quand il est plein je le vide," only partially reproduces the original double rhyme (*plains–plein* and *vide–vide*). *Trans.*]

4. *Since then, this one-pint *pot* has gotten a promotion in Lyons restaurants. People sell them in antique and secondhand shops, and the owners of the *bouchons* [Lyons restaurants] downtown have put them back on their menus and their tables, as a witness to the place's cultural identity.

5. See Paul Fournel, *L'Histoire véritable de Guignol* (Lyons: Fédérop, 1975).

6. [François Rabelais, *Gargantua and Pantagruel*, trans. Burton Raffel (New York and London: W. W. Norton, 1990), 22. *Trans.*]

7. *When I was writing these pages, wine still had a considerable symbolic value. I am not certain that it has preserved it. The poetics of wine, the "lifeblood of the worker," has gone out of fashion. While appreciating the book by Pierre Sansot, *Les gens de peu* (Paris: PUF, 1991), I do not share his "appreciative," even euphoric, point of view on the "public drunkard" (chap. 9). According to my study, the drunkard was and still is considered, even by hearty drinkers, as the cause or the consequence of a disastrous social and personal situation. It also seems to me that the "elbow sportsmen," whose principal activity consists in "bending their elbows," are now more often standing at the bar than sitting at tables, in other words, more solitary. Over the years, I noticed that people were drinking less and less alcohol (beer, aperitifs, liqueurs) and wine, whether at home, in "just passing by" cafés, or in "neighborhood" cafés. This recent modification of social behaviors in relation to drinking isolates the heavy drinkers even more; reprobation is no longer moral, directed toward others, but "health smart" and even ecological, directed toward oneself. Whatever the case, the statistics are crystal clear: people drink less wine, and choose it more carefully (like bread). Thus, consumption at home per person and per year was 91 liters of wine, of which 84 liters of ordinary wine, in 1965; it was still 55 liters, of which 48 liters of ordinary wine, in 1979; in 1989, it is 32 liters, of which 21 liters of ordinary wine. The quantities have thus been divided by three for wine in general, by four for ordinary wine. In this regular decline, one notices that the "volume indicator, base 100 in 1980" is clearly favorable to corked wine (Vin de Qualité Supérieure, Appellation d'Origine Contrôlée), as the data in table 13 show.

8. See Pierre Mayol, "Le jeu: Approche anthropologique," *Éducation 2000*, no. 11 (December 1978).

9. *This reference is an allusion to the book by the psychoanalyst Denis Vasse, *Le temps du désir* (Paris: Seuil, 1969).

Table 13

	AOC and VDQS wine	Ordinary wine
1970	79.2	115.6
1975	81.3	109.3
1980	100.0	100.0
1985	130.4	85.3
1990	162.3	62.0

Sources: Michèle Bertrand, *Consommation et lieux d'achat des produits alimentaires en 1989,* INSEE (August 1992): 31; Monique Gombert et al., *La consommation des ménages en 1991,* Résultats, no. 177–78, Consommation—Modes de vie, no. 39–40, INSEE (May 1992).

6. The End of the Week

1. *The Saturday euphoria was linked to the recent decrease of work time in social life. It has become effective for Joseph and his fellow factory workers, as well as for a number of his neighbors and salaried friends, through the progressive conquest first of Saturday afternoon, then an entire Saturday once every two weeks, and finally with the entire day every week. The "weekly effective work duration for workers" was on average around forty-seven hours from 1950 to 1968, and then it began to decrease: forty-two hours in 1975, forty in 1978 (and thirty-nine beginning in January 1982). In addition, for people who began to work very young "in the factory" after World War II, one must remember that the third week of paid vacation dates from the law of March 27, 1957, and the fourth from that of May 16, 1959 (the fifth week is the result of the edict of January 16, 1982, which also institutes the thirty-nine-hour workweek). My research is situated right in the middle of the period of experimentation with "freed time," taking over the "constrained time" of work; hence, my emphasis on the appropriation of the city as market space, up till then accessible with difficulty, suddenly revealed in all its glory thanks to the brand-new freedom of Saturdays.

2. I remind the reader that this study was completed before the Part-Dieu neighborhood became dominant.

3. [These remarks from Madame Marie are taken from her conversation with Mayol transcribed in chapter 7. The citation here differs slightly in punctuation and because of minor editorial omissions. *Trans.*]

4. [The word *crèche* in the name of this café has several distinct connotations in French. First, it can be a day-care center, hence the parenthetical reference to a nursery school. Second, it refers to a crib, more specifically to the manger where Jesus lay, whose circumstances and disposition are still displayed at churches and with special store-window displays in December. Finally, in contemporary informal usage, one's *crèche* refers to one's apartment. All these connotations will be exploited in the discussion that follows. *Trans.*]

7. "And So for Shopping, There's Always Robert?"

1. The materials taken from these interviews have been used in chapters 3–6.

2. Robert runs a grocery store where he also sells bread.

3. She is referring to Robert.

4. On the rue Saint-Jean, see chapter 3, "The R. Family in Its Neighborhood."

5. Madame Marie is confusing the generations. Jean, her grandson, twenty-five years old at the time, did not attend the same school as her two sons, Maurice and Joseph.

6. The current location of the bus station on the square.

7. The neighborhood movie theater.

8. [Puvis de Chavannes is a nineteenth-century French painter (1824–98). *Trans.*]

9. Madame Marguerite had a sister.

10. [See chap. 3, note 29. *Trans.*]

11. He ran a hardware store in the rue Jean-Baptiste Say.

12. [The French text plays on three pronunciations of the word *cubbyhole*: *soupente*, *suspente*, and *sus-pente*. This play cannot be easily reproduced in English, but seems to stress the notion of above (*sus*) as opposed to below (*sous*), inherent in the reference to these sorts of mezzanines built "above" the rest of the apartment. *Trans.*]

13. This was the neighborhood for prostitutes.

14. ["To paw" is undoubtedly an inadequate translation of the dated Lyons slang word *pétafiner*. It means something like *tripoter*, "to grope." *Trans.*]

15. A curious expression used by Madame Marguerite to refer to the fact that a young woman has sexual relations before marriage. [This curious expression (*Voir péter le loup sur la pierre de bois*) seems to be related to another slang phrase, *Avoir vu le loup*, which means to lose one's virginity. Because the former expression is so "curious," I decided to do a translation as literal as possible into English in order to emphasize the bizarre, bordering on incomprehensible, nature of the original phrase. *Trans.*]

16. On the *ficelle*, see later in this section.

17. Madame Marguerite refers to the buildings constructed on the plateau in the last twenty years, especially the public housing tower erected on the site of the former Croix-Rousse train station and the Saint Bernard residence, a building of luxury apartments at the end of the boulevard on the site of the former Teppaz factories.

18. Postcards from the period show this train maneuvering down the middle of the boulevard de la Croix-Rousse. Created in 1864 by the Compagnie des Dombes, it went from Lyon–Croix-Rousse to Bourg-en-Bresse. Its station was located next to the current exit for the highway tunnel coming from the rue Terme.

19. Madame Marguerite is in error. The first funicular was on the rue Terme, inaugurated on June 3, 1862; the second would not begin running until 1891.

20. By "sweet wine," she refers to new wine and not sugared wine. At the fair, people also used to eat a sort of thick, very nutritious pancake called a *matefaim*.

21. Further on, Madame Marguerite writes: "My father, undoubtedly through a spirit for contradiction and so as to not do like everyone else, had refused to have electricity installed, which at that time was done for free. We thus continued to live with an oil lamp suspended over our heads that smoked for all it was worth. In the

store, there was a gas lamp that required the lamplighter to climb up on a chair in order to light it or put it out."

22. The store was open at six o'clock in the morning in the summer, a half hour later in the winter; they closed at nine o'clock at night. In the winter, there were no days off, not even on Sunday. In the summer, they closed on Sundays at two o'clock. Madame Marguerite remembers: "Once a year, on Easter Monday, we would close for the whole day. On that day, we would go to the old folks' home in Albigny to visit a very old female relative who had a wooden leg. With this once-a-year visit, my father thought himself to be the benefactor of the infirm and so his conscience was at rest. We used to take a train from the Saint Paul station, an old rattletrap with no conveniences; it was perhaps a half-hour or forty-five-minute trip with the train moving along step by step and stopping often. In spite of the short duration of the trip, my mother used to bring a snack. This single annual trip had to be given the allure of a true journey!"

23. Located along the Saône north of Lyons, Île-Barbe was a place to take walks that was very crowded on Sundays. "The Guillotine" was a nickname given to the steam power unit that towed the trains on the banks of the Saône between Lyons and Neuville-sur-Saône. In 1932, a high-capacity tramway was substituted, which remained in service until 1957 and which was instead nicknamed the Blue Train. See Jean Arrivetz, *Histoire des transports à Lyon* (Lyons: Éditions Réalisation, 1966).

8. Ghosts in the City

1. Jean-Claude Jolain, "Inventer du nouveau sans défigurer l'ancien," *Le Monde*, February 15, 1979.

2. On the quai des Célestins, see F. Chaslin, "Réhabilitation par le vide," *Le Monde*, February 18, 1982; on the Saint Paul block, see A. Jacob, "Du neuf dans le vieux pour le IVe arrondissement," *Le Monde*, November 22, 1979.

3. Volker Plageman, *Das deutsche Kunstmuseum 1790–1870* (Munich: Prestel, 1967), on the organization of German museums during the nineteenth century: these pedagogical displays combine progress of the mind with the promotion of the fatherland.

4. P. Maillard, "L'art s'installera-t-il dans l'usine à gaz?" *Le Monde*, April 7, 1982.

5. M. Champenois, *Le Monde*, September 12, 1979.

6. Pierre-Jakez Helias, *Le Cheval d'orgueil* (Paris: Plon, 1975), 14–16.

7. [The *bigouden* costume refers to a festival costume worn in the Finistère department in Brittany. *Trans.*]

8. Jules Michelet, *La Sorcière* (Paris: Calmann-Lévy, n.d.), 23ff.

9. See Dominique Poulot, "L'avenir du passé: Les musées en mouvement," *Le Débat*, no. 12 (May 1981): 105–15; or Jean Clair, "Érostrate, ou le musée en question," *Revue d'esthétique*, no. 3–4 (1974): 185–206.

10. On the Marais, see D. Benassaya, "Un luxe sur le dos des pauvres," *Le Monde*, May 15, 1979. The same problem exists in other cities, for example, the rue des Tanneurs in Colmar.

11. See *Le Monde*, November 20, 1979.

12. Ibid.

13. See Michel de Certeau, *La Culture au pluriel*, new ed. (Paris: Seuil, Points, 1993), chap. 3, "La beauté du mort." [In Michel de Certeau, *Heterologies: Discourse on the Other*, trans. Brian Massumi (Minneapolis: University of Minnesota Press, 1986), 119–36. *Trans.*]

14. J. de Barrin, "Le musée d'un paysan," *Le Monde*, April 9, 1977.

15. See Michel de Certeau, *The Practice of Everyday Life*, trans. Steven Rendall (Berkeley: University of California Press, 1984).

16. See Jean-Pierre Faye, *Langages totalitaires* (Paris: Hermann, 1972).

17. Pierre Janet, *L'Évolution de la mémoire* (Paris: Chahine, 1928), 288.

9. Private Spaces

1. Marie-Claire Ferrier, *Enfants de justice* (Paris: Maspero, 1981), 123.

2. Luce Giard, "Voyageuse raison," *Esprit*, special issue titled "L'utopie ou la raison dans l'imaginaire" (April 1974): 557–66; and Gérard Raulet, ed., *Stratégies de l'utopie* (Paris: Galilée, 1979); Michel de Certeau and Luce Giard contributed to this work.

Part II. Doing-Cooking

1. [This expression is a rather awkward translation of the unique phrase that Luce Giard uses to specify the practice of cooking. She uses the inventive term *faire-la-cuisine* ("doing-cooking") to resonate with the underlying theme for both volumes provided by Michel de Certeau in the expression *arts de faire*. *Trans.*]

10. The Nourishing Arts

1. Luce Giard, "La fabrication des filles," *Esprit* (June 1976): 1108–23; and in collaboration, "Note conjointe sur l'éminente relativité du concept de femme," *Esprit* (June 1976): 1079–85.

2. Marcel Mauss, *Sociology and Psychology*, trans. Ben Brewster (London: Routledge and Kegan Paul, 1979), 95–123.

3. Chantal Akerman, interview in *Télérama*, cited in *Études* (April 1976): 564.

4. Chantal Akerman, a conversation with Jacques Siclier, *Le Monde*, January 22, 1976; this interview was preceded by an article by Louis Marcorelles, "Comment dire chef-d'œuvre au féminin?"

5. Interview with Chantal Akerman, *Cahiers du cinéma*, no. 278 (July 1977): 41.

6. Freddy Laurent, *La Revue nouvelle* (March 1974): 296.

7. Le Théâtre des cuisines, *Môman travaille pas, a trop d'ouvrage!* (Montreal: Éditions du Remue-ménage, 1976).

8. On Rabelais, Noëlle Châtelet, *Le Corps à corps culinaire* (Paris: Seuil, 1977), 55–92.

9. "This narrative, but also all the others, and this one with no exception, are interlarded with long lists of mounds of food, as in Dickens, Rabelais, Cervantes... For Verne, as for those writers, there is a naive and simple fantasy of feeling full, the horror of emptiness.... nature is the mother and she provides food. She is full everywhere, as Leibniz said, and she cannot be hungry. Man is the hole in Nature,

he is the hunger of the world" (Michel Serres, *Jouvences sur Jules Verne* [Paris: Minuit, 1974], 176).

10. Robert Courtine, *Balzac à table* (Paris: Laffont, 1976).

11. Robert Courtine, *Le Cahier de recettes de Mme Maigret* (Paris: Laffont, 1974), with a preface by Georges Simenon; and *Zola à table: trois cents recettes* (Paris: Laffont, 1978).

12. Pierre Bonte, *Le Bonheur est dans le pré* (Paris: Stock, 1976), 232. See the book review by Catherine B. Clément, "Pierre Bonte et ses philosophes du matin: le Christophe Colomb de Chavignol," *Le Monde*, February 15–16, 1976.

13. Nicole, "Les pommes de terre," *Les Temps modernes*, issue titled "Les femmes s'entêtent" (April–May 1974): 1732–34.

14. Our method seems very close to that of Claudine Herzlich, *Santé et maladie: Analyse d'une représentation sociale*, 2d ed. (Paris and The Hague: Mouton, 1975), 25–28.

15. See chapter 14.

16. André Villeneuve, *La Consommation alimentaire des Français, année 1972*, series M, 34 (INSEE, 1974); André Villeneuve and Georges Bigata, *Repas à l'extérieur et repas au domicile en 1971*, series M, 49 (INSEE, 1975). Cf. also Annie Fouquet, *Les Grandes tendances de la consommation alimentaire (exercice pour 1980)*, series M, 54 (INSEE, 1976).

17. On this method, see Villeneuve, *La Consommation*, 7–11; Villeneuve and Bigata, *Repas*, 9–11.

18. Jean Claudian, Yvonne Serville, and Fernand Trémolières, "Enquête sur les facteurs de choix des aliments," *Bulletin de l'INSERM* 24.5 (1969): 1277–1390. Two complementary texts can be added: Jean Claudian and Yvonne Serville, "Aspects de l'évolution récente du comportement alimentaire en France: composition des repas et urbanisation," in Jean-Jacques Hémardinquer, ed., *Pour une histoire de l'alimentation* (Paris: Armand Colin, 1970), 174–87; and Jean Claudian and Yvonne Serville, "Les aliments du dimanche et du vendredi: Études sur le comportement alimentaire actuel en France," in Hémardinquer, *Pour une histoire*, 300–306. On the large study cited first, a convenient summary has been given by Michelle de Wilde, "La nourriture en famille," *L'École des parents*, no. 10 (December 1972): 21–29.

19. Claudian, Serville, and Trémolières, "Enquête," 1277–79, 1281, 1283, 1358, 1366.

20. Arlette Jacob, *La Nutrition* (Paris: PUF, "Que sais-je?" 1975); contains a clear and precise account of these questions.

21. Jean Trémolières, "Dénutrition," in *Encyclopaedia universalis* (Paris: Encyclopaedia Universalis France, 1968).

22. Jacob, *La Nutrition*, 108–16.

23. Jean Claudian, "L'alimentation," in Michel François, ed., *La France et les Français* (Paris: Gallimard, Pléiade, 1972), 152–53; and Maurice Aymard, "Pour l'histoire de l'alimentation: quelques remarques de méthode," *Annales ESC* 30 (1975): 435, 439–42.

24. John Dobbing, "Malnutrition et développement du cerveau," *La Recherche*, no. 64 (February 1976): 139–45; and Ciba Foundation Symposium, *Lipids, Malnutrition and the Developing Brain* (Amsterdam: North Holland, 1972).

25. Emmanuel Le Roy Ladurie, "L'aménorrhée de famine (XVIIᵉ–XXᵉ siècle)," *Annales ESC* 24 (1969), special issue, *Histoire biologique et société*, 1589–1601.

26. Tom Brewer, *Metabolic Toxemia of Late Pregnancy* (Springfield, Ill.: C. C. Thomas, 1966); Tom Brewer, "Consequences of Malnutrition in Human Pregnancy," *Ciba Review: Perinatal Medicine* (1975): 5–6.

27. Dr. Escoffier-Lambiotte, "Vers une prévention des affections et des cancers intestinaux?" *Le Monde*, September 17, 1975. On the great number of stomach cancers in Japan linked, it would seem, to a certain type of food diet, see J.-D. Flaysakier, "Au Japon, le cancer de l'estomac: un exemple réussi de prévention," *Le Monde*, October 3, 1979.

28. M. D., "L'alimentation et la préservation de la santé," *Le Monde*, September 29, 1976.

29. Dr. Escoffier-Lambiotte, "Graisses alimentaires et fibres végétales," *Le Monde*, February 16, 1977, according to the dissertation by F. Meyer (Lyons).

30. Henri Dupin, *l'Alimentation des Français: Évolution et problèmes nutritionnels* (Paris: Éditions Sociales Françaises, 1978).

31. This discovery earned its author, Daniel Carleton Gajdusek, a Nobel Prize in 1976; see Edmond Schuller, "Virologie tous azimuts: du cerveau de l'anthropophage … ," *La Recherche*, no. 73 (December 1976): 1061–63.

32. Jacob, *La Nutrition*, 117–19.

33. Yvonne Rebeyrol, "Y a-t-il encore des explorateurs?" *Le Monde*, September 14, 1977. This article details François Lupu's trip into the Sepik Valley [New Guinea], where people eat the parasitic worms of sago palm trees.

34. Léo Moulin, *L'Europe à table: Introduction à une psychosociologie des pratiques alimentaires* (Paris and Brussels: Elsevier Sequoia, 1975), 20–26, 129–30, 136–38.

35. In this specific case, it seems that biological factors come into play: European ethnic groups may be the only ones to retain until adulthood the capacity to produce an enzyme necessary for the complete digestion of raw milk.

36. Roland Barthes, "Pour une psychosociologie de l'alimentation contemporaine," in Hémardinquer, *Pour une histoire*, 309–10.

37. Aymard, "Pour l'histoire de l'alimentation," 431ff.

11. Plat du jour

1. Paul Leuilliot, preface to Guy Thuillier, *Pour une histoire du quotidien au XIXᵉ siècle en Nivernais* (Paris and The Hague: Mouton, 1977), xii.

2. Mary Douglas, *Purity and Danger: An Analysis of the Concepts of Pollution and Taboo* (London and New York: Routledge, 1992), 5, 35, 38.

3. Jean Claudian, "L'alimentation," in Michel François, ed., *La France et les Français* (Paris: Gallimard, Pléiade, 1972), 160. On the improvement of agricultural techniques, see Roland Mousnier, *Progrès scientifique et technique au XVIIIᵉ siècle* (Paris: Plon, 1958).

4. François Sigaut, *Les Réserves de grains à long terme: Techniques de conservation et fonctions sociales dans l'histoire* (Lille and Paris: University of Lille III and Maison des Sciences de l'Homme, 1978); and Marceau Gast and François Sigaut, *Les Techniques de conservation des grains à long terme* (Paris: Centre National de la Recherche Scientifique, 1979).

5. Guy Thuillier, "L'alimentation en Nivernais au XIXᵉ siècle," in Jean-Jacques Hémardinquer, ed., *Pour une histoire de l'alimentation* (Paris: Armand Colin, 1970), 161–62.

6. Andrzej Wyczanski, "La consommation alimentaire en Pologne au XVIe siècle," in ibid., 45–46.

7. Jean-Jacques Hémardinquer, "Faut-il 'démythifier' le porc familial d'Ancien Régime?" *Annales ESC* 25 (November–December 1970): 1745–66; and Bartolomé Bennassar and Joseph Goy, "Contribution à l'histoire de la consommation alimentaire du XIVe au XIXe siècle," *Annales ESC* 30 (March–June 1975): 416.

8. Michel Morineau, "La pomme de terre au XVIIIe siècle," *Annales ESC* 25 (November–December 1970): 1767–85.

9. Jean-Paul Aron, *Le Mangeur du XIXe siècle* (Paris: Denoël Gonthier, Médiations, 1976), 115.

10. Arlette Farge, *Délinquance et criminalité: le vol d'aliments au XVIIIe siècle* (Paris: Plon, 1974), 93, 116–17, 128, 156–58.

11. Aron, *Le Mangeur du XIXe siècle*, 215–17, 259–62; and Jean-Paul Aron, "Sur les consommations avariées à Paris dans la deuxième moitié du XIXe siècle," *Annales ESC* 30 (March–June 1975): 553–62.

12. *Cinq siècles d'imagerie française* (Paris: Musée des Arts et Traditions Populaires, 1973), no. 3, 9, on "Le Pays de Cocagne."

13. Geneviève Bollème, *La Bible bleue: Anthologie d'une littérature "populaire"* (Paris: Flammarion, 1975), 16–18, 243–54.

14. Lotte Schwarz, *Je veux vivre jusqu'à ma mort* (Paris: Seuil, 1979), 165.

15. Claudian, "L'alimentation," 150–51.

16. Serge Grafteaux, *La Mère Denis* (Paris: Jean-Pierre Delarge, 1976), 17–18, 20, 23–24, 72, 74, 75, 81–82, 141, 160, 188–90.

17. Immanuel Kant, *Anthropology from a Pragmatic Point of View*, trans. Victor Lyle Dowdell (Carbondale and Edwardsville: Southern Illinois Press, 1978), 47.

18. Serge Grafteaux, *Mémé Santerre* (Verviers: Marabout, 1976), 9, 11, 12, 13, 40–41.

19. Mary Chamberlain, *Fenwomen: A Portrait of Women in an English Village* (London: Quartet for Virago, 1975).

20. Julien Nussbaum, "Aspects technologiques de la cuisine rurale alsacienne d'autrefois," *Revue des sciences sociales de la France de l'Est*, special issue (1977): 131, 136.

21. Bennassar and Goy, "Contribution," 417.

22. On the methods for this study, see chapter 10, the section titled "Other Sources."

23. Jean Claudian and Yvonne Serville, "Aspects de l'évolution récente du comportement alimentaire en France: composition des repas et 'urbanisation'" in Hémardinquer, *Pour une histoire*, 182–84.

24. Thuillier, *Pour une histoire du quotidien*, 54.

25. Ibid., 65.

26. Abel Poitrineau, "L'alimentation populaire en Auvergne au XVIIIe siècle," in Hémardinquer, *Pour une histoire*, 151.

27. Micheline Baulant, "Niveaux de vie paysans autour de Meaux en 1700 et 1750," *Annales ESC* 30 (March–June 1975): 514.

28. Thuillier, "L'alimentation," in Hémardinquer, *Pour une histoire*, 164.

29. Willem Frijhoff and Dominique Julia, "L'alimentation des pensionnaires à la fin de l'Ancien Régime," *Annales ESC* 30 (March–June 1975): 499.

30. Nussbaum, "Aspects technologiques," 120.

31. E. N. Anderson, "Réflexions sur la cuisine," *L'Homme* 10 (April–June 1970): 122–24; and Mark Elvin, "The Sweet and the Sour," *Times Literary Supplement*, August 8, 1977.

32. Paul Valéry, *Monsieur Teste*, in *The Collected Works of Paul Valéry*, vol. 6, trans. Jackson Mathews (Princeton, N.J.: Princeton University Press, 1973), 9.

33. Claude Lévi-Strauss, *From Honey to Ashes*, trans. John Weightman and Doreen Weightman (New York: Harper and Row, 1973), 323.

34. Claude Lévi-Strauss, *The Origin of Table Manners*, trans. John Weightman and Doreen Weightman (New York: Harper and Row, 1978), 495.

35. Ibid., 469.

36. Ibid., 505.

37. Ibid., 507.

38. Francis Martens, "Diététique ou la cuisine de Dieu," *Communications*, no. 26 (1977): 16–45, especially 27–28.

39. Ibid., 45.

40. Pierre Bourdieu, *Distinction: A Social Critique of the Judgement of Taste*, trans. Richard Nice (London: Routledge and Kegan Paul, 1984), 208.

41. Ibid., 78.

42. Ibid., 209.

43. Ibid., 79.

44. Ibid., 193.

45. Ibid., 194, 196.

46. Léo Moulin, *L'Europe à table: Introduction à une psychosociologie des pratiques alimentaires* (Paris and Brussels: Elsevier Sequoia, 1975), 10–11.

47. Michèle Dacher and Micheline Weinstein, *Histoire de Louise: Des vieillards en hospice* (Paris: Seuil, 1979), 81, 83.

48. Joëlle Bahloul, "Nourritures juives," *Les Temps modernes*, no. 394 bis, titled "Le second Israël" (1979): 387.

49. Ibid., 388.

50. Claudine Herzlich, *Santé et maladie: Analyse d'une représentation sociale*, 2d ed. (Paris and The Hague: Mouton, 1975), 128–29.

51. Jean Claudian, Yvonne Serville, and Fernand Trémolières, "Enquête sur les facteurs de choix des aliments," *Bulletin de l'INSERM* 24.5 (1969): 1298.

52. Bourdieu, *Distinction*, 177–78.

53. Cited by Jean Trémolières, "Diététique," in *Encyclopaedia universalis* (Paris: Encyclopaedia Universalis France, 1968).

54. Fernand Braudel, "Alimentation et catégories de l'histoire" in Hémardinquer, *Pour une histoire*, 15, 27–28.

55. Jean Anthelme Brillat-Savarin, *The Physiology of Taste*, trans. M. F. K. Fisher (New York and London: Harcourt Brace Jovanovich, 1978), 38.

56. Michel Tournier, interviewed by Gilles Lapouge, on the program *Agora* (France-Culture, October 15, 1979, 12:00 A.M.).

57. Aron, *Le Mangeur du XIXᵉ siècle*, 117–20.

58. [The wordplay here is untranslatable in English. The original sentence ("Pour trouver des coings, mesdames, suivez les côtés") plays on the homonyms

coins (corners) and *coings* (quinces). A more direct translation of the statement would be "To find the corners (*coins–coings*), ladies, follow the sides." *Trans.*]

59. The INSERM study provides statistical proof for this for the four departments outside of the Paris region that it studied (Claudian, Serville, and Trémolières, "Enquête," 1349; table 34, 1350). The statistics measure the frequency of a dish made with the food mentioned for the meal in question, as table 14 demonstrates.

60. Dr. Henri Dupin (professor of human nutrition at the University of Rennes), "Apprendre à manger," *Le Monde*, November 14–15, 1976.

61. Advertisement for mineral water posted on Parisian buses in September 1977.

62. A classified ad that appeared in *L'Enseignement public* 35.1 (September–October 1977).

63. Gaston Bachelard, *The Right to Dream*, trans. J. A. Underwood (Dallas: Dallas Institute Publications, 1988), 181.

64. Dacher and Weinstein, *Histoire de Louise*, 92–93.

65. Mary Barnes and Joseph Berke, *Mary Barnes: Two Accounts of a Journey through Madness* (London: MacGibbon and Kee, 1971), 21.

66. Ibid.

67. Gaston Bachelard, *La Terre et les Rêveries de la volonté* (Paris: José Corti, 1948), 86.

68. Fanny Deschamps, *Croque-en-bouche* (Paris: Albin Michel, 1976), 236.

69. Mme C. F., "La cuisinière au bois," *Le Monde Dimanche*, September 30, 1979.

70. Charles Vial, "Les jeunes dans leur corps. II: 'La Bouffe? Bof...,'" *Le Monde*, August 10, 1978.

71. Marie-Claire Cèlerier, "La boulimie compulsionnelle," *Topique*, no. 18 (January 1977): 95.

72. Ibid., 102–4, 109, 112.

73. Jean Trémolières, *L'Obésité: Actualités diététiques*, no. 1 (July 1970).

74. *Le Monde* devoted the health page to this problem on July 6, 1977.

75. Claire Brisset, "Et mourir de maigrir," *Le Monde*, June 4–6, 1978; letters to the editor on this topic, ibid., July 19, 1978; and the dossier in *L'Impatient*, no. 4 (February 1978): 16–22, 36.

Table 14

Dish	Noon	Evening
Fish	ordinary day: 6%	3.5%
	Friday: 78%	20%
Meat	ordinary day: 65%	15%
	Friday: 8.5%	3.5%
Poultry	ordinary day: 9%	2%
	Friday: 1%	1%
Deli meat	ordinary day: 23.5%	25%
	Friday: 4.5%	7%

76. Mario Bensasson and Jean-Paul Dugas, *Je ne veux pas maigrir idiot!* (Paris: Fayard, 1978).

77. An astonishing description of this, from lived experience between age fourteen and sixteen and through successive episodes, can be found in Valérie Valère, *Le Pavillon des enfants fous* (Paris: Stock, 1978).

78. Noëlle Châtelet, *Le Corps à corps culinaire* (Paris: Seuil, 1977), 155.

79. Claude Lévi-Strauss, *The Raw and the Cooked*, trans. John Weightman and Doreen Weightman (New York: Harper and Row, 1969), 296 n. 7.

80. Frédéric Lange, *Manger ou les jeux et les creux du plat* (Paris: Seuil, 1975), 36.

12. Gesture Sequences

1. Delphine Seyrig, interview by Alain Remond in *Télérama*, no. 1454, November 23, 1977.

2. *Les Secrets de la mère Brazier*, with the collaboration of Roger Moreau (Paris: Solar, 1977), 37.

3. Pierre-Jakez Helias, *Le Cheval d'orgueil* (Paris: Plon, 1975); Yvonne Verdier, *Façons de dire, façons de faire* (Paris: Gallimard, 1979); Anne Merlin and Alain-Yves Beaujour, *Les Mangeurs de Rouergue* (Paris and Gembloux: Duculot, 1978).

4. Guy Thuillier, *Pour une histoire du quotidien au XIXe siècle en Nivernais* (Paris and The Hague: Mouton, 1977), 162.

5. Marcel Mauss, *Sociology and Psychology: Essays*, trans. Ben Brewster (London: Routledge and Kegan Paul, 1979), 97. See also the Musée des Arts et Traditions Populaires, *Religions et traditions populaires* (Paris: Réunion des Musées Nationaux, 1979).

6. See, for example, Marcel Detienne and Jean-Pierre Vernant, *La Cuisine du sacrifice en pays grec* (Paris: Gallimard, 1979).

7. Jean-Noël Pelen, *La Vallée longue en Cévenne: Vie, traditions et proverbes du temps passé* (n.p., n.d., *Causses et Cévennes*, special edition), 39–46.

8. Merlin and Beaujour, *Les Mangeurs de Rouergue*, 64–65. [On the *matefaim*, see chap. 7, n. 20. *Trans.*]

9. Ibid., 70.

10. Verdier, *Façons de dire*, 19–40; Merlin and Beaujour, *Les Mangeurs de Rouergue*, 89–106.

11. Dominique Simonnet and Jean-Paul Ribes, "Savez-vous vraiment ce que vous mangez?" *L'Express*, no. 1427, November 18, 1978. For information from the point of view of professionals, see *Les Industries agro-alimentaires* (Paris: Larousse, Encyclopoche, 1979).

12. Aristotle, *Aristotle's 'De Anima': Books II and III*, trans. D. W. Hamlyn (Oxford: Clarendon, 1968), 65; *Parts of Animals*, trans. A. L. Peck (Cambridge, Mass., and London: Harvard University Press and William Heinemann, 1968), 373; and so on. Also, the parallel texts of Galen, *De l'utilité des parties du corps humain*. On the gesture and the tool, see the admirable work of André Leroi-Gourhan, *Milieu et techniques* (Paris: Albin Michel, 1973), 142–91, and *La mémoire et les rythmes* (Paris: Albin Michel, 1977).

13. Suzanne Tardieu, *Équipement et activités domestiques* (Paris: Musées Nationaux, Musée des Arts et Traditions Populaires, guide ethnologique, 1972).

14. *L'Utile: Préparation des aliments, choix et usage des appareils et des ustensiles* (Paris: Centre Georges Pompidou, Centre de Création Culturelle, 1978).

15. There are a few indications in *L'Objet industriel* (Paris: Centre Georges Pompidou, Centre de Création Culturelle, 1980). The best source of information remains the annual mail-order catalogs (*La Redoute*, or *Les trois Suisses*, or *La Camif*, a marvelous repertoire of the objects that are available and considered desirable in private space). See Jany Aujame, "La cuisine en batterie," *Le Monde*, April 18, 1979; and "Bonnes casseroles, bonne cuisine," *Le Monde*, May 3, 1980; François Cérésa, "Le mystère de la bonne cuisine," *Le Nouvel Observateur*, no. 802, March 24, 1980.

16. Jany Aujame, "Les hautes techniques dans les mains de toutes les maîtresses de maison," *Le Monde*, March 8, 1978; and "Le ménage à l'électronique," *Le Monde*, March 1, 1980.

17. The history of the social and technical relationship with water in domestic space and of its modification in everyday cleaning operations (personal hygiene, meals, laundry, etc.) has yet to be written. Thuillier, *Pour une histoire*, 11–30, devotes a very interesting chapter to it on local customs.

18. Ibid., 127.

19. Marc Ambroise-Rendu, "Un week-end dans le pétrin," *Le Monde*, March 3, 1979.

13. The Rules of the Art

1. Ludwig Wittgenstein, *Zetel*, trans. G. E. M. Anscombe (Berkeley and Los Angeles: University of California Press, 1967), 59e.

2. Molière, *The Learned Ladies*, trans. Richard Wilbur (New York: Harcourt Brace Jovanovich, 1978), vol. 2, 7, 49.

3. Menon, *La Cuisinière bourgeoise* (Paris, 1746), cited in *Le Livre dans la vie quotidienne* (Paris: Bibliothèque Nationale, 1975), exhibition catalog, no. 85, 26.

4. Claude Sarraute, "In corpore sano" *Le Monde*, September 14, 1976.

5. At the time of this study (1979), I had consulted the last reissue available (Paris: Taride, 1977). A 1986 reissue is currently available in bookstores.

6. Cited by La Reynière, "Ces dames au 'piano,'" *Le Monde*, May 21, 1977.

7. [This idiomatic expression means something along the lines of "Let's move on to something else." The culinary reference (*muscade* is nutmeg) is not easily translated into a corresponding English idiom. The translation I propose here unfortunately does not convey the ironic intent of this expression in relation to the preceding citation from Paul Bocuse. *Trans.*]

8. Paul Valéry, "Variété," in *Œuvres*, vol. 1 (Paris: Gallimard, Pléiade, 1971), 732.

9. Laurent Grimod de La Reynière, *Écrits gastronomiques* (Paris: 10–18, 1978). I am citing a phrase from the excellent introduction by Jean-Claude Bonnet for this reedition, 7–92.

10. Ibid., 47.

11. Jean-Paul Aron, *Le Mangeur du XIXᵉ siècle* (Paris: Denoël Gonthier, Médiations, 1976), 9, 11, 74, 284–89.

12. Jean-Claude Bonnet, "Le réseau culinaire de l'Encyclopédie," *Annales ESC* 31 (September–October 1976): 907.

13. Jean Baillon and Jean-Paul Ceron, "La durabilité de l'équipement ménager," *La Société de l'éphémère* (Paris and Grenoble, Maison des Sciences de l'Homme and PUG, 1979), 139, 145, 156.

14. Aron, *Le Mangeur du XIXe siècle*, 155.

15. Grimod de La Reynière, *Écrits gastronomiques*, 35–37.

16. [The French text indicates that the March 8, 1941, diary entry was written *four* days before Virginia Woolf's death. Woolf committed suicide on March 28, 1941, *twenty* days after this diary entry. *Trans.*]

17. Virginia Woolf, *The Diary of Virginia Woolf*, ed. Anne Olivier Bell with Andrew McNeillie (San Diego, New York, and London: Harcourt Brace Jovanovich, 1984), 358. [Luce Giard cited the 1959 Hogarth edition of Virginia Woolf's diary, one that contained only excerpts. In this more recent edition, the cited entry is in fact not the last one. *Trans.*]

14. "When It Comes Down to It, Cooking Worries Me . . ."

1. All the first names and place-names, with the exception of Paris, are fictional in order to respect the anonymity of the interview. The notes were done by Luce Giard. For information on collecting the interviews, see chapter 10, the section titled "Women's Voices."

2. Jean makes a mistake here: Pierre, the heartier eater, is also the youngest.

3. Irène is the oldest in a family with four children: her younger sister is so by two years, then comes a brother two years younger than her sister, followed by the youngest sister, who is twelve years younger than Irène.

4. [I have chosen to keep the French in this passage because a literal translation of *gourmand* and *gourmandise* as glutton and gluttony would overshadow what contemporary French expresses as the positive side of eating hearty and well (and not simply the connotation of excess as in the seven deadly sins). In this context, there is little difference between the word *gourmand* and what is understood in English as "gourmet." *Trans.*]

5. Jean has made several trips to the hospital.

6. Paul is one of Irène's first cousins. He also lives in Paris with his wife and their numerous children. The two families are very close.

7. Marie was single at the time and traveled a lot for professional reasons.

8. Irène and Jean reside in an old neighborhood of Paris, currently in the midst of transformation, and whose former modest-income inhabitants are being chased away little by little because of renovation work and the accompanying rise in rents. See chapter 8, the section titled "A Policy of Authors: Inhabitants."

9. [The actual figure in the original text is twenty francs, which would be more like five dollars at the 1997 exchange rate. I use fifteen dollars not as an accurate mathematical conversion, but to better illustrate Jean's claim that this figure indicates a seemingly "expensive," good-quality bottle of wine. One must keep in mind a difference in price resulting both from inflation (these remarks were made before 1980) and from the fact that wine is generally less expensive in France than it is in the United States. *Trans.*]

10. [SEB is a rather widespread brand-name of cooking appliances in France. *Trans.*]

11. Finding a printer's error in a cooking recipe amuses Irène all the more so because, in so doing, she encounters within her private space (her kitchen) her professional life (at the office), where, every month, she proofreads publications in the process of being printed.

12. Irène has long workdays at the office; sometimes, in order to meet publication deadlines, she has to bring texts home to proofread over the weekend.

13. At the time of this interview, Sarah was out of town during a short school vacation.

14. A friend and neighbor of the family.

15. An allusion to the period of time preceding Jean and Irène's marriage.

16. [*Borel* refers to a generally mediocre fast-food restaurant chain often found along major highways in France. *Trans.*]

17. [ORTF refers to the Office de la Radiodiffusion-Télévision Française, the office of French television and radio broadcasting, located in Paris's sixteenth arrondissement. *Trans.*]

18. The interview was recorded in the family's apartment after a dinner shared with Marie.

19. By deliberate choice, the family does not have a television set.

20. A small room adjoining the kitchen serves as a dining room; the rest of the apartment is arranged around this same room, which opens onto the kitchen on one side, the parents' bedroom on the other, and a small sitting room in the back that must be crossed to gain access to Sarah's room.

21. An allusion to the conversation exchanged during dinner, just before recording the interview.

22. Jean's mother's untimely death left behind five young children, hence the presence of a cook-governess to take care of the house in Saint-André for Jean's father.

23. [The reference in French is to a *pâtisserie*, where one generally finds only pastries, as opposed to a *boulangerie*, where one buys bread and occasionally pastries as well. Because the same distinction is not as systematic in English, I have used the more general term *bakery*. *Trans.*]

24. A friend of the couple who lives in the same building, one floor down; one passes in front of her windows in order to reach the stairs leading to Irène's apartment.

25. The small room adjoining the kitchen; see note 20.

Envoi. A Practical Science of the Singular

1. Jacques Mehler et al., "La reconnaissance de la voix maternelle par le nourrisson," *La Recherche*, no. 70 (September 1976): 786–88; Jacques Mehler, "La perception du langage chez le nourrisson," *La Recherche*, no. 88 (April 1978): 324–30; and Bénédicte de Boysson-Bardies, "Les bébés babillent-ils dans leur langue maternelle?" *La Recherche*, no. 129 (January 1982): 102–4.

2. Michel de Certeau, *The Practice of Everyday Life*, trans. Steven Rendall, paperback edition (Berkeley: University of California Press, 1988), 169.

3. See *Traverses*, no. 20, titled "La voix, l'écoute" (November 1980), and the activities program of FNAC in Paris (January 1982), "La voix, instrument du XXe siècle."

4. See *Communications*, no. 30, titled "La conversation" (1979). On the role of informal exchanges in a research laboratory, see André Lwoff and Agnès Ullmann, eds., *Un hommage à Jacques Monod: Les origines de la biologie moléculaire* (Paris and Montreal: Études Vivantes, 1980).

5. See, for example, Aaron V. Cicourel, *Cognitive Sociology: Language and Meaning in Social Interaction* (New York: Free Press, 1974).

6. Pierre Bourdieu, *Ce que parler veut dire: L'économie des échanges linguistiques* (Paris: Fayard, 1982). [*Language and Symbolic Power*, trans. Gino Raymond and Matthew Adamson (Cambridge: Harvard University Press, 1991). *Trans.*]

7. Mathilde La Bardonnie, "Les folies langagières," *Le Monde*, February 17, 1982; Colette Godard, "Un entretien avec Gildas Bourdet," *Le Monde*, December 1, 1982. [The textual reference is to Gildas Bourdet, *Le Saperleau* (Paris: Solin, 1982). *Trans.*]

8. David Charrasse, *Lorraine Cœur d'Acier* (Paris: Maspero, 1981).

9. Marcel, forty-five, a rolling mill operator since the age of seventeen, on the radio program *Nous tous chacun*, November 19 and 22, 1982 (France-Culture, 12:00–12:30, Jean-Claude Bringuier, producer). On this trade unionist, see ibid., *Lorraine*, 181–85.

10. Certeau, *The Practice of Everyday Life*, chaps. 1–3.

Index

[This index is based on Luce Giard's index for the 1994 French edition of volume 2. Giard created primarily a proper name index that also included the titles of anonymous works and those of special journal editions. The list of proper names includes real people, fictive characters, and any cited authors. Following Giard's practice, I have placed a single asterisk before the names of people interviewed for Pierre Mayol's study and a double asterisk before the names of those whose interviews were cited in Giard's own study. Given that the latter two groups are only cited by first names, the family or friend ties of these people have been specified in parentheses. Although Giard included the names of the three main authors of volume 2 in her index, I have chosen to omit them here. *Trans.*]

Michel de Certeau was born in Chambéry in 1925. He authored numerous articles and books, including *The Writing of History*, *The Mystic Fable*, *The Stranger: Union in Difference*, *Heterologies: Discourse on the Other* (Minnesota, 1986), *Culture in the Plural* (Minnesota, 1997), and *The Capture of Speech and Other Political Writings* (Minnesota, 1997). A historian of religion and a student of ethnography, Michel de Certeau was a professor at both the École des Hautes Études en Sciences Sociales, Paris, and the University of California, San Diego. He died in 1986.

Luce Giard is a research fellow at the Centre National de la Recherche Scientifique and is affiliated with the Centre de Recherches Historiques at the École des Hautes Études en Sciences Sociales, Paris. She regularly serves as a visiting professor in the Department of History at the University of California, San Diego. Giard's studies focus on the history of science and philosophy of the medieval and Renaissance periods. Michel de Certeau entrusted her with the editorial responsibility of his work.

Pierre Mayol specialized in urban anthropology and the sociology of culture after obtaining a doctorate in anthropology and studying French language, literature, and philosophy at the University of Paris-VII. He is a member of the editorial board of the journal *Esprit* and is currently a researcher at the French Ministry of Culture in the Department of Research and Futurology.

Timothy J. Tomasik is a freelance translator pursuing a Ph.D. in French literature at Harvard University.